Hands-On Design Patterns with C++

Solve common C++ problems with modern design patterns and build robust applications

Fedor G. Pikus

BIRMINGHAM - MUMBAI

Hands-On Design Patterns with C++

Commissioning Editor: Richa Tripathi
Acquisition Editor: Shriram Shekhar
Content Development Editor: Manjusha Mantri
Technical Editor: Royce John
Copy Editor: Safis Editing
Project Coordinator: Prajakta Naik
Proofreader: Safis Editing
Indexer: Tejal Daruwale Soni
Graphics: Jisha Chirayil
Production Coordinator: Aparna Bhagat

First published: January 2019

Production reference: 1280119

Published by Packt Publishing Ltd.
Livery Place
35 Livery Street
Birmingham
B3 2PB, UK.

ISBN 978-1-78883-256-4

www.packtpub.com

`mapt.io`

Mapt is an online digital library that gives you full access to over 5,000 books and videos, as well as industry leading tools to help you plan your personal development and advance your career. For more information, please visit our website.

Why subscribe?

- Spend less time learning and more time coding with practical eBooks and videos from over 4,000 industry professionals

- Improve your learning with skill plans designed especially for you

- Get a free eBook or video every month

- Mapt is fully searchable

- Copy and paste, print, and bookmark content

Packt.com

Did you know that Packt offers eBook versions of every book published, with PDF and ePub files available? You can upgrade to the eBook version at `www.packt.com` and, as a print book customer, you are entitled to a discount on the eBook copy. Get in touch with us at `customercare@packtpub.com` for more details.

At `www.packt.com`, you can also read a collection of free technical articles, sign up for a range of free newsletters, and receive exclusive discounts and offers on Packt books and eBooks.

Contributors

About the author

Fedor G. Pikus is a chief engineering scientist in the Design-to-Silicon division of Mentor Graphics (a Siemens business), and is responsible for the long-term technical direction of Calibre products, the design and architecture of software, and research into new software technologies. His earlier positions include senior software engineer at Google and chief software architect at Mentor Graphics. Fedor is a recognized expert on high-performance computing and C++. He has presented his works at CPPCon, SD West, DesignCon, and in software development journals, and is also an O'Reilly author. Fedor has over 25 patents, and over 100 papers and conference presentations on physics, EDA, software design, and C++.

This book would not be possible without the support of my wife, Galina, who made me go on in the moments of self-doubt. Thank you to my sons, Aaron and Benjamin, for their enthusiasm, and to my cat, Pooh, for letting me use his warming pad as my laptop.

About the reviewer

Cale Dunlap has been writing code in various languages since high school, when he wrote his first video game mod for Half-Life in 1999. In 2002, he contributed to the semi-popular Firearms mod for Half-Life and eventually helped bring that same video game mod to the Source Engine as Firearms—Source. He's earned an associate's degree in computer information systems and a bachelor's degree in game and simulation programming. He's worked professionally as a software developer for small companies since 2005, contributing to software ranging from web applications to military simulations. He currently works as a senior interactive developer for a creative agency based in Orange County, California, called Column Five.

Thank you to my fiancé Elizabeth, our son, Mason, and the rest of our family, for supporting me through my first book review.

Packt is searching for authors like you

If you're interested in becoming an author for Packt, please visit `authors.packtpub.com` and apply today. We have worked with thousands of developers and tech professionals, just like you, to help them share their insight with the global tech community. You can make a general application, apply for a specific hot topic that we are recruiting an author for, or submit your own idea.

Table of Contents

Preface

Another book on design patterns in C++? Why that, and why now? Hasn't everything there is to know about design patterns been written already?

There are several reasons why yet another book on *design patterns* has been written, but first of all, this is very much a C++ book—this is not a book on *design patterns* in C++ but a book on design patterns *in* C++, and the emphasis sets it apart. C++ has all the capabilities of a traditional object-oriented language, so all the classic object-oriented design patterns, such as Factory and Strategy, can be implemented in C++. A few of those are covered in this book. But the full power of C++ is realized when you utilize its generic programming capabilities. Remember that design patterns are frequently occurring design challenges and the commonly accepted solution—both sides are equally important in a pattern. It stands to reason that when new tools become available, new solutions become possible. Over time, the community settles on some of these solutions as the most advantageous overall, and a new variation of an old design pattern is born—the same challenge, but a different preferred solution. But expanding capabilities also open up new frontiers—with new tools at our disposal, new design challenges arise.

In this book, we focus on design patterns where C++ has something essential to add to at least one of the two sides of the pattern. On the one hand, we have patterns such as Visitor, where the generic programming capabilities of C++ allow for a better solution. That better solution was made possible by new features added in recent versions of the language, from C++11 to C++17. On the other hand, generic programming is still programming (only the execution of the program happens at compile time); programming requires design, and design has common challenges that are not all that dissimilar to the challenges of traditional programming. Thus, many of the traditional patterns have their twins, or at least close siblings, in generic programming, and we largely focus on those patterns in this book. A prime example is the Strategy pattern, better known in the generic programming community by its alternative name, the Policy pattern. Finally, a language as complex as C++ is bound to have a few idiosyncrasies of its own that often lead to C++, specific challenges that have common, or *standard*, solutions. While not quite deserving of being called *patterns*, these C++-specific idioms are also covered in this book.

All that said, there are three main reasons why this book has been written:

- To cover C++, specific solutions for otherwise general, *classic* design patterns
- To show C++, specific pattern variants that occur when old design challenges arise in the new domain of generic programming
- To keep our patterns up to date with the language's evolution

Who this book is for

This book is intended for C++ programmers who want to learn from *the wisdom of the community*—from commonly-recognized good solutions to frequently occurring design problems. Another way to put it is that this book is a way for a programmer to learn from someone else's mistakes.

This is not a *learn C++* book; the target audience is mostly programmers who are reasonably familiar with the tools and the syntax of the language, and who are more interested in learning how and why these tools should be used. However, this book will also be useful for programmers wanting to learn more about C++, but wishing that their study could be guided by concrete and practical examples (for such programmers, we recommend having a C++ reference book close to hand as well). Finally, programmers who want to learn not just what's new in C++11, C++14, and C++17, but what all these new features can be used for, will hopefully find this book illuminating as well.

What this book covers

Chapter 1, *An Introduction to Inheritance and Polymorphism*, provides a brief overview of the object-oriented features of C++. This chapter is not intended as a reference for object-oriented programming in C++, but, rather, highlights the aspects of it that are important for the subsequent chapters.

Chapter 2, *Class and Function Templates*, provides an overview of the generic programming facilities of C++—class templates, function templates, and lambda expressions. This chapter covers template instantiations and specializations, along with template function argument deduction and overload resolution, and prepares you for more complex uses of templates in later chapters.

Chapter 3, *Memory Ownership*, describes modern idiomatic ways of expressing different kinds of memory ownership in C++. This is a collection of conventions or idioms—the compiler does not enforce these rules, but programmers will find it easier to understand each other if they use the shared idiomatic vocabulary.

Chapter 4, *Swap - From Simple to Subtle*, explores one of the most basic C++ operations, the swap, or exchange, of two values. This operation has surprisingly complex interactions with other C++ features that are discussed in the chapter.

Chapter 5, *A Comprehensive Look at Resource Acquisition is Initialization*, explores in detail one of the fundamental concepts of C++, that of resource management, and introduces what may be the most popular C++ idiom, RAII, which is the standard C++ approach to managing resources.

Chapter 6, *Understanding Type Erasure*, provides insight into a C++ technique that has been available in C++ for a long time, but has grown in popularity and importance since the introduction of C++11. Type erasure allows the programmer to write abstract programs that do not explicitly mention certain types.

Chapter 7, *SFINAE and Overload Resolution Management*, discusses SFINAE—a C++ idiom that is, on the one hand, essential to the use of templates in C++ and *just happens* transparently, while on the other hand, requires a very thorough and subtle understanding of C++ templates when used purposefully.

Chapter 8, *The Curiously Recurring Template Pattern*, describes a *mind-wrapping* template-based pattern that combines the benefits of object-oriented programming with the flexibility of templates. The chapter explains the pattern and teaches you how to use it properly to solve practical problems. Lastly, this chapter prepares you for recognizing this pattern in later chapters.

Chapter 9, *Named Arguments and Method Chaining*, covers an unusual technique for calling functions in C++, using named arguments instead of positional ones. This is another one of those idioms we use implicitly in every C++ program, but its explicit purposeful use takes some thought.

Chapter 10, *Local Buffer Optimization*, is the only purely performance-oriented chapter in this book. Performance and efficiency are critical considerations that influence every design decision that affects the language itself—there is not a feature in the language that was not reviewed from the point of view of efficiency before being accepted into the standard. It is only fair that a chapter is dedicated to a common idiom used to improve the performance of C++ programs.

Chapter 11, *ScopeGuard*, introduces an old C++ pattern that has changed almost beyond recognition with the recent versions of C++. The chapter teaches you about a pattern for easily writing exception-safe, or, more generally, error-safe code in C++.

Chapter 12, *Friend Factory*, describes another old pattern that finds new uses in modern C++. This pattern is used to generate functions *associated* with templates, such as arithmetic operators for every type generated by a template.

Chapter 13, *Virtual Constructors and Factories*, covers another classic object-oriented programming pattern as applied to C++, the Factory pattern. In the process, the chapter also shows you how to get the appearance of polymorphic behavior from C++ constructors, even though constructors cannot be virtual.

Chapter 14, *The Template Method Pattern and the Non-Virtual Idiom*, describes an interesting crossover between a classic object-oriented pattern, the template, and a very C++-centric idiom. Together, they form a pattern that describes the optimal use of virtual functions in C++.

Chapter 15, *Singleton, a Classic OOP Pattern*, explains another classic object-oriented pattern, the Singleton, as it applies to C++. The chapter discusses when the pattern can be reasonably applied and when it should be avoided, and demonstrates several common implementations of the Singleton.

Chapter 16, *Policy-Based Design*, covers one of the jewels of C++ design patterns, the Policy pattern (more commonly known as the Strategy pattern), applied at compile time, that is, as a generic programming pattern instead of an object-oriented pattern.

Chapter 17, *Adapters and Decorators*, discusses the two very broad and closely related patterns as they apply to C++. The chapter considers the use of these patterns in object-oriented designs, as well as in generic programs.

Chapter 18, *Visitor and Multiple Dispatch*, rounds off our gallery of the classic object-oriented programming patterns with the perennially popular Visitor pattern. The chapter explains the pattern itself, then focuses on the ways that modern C++ makes the implementation of Visitor simpler, more robust, and less error-prone.

To get the most out of this book

To run examples from this book, you will need a computer running Windows, Linux, or macOS (C++ programs can be built on something as small as a Raspberry Pi). You will also need a modern C++ compiler, such as GCC, Clang, Visual Studio, or another compiler that supports the C++ language up to C++17. You will need a basic knowledge of GitHub and Git in order to clone a project with examples.

Download the example code files

You can download the example code files for this book from your account at www.packt.com. If you purchased this book elsewhere, you can visit www.packt.com/support and register to have the files emailed directly to you.

You can download the code files by following these steps:

1. Log in or register at www.packt.com.

2. Select the **SUPPORT** tab.

3. Click on **Code Downloads & Errata**.

4. Enter the name of the book in the **Search** box and follow the onscreen instructions.

Once the file is downloaded, please make sure that you unzip or extract the folder using the latest version of:

- WinRAR/7-Zip for Windows

- Zipeg/iZip/UnRarX for Mac

- 7-Zip/PeaZip for Linux

The code bundle for the book is also hosted on GitHub at https://github.com/PacktPublishing/Hands-On-Design-Patterns-with-CPP. In case there's an update to the code, it will be updated on the existing GitHub repository.

We also have other code bundles from our rich catalog of books and videos available at https://github.com/PacktPublishing/. Check them out!

Conventions used

There are a number of text conventions used throughout this book.

`CodeInText`: Indicates code words in the text, database table names, folder names, filenames, file extensions, pathnames, dummy URLs, user input, and Twitter handles. Here is an example—*The* `overload_set` *is a variadic class template.*

A block of code is set as follows:

```
template <typename T>
T increment(T x) { return x + 1; }
```

Get in touch

Feedback from our readers is always welcome.

General feedback: If you have questions about any aspect of this book, mention the book title in the subject of your message and email us at `customercare@packtpub.com`.

Errata: Although we have taken every care to ensure the accuracy of our content, mistakes do happen. If you have found a mistake in this book, we would be grateful if you would report this to us. Please visit `www.packt.com/submit-errata`, selecting your book, clicking on the Errata Submission Form link, and entering the details.

Piracy: If you come across any illegal copies of our works in any form on the internet, we would be grateful if you would provide us with the location address or website name. Please contact us at `copyright@packt.com` with a link to the material.

If you are interested in becoming an author: If there is a topic that you have expertise in and you are interested in either writing or contributing to a book, please visit `authors.packtpub.com`.

Reviews

Please leave a review. Once you have read and used this book, why not leave a review on the site that you purchased it from? Potential readers can then see and use your unbiased opinion to make purchase decisions, we at Packt can understand what you think about our products, and our authors can see your feedback on their book. Thank you!

For more information about Packt, please visit `packt.com`.

1
An Introduction to Inheritance and Polymorphism

C++ is, first and foremost, an object-oriented language, and objects are the fundamental building blocks of a C++ program. Class hierarchies are used to express relationships and interactions between different parts of a software system, define and implement the interfaces between components, and organize data and code. While this isn't a book for teaching C++, the aim of this chapter is to give the reader enough knowledge about C++ language features as they relate to classes and inheritance, which will be used in later chapters. To that end, we don't attempt to completely describe the C++ tools for working with classes but introduce the concepts and language constructs that will be used throughout this book.

The following topics will be covered in this chapter:

- What are classes and what is their role in C++?
- What are class hierarchies and how does C++ use inheritance?
- What is runtime polymorphism and how is it used in C++?

Classes and objects

Object-oriented programming is a way to structure a program by combining the algorithms and the data that the algorithms operate on into single entities called **objects**. Most object-oriented languages, including C++, are class-based. A class is a definition of an object—it describes the algorithms and the data, its format, and relations to other classes. An object is a concrete instantiation of a class, that is, a variable. An object has an address, which is a location in memory. A class is a user-defined type. In general, any number of objects can be instantiated from the definition provided by the class (some classes limit the number of objects that can be created, but this is an exception, not the norm).

In C++, the data contained in a class is organized as a collection of data members, variables of different types. The algorithms are implemented as functions—the methods of the class. While there's no language requirement that the data members of a class should be somehow relevant to the implementation of its methods, it's one of the signs of good design when the data is well encapsulated in the classes, and the methods have limited interaction with external data.

This concept of encapsulation is central to the classes in C++—the language allows us to control which data members and methods are public—visible outside of the class, and which are internal—private to the class. A well-designed class has mostly, or only, private data members, and the only public methods are those needed to express the public interface of the class—in other words, what the class does. This public interface is like a contract—the class designer promises that this class provides certain features and operations. The private data and methods of the class are part of the implementation, and they can be changed as long as the public interface, the contract we've committed to, remains valid. For example, the following class represents a rational number and supports the increment operation, as exposed by its public interface:

```
class Rational {
    public:
    Rational& operator+=(const Rational& rhs);
};
```

A well-designed class doesn't expose any more of the implementation details than it has to through its public interface. The implementation isn't part of the contract, although the documented interface may impose some restrictions on it. For example, if we promise that all rational numbers don't contain any common multipliers in the numerator and denomination, the addition should include the step of canceling them. That would be a good use of a private member function—the implementation of several other operations will need to call it, but the client of the class never needs to call it because every rational number is already reduced to its lowest terms before it's exposed to the callers:

```
class Rational {
    public:
    Rational& operator+=(const Rational& rhs);
    private:
    long n_;      // numerator
    long d_;      // denominator
    void reduce();
};
Rational& Rational::operator+=(const Rational& rhs) {
    n_ = n_*rhs.d_ + rhs.n_*d_;
    d_ = d_*rhs.d_;
    reduce();
```

```
        return *this;
    }
    Rational a, b;
    a += b;
```

The class methods have special access to the data members—they can access the private data of the class. Note the distinction between the class and the object here—operator+=() is a method of the Rational class and is invoked on the object, a. However, it has access to the private data of the b object as well, because a and b are objects of the same class. If a member function references a class member by name without any additional qualifiers, then it's accessing a member of the same class it's invoked on (we can make it explicit by writing this->n_ and this->d_). Accessing members of another object of the same class requires a pointer or a reference to that object, but is otherwise not restricted, as would have been the case if we tried to access a private data member from a non-member function.

By the way, C++ also supports C-style structs. But in C++, a struct isn't limited to just an aggregate of data members—it can have methods, public and private access modifiers, and anything else classes have. From a language point of view, the only difference between a class and a struct is the default access—in a class, all members and methods are private by default, while in a struct they're public. Beyond that, the use of structs instead of classes in a matter of convention—traditionally, structs are used for C-style structs (structs that would be legal in C) as well as *almost* C-style structs, for example, a struct with only a constructor added. Of course, this boundary isn't precise and is a matter of coding styles and practices in each project or team.

In addition to the methods and data members we've seen, C++ also supports static data and methods. A static method is very similar to a regular non-member function—it isn't invoked on any particular object, and the only way it can get access to an object of any type is through its arguments. However, unlike a non-member function, a static method retains its privileged access to the private data of the class.

Classes by themselves are a useful way to group together the algorithms and the data they operate on and to limit access to some data. However, the most powerful object-oriented features of C++ are inheritance and the resulting class hierarchies.

Inheritance and class hierarchies

Class hierarchies in C++ serve a dual purpose. On the one hand, they allow us to express relations between objects. On the other hand, they let us compose more complex types from simpler ones. Both uses are accomplished through inheritance.

The concept of inheritance is central to the C++ use of classes and objects. Inheritance allows us to define new classes as extensions of existing ones. When a derived class is inherited from the base class, it contains, in some form, all of the data and the algorithms that were in the base class, and it adds some of its own. In C++, it's important to distinguish between two primary types of inheritance—public and private.

Public inheritance inherits the public interface of the class. It also inherits the implementation—the data members of the base class are also a part of the derived class. But the inheritance of the interface is what distinguishes public inheritance—the derived class has, as a part of its public interface, the public member functions of the base class.

Remember that the public interface is like a contract—we promise to the clients of the class that it supports certain operations, maintains some invariants, and obeys the specified restrictions. By publicly inheriting from the base class, we bind the derived class to the same contract (plus any extensions of the contract, should we decide to define additional public interfaces). Because the derived class also respects the interface contract of the base class, we could use a derived class in any place in the code where a base class is expected—we would not be able to use any of the extensions to the interface (the code expects the base class, we don't know about any extensions at that point), but the base class interface and its restrictions have to be valid.

This is often expressed as the *is-a principle*—an instance of a derived class is also an instance of the base class. However, the way we interpret the *is-a* relationship in C++ isn't exactly intuitive. For example, is a square a rectangle? If it is, then we can derive the `Square` class from the `Rectangle` class:

```
class Rectangle {
    public:
    double Length() const { return length_; }
    double Width() const { return width_; }
    ...
    private:
    double l_;
    double w_;
};
class Square : public Rectangle {
    ...
};
```

Right away, there's something that doesn't seem right—the derived class has two data members for dimensions, but it really needs only one. We would have to somehow enforce that they're always the same. This doesn't seem so bad—the Rectangle class has the interface that allows for any positive values of length and width, and the Square imposes additional restrictions. But it's worse than that—the Rectangle class has a contract that allows the user to make the dimensions different. This can be quite explicit:

```
class Rectangle {
    public:
    void Scale(double sl, double sw) {    // Scale the dimensions
        length_ *= sl;
        width_ *= sw;
    }
    ...
};
```

Now, we have a public method that allows us to distort the rectangle, altering its aspect ratio. Like any other public method, it's inherited by the derived classes, so now the Square class has it too. In fact, by using public inheritance, we assert that a Square object can be used anywhere a Rectangle object is used, without even knowing that it's really a Square. Clearly, this is a promise we can't keep—when the client of our class hierarchy tries to change the aspect ratio of a square, we can't do it. We could ignore the call or report an error at runtime. Either way, we've violated the contract provided by the base class. There's only one solution—in C++, a square isn't a rectangle. Note that a rectangle is usually not a square, either—the contract provided by the Square interface could contain any number of guarantees that we can't maintain if we derive the Rectangle class from Square.

Similarly, a penguin isn't a bird in C++ if the bird interface includes flying. The correct design for such cases usually includes a more abstract base class, Bird, that doesn't make any promises that at least one derived class can't keep (for example, a Bird object doesn't make a guarantee that it can fly). Then, we create intermediate-based classes, such as FlyingBird and FlightlessBird, that are derived from the common base class and serve as base classes for the more specific classes such as Eagle or Penguin. The important lesson here is that whether or not a penguin is a bird in C++ depends on how we define what a bird is, or, in C++ terms, what the public interface of the Bird class is.

Because the public inheritance implies the *is-a* relationship, the language allows a wide range of conversions between references and pointers to different classes in the same hierarchy. First of all, a conversion from a pointer to a derived class into a pointer to the base class is implicit (this is the same for references):

```
class Base { ... };
class Derived : public Base { ... };
```

```
Derived* d = new Derived;
Base* b = d;    // Implicit conversion
```

This conversion is always valid because an instance of the derived class is also an instance of the base class. The inverse conversion is possible but has to be made explicit:

```
Base* b = new Derived;    // *b is really Derived
Derived* d = b;           // Does not compile, not implicit
Derived* d = static_cast<Derived*>(b);    // Explicit conversion
```

The reason this conversion isn't implicit is that it's valid only if the base class pointer really points to a derived object (otherwise, the behavior is undefined). The programmer, therefore, must explicitly assert, using the static cast, that somehow, through the logic of the program or a prior test or by some other means, it's known that this conversion is valid. If you aren't sure that the conversion is valid, there's a safer way to try it without causing undefined behavior; we'll learn about this in the next section.

The other kind of inheritance in C++ is private inheritance. When inheriting privately, the derived classes don't extend the public interface of the base class—all base class methods become private in the derived class. Any public interface has to be created by the derived class, starting from a clean slate. There's no assumption that an object of the derived class can be used in place of an object of the base class. What the derived class does get from the base class is the implementation details—both the methods and the data members can be used by the derived class to implement its own algorithms. It's said, therefore, that private inheritance implements a *has-a* relationship—the derived object has an instance of the base class contained inside of it.

The relation of the privately derived class to its base class is, therefore, similar to that of the relationship of a class to its data members. The latter implementation technique is known as composition—an object is composed from any number of other objects, which are all used as its data members. In the absence of any reason to do otherwise, the composition should be preferred to private inheritance. What, then, might be the reasons to use private inheritance? There are several possibilities. First of all, it's possible, within the derived class, to re-expose one of the public member functions of the base class with the help of the using declaration:

```
class Container : private std::vector<int> {
    public:
    using std::vector<int>::size;
    ...
};
```

This can be useful in rare cases, but it's also equivalent to an inline forwarding function:

```
class Container {
    private:
    std::vector<int> v_;
    public:
    size_t size() const { return v_.size(); }
    ...
};
```

Second, a pointer or reference to a derived object can be converted into a pointer or reference to the base object, but only inside a member function of the derived class. Again, the equivalent functionality for composition is provided by taking the address of a data member. So far, we haven't seen a good reason to use private inheritance, and indeed, the common advice is to prefer composition. But the next two reasons are more significant, and either one could be motivation enough to use private inheritance.

One good reason to use private inheritance has to do with the size of the composed or derived objects. It isn't uncommon to have base classes that provide only methods but no data members. Such classes have no data of their own and, therefore, should not occupy any memory. But in C++, they have to be given a non-zero size. This has to do with the requirement that any two different objects or variables have different and unique addresses. Typically, if we have two variables declared one after the other, the address of the second one is the address of the first one, plus the size of the first one:

```
int x;      // Created at address 0xffff0000, size is 4
int y;      // Created at address 0xffff0004
```

To avoid the need to handle zero-sized objects differently, C++ assigns an empty object the size of one. If such an object is used as a data member of a class, it occupies at least 1 byte (the alignment requirements for the next data member may increase this value). This is wasted memory; it'll never be used for anything. On the other hand, if an empty class is used as a base class, there's no requirement that the base part of an object must have a non-zero size. The entire object of the derived class must have a non-zero size, but the address of a derived object, its base object, and its first data member can all be at the same address. Therefore, it's legal in C++ to allocate no memory for an empty base class, even though `sizeof()` returns 1 for this class. While legal, such empty base class optimization isn't required and is considered an optimization. Nonetheless, most modern compilers do this optimization:

```
class Empty {
    public:
    void useful_function();
};
class Derived : private Empty {
```

```
    int i;
};     // sizeof(Derived) == 4
class Composed {
    int i;
    Empty e;
};     // sizeof(Composed) == 8
```

If we create many derived objects, the memory saved by the empty base optimization can be significant.

The second reason to possibly use private inheritance has to do with virtual functions, and this will be explained in the next section.

Polymorphism and virtual functions

When we discussed public inheritance earlier, we mentioned that a derived object can be used in any place where a base object is expected. Even with this requirement, it's often useful to know what the actual type of the object is—in other words, what type the object was created as:

```
Derived d;
Base& b = d;
...
b.some_method(); // b is really a Derived object
```

`some_method()` is a part of the public interface of the `Base` class and has to be valid for the `Derived` class as well. But, within the flexibility allowed by the contract of the base class interface, it can do something different. As an example, we've already used the avian hierarchy before to represent different birds, in particular, birds that can fly. The `FlyingBird` class can be assumed to have a `fly()` method, and every specific bird class derived from it has to support flight. But eagles fly differently from vultures, and so the implementation of the `fly()` method in the two derived classes, `Eagle` and `Vulture`, can be different. Any code that operates on arbitrary `FlyingBird` objects can call the `fly()` method, but the results will vary depending on the actual type of the object.

This functionality is implemented in C++ using virtual functions. A virtual public function must be declared in the base class:

```
class FlyingBird : public Bird {
    public:
    virtual void fly(double speed, double direction) {
        ... move the bird at the specified speed in the given direction ...
    }
```

```
    . . .
};
```

A derived class inherits both the declaration and the implementation of this function. The declaration and the contract it provides must be respected. If the implementation meets the needs of the derived class, there's no need to do anything more. But if the derived class needs to change the implementation, it can override the implementation of the base class:

```
class Vulture : public FlyingBird {
    public:
    virtual void fly(double speed, double direction) {
        ... move the bird but accumulate exhaustion if too fast ...
    }
};
```

When a virtual function is called, the C++ runtime system must determine what the real type of the object is. Usually, this information isn't known at compile time and must be determined at runtime:

```
void hunt(FlyingBird& b) {
    b.fly(...);    // Could be Vulture or Eagle
    . . .
};
Eagle e;
hunt(e);    // Now b in hunt() is Eagle, FlyingBird::fly() is called
Vulture v;
hunt(v);    // Now b in hunt() is Vulture, Vulture::fly() is called
```

The programming technique where some code operates on any number of base objects and invokes the same methods, but the results depend on the actual type of these objects, is known as runtime polymorphism, and the objects that support this technique are **polymorphic**. In C++, polymorphic objects must have at least one virtual function, and only the parts of their interface that use the virtual functions for some or all of the implementation are polymorphic.

It should be evident from this explanation that the declaration of the virtual function and its overrides should be identical—the programmer calls the function on a base object, but the version that's implemented in the derived class runs instead. This can happen only if the two functions have identical arguments and return types (one exception is that if a virtual function in the base class returns a pointer or a reference to an object of some type, the override can return a pointer or a reference to an object derived from that type).

A very common special case of polymorphic hierarchies is one where the base class doesn't have a good *default* implementation of the virtual function. For example, all flying birds fly, but they all fly at different speeds, so there's no reason to select one speed as the default. In C++, we can refuse to provide any implementation for a virtual function in the base class. Such functions are called pure virtual, and any base class that contains a pure virtual function is known as an abstract class:

```
class FlyingBirt {
    public:
    virtual void fly(...) = 0;    // Pure virtual function
};
```

An abstract class defines an interface only; it's the job of the concrete derived classes to implement it. If the base class contains a pure virtual function, every derived class that's instantiated in the program must provide an implementation. In other words, an object of a base class can't be created. We can, however, have a pointer or a reference to an object of a base class—they really point to a derived class, but we can operate on it through the base class interface.

A few notes on the C++ syntax—when overriding a virtual function, it isn't required to repeat the virtual keyword. If the base class declares a virtual function with the same name and arguments, the one in the derived class will always be a virtual function and will override the one from the base class. Note that, if the arguments differ, the derived class function doesn't override anything and instead shadows the name of the base class function. This can lead to subtle bugs where the programmer intended to override a base class function but didn't copy the declaration correctly:

```
class Eagle : public FlyingBird {
    public:
    virtual void fly(int speed, double direction);
};
```

Here, the types of the arguments are slightly different. The Eagle::fly() function is also virtual, but it doesn't override FlyingBird::fly(). If the latter is a pure virtual function, the bug will be caught because every pure virtual function must be implemented in a derived class. But if FlyingBird::fly() has the default implementation, then the bug will go undetected by the compiler. C++11 provides a very useful feature that greatly simplifies finding such bugs—any function that's intended to be an override of a base class virtual function can be declared with the override keyword:

```
class Eagle : public FlyingBird {
    public:
    void fly(int speed, double direction) override;
};
```

The virtual keyword is still optional, but if the FlyingBird class doesn't have a virtual function that we could be overriding with this declaration, this code won't compile.

The most common use of virtual functions, by far, is in hierarchies that use public inheritance—since every derived object is also a base object (*is-a* relationship), a program can often operate on a collection of derived objects as if they were all of the same type, and the virtual function overrides ensure that the right processing happens for every object:

```
void MakeLoudBoom(std::vector<FlyingBird*> birds) {
    for (auto bird : birds) {
        bird->fly(...);    // Same action, different results
    }
}
```

But virtual functions can also be used with private inheritance. The use is less straightforward (and much less common)—after all, an object that's derived privately can't be accessed through a base class pointer (a private base class is referred to as an *inaccessible base*, and an attempt to cast a derived class pointer to the base class will fail). However, there's one context in which this cast is permitted, and that's within a member function of the derived class. Here's, then, the way to arrange a virtual function call from a privately inhered base class to the derived one:

```
class Base {
    public:
    virtual void f() { std::cout << "Base::f()" << std::endl; }
    void g() { f(); }
};
class Derived : private Base {
    virtual void f() { std::cout << "Derived::f()" << std::endl; }
    void h() { g(); }
};
Derived d;
d.h(); // Prints "Derived::f()"
```

The public methods of the Base class become private in the Derived class, so we can't call them directly. We can, however, call them from another method of the Derived class, such as the public method, h(). We can then call f() directly from h(), but that doesn't prove anything—it would come as no surprise if Derived::h() invoked Derived::f(). Instead, we call the Base::f() function that's inherited from the Base class. Inside that function, we're in the Base class—the body of this function may have been written and compiled long before the Derived class was implemented. And yet, in this context, the virtual function override works correctly and Derived::f() is called, just as it would if the inheritance was public.

In the previous section, we recommended that the composition is preferred to private inheritance unless there's a reason to do otherwise. There's no good way to implement similar functionality using composition; so, if the virtual function behavior is desired, private inheritance is the only way to go.

A class with a virtual method has to have its type encoded into every object—this is the only way to know, at runtime, what was the type of the object when it was constructed, after we converted the pointer into a base class pointer and lost any other information about the original type. That type information isn't free; it takes space—a polymorphic object is always larger than an object with the same data members but no virtual methods (usually by the size of a pointer). The extra size doesn't depend on how many virtual functions the class has—at long as it has one, the type information must be encoded in the object. Now, recall that a pointer to the base class can be converted into a pointer to the derived class, but only if we know the correct type of the derived class. With the static cast, there's no way to test whether our knowledge is correct. For non-polymorphic classes (classes without any virtual functions), there can be no better way; once their original type is lost, there is no way to recover it. But for polymorphic objects, the type is encoded in the object, so there has to be a way to use that information to check whether our assumption is correct about which derived object this really is. Indeed, there is a way. It's provided by the dynamic cast:

```
class Base { ... };
class Derived : public Base { ... };
Base* b1 = new Derived;    // Really Derived
Base* b2 = new Base;       // Not Derived
Derived* d1 = dynamic_cast<Derived*>(b1);    // Succeeds
Derived* d2 = dynamic_cast<Derived*>(b2);    // d2 == nullptr
```

The dynamic cast doesn't tell us what the real type of the object is; rather, it allows us to ask the question—*Is the real type* Derived? If our guess at the type is correct, the cast succeeds and returns the pointer to the derived object. If the real type is something else, the cast fails and returns a null pointer. The dynamic cast can also be used with references, with similar effects, save one—there's no *null reference*. A function that returns a reference must always return a reference to some valid object. Since the dynamic cast can't return a reference to a valid object if the requested type doesn't match the actual type. The only alternative is to throw an exception.

So far, we've limited ourselves to only one base class. While it's much easier to think about class hierarchies if we imagine them as trees, with the base class and the root and branches where multiple classes are derived from the same base, C++ doesn't impose such limitations. Next, we'll learn about inheriting from several base classes at once.

Multiple inheritance

In C++, a class can be derived from several base classes. Going back to our birds, let's make an observation—while flying birds have a lot in common with each other, they also have something in common with other flying animals, specifically, the ability to fly. Since flight isn't limited to birds, we may want to move the data and the algorithms related to processing flight into a separate base class. But there's also no denying that an eagle is a bird. We could express this relation if we used two base classes to construct the `Eagle` class:

```
class Eagle : public Bird, public FlyingAnimal { ... };
```

In this case, the inheritance from both base classes is public, which means that the derived class inherits both interfaces and must fulfill two separate contracts. What happens if both interfaces define a method with the same name? If this method isn't virtual, then an attempt to invoke it on the derived class is ambiguous, and the program doesn't compile. If the method is virtual and the derived class has an override for it, then there's no ambiguity since the method of the derived class is called. Also, `Eagle` is now both `Bird` and `FlyingAnimal`:

```
Eagle* e = new Eagle;
Bird* b = e;
FlyingAnimal* f = e;
```

Both conversions from the derived class into the base class pointer are allowed. The reverse conversions must be made explicitly using a static or a dynamic cast. There's another interesting conversion—if we have a pointer to a `FlyingAnimal` class that's also a `Bird` class, can we cast from one to the other? Yes, we can with a dynamic cast:

```
Bird* b = new Eagle;    // Also a FlyingAnimal
FlyingAnimal* f = dynamic_cast<FlyingAnimal*>(b);
```

When used in this context, the dynamic cast is sometimes called a **cross-cast**—we aren't casting up or down the hierarchy (between derived and based classes) but across the hierarchy—between the classes on different branches of the hierarchy tree.

Multiple inheritance is often maligned and disfavored in C++. Much of this advice is outdated and stems from the time when compilers implemented multiple inheritance poorly and inefficiently. Today, with modern compilers, this isn't a concern. It's often said that multiple inheritance makes the class hierarchy harder to understand and reason about. Perhaps it would be more accurate to say that it's harder to design a good multiple inheritance hierarchy that accurately reflects the relations between different properties, and that a poorly designed hierarchy is difficult to understand and reason about.

These concerns mostly apply to hierarchies that use public inheritance. Multiple inheritance can be private as well. There's even less reason to use multiple private inheritance instead of composition than there was to use single private inheritance. However, the empty base optimization can be done on multiple empty base classes and remains a valid reason to use private inheritance, if it applies:

```
class Empty1 {};
class Empty2 {};
class Derived : private Empty1, private Empty2 {
    int i;
};    // sizeof(Derived) == 4
class Composed {
    int i;
    Empty1 e1;
    Empty2 e2;
};    // sizeof(Composed) == 8
```

Multiple inheritance can be particularly effective when the derived class represents a system that combines several unrelated, non-overlapping attributes. We'll encounter such cases throughout this book when we explore various design patterns and their C++ representations.

Summary

While by no means a complete guide or reference to classes and objects, this chapter introduces and explains the concepts the reader will need to understand the examples and explanations in the rest of this book. As our interest is and will be in representing design patterns in C++, this chapter focuses on the proper use of classes and inheritance. We pay particular attention to what relations are expressed through different C++ features—it's through these features we'll express relations and interactions between different components that form a design pattern.

The next chapter will similarly cover knowledge of C++ templates, which will be necessary to understand the subsequent chapters of this book.

Questions

- What is the importance of objects in C++?
- What relation is expressed by public inheritance?
- What relation is expressed by private inheritance?
- What is a polymorphic object?

Further reading

For more information on what was covered in this chapter, check out the following links:

- **C++ Fundamentals**: https://www.packtpub.com/application-development/c-fundamentals
- **C++ Data Structures and Algorithms**: https://www.packtpub.com/application-development/c-data-structures-and-algorithms
- **Mastering C++ Programming**: https://www.packtpub.com/application-development/mastering-c-programming
- **Beginning C++ Programming**: https://www.packtpub.com/application-development/beginning-c-programming

Class and Function Templates

The template programming features of C++ form a large and complex subject, with many books dedicated exclusively to teaching these features. In this book, we will use many of the advanced C++ generic programming features. How, then, should we prepare the reader to understand these language constructs as they make their appearance throughout this book? This chapter takes an informal approach—instead of precise definitions, we demonstrate the use of templates through examples and explain what the different language features do. If you find your knowledge lacking at this point, you're encouraged to seek a deeper understanding and read one or more of the books dedicated entirely to the C++ language that's focused on explaining its syntax and semantics. Of course, the reader wishing for more precise, formal description is referred to the C++ standard or a reference book.

The following topics will be covered in this chapter:

- Templates in C++
- Class and function templates
- Template instantiations
- Template specializations
- Overloading of template functions
- Variadic templates
- Lambda expressions

Templates in C++

One of the greatest strengths of C++ is its support for generic programming. In generic programming, the algorithms and data structures are written in terms of generic types that will be specified later. This allows the programmer to implement a function or a class once, and later, instantiate it for many different types. Templates are a C++ feature that allows classes and functions to be defined on generic types. C++ supports three kinds of templates—function, class, and variable templates.

Function templates

Function templates are generic functions—unlike the regular functions, a template function does not declare its argument types. Instead, the types are template parameters:

```
template <typename T>
T increment(T x) { return x + 1; }
```

This `template` function can be used to increment a value of any type by one, for which adding one is a valid operation:

```
increment(5);      // T is int, returns 6
increment(4.2);    // T is double, return 5.2
char c[10];
increment(c);      // T is char*, returns &c[1]
```

Most template functions have some limitations on the types that are used as their template parameters. For example, our `increment()` function requires that the expression x + 1 is valid for the type of x. Otherwise, the attempt to instantiate the template will fail, with a somewhat verbose compilation error.

Both non-member and class member functions can be function templates; however, virtual functions cannot be templates. The generic types can be used not only to declare function parameters, but to declare any variables inside the body of the function:

```
template <typename T>
T sum(T from, T to, T step) {
    T res = from;
    while ((from += step) < to) { res += from; }
    return res;
}
```

We will see more of the function templates later, but let's introduce the class template next.

Class templates

Class templates are classes that use generic types, usually to declare its data members, but also to declare methods and local variables inside them:

```cpp
template <typename T>
class ArrayOf2 {
    public:
    T& operator[](size_t i) { return a_[i]; }
    const T& operator[](size_t i) const { return a_[i]; }
    T sum() const { return a_[0] + a_[1]; }
    private:
    T a_[2];
};
```

This class is implemented once, and can then be used to define an array of two elements of any type:

```cpp
ArrayOf2<int> i;
i[0] = 1; i[1] = 5;
std::cout << i.sum();        // 6

ArrayOf2<double> x;
x[0] = -3.5; x[1] = 4;
std::cout << x.sum();        // 0.5

ArrayOf2<char*> c;
char s[] = "Hello";
c[0] = s; c[1] = s + 2;
```

Pay particular attention to the last example—you might expect the ArrayOf2 template not to be valid with a type such as char*—after all, it has a method, sum(), that does not compile if the type of a_[0] and a_[1] is a pointer. However, our example compiles as written—a method of a class template does not have to be valid until we try to use it. If we never call c.sum(), then the fact that it would not compile never comes up, and the program remains valid.

Variable template

The last kind of template in C++ is the variable template, which was introduced in C++14. This template allows us to define a variable with a generic type:

```cpp
template <typename T>
constexpr T pi =
T(3.1415926535897932384626433832795028841971693993751058209749445923078L);
```

```
pi<float>;      // 3.141592
pi<double>;     // 3.141592653589793
```

Variable templates are not used in the rest of this book, so we will not mention them again.

Non-type template parameters

Usually, template parameters are types, but C++ also allows for several kinds of non-type parameters. First of all, template parameters can be values of integer or enumeration types:

```
template <typename T, size_t N> class Array {
    public:
    T& operator[](size_t i) {
        if (i >= N) throw std::out_of_range("Bad index");
        return data_[i];
    private:
    T data_[N];
};
Array<int, 5> a;        // OK
cin >> a[0];
Array<int, a[0]> b;     // Error
```

This is a template with two parameters—the first is a type, but the second is not. It is a value of type `size_t` that determines the size of the array; the advantage of such a template over a built-in C-style array is that it can do range checking. The C++ standard library has a `std::array` class template that should be used instead of implementing your own array in any real program, but it does make for an easy-to-follow example.

The values of non-type parameters that are used to instantiate a template must be compile-time constants or `constexpr` values—the last line in the preceding example is invalid because the value of `a[0]` is not known until the program reads it in at runtime. The numeric template parameters used to be very popular in C++ because they allow complex compile-time calculations to be implemented, but in the recent versions of the standard, the `constexpr` functions can be used to the same effect and are much easier to read.

The second kind of non-type template parameter worth mentioning is the *template template* parameter—a template parameter that is itself a template. We will need them in the later chapters of this book. This template parameter is substituted—not with a name of a class, but a name of an entire template. Here is a function template that has two *template template* parameters:

```
template <template <typename> class Out_container,
          template <typename> class In_container,
          typename T>
```

```
Out_container<T> resequence(const In_container<T>& in_container) {
    Out_container<T> out_container;
    for (auto x : in_container) {
        out_container.push_back(x);
    }
    return out_container;
}
```

This function takes an arbitrary container as an argument and returns another container, a different template, but instantiated on the same type, with the values copied from the input container:

```
std::vector<int> v { 1, 2, 3, 4, 5 };
auto d = resequence<std::deque>(v); // deque with 1, 2, 3, 4, 5
```

Templates are a kind of recipe for generating code. Next, we will see how we can convert these recipes into actual code we can run.

Template instantiations

The template name is not a type and cannot be used to declare a variable or call a function. To create a type or a function, the template must be instantiated. Most of the time, the templates are instantiated implicitly when they are used. We will again start with the function templates.

Function templates

To use a function template to generate a function, we have to specify which types should be used for all template type parameters. We can just specify the types directly:

```
template <typename T>
T half(T x) { return x/2; }
int i = half<int>(5);
```

This instantiates the `half` function template with the `int` type. The type is explicitly specified; we could call the function with an argument of another type, as long as it is convertible to the type we requested:

```
double x = half<double>(5);
```

Even though the argument is an `int`, the instantiation is that of `half<double>`, and the return type is `double`. The integer value 5 is implicitly converted to `double`.

Even though every function template can be instantiated by specifying all its type parameters, this is rarely done. Most of the uses of function templates involve the automatic deduction of types. Consider the following:

```
auto x = half(8);     // int
auto y = half(1.5);   // double
```

The template type can be deduced only from the template function arguments—the compiler will attempt to select the type for the `T` parameter to match the type of the function argument that is declared with the same type. In our case, the function template has the argument x of the `T` type. Any call to this function has to provide some value for this argument, and this value must have a type. The compiler will deduce that `T` must be that type. In the first call in the preceding code block, the argument is 5, and its type is `int`. There is nothing better to do than to assume that `T` should be `int` in this particular template instantiation. Similarly, in the second call, we can deduce that `T` must be `double`.

After this deduction, the compiler performs type substitution: all other mentions of the `T` type are replaced by the type that was deduced; in our case, there is only one other use of `T`, which is the return type.

Template argument deduction is widely used to capture types that we cannot easily determine:

```
long x = ...;
unsigned int y = ...;
auto x = half(y + z);
```

Here, we deduce the `T` type to be whatever the type of the expression y + z is (it's `long`, but with template deduction, we don't need to specify that explicitly, and the deduced type will *follow* the argument type if we ever change the types of y and z). Consider the following example:

```
template <typename U> auto f(U);
half(f(5));
```

We deduce `T` to match whatever type the `f()` template function returns for an `int` argument (of course, the definition of the `f()` template function has to be provided before it can be called, but we do not need to dig into the header files where `f()` is defined, as the compiler will deduce the right type for us).

Only the types that are used to declare function arguments can be deduced. There is no rule that all template type parameters must be somehow present in the argument list, but any parameters that cannot be deduced must be explicitly specified:

```
template <typename U, typename V>
U half(V x) { return x/2; }
auto y = half<double>(8);
```

Here, the first template type parameter is explicitly specified, so U is double, and V is deduced to be int.

Sometimes, the compiler cannot deduce the template type parameters, even if they are used to declare arguments:

```
template <typename T>
T Max(T x, T y) { return (x > y) ? x : y; }
auto x = Max(7L, 11);
```

Here, we can deduce from the first argument that T must be long, but from the second argument, we deduce that T must be int. It is often surprising to the programmers who learn their way around the templates that the long type is not deduced in this case—after all, if we substitute long for T everywhere, the second argument will be implicitly converted, and the function will compile fine. So why isn't the *larger* type deduced? Because the compiler does not attempt to find a type for which all argument conversions are possible: after all, there is usually more than one such type. In our example, T could be double or unsigned long, and the function would still be valid. If a type can be deduced from more than one argument, the result of all these deductions must be the same. Otherwise, the template instantiation is considered ambiguous.

The type deduction is not always as straightforward as using the type of the argument for a type parameter. The argument may be declared with a type that's more complex than a type parameter itself:

```
template <typename T>
T decrement(T* p) { return --(*p); }
int i = 7;
decrement(&i);     // i == 6
```

Here, the type of the argument is *pointer to* int, but the type that is deduced for T is int. The deduction of types can be arbitrarily complex, as long as it's unambiguous:

```
template <typename T>
T first(const std::vector<T>& v) { return v[0]; }
std::vector<int> v{11, 25, 67};
first(v);          // T is int, returns 11
```

Here, the argument is an instantiation of another template, `std::vector`, and we have to deduce the template parameter type from the type that was used to create this vector instantiation.

As we have seen, if a type can be deduced from more than one function argument, the result of these deductions must be the same. On the other hand, one argument can be used to deduce more than one type:

```
template <typename U, typename V>
std::pair<V, U> swap12(const std::pair<U, V>& x) {
    return std::pair<V, U>(x.second, x.first);
}
swap12(std::make_pair(7, 4.2); // pair of 4.2, 7
```

Here, we deduce two types, `U` and `V`, from one argument, then use these two types to form a new type, `std::pair<V, U>`. This example is unnecessarily verbose, and we can take advantage of a few more C++ features to make it both more compact and easier to maintain. First of all, the standard already has a function that deduces the argument types and uses them to declare a pair, and we have even used this function—`std::make_pair()`. Secondly, the return type of the function can be deduced from the expression in the return statement (a C++14 feature). The rules of this deduction are similar to the rules of the template argument type deduction. With these simplifications, our example becomes the following:

```
template <typename U, typename V>
auto swap12(const std::pair<U, V>& x) {
    return std::make_pair(x.second, x.first);
}
```

Note that we don't explicitly use the types `U` and `V` anymore. We still need this function to be a templates, since it operates on a generic type, that is, a pair of two types that we don't know until we instantiate the function. We could, however, use only one template parameter that would stand for the type of the argument:

```
template <typename T>
auto swap12(const T& x) {
    return std::make_pair(x.second, x.first);
}
```

There is a significant difference between these two variants—the last function template will have its type deduced successfully from any call with one argument, no matter the type of that argument. If that argument is not an `std::pair`, or, more generally, if the argument is not a class or a struct or it does not have the `first` and `second` data members, the deduction will still succeed, but the type substitution will fail. On the other hand, the previous version will not even be considered for arguments that are not a pair of some types. For any `std::pair` argument, the pair types are deduced, and the substitution should proceed without a problem.

Member function templates are very similar to the non-member function templates, and their arguments are similarly deduced. Member function templates can be used in classes or class templates, which we will review next.

Class templates

Instantiation of class templates is similar to that of the function templates—the use of the template to create a type implicitly instantiates the template. To use a class template, we need to specify the type arguments for the template parameters:

```
template <typename N, typename D>
class Ratio {
    public:
    Ratio() : num_(), denom_() {}
    Ratio(const N& num, const D& denom) : num_(num), denom_(denom) {}
    explicit operator double() const {
        return double(num_)/double(denom_);
    }
    private:
    N num_;
    D denom_;
};
Ratio<int, double> r;
```

The definition of the `r1` variable implicitly instantiates the `Ratio` class template for the `int` and `double` types. It also instantiates the default constructor of this class. The second constructor is not used in this code and is not instantiated. It is this feature of class templates—instantiating a template instantiates all data members, but does not instantiate the methods until they are used—that allows us to write class templates where only some of the methods compile for certain types. If we use the second constructor to initialize the values of `Ratio`, then that constructor is instantiated, and must be valid for the given types:

```
Ratio<int, double> r(5, 0.1);
```

In C++17, these constructors can be used to deduce the types of the class template from the constructor arguments:

```
Ratio r(5, 0.1);
```

Of course, this works only if there are enough constructor arguments to deduce the types. For example, the default-constructed `Ratio` object has to be instantiated with explicitly specified types; there is simply no other way to deduce them. Prior to C++17, a helper function template was often used to construct an object whose type can be deduced from the arguments. Similarly to `std::make_pair()`, which we looked at previously, we can implement a `make_ratio` function that will do the same thing as the C++17 constructor argument deduction:

```
template <typename N, typename D>
Ratio<N, D> make_ratio(const N& num, const D& denom) {
    return { num, denom };
}
auto r(make_ratio(5, 0.1));
```

The C++17 way of deducing template arguments should be preferred, if it is available: it does not require writing another function that essentially duplicates the class constructor, and does not make an additional call to the copy or move constructor to initialize the object (although in practice most compilers will optimize away that call).

When a template is used to generate a type, it is instantiated implicitly. Both class and function templates can be explicitly instantiated as well. Doing so instantiates a template without using it:

```
template class Ratio<long, long>;
template Ratio<long, long> make_ratio(const long&, const long&);
```

Explicit instantiations are rarely needed, and will not be used elsewhere in this book.

Class templates, as we have used them so far, allow us to declare generic classes, that is, classes that can be instantiated with many different types. So far, all of these classes look exactly the same, except for the types, and generate the same code. This is not always desirable—different types may need to be handled somewhat differently.

For example, let's say that we want to be able to represent not only a ratio of two numbers stored in the `Ratio` object, but also a ratio of two numbers stored elsewhere, with the `Ratio` object containing pointers to these numbers. Clearly, some of the methods of the `Ratio` object, such as the conversion operator to double, need to be implemented differently if the object stores pointers to the numerator and denominator. In C++, this is accomplished by specializing the template, which we will do next.

Template specializations

Template specializations allow us to make the generated template code differently for some types—not just the same code with different types substituted, but completely different code. There are two kinds of template specialization in C++—the explicit, or full, specialization and the partial specialization. Let's start with the former.

Explicit specialization

Explicit template specialization defines a special version of the template for a particular set of types. In an explicit specialization, all generic types are replaced by specific, concrete types. Since the explicit specialization is not a generic class or function, it does not need to be instantiated later. For the same reason, it is sometimes called **full specialization**. If the generic types are fully substituted, there is nothing generic left. The explicit specialization should not be confused with the explicit template instantiation—while both create an instantiation of a template for a given set of type arguments, the explicit instantiation creates an instantiation of the generic code, with the generic types substituted by the specific types. The explicit specialization creates an instantiation of the function or class with the same name but it overrides the implementation, so the resulting code can be completely different. An example should help us understand this distinction.

Let's start with a class template. Let's say that, if both the numerator and the denominator of `Ratio` are `double`, we want to compute the ratio and store it as a single number. The generic Ratio code should remain the same, but for one particular set of types, we want the class to look entirely different. We can do this with an explicit specialization:

```
template <>
class Ratio<double, double> {
    public:
    Ratio() : value_() {}
    template <typename N, typename D>
    Ratio(const N& num, const D& denom) :
        value_(double(num)/double(denom)) {}
    explicit operator double() const { return value_; }
    private:
    double value_;
};
```

Both template type parameters are specified to be `double`. The class implementation is totally unlike the generic version—instead of two data members, we have just one; the conversion operator simply returns the value, and the constructor now computes the ratio of the numerator and the denominator. But it is not even the same constructor—instead of the non-template constructor `Ratio(const double&, const double&)` that the generic version would have if it was instantiated for two `double` template arguments, we provided a template constructor that can take two arguments of any types as long as they are convertible to `double`.

Sometimes, we don't need to specialize the whole class template, because most of the generic code is still applicable. However, we may want to change the implementation of one or a few member functions. We can explicitly specialize the member function as well:

```
template <>
Ratio<float, float>::operator double() const { return num_/denom_; }
```

Template functions can be explicitly specialized as well. Again, unlike the explicit instantiation, we get to write the body of the function, and we can implement it any way we want:

```
template <typename T>
T do_something(T x) { return ++x; }
template <>
double do_something<double>(double x) { return x/2; }

do_something(3);     // 4
do_something(3.0);   // 1.5
```

We cannot, however, change the number or the types of arguments or the return type—they must match the result of the substitution of the generic types, so the following does not compile:

```
template <>
long do_something<int>(int x) { return x*x; }
```

An explicit specialization must be declared before the first use of the template that would cause an implicit instantiation of the generic template for the same types. This makes sense—the implicit instantiation would create a class or a function with the same name and the same types as the explicit specialization. We would now have two versions of the same class or function in the program, and this violates the one definition rule and makes the program ill-formed.

Explicit specializations are useful when we have one or a few types for which we need the template to behave very differently. However, this does not solve our problem with the ratio of pointers—we want a specialization that is still *somewhat generic*, that is, it can handle pointers to any types, just not any other types. This is accomplished by a partial specialization, which we will look at next.

Partial specialization

Now, we are getting to the really interesting part of the C++ template programming—partial template specializations. When a class template is partially specialized, it remains as generic code, but *less generic* than the original template. The simplest form of the partial template is one where some of the generic types are replaced by concrete types, but other types remain generic:

```
template <typename N, typename D>
class Ratio {
    .....
};

template <typename D>
class Ratio<double, D> {
    public:
    Ratio() : value_() {}
    Ratio(const double& num, const D& denom) : value_(num/double(denom)) {}
    explicit operator double() const { return value_; }
    private:
    double value_;
};
```

Here, we convert the `Ratio` to a `double` value if the numerator is `double`, regardless of the denominator type. More than one partial specialization can be defined for the same template. For example, we can also specialize for the case when the denominator is `double` and the numerator is anything:

```
template <typename N>
class Ratio<N, double> {
    public:
    Ratio() : value_() {}
    Ratio(const N& num, const double& denom) : value_(double(num)/denom) {}
    explicit operator double() const { return value_; }
    private:
    double value_;
};
```

When the template is instantiated, the best specialization for the given set of types is selected. In our case, if neither the numerator or the denominator is `double`, then the general template has to be instantiated—there are no other choices. If the numerator is `double`, then the first partial specialization is a better (more specific) match than the general template. If the denominator is `double`, then the second partial specialization is a better match. But what happens if both terms are `double`? In this case, the two partial specializations are equivalent; neither is more specific than the other. This situation is considered ambiguous and the instantiation fails. Note that only this particular instantiation, `Ratio<double, double>`, fails—it is not an error (at least, not a syntax error) to define both specializations, but it is an error to request an instantiation that cannot be uniquely resolved to the narrowest specialization. To allow any instantiation of our template, we have to remove this ambiguity, and the only way to do that is to provide an even more narrow specialization that would be preferred over the other two. In our case, there is only one option—a full specialization for `Ratio<double, double>`:

```
template <>
class Ratio<double, double> {
    public:
    Ratio() : value_() {}
    template <typename N, typename D>
    Ratio(const N& num, const D& denom) :
        value_(double(num)/double(denom)) {}
    explicit operator double() const { return value_; }
    private:
    double value_;
};
```

Now, the fact that the partial specializations are ambiguous for the instantiation of `Ratio<double, double>` is no longer relevant—we have a more specific version of the template than either of them, so that version is preferred over both.

Partial specializations do not have to specify some of the generic types fully. Therefore, can keep all types generic, but impose some restrictions on them. For example, we still want a specialization where both the numerator and the denominator are pointers. They can be pointers to anything, so they are generic types, but *less generic* than the arbitrary types of the general template:

```
template <typename N, typename D>
class Ratio<N*, D*> {
    public:
    Ratio(N* num, D* denom) : num_(num), denom_(denom) {}
    explicit operator double() const {
        return double(*num_)/double(*denom_);
    }
}
```

```
    private:
    N* const num_;
    D* const denom_;
};
int i = 5; double x = 10;
auto r(make_ratio(&i, &x));    // Ratio<int*, double*>
double(r);                     // 0.5
x = 2.5;
double(r);                     // 2
```

This partial specialization still has two generic types, but they are both pointer types, `N*` and `D*`, for any `N` and `D` types. The implementation is totally unlike that of the general template. When instantiated with two pointer types, the partial specialization is *more specific* than the general template and is considered a better match. Note that, in our example, the denominator is `double`. So why isn't a partial specialization for the `double` denominator considered? That is because, while the denominator is `double` as far as the program logic is concerned, technically it is `double*`, a completely different type, and we do not have a specialization for that.

To define a specialization, the general template must first be declared. It does not, however, need to be defined—it is possible to specialize a template that does not exist in the general case. To do so, we must forward-declare the general template, then define all the specializations we need:

```
template <typename T> class Value; // Declaration
template <typename T> class Value<T*> {
    public:
    explicit Value(T* p) : v_(*p) {}
    private:
    T v_;
};
template <typename T> class Value<T&> {
    public:
    explicit Value(T& p) : v_(p) {}
    private:
    T v_;
};

int i = 5;
int* p = &i;
int& r = i;

Value<int*> v1(p); // T* specialization
Value<int&> v2(r); // T& specialization
```

Here, we have no general `Value` template, but we have them for any pointer or reference types. If we try to instantiate the template on some other type, like `int`, we will get an error stating that the `Value<int>` type is incomplete—this is no different than trying to define an object with only a forward declaration of the class.

So far, we have seen only the examples of partial specialization for class templates. Unlike the earlier discussion of the full specializations, we have not seen a single function specialization here. There is a very good reason for that—a partial function template specialization does not exist in C++. What is sometimes incorrectly called a partial specialization is nothing more than overloading template functions. On the other hand, overloading template functions can get quite complex and is worth learning about—we will cover this next.

Template function overloading

We are used to regular functions, or class methods, being overloaded—multiple functions with the same name have different parameter types. Each call invokes the function with the best match of the parameter types to the call arguments, as show in the following example:

```
void whatami(int x) { std::cout << x << " is int" << std::endl; }
void whatami(long x) { std::cout << x << " is long" << std::endl; }
whatami(5);      // 5 is int
whatami(5.0);    // Compilation error
```

If the arguments are a perfect match for one of the overloaded functions with the given name, that function is called. Otherwise, the compiler considers conversions to the parameter types of the available functions. If one of the functions offers *better* conversions, that function is selected. Otherwise, the call is ambiguous, just as in the last line of the preceding example. The precise definition of what constitutes as the *best* conversion can be found in the standard. Generally, the *cheapest* conversions are the ones such as adding const or removing a reference; then, there are conversions between built-in types, conversions from derived to base class pointers, and so on. In the case of multiple arguments, each argument for the chosen function must have the best conversion. There is no *voting*—if a function has three arguments, and two are an exact match for the first overload, while the third one is an exact match for the second overload, then even if the remaining arguments are implicitly convertible to their corresponding parameter types, the overloaded call is ambiguous.

The presence of templates makes the overload resolution much more complex. Multiple function templates with the same name and, possibly, the same number of arguments, can be defined, in addition to non-template functions. All of these functions are the candidates for an overloaded function call, but the function templates can generate functions with different parameter types, so how do we decide what the actual overloaded functions are? The exact rules are even more complex than the ones for non-template functions, but the basic idea is this—if there is a non-template function that is a near-perfect match to the call arguments, that function is selected. The standard, of course, uses much more precise terms than *near-perfect*, but *trivial* conversions, such as adding `const`, fall under that category—you get them *at no cost*. If there is no such function, the compiler will attempt to instantiate all function templates with the same name to a near-perfect match, using the template argument deduction. If exactly one of the templates was instantiated, the function created by this instantiation is called. Otherwise, overload resolution continues the usual way among the non-template functions.

This is a very simplified description of a very complex process, but there are two important points—firstly, if there is an equally good match of a call to a template and a non-template function, the non-template function is preferred, and secondly, the compiler does not attempt to instantiate the function templates into something that might be convertible to the types we need. The template functions must match the call almost perfectly after the argument type deduction, or they are not called at all. Let's add a template to our previous example:

```
template <typename T>
void whatami(T* x) { std::cout << x << " is pointer" << std::endl; }

int i = 5;
whatami(i);      // 5 is int
whatami(&c);     // 0x???? is a pointer
```

Here, we have what looks like partial specialization of a function template. But it really isn't—it is just a function template—there is no general template for which it could be a specialization. Instead, it is simply a function template whose type parameter is deduced from the same arguments, but using different rules. The template can have its type deduced if the argument is a pointer of any kind. This includes a pointer to `const`—T could be a `const` type, so if we call `whatami(ptr)`, where `ptr` is `const int*`, that first template overload is a perfect match when `T` is `const int`. If the deduction succeeds, the function generated by the template, that is, the template instantiation, is added to the overload set.

For the `int *` argument, it is the only overload that works, so it is called. But what happens if more than one function template can match the call, and both instantiations are valid overloads? Let's add one more template:

```
template <typename T>
void whatami<T&& x> { std::cout << "Something weird" << std::endl; }

class C { ..... };
C c;
whatami(&c);      // 0x???? is a pointer
whatami(c);       // Something weird
```

This template function accepts its arguments by the universal reference, so it can be instantiated for any call to `whatami()` with one argument. The first call, `whatami(c)`, is easy—the last overload, with `T&&`, is the only one that can be called. There are no conversions from `c` to a pointer or an integer. But the second call is tricky—we have not one, but two template instantiations that are a perfect match for the call, with no conversions needed. So why is this not an ambiguous overload? Because the rules for resolving overloaded function templates are different than the rules for non-template functions, and resemble the rules for selecting the partial specialization of a class template (which is another reason why the function template overloads are often confused with partial specializations). The template that is more specific is a better match.

In our case, the first template is more specific—it can accept any pointer argument, but only pointers. The second template can accept any argument at all, so any time the first template is a possible match, the second is too, but not the reverse. If the more specific template can be used to instantiate a function that is a valid overload, then this template is used. Otherwise, we have to fall back to the more general template.

The very general template functions in the overload set sometimes lead to unexpected results. Let's say we have the following three overloads for `int`, `double`, and anything:

```
void whatami(int x) { std::cout << x << " is int" << std::endl; }
void whatami(double x) { std::cout << x << " is double" << std::endl; }
template <typename T>
    void whatami<T&& x> { std::cout << "Something weird" << std::endl; }
int i = 5;
float x = 4.2;
whatami(i);      // i is int
whatami(x);      // Something weird
```

The first call has an `int` argument, so `whatami(int)` is a perfect match. The second call would have gone to `whatami(double)` if we did not have the template overload—the conversion from `float` to `double` is implicit (so is the conversion from `float` to `int`, but the conversion to `double` is preferred). But it's still a conversion, so when the function template instantiates to a perfect match of `whatami(double&&)`, that is the best match and the chosen overload.

Finally, there is one more kind of function that has a special place in the overload resolution order—the variadic function.

The variadic function is declared with . . . instead of arguments, and it can be called with any number of arguments of any type (`printf` is one such function). This function is the overload of the last resort—it is called only if no other overloads can be used:

```
void whatami(...) {
    std::cout << "It's something or somethings" << std::endl;
}
```

As long as we have the overload `whatami(T&& x)` available, the variadic function will never be the preferred overload, at least not for any calls to `whatami()` with one argument. Without that template, `whatami(...)` is called for any argument that is not a number or a pointer. The variadic functions were around since the days of C, and are not to be confused with variadic templates that were introduced in C++11, and this is what we'll talk about next.

Variadic templates

Probably the greatest difference between generic programming in C and C++ is type safety. It is possible to write generic code in C—the standard function `qsort()` is a perfect example—it can sort values of any type and they are passed in using a `void*` pointer, which can really be a pointer to any type. Of course, the programmer has to know what the real type is and cast the pointer to the right type. In a generic C++ program, the types are either explicitly specified or deduced at the time of the instantiation, and the type system for generic types is as strong as it is for regular types. Unless we want a function with an unknown number of arguments, that is, prior to C++11, the only way was the old C-style variadic functions where the compiler had no idea what the argument types were; the programmer just had to know and unpack the variable arguments correctly.

C++11 introduced the modern equivalent to the variadic function—the variadic template. We can now declare a generic function with any number of arguments:

```
template <typename ... T>
auto sum(const T& ... x);
```

This function takes one or more arguments, possibly of different types, and computes their sum. The return type is not easy to determine, but, fortunately, we can let the compiler figure it out—we just declare the return type as `auto`. How do we actually implement the function to add up the unknown number of values whose types we can't name, not even as generic types? In C++17, it's easy, because it has fold expressions:

```
template <typename ... T>
auto sum(const T& ... x) {
    return (x + ...);
}
sum(5, 7, 3);       // 15, int
sum(5, 7L, 3);      // 15, long
sum(5, 7L, 2.9);    // 14.9, double
```

In C++14, as well as in C++17, when a fold expression is not sufficient (and they are useful only in limited contexts, mostly when the arguments and combines using binary or unary operators), the standard technique is recursion, which is ever-popular in template programming:

```
template <typename T1>
auto sum(const T& x1) {
    return x1;
}
template <typename T1, typename ... T>
auto sum(const T1& x1, const T& ... x) {
    return x1 + sum(x ...);
}
```

The first overload (not a partial specialization!) is for the `sum()` function with one argument of any type. That value is returned. The second overload is for more than one argument, and the first argument is explicitly added to the sum of the remaining arguments. The recursion continues until there is only one argument left, at which point the other overload is called and the recursion stops. This is the standard technique for unraveling the parameter packs in variadic templates, and we will see this many times in this book. The compiler will inline all the recursive function calls and generate the straightforward code that adds all arguments together.

The class templates can also be variadic—they have an arbitrary number of type arguments and can build the classes from a varying number of objects of different types. The declaration is similar to that of a function template. For example, let's build a class template, `Group`, that can hold any number of objects of different types and return the right object when it's converted to one of the types it holds:

```
template <typename ... T>
struct Group;
```

The usual implementation of such templates is again recursive, using deeply nested inheritance, although a non-recursive implementation is sometimes possible. We will see one in the next section. The recursion has to be terminated when there is only one type parameter left. This is done using a partial specialization, so we will leave the general template we showed previously as a declaration only, and define the specialization for one type parameter:

```
template <typename T1>
struct Group<T1> {
    T1 t1_;
    Group() = default;
    explicit Group(const T1& t1) : t1_(t1) {}
    explicit Group(T1&& t1) : t1_(std::move(t1)) {}
    explicit operator const T1&() const { return t1_; }
    explicit operator T1&() { return t1_; }
};
```

This class holds the value of one type, `T1`, initializes it by copy or move, and returns a reference to it when converted to the `T1` type. The specialization for an arbitrary number of type parameters contains the first one as a data member, together with the corresponding initialization and conversion methods, and inherits from the `Group` class template of the remaining types:

```
template <typename T1, typename ... T>
struct Group<T1, T ...> : Group<T ...> {
    T1 t1_;
    Group() = default;
    explicit Group(const T1& t1, T&& ... t) :
        Group<T ...>(std::forward<T>(t) ...), t1_(t1) {}
    explicit Group(T1&& t1, T&& ... t) :
        Group<T ...>(std::forward<T>(t) ...), t1_(std::move(t1)) {}
    explicit operator const T1&() const { return t1_; }
    explicit operator T1&() { return t1_; }
};
```

For every type contained in a `Group` class, there are two possible ways it can be initialized—copy or move. Fortunately, we do not have to spell out the constructors for every combination of copy and move operations. Instead, we have two versions of the constructor for the two ways to initialize the first argument (the one stored in the specialization); we use perfect forwarding for the remaining arguments.

Now, we can use our `Group` class template to hold some values of different types (it cannot handle multiple values of the same type, since the attempt to retrieve this type would be ambiguous):

```
Group<int, long> g(3, 5);
int(g);      // 3
long(t);     // 5
```

It is rather inconvenient to write all the group types explicitly and to make sure they match the argument types. The usual solution to this problem is to use a helper function template (a variadic template, of course) to take advantage of the template argument deduction:

```
template <typename ... T>
auto makeGroup(T&& ... t) {
    return Group<T ...>(std::forward<T>(t) ...);
}
auto g = makeGroup(3, 2.2, std::string("xyz"));
int(g);              // 3
double(g);           // 2.2
std::string(g);      // "xyz"
```

Note that the C++ standard library contains a class template, `std::tuple`, which is a much more complete and full-featured version of our `Group`.

The variadic templates, especially combined with perfect forwarding, are extremely useful for writing very general template classes—for example, a vector can contain objects of an arbitrary type, and, to construct these objects in place instead of copying them, we have to call constructors with a different number of arguments. When the vector template is written, there is no way to know how many arguments are needed to initialize the objects the vector will contain, so a variadic template has to be used (indeed, the in-place constructors of `std::vector`, such as `emplace_back`, are variadic templates).

There is one more kind of template-like entity in C++ that we have to mention, one that has the appearance of both a class and a function—the lambda expression. The next section is dedicated to this.

Lambda expressions

In C++, the regular function syntax is extended with the concept of a *callable*, short for *callable entity*—a callable is something that can be called in the same way as a function. Some examples of callables are functions (of course), function pointers, or objects with `operator()`, also known as **functors**:

```
void f(int i);
struct G {
    void operator()(int i);
};
f(5);              // Function
G g; g(5);         // Functor
```

It is often useful to define a callable entity in a local context, right next to the place it is used. For example, to sort a sequence of objects, we may want to define a custom comparison function. We can use an ordinary function for this:

```
bool compare(int i, int j) { return i < j; }
void do_work() {
    std::vector<int> v;
    .....
    std::sort(v.begin(), v.end(), compare);
}
```

However, in C++, functions cannot be defined inside other functions, so our `compare()` function may have to be defined quite far from the place it is used. If it is a single-use comparison function, such separation is inconvenient and reduces the readability and maintainability of the code.

There is a way around this limitation—while we cannot declare functions inside functions, we can declare classes, and classes can be callable:

```
void do_work() {
    std::vector<int> v;
    .....
    struct compare {
        bool operator()(int i, int j) const { return i < j; }
    };
    std::sort(v.begin(), v.end(), compare());
}
```

This is compact and local, but too verbose. We do not actually need to give this class a name, and we only ever want one instance of this class. In C++11, we have a much better option, the lambda expression:

```
void do_work() {
    std::vector<int> v;
    .....
    auto compare = [](int i, int j) { return i < j; };
    std::sort(v.begin(), v.end(), compare);
}
```

This is as compact as it gets. The return type can be specified, but can usually be deduced by the compiler. The lambda expression creates an object, so it has a type, but that type is generated by the compiler, so the object declaration must use auto.

The lambda expressions are objects, so they can have data members. Of course, a local callable class can also have data members. Usually, they are initialized from the local variables in the containing scope:

```
void do_work() {
    std::vector<double> v;
    .....
    struct compare_with_tolerance {
        const double tolerance;
        explicit compare_with_tolerance(double tol) :
            tolerance(tol) {}
        bool operator()(double x, double y) const {
            return x < y && std::abs(x - y) > tolerance;
        }
    };
    double tolerance = 0.01;
    std::sort(v.begin(), v.end(), compare_with_tolerance(tolerance));
}
```

Again, this is a very verbose way to do something simple. We have to mention the tolerance variable three times—as a data member, a constructor argument, and in the member initialization list. A lambda expression makes this code simpler as well because it can capture local variables. In local classes, we are not allowed to reference variables from the containing scope, except by passing them through the constructor arguments, but for the lambda expressions, the compiler automatically generates a constructor to capture all local variables mentioned in the body of the expression:

```
void do_work() {
    std::vector<double> v;
    .....
    double tolerance = 0.01;
```

```
    auto compare_with_tolerance = [=](auto x, auto y) {
        return x < y && std::abs(x - y) > tolerance;
    }
    std::sort(v.begin(), v.end(), compare_with_tolerance);
}
```

Here, the name `tolerance` inside the lambda expression refers to the local variable with the same name. The variable is captured by value, which is specified in the lambda expression's capture clause `[=]` (we could have captured by reference using `[&]` instead). Also, instead of changing the arguments of the lambda expression from `int` in the earlier example to `double`, we can declare them as `auto`, which effectively makes the `operator()` of the lambda expression a template (this is a C++14 feature).

Lambda expressions are most commonly used as local functions. However, they are not really functions; they are callable objects, and so they are missing one feature that the functions have—the ability to overload them. The last trick we will learn in this section is how to work around that and create an overload set from lambda expressions.

First, the main idea—it is indeed impossible to overload callable objects. On the other hand, it is very easy to overload several `operator()` methods in the same object—methods are overloaded like any other function. Of course, the `operator()` of a lambda expression object is generated by the compiler, not declared by us, so it is not possible to force the compiler to generate more than one `operator()` in the same lambda expression. But classes have their own advantages, the main one being that we can inherit from them. Lambda expressions are objects—their types are classes, so we can inherit from them too. If a class inherits publicly from a base class, all public methods of the base class become public methods of the derived class. If a class inherits publicly from several base classes (multiple inheritance), its public interface is formed from all the public methods of all the base classes. If there are multiple methods with the same name in this set, they become overloaded and the usual overloading resolution rules apply (in particular, it is possible to create an ambiguous set of overloads, in which case the program will not compile).

So, we need to create a class that automatically inherits from any number of base classes. We have just seen the right tool for that—the variadic templates. As we have learned in the previous section, the usual way to iterate over the arbitrary number of items in the parameter pack of a variadic template is through recursion:

```
template <typename ... F> struct overload_set;

template <typename F1>
struct overload_set<F1> : public F1 {
    overload_set(F1&& f1)      : F1(std::move(f1)) {}
    overload_set(const F1& f1) : F1(f1) {}
    using F1::operator();
```

```
};

template <typename F1, typename ... F>
struct overload_set<F1, F ...> : public F1, public overload_set<F ...> {
    overload_set(F1&& f1, F&& ... f) :
        F1(std::move(f1)), overload_set<F ...>(std::forward<F>(f) ...) {}
    overload_set(const F1& f1, F&& ... f) :
        F1(f1), overload_set<F ...>(std::forward<F>(f) ...) {}
    using F1::operator();
};

template <typename ... F>
auto overload(F&& ... f) {
    return overload_set<F ...>(std::forward<F>(f) ...);
}
```

The overload_set is a variadic class template; the general template has to be declared
before we can specialize it, but it has no definition. The first definition is for the special case
of only one lambda expression—the overload_set class inherits from the lambda
expression and adds its operator() to its public interface. The specialization for N lambda
expressions (N>1) inherits from the first one and from the overload_set constructed from
the remaining N-1 lambda expressions. Finally, we have a helper function that constructs
the overload set from any number of lambda expressions—in our case, this is a necessity
and not a mere convenience, since we cannot explicitly specify the types of the lambda
expressions, but have to let the function template deduce them. Now, we can construct an
overload set from any number of lambda expressions:

```
int i = 5;
double d = 7.3;
auto l = overload(
    [](int* i) { std::cout << "i=" << *i << std::endl; },
    [](double* d) { std::cout << "d=" << *d << std::endl; }
);
l(&i);     // i=5
l(&d);     // d=5.3
```

This solution is not perfect, because it does not handle ambiguous overloads well. In C++17,
we can do better, and it gives us a chance to demonstrate the alternative way of using a
parameter pack that does not need recursion. Here is the C++17 version:

```
template <typename ... F>
struct overload_set : public F ... {
    overload_set(F&& ... f) : F(std::forward<F>(f)) ... {}
    using F::operator() ...;     // C++17
};
```

```
template <typename ... F>
auto overload(F&& ... f) {
    return overload_set<F ...>(std::forward<F>(f) ...);
}
```

The variadic template does not rely on partial specializations anymore; instead, it inherits directly from the parameter pack (this part of the implementation works in C++14 as well, but the `using` declaration needs C++17). The template helper function is the same—it deduces the types of all lambda expressions and constructs an object from the `overload_set` instantiation with these types. The lambda expressions themselves are passed to the base classes using perfect forwarding, where they are used to initialize all the base objects of the `overload_set` objects (lambda expressions are movable). Without the need for recursion or partial specialization, this is a much more compact and straightforward template. Its use is identical to the previous version of the `overload_set`, but it handles near-ambiguous overloads better.

We will see their use in later chapters of this book, when we will need to write a fragment of code and attach it to an object so that it can be executed later.

Summary

Templates, variadic templates, and lambda expressions are all powerful features of C++, offering simplicity in use, but are rich in complex details. The examples in this chapter should serve to prepare the reader for the later chapters of this book, where we use these techniques to implement design patterns, both classic and novel, with the tools of the modern C++ language. The reader wishing to learn the art of using these complex and powerful tools to their fullest potential is referred to other books that are dedicated to teaching these subjects, some of which can be found at the end of this chapter.

The reader is now ready to learn the common C++ idioms, starting with the idioms for expressing memory ownership, in the next chapter.

Questions

1. What is the difference between a type and a template?
2. What kind of templates does C++ have?
3. What kinds of template parameters do C++ templates have?
4. What is the difference between a template specialization and a template instantiation?
5. How can you access the parameter pack of the variadic template?
6. What are lambda expressions used for?

Further reading

- C++ Fundamentals: `https://www.packtpub.com/application-development/c-fundamentals`
- C++ Data Structures and Algorithms: `https://www.packtpub.com/application-development/c-data-structures-and-algorithms`
- Mastering C++ Programming: `https://www.packtpub.com/application-development/mastering-c-programming`

Memory Ownership **3**

Memory mismanagement is one of the most common problems in C++ programs. Many of these problems boil down to incorrect assumptions about which part of the code or which entity owns a particular memory. Then, we get memory leaks, accessing unallocated memory, excessive memory use, and other problems that are difficult to debug. Modern C++ has a set of memory ownership idioms that, taken together, allow the programmer to clearly express their design intent when it comes to memory ownership. This, in turn, makes it much easier to write code that correctly allocates, accesses, and deallocates memory.

The following topics are covered in this chapter:

- What is memory ownership?
- What are the characteristics of well-designed resource ownership?
- When and how should we be agnostic about resource ownership?
- How do we express exclusive memory ownership in C++?
- How do we express shared memory ownership in C++?
- What is the cost of different memory ownership language constructs?

Technical requirements

You can find the C++ Core Guidelines at `https://github.com/isocpp/CppCoreGuidelines/blob/master/CppCoreGuidelines.md`.

You can find the C++ **Guideline Support library (GSL)** at `https://github.com/Microsoft/GSL`.

What is memory ownership?

In C++, the term **memory ownership** refers to the entity that is responsible for enforcing the lifetime of a particular memory allocation. In reality, we rarely talk about the ownership of raw memory. Usually, we manage the ownership and the lifetime of the objects that reside in said memory, and memory ownership is really just shorthand for *object ownership*. The concept of memory ownership is closely tied to that of *resource ownership*. First of all, memory is a resource. It is not the only resource a program can manage, but it is by far the most commonly used one. Second, the C++ way of managing resources is to have objects own them. Thus, the problem of managing resources is reduced to the problem of managing the owning objects, which, as we just learned, is what we really mean when we talk about memory ownership. In this context, memory ownership is about owning more than memory, and mismanaged ownership can leak, miscount, or lose track of any resource that can be controlled by the program—memory, mutexes, files, database handles, cat videos, airline seat reservations, or nuclear warheads.

Well-designed memory ownership

What does well-designed memory ownership look like? The naive answer that first comes up is that, at every point in the program, it is clear who owns what object. This, however, is overly constraining—most of the program does not deal with ownership of resources, including memory. These parts of the program merely use resources. When writing such code, it is sufficient to know that a particular function or class does not own the memory. It is completely irrelevant to know who does what:

```
struct MyValues { long a, b, c, d; }
void Reset(MyValues* v) { // Don't care who owns v, as long as we don't
    v->a = v->b = v->c = v->d = 0;
}
```

How about this, then—at every point in the program, is it clear who owns that object, or is it clear that the ownership is not changing? This is better, since most of the code will fall under the second part of our answer. However, it's still too constraining—when taking ownership of an object, it is usually not important to know who it is taken from:

```
class A {
    public:
    A(std::vector<int>&& v) :
        v_(std::move(v)) {}    // Transfers ownership from whomever
    private:
    std::vector<int> v_;       // We own this now
};
```

Similarly, the whole point of the shared ownership (expressed through the reference-counted `std::shared_ptr`) is that we don't need to know who else owns the object:

```
class A {
    public:
    A(std::shared_ptr<std::vector<int>> v) : v_(v) {}
                // No idea who owns v, don't care
    private:
    std::shared_ptr<std::vector<int>> v_;
                // Sharing ownership with any number of owners
};
```

A more accurate description of well-designed memory ownership takes more than one quoted sentence. Generally, the following are the attributes of good memory ownership practices:

- If a function or a class does not alter memory ownership in any way, this should be clear to every client of this function or class, as well as the implementer
- If a function or a class takes exclusive ownership of some of the objects passed to it, this should be clear to the client (we assume that the implementer knows this already, since he/she has to write the code)
- If a function or a class shares ownership of an object passed to it, this should be clear to the client (or anyone who reads the client code, for that matter)
- For every object that is created, at every point that it's used, it is clear whether this code is expected to delete it or not

Poorly designed memory ownership

Just like good memory ownership defies a simple description and instead is characterized by a set of criteria it satisfies, so can bad memory ownership practices be recognized by their common manifestations. In general, where good design makes it clear whether a particular piece of code owns a resource or not, a bad design requires additional knowledge that cannot be deduced from the context. For example, who owns the object returned by the following `MakeWidget()` function?

```
Widget* w = MakeWidget();
```

Is the client expected to delete the widget when it's no longer needed? If yes, how should it be deleted? If we decide to delete the widget and do it in the wrong way, for example, by calling `operator delete` on a widget that was not, in fact, allocated by `operator new`, memory corruption will certainly result. In the best case scenario, the program will just crash:

```
WidgetFactory WF;
Widget* w = WF.MakeAnother();
```

Does the Factory own the widgets it created? Will it delete them when the Factory object is deleted? Alternatively, is the client expected to do that? If we decide that the Factory probably knows what it created, and will delete all such objects in due time, we may end up with a memory leak (or worse, if the objects owned some other resources):

```
Widget* w = MakeWidget();
Widget* w1 = Transmogrify(w);
```

Does `Transmogrify()` take ownership of the widget? Is the `w` widget still around after `Transmogrify()` is done with it? If the widget is deleted to construct the new, transmogrified, `w1` widget, we now have a dangling pointer. If the widget is not deleted, but we assume it might be, we have a memory leak.

Lest you think that all bad memory management practices can be recognized by the presence of raw pointers somewhere, here is an example of a rather poor approach to memory management that often arises as a knee-jerk response to the problems caused by the use of raw pointers:

```
void Double(std::shared_ptr<std::vector<int>> v) {
    for (auto& x : *v) {
        x *= 2;
    }
};
    ...
std::shared_ptr<std::vector<int>> v(...);
Double(v);
    ...
```

The `Double()` function is claiming in its interface that it takes shared ownership of the vector. However, that ownership is entirely gratuitous—there is no reason for `Double()` to own its argument—it does not attempt to extend its lifetime, it does not transfer ownership to anyone else; it merely modifies a vector passed in by the caller. We can reasonably expect that the caller owns the vector (or that somebody else even higher in the call stack does), and that the vector will still be around when `Double()` returns control to the caller—after all, the caller wanted us to double the elements, presumably so that he/she can do something else with them.

While this list is hardly complete, it serves to demonstrate the spectrum of the problems that can be caused by a slap-dash approach to memory ownership.

Expressing memory ownership in C++

Throughout its history, the C++ language has evolved in its approach to expressing memory ownership. The same syntactic constructs have been, at times, imbued with different assumed semantics. This evolution was partially driven by the new features added to the language (it's hard to talk about shared memory ownership if you don't have any shared pointers). On the other hand, most of the memory management tools added in C++ 11 and later were not new ideas or new concepts. The notion of a shared pointer has been around for a long time. This language support makes it easier to implement one (and having a shared pointer in the standard library makes most custom implementations unnecessary), but shared pointers were used in C++ long before C++ 11 added them to the standard. The more important change that has occurred was the evolution of the understanding of the C++ community, and the emergence of common practices and idioms. It is in this sense, as a set of conventions and semantics commonly associated with different syntactic features, that we can talk about the set of memory management practices as a design pattern of the C++ language. Let's now learn the different ways that we can express different types of memory ownership.

Expressing non-ownership

Let's start with the most common kind of memory ownership. Most code does not allocate, deallocate, construct, or delete. It just does its work on objects that were created by someone else earlier and will be deleted by someone else later. How do you express the notion that a function is going to operate on an object but will not attempt to delete it or, conversely, extend its lifetime past the completion of the function itself?

Very easily, in fact, and every C++ programmer has done it many times:

```cpp
void Transmogrify(Widged* w) {         // I will not delete w
    ...
}
void MustTransmogrify(Widget& w) {     // Neither will I
    ...
}
class WidgetProcessor {
    public:
    WidgetProcessor(Widget* w) : w_(w) {}
    ...
    Widget* w_;                        // I do not own w
};
```

Non-owning access to an object should be granted by using raw pointers or references. Yes, even in C++ 17, with all its smart pointers, there is a place for raw pointers. Not only that, but in the bulk of the code, the majority of pointers will be raw pointers—all the non-owning ones.

You might reasonably point out at this time that the preceding example of the recommended practices for granting non-owning access looks exactly like one of the examples of bad practices shown earlier. The distinction is in the context—in a well-designed program, only non-owning access is granted through raw pointers and references. Actual ownership is always expressed in some other way. Thus, it is clear that, when a raw pointer is encountered, the function or class is not going to mess with the ownership of the object in any way. This, of course, creates some confusion when it comes to converting old legacy code, with raw pointers everywhere, to the modern practices. As a matter of clarity, it is recommended to convert such code in parts, with clearly indicated transitions between the code that follows the modern guidelines and the ones that do not.

Another issue to discuss here is the use of pointers versus references. As a matter of syntax, the reference is basically a pointer that cannot be NULL (or nullptr) and cannot be left uninitialized. It is tempting to adopt a convention that any pointer passed to a function may be NULL and must, therefore, be checked, and any function that cannot accept a NULL pointer must instead take a reference. It is a good convention, and widely used, but not widely enough to be considered an accepted design pattern. Perhaps in recognition of this, the C++ Core Guidelines library offers an alternative for expressing non-NULL pointers—not_null<T*>. Note that this is not a part of the language itself, but can be implemented in standard C++ without any language extension.

Expressing exclusive ownership

The second most common type of ownership is exclusive ownership—the code creates an object and will delete it later. The task of deletion will not be delegated to someone else, as neither an extension of the lifetime or the object is permitted. This type of memory ownership is so common that we do it all the time without even thinking about it:

```
void Work() {
    Widget w;
    Transmogrify(w);
    Draw(w);
}
```

All local (stack) variables express unique memory ownership! Note that ownership in this context does not mean that someone else will not modify the object. It merely means that when the creator of the w widget—the `DoWork()` function, in our case—decides to delete it; the deletion will succeed (nobody has deleted it already) and the object will actually be deleted (nobody attempted to keep the object alive after the end of its scope).

This is the oldest way to construct an object in C++, and it's still the best one. If a stack variable does what you need, use it. C++ 11 provides another way to express unique ownership, and it is mainly used in cases where an object cannot be created on the stack but must be allocated on the heap. Heap allocation often happens when the ownership is shared or transferred—after all, the stack-allocated object will be deleted at the end of the containing scope; there is no way around it. If we need to keep the object alive for longer, it has to be allocated somewhere else. But we are talking about exclusive ownership here, the one that is not shared or given away. The other reason to create objects on the heap is that the size or type of the object may not be known at compile time. This usually happens when the object is polymorphic—a derived object is created, but the base class pointer is used. We now have a way of expressing the exclusive ownership of such objects using `std::unique_ptr`:

```
class FancyWidget : public Widget { ... };
std::unique_ptr<Widget> w(new FancyWidget);
```

What if the way to create an object is more complex than just `operator new`, and we need a Factory function? That is the type of ownership we will consider next.

Expressing transfer of exclusive ownership

In the preceding example, a new object was created and immediately bound to a unique pointer, `std::unique_ptr`, which guarantees exclusive ownership. The client code looks exactly the same if the object is created by a Factory:

```
std::unique_ptr<Widget> w(WidgetFactory());
```

But what should the Factory function return? It could certainly return a raw pointer, `Widget*`. After all, that is what `new` returns. But this opens the way to incorrect use of the `WidgetFactory`—for example, instead of capturing the returned raw pointer in a unique pointer, we could pass it to a function such as `Transmogrify` that takes a raw pointer because it does not deal with the ownership. Now, nobody owns the widget, and it ends up as a memory leak. Ideally, `WidgetFactory` would be written in a way that would force the caller to take ownership of the returned object.

What we need here is an ownership transfer—`WidgetFactory` is certainly an exclusive owner of the object it constructs, but at some point, it needs to hand off that ownership to a new, also exclusive, owner. The code to do so is very simple:

```
std::unique_ptr<Widget> WidgetFactory() {
    Widget* new_w = new Widget;
        ...
    return std::unique_ptr<Widget>(new_w);
}
std::unique_ptr<Widget> w(WidgetFactory());
```

This works exactly the way we want it to, but why? Doesn't the unique pointer provide exclusive ownership? The answer is, it does, but it is also a movable object. Moving the content of a unique pointer into another one transfers the ownership of the object; the original pointer is left in the moved-from state (its destruction will not delete any objects). What is so good about this idiom? It clearly expresses, and forces at compile-time, that the Factory expects the caller to take exclusive (or shared) ownership of the object. For example, the following code, which would have left the new widget with no owner, does not compile:

```
void Transmogrify(Widget* w);
Transmogrify(WidgetFactory());
```

So, how do we call `Transmogrify()` on a widget, after we properly assumed ownership? This is still done with a raw pointer:

```
std::unique_ptr<Widget> w(WidgetFactory());
Transmogrify(&*w);   // or w.get()-same thing, gives non-owning access
```

But what about the stack variables? Can the exclusive ownership be transferred to someone else before the variable is destroyed? This is going to be slightly more complicated—the memory for the object is allocated on the stack and is going away, so some amount of copying is involved. Exactly how much copying depends on whether the object is movable. Moving, in general, transfers the ownership from the moved-from object to the moved-to one. This can be used for return values, but is more often used for passing arguments to functions that take exclusive ownership. Such functions must be declared to take the parameters by the `rvalue` reference `T&&`:

```
void Consume(Widget&& w) { auto my_w = std::move(w); ... }
Widget w, w1;
Consume(std::move(w));     // No more w - it's in moved-from state now
Consume(w1);               // Does not compile - must consent to move
```

Note that the caller must explicitly give up the ownership by wrapping the argument in `std::move`. This is one of the advantages of this idiom; without it, an ownership-transferring call would look exactly the same as a regular call.

Expressing shared ownership

The last type of ownership we need to cover is shared ownership, where multiple entities own the object equally. First, a word of caution—shared ownership is often misused, or over-used. Consider the preceding example, where a function was passed a shared pointer to an object it did not need to own. It is tempting to let the reference counting deal with the ownership of objects and *not worry about deletion*. However, this is often a sign of a poor design. In most systems, at some level, there is a clear ownership of resources, and it should be reflected in the chosen design of resource management. The *not worry about deletion* concern remains valid; explicit deletion of objects should be rare, but automatic deletion does not require shared ownership, merely a clearly expressed one (unique pointers, data members, and containers provide automatic deletion just as well).

That being said, there are definite cases for shared ownership. The most common valid applications of shared ownership are at a low level, inside data structures such as lists, trees, and more. A data element may be owned by other nodes of the same data structure, by any number of iterators currently pointing to it, and, possibly, by some temporary variables inside data structure member functions that operate on the entire structure or a part of it (such as rebalancing a tree). The ownership of the entire data structure is usually clear in a well-thought-out design. But the ownership of each node, or data element, may be truly shared in the sense that any owner is equal to any other; none is privileged or primary.

In C++, the notion of shared ownership is expressed through a shared pointer, `std::shared_ptr`:

```
struct ListNode {
    T data;
    std::shared_ptr<ListNode> next, prev;
};
class ListIterator {
    ...
    std::shared_ptr<ListNode> node_p;
};
```

The advantage of this design is that a list element that was unlinked from the list remains alive for as long as there is a way to access it through an iterator. This is not the way `std::list` is done, and it does not provide such guarantees. However, it may be a valid design for certain applications, for example, for a thread-safe list. Note that this particular application would also require atomic shared pointers, which are only available in C++ 20 (or you can write your own using C++ 11).

Now, what about functions taking shared pointers as parameters? In a program that follows good memory ownership practices, such a function conveys to the caller that it intends to take partial ownership that lasts longer than the function call itself—a copy of the shared pointer will be created. In the concurrent context, it may also indicate that the function needs to protect the object from deletion by another thread for at least as long as it's executing.

There are several disadvantages to shared ownership that you must keep in mind. The best-known one is the bane of shared pointers, that is, the circular dependency. If two objects with shared pointers point to each other, the entire pair remains *in use* indefinitely. C++ offers a solution to that in the form of `std::weak_ptr`, a counterpart to the shared pointer that provides a safe pointer to an object that may have already been deleted. If the previously mentioned pair of objects uses one shared and one weak pointer, the circular dependency is broken.

The circular dependency problem is real, but it happens more often in designs where shared ownership is used to conceal the larger problem of unclear resource ownership. However, there are other downsides to shared ownership. The performance of a shared pointer is always going to be lower than that of a raw pointer. On the other hand, a unique pointer can be just as efficient as a raw pointer (and in fact, `std::unique_ptr` is). When the shared pointer is first created, an additional memory allocation for the reference count must take place.

In C++ 11, `std::make_shared` can be used to combine the allocations for the object itself and the reference counter, but this implies that the object is created with the intent to share (often, the object Factory returns unique pointers, some of which are later converted to shared pointers). Copying or deleting a shared pointer must also increment or decrement the reference counter. Shared pointers are often attractive in concurrent data structures, where, at least at the low level, the notion of ownership may indeed be fuzzy, with several accesses to the same object happening at the same time. However, designing a shared pointer to be thread-safe in all contexts is not easy and carries additional runtime overhead.

Summary

In C++, memory ownership is really just shorthand for object ownership, which, in turn, is the way to manage arbitrary resources, their ownership, and access. We have reviewed the contemporary idioms that the C++ community has developed to express different types of memory ownership. C++ allows the programmer to express exclusive or shared memory ownership. Just as important is expressing *non-ownership* in programs that are agnostic about the ownership of resources. We have also learned about the practices and attributes of resource ownership in a well-designed program.

We now have the idiomatic language to clearly express which entity in the program owns each object or resource. The next chapter covers the idiom for the simplest operation on resources: the exchange, or swap.

Questions

- Why is it important to clearly express memory ownership in a program?
- What are the common problems that arise from unclear memory ownership?
- What types of memory ownership can be expressed in C++?
- How do you write non-memory-owning functions and classes?
- Why should exclusive memory ownership be preferred to the shared one?
- How do you express exclusive memory ownership in C++?
- How do you express shared memory ownership in C++?
- What are the potential downsides of shared memory ownership?

Further reading

C++ – From Beginner to Expert [Video] by Arkadiusz Wlodarczyk:
https://www.packtpub.com/application-development/c-beginner-expert-video

C++ Data Structures and Algorithms by Wisnu Anggoro:
https://www.packtpub.com/application-development/c-data-structures-and-algorithms

Expert C++ Programming by Jeganathan Swaminathan, Maya Posch, and Jacek Galowicz:
https://www.packtpub.com/application-development/expert-c-programming

4
Swap - From Simple to Subtle

We begin our exploration of basic C++ idioms with a very simple, even humble, operation—swap. The notion of swap refers to two objects exchanging places—after the swap, the first object keeps its name, but otherwise looks like the second object used to, and vice versa. This operation is so fundamental to C++ classes that the standard provides a template, std::swap, to do just that. Rest assured that C++ manages to turn even something as basic as a swap into a complex issue with subtle nuances.

The following topics are covered in this chapter:

- How is swap used by the standard C++ library?
- What are the applications of swap?
- How can we write exception-safe code using swap?
- How can we implement swap for our own types correctly?
- How can we correctly swap variables of an arbitrary type?

Technical requirements

Example code: https://github.com/PacktPublishing/Hands-On-Design-Patterns-with-CPP/tree/master/Chapter04

C++ Core Guidelines: https://github.com/isocpp/CppCoreGuidelines/blob/master/CppCoreGuidelines.md

C++ **Guideline Support Library (GSL):** https://github.com/Microsoft/GSL

Swap and the standard template library

The swap operation is widely used in the C++ standard library. All **Standard Template Library (STL)** containers provide swap functionality, and there is a non-member function template, `std::swap`. There are also uses of swap in STL algorithms. The standard library is also a template for implementing custom features that resemble standard ones. Therefore, we'll begin our study of the swap operation with a look at the functionality provided by the standard.

Swap and STL containers

Conceptually, swap is equivalent to the following operation:

```
template <typename T> void swap(T& x, T& y) {
    T tmp(x);
    x = y;
    y = tmp;
}
```

After the `swap()` is called, the contents of the x and y objects are swapped. This, however, is probably the worst possible way to actually implement swap. The first and most obvious problem with this implementation is that it copies both objects unnecessarily (it actually does three copy operations). The execution time of this operation is proportional to the size of the T type. For an STL container, the size would refer to the size of the actual container, not to the type of the element:

```
void swap(std::vector<int>& x, std::vector<int>& y) {
    std::vector<int> tmp(x);
    x = y;
    y = tmp;
}
```

Note that this code compiles, and, in most cases, even does the right thing. However, it copies every element of the vector several times. The second problem is that it temporarily allocates resources—for example, during the swap, we create a third vector that uses as much memory as one of the vectors being swapped. This allocation seems unnecessary, given that, in the final state, we have exactly as much data as we started with; only the names we use to access this data have been changed. The last problem with naive implementation is revealed when we consider what happens if, for example, the memory allocation we just mentioned fails.

The entire swap operation, which should have been as simple and foolproof as exchanging the names used to access vector elements, instead fails with a memory allocation failure. But that's not the only way it can fail—the copy constructor and the assignment operator can both throw exceptions.

All STL containers, including `std::vector`, provide the guarantee that they can be swapped in constant time. The way this is accomplished is rather straightforward if you consider that the STL container objects themselves contain only pointers to the data, plus some state, such as object size. To swap these containers, we need only to swap the pointers (and the rest of the state, of course)—the elements of the container remain exactly where they always were, in dynamically allocated memory, and do not need to be copied or even accessed. The implementation of the swap needs only to swap the pointers, the sizes, and other state variables (in a real STL implementation, a container class, such as a vector, does not directly consist of data members of built-in types, such as pointers, but has one or more class data members that, in turn, are made from pointers and other built-in types).

Since any pointers or other vector data members are not publicly accessible, the swap has to be implemented as a member function of the container, or be declared a friend. The STL takes the former approach—all STL containers have a `swap()` member function that swaps the object with another object of the same type.

The implementation of this by swapping pointers takes care, indirectly, of the two other problems we mentioned. First of all, because only the data members of the containers are swapped, there is no memory allocation. Secondly, copying pointers and other built-in types cannot throw an exception, and so the entire swap operation does not throw (and cannot otherwise fail).

The simple and consistent picture we have described so far is only mostly true. The first complication, and by far the simpler one, applies only to containers that are parameterized not just on the element type, but also on a callable object of some sort. For example, the `std::map` container accepts the optional comparison function for comparing the elements of the map, which, by default, is `std::less`. Such callable objects have to be stored with the container. Since they are invoked very often, it is highly desirable, for performance reasons, to keep them in the same memory allocation as the container object itself, and indeed they are made data members of the container class.

However, that optimization comes with a price—swapping two containers now requires exchanging the compare functions; that is, the actual objects, not the pointers to them. The comparison objects are implemented by the client of the library, so there is no guarantee that swapping them is possible, let alone that it will not throw an exception.

Therefore, for `std::map`, the standard provides the following guarantee—in order for the map to be swappable, the callable objects must also be swappable. Furthermore, swapping two maps does not throw an exception, unless swapping comparison objects may throw, in which case, any exception thrown by that swap is propagated from the `std::map` swap. This consideration does not apply to containers, such as `std::vector`, that do not use any callable objects, and swapping these containers still does not throw an exception (as far as we know up to now).

The other complication in the otherwise consistent and natural behavior of the swap is due to the allocators, and that is a hard one to resolve. Consider the problem—the two swapped containers must, necessarily, have allocators of the same type, but not necessarily the same allocator object. Each container has its elements allocated by its own allocator, and they must be deallocated by the same allocator. After the swap, the first container owns the elements from the second one and must eventually deallocate them. This can only be done (correctly) using the allocator of the first container; therefore, the allocators must also be exchanged.

C++ standards prior to C++11 ignore the problem entirely, and decree that any two allocator objects of the same type must be able to deallocate each other's memory. If it's true, then we do not have to swap allocators at all. If it is not true, then we have already violated the standard and are in undefined behavior territory. C++11 allows allocators to have a non-trivial state, which must, therefore, be swapped too. But the allocator objects do not have to be swappable. The standard addresses the problem in the following way—if, for any `allocator_type` allocator class, there is a `trait` class that defines, among other things, the `std::allocator_traits<allocator_type>::propagate_on_container_swap::value` trait property, and if this value is true, then the allocators are exchanged using an unqualified call to a non-member swap; that is, simply a `swap(allocator1, allocator2)` call (see the next section to learn what that call actually does). If this value is not true, then the allocators are not swapped at all, and both container objects must use the same allocator. If that is not true either, then we are back to undefined behavior. C++17 puts a more formal veneer on this by declaring `swap()` member functions of STL containers to be conditionally `noexcept()`, with the same limitations.

The requirement that swapping two containers cannot throw an exception, at least as long as the allocators are not involved and the container does not use callable objects or uses non-throwing ones, ends up imposing a rather subtle limitation on the implementation of the container—it prevents the use of local buffer optimization.

We will talk about this optimization in great detail in `Chapter 10`, *Local Buffer Optimization*, but in a nutshell, the idea is to avoid dynamic memory allocation for containers of very few elements, such as short strings, by defining a buffer inside the container class itself. This optimization, however, is generally incompatible with the notion of a non-throwing swap, since the elements inside the container object can no longer be exchanged by merely swapping pointers, but have to be copied between the containers.

Non-member swap

The standard also provides a template `std::swap()` function. Prior to C++11, it was declared in the `<algorithm>` header; in C++11, it was moved to `<utility>`. The declaration of the function is as follows:

```
template <typename T>
    void swap (T& a, T& b);
template <typename T, size_t N>
    void swap(T (&a)[N], T (&b)[N]);     // Since C++11
```

The overload for arrays was added in C++11. In C++20, both versions are additionally declared `constexpr`. For STL containers, `std::swap()` calls the member function `swap()`. As we will see in the following section, the behavior of `swap()` can be customized for other types as well, but without any special efforts, the default implementation is used. This implementation does a swap using a temporary object. Before C++11, the temporary object was copy-constructed, and the swap was done with two assignments, just as we did in the preceding section. The type has to be copyable (both copy-constructible and copy-assignable), otherwise `std::swap()` will not compile. In C++11, `std::swap()` has been redefined to use move construction and move assignment. As usual, if the class is copyable, but does not have move operations declared at all, then the copy constructor and assignment are used. Note that if the class has copy operations declared and move operations declared as deleted, there is no automatic fallback to copying—that class is a non-movable type and `std::swap()` will not compile for it.

Since copying an object can, in general, throw an exception, swapping two objects for which a custom swap behavior is not provided can throw an exception as well. Move operations do not usually throw exceptions, and in C++11, if the object has a move constructor and an assignment operator and neither throw an exception, `std::swap()` also provides the no-throw guarantee. That behavior has been formalized in C++17 with a conditional `noexcept()` specification.

Swapping like the standard

From the preceding review of how the standard library handles a swap, we can deduce the following guidelines:

- Classes that support swap should implement `swap()` member functions that perform the operation in constant time
- A free-standing `swap()` non-member function should also be provided for all types that can be swapped
- Swapping two objects should not throw exceptions or otherwise fail

The latter guideline is less strict, and it is not always possible to follow it. In general, if the type has move operations that do not throw an exception, a non-throwing swap implementation is also possible. Note also that many exception-safety guarantees, and in particular those provided by the standard library, require that move and swap operations do not throw an exception.

When and why to use swap

What is so important about the swap functionality that it deserves its own chapter? For that matter, why even use swap, and not continue to refer to an object by its original name? Mostly, it has to do with exception safety, which is also why we keep mentioning when swap can and cannot throw an exception.

Swap and exception safety

The most important application of swap in C++ has to do with writing exception-safe code, or, more generally, error-safe code. Here is the problem, in a nutshell—in an exception-safe program, throwing an exception should never leave the program in an undefined state. More generally, an error condition should never leave the program in an undefined state. Note that the error does not need to be handled by means of an exception—for example, returning an error code from a function should also be handled without creating undefined behavior. In particular, if an operation causes an error, the resources already consumed by the operation in progress should be released. Often, an even stronger guarantee is desired—every operation either succeeds or is entirely rolled back.

Let's consider an example where we will apply a transform to all elements of a vector, and store the results in a new vector:

```
class C; // Our element type
C transmogrify(C x) { return C(...); }    // Some operation on C
void transmogrify(const std::vector<C>& in, std::vector<C>& out) {
    out.resize(0);
    out.reserve(in.size());
    for (const auto& x : in) {
        out.push_back(transmogrify(x));
    }
}
```

Here, we return the vector via an output parameter (in C++17, we could return via a value and count on the copy elision, but in earlier versions of the standard copy, elision is not guaranteed). The vector is made empty at first, and grows to the same size as the input vector. Any data the out vector may have had is gone. Note the reserve() call that is used to avoid repeated deallocations of the growing vector.

This code works fine as long as there are no errors, that is, no exceptions are thrown. But this is not guaranteed. First of all, reserve() does a memory allocation, which may fail. If this happens, the transmogrify() function will exit via the exception, and the output vector will be empty, since the resize(0) call has already executed. The initial content of the output vector is lost, and nothing is written to replace it. Secondly, any iteration of the loop over the elements of the vector may throw an exception. The exception could be thrown by the copy constructor of the new element of the output vector, or by the transformation itself. Either way, the loop is interrupted. STL guarantees that the output vector is not left in an undefined state even if the copy constructor inside the push_back() call fails—the new element is not *partially* created, and vector size is not increased. However, the elements already stored will remain in the output vector (and any elements that were there originally are gone). This may not be what we intended—it is not unreasonable to request that the transmogrify() operation either succeeds and applies the transform to the entire vector, or fails and changes nothing.

The key to such exception-safe implementation is the swap:

```
void transmogrify(const std::vector<C>& in, std::vector<C>& out) {
    std::vector<C> tmp;
    tmp.reserve(in.size());
    for (const auto& x : in) {
        tmp.push_back(transmogrify(x));
    }
    out.swap(tmp);          // Must not throw!
}
```

In this example, we have changed the code to operate on a temporary vector during the entire transformation. Note that, in a typical case of an output vector that is empty on input, this does not increase the amount of memory in use. If the output vector has some data in it, both the new data and the old data exist in memory until the end of the function. This is necessary to provide the guarantee that the old data will not be deleted unless the new data can be fully computed. If desired, this guarantee can be traded for lower overall memory use, and the output vector can be emptied at the beginning of the function (on the other hand, any caller who wants to make such a trade-off can just empty the vector before calling `transmogrify()`).

If an exception is thrown at any time during the execution of the `transmogrify()` function, right up until the last line, then the temporary vector is deleted, as would be any local variable allocated on the stack (see Chapter 5 *A Comprehensive Look at RAII* later in this book). The last line is the key to exception safety—it swaps the content of the output vector with that of the temporary one. If that line can throw an exception, then our entire work is for nothing—the swap has failed, and the output vector is left in an undefined state, since we do not know how much of the swap had succeeded before the exception was thrown. But if the swap does not throw an exception, as in the case for the `std::vector`, then, as long as the control reached the last line, the entire `transmogrify()` operation has succeeded, and the result will be returned to the caller. What happens to the old content of the output vector? It is now owned by the temporary vector, which is about to be deleted, implicitly, on the next line (the closing brace). Assuming the destructor of C follows the C++ guidelines and does not throw an exception, and to do otherwise would be to invite the dreaded specter of undefined behavior, our entire function has been made exception-safe.

This idiom is sometimes known as **copy-and-swap** and is, perhaps, the easiest way to implement an operation with commit-or-rollback semantics, or the strong exception-safety guarantee. The key to the idiom is the ability to swap objects cheaply and without exceptions being thrown.

Other common swap idioms

There are a few more commonly used techniques that rely on swap, although none are as critically important as the use of swap for exception safety.

Let's start with a very simple way to reset a container, or any other swappable object, to its default-constructed state:

```
C c = ....;          // Object with stuff in it
{
    C tmp;
    c.swap(tmp);     // c is now empty
}                    // Old c is now gone
```

Note that this code explicitly creates an empty object just to swap with it, and uses an extra scope (a pair of curly braces) to ensure that that object is deleted as soon as possible. We can do better by using a temporary object, without a name, to swap with:

```
C c = ....;      // Object with stuff in it
C().swap(c);     // Temporary is created and deleted
```

The temporary object here is created and deleted within the same line of code and takes the old content of the object c with it. Note that the order of what is swapped with what is very important—the swap() member function is called on the temporary object. An attempt to do the reverse will not compile:

```
C c = ....;      // Object with stuff in it
c.swap(C());     // Close but does not compile
```

This is because the swap() member function takes its argument by a C& non-const reference, and non-const references cannot be bound to temporary objects (more generally, to r-values). Note that, for the same reason, the swap() non-member function cannot be used to swap an object with a temporary object either, so, if the class does not have a swap() member function, then an explicitly named object must be created.

A more general form of this idiom is used to apply transforms to the original object without changing its name in the program. Let's suppose that we have a vector in our program to which we want to apply the preceding transmogrify() function; however, we do not want to create a new vector. Instead, we want to continue using the original vector (or at least its variable name) in the program, but with the new data in it. This idiom is an elegant way to achieve the desired result:

```
std::vector<C> vec;
... // Write data into the vector
{
    std::vector<C> tmp;
    transmogrify(vec, tmp);     // tmp is the result
    swap(vec, tmp);             // Now vec is the result!
}                              // and now old vec is destroyed
... // Continue using vec, with new data
```

This pattern can be repeated as many times as needed, replacing the content of the object without introducing new names into the program. Contrast it with the more traditional, C-like way that does not use swap:

```
std::vector<C> vec;
...                              // Write data into the vector
std::vector<C> vec1;
transmogrify(vec, vec1);         // Must use vec1 from now on!
std::vector<C> vec2;
transmogrify_other(vec1, vec2); // Must use vec2 from now on!
```

Note that the old names, vec and vec1, are still accessible after the new data is computed. It would be an easy mistake to use vec in the following code, when vec1 should be used instead. With the previously demonstrated swap technique, the program is not polluted with new variable names.

How to implement and use swap correctly

We have seen how swap functionality is implemented by the standard library, and what the expectations are for a swap implementation. Let's now see how to correctly support swap for your own types.

Implementing swap

We have seen that all STL containers, and many other standard library types (for example, std::thread), provide a swap() member function. While not required, it is the easiest way to implement swap that needs access to the private data of the class, and also the only way to swap an object with a temporary object of the same type. The proper way to declare the swap() member function is like this:

```
class C {
    public:
    void swap(C& rhs) noexcept;
};
```

Of course, the noexcept specification should only be included if a no-throw guarantee can indeed be given; in some cases, it may need to be conditional, based on properties of other types.

How should the swap be implemented? There are several ways. For many classes, we can simply swap the data members, one at a time. This delegates the problem of swapping the objects to their contained types, which, if they follow the pattern, will eventually end up swapping the built-in types that everything is made of. If you know that your data member has a `swap()` member function, then you can call that. Otherwise, you have to call the non-member swap. This is likely to call an instantiation of the `std::swap()` template, but you should not invoke it by that name for reasons that will be explained in the next section. Instead, you should bring the name into the containing scope, and call `swap()` without the `std::` qualifier:

```
#include <utility>       // <algorithm> before C++11
...
class C {
    public:
    void swap(C& rhs) noexcept {
        using std::swap;       // Brings in std::swap into this scope
        v_.swap(rhs.v_);
        swap(i_, rhs.i_);       // Calls std::swap
    }
    ...
    private:
    std::vector<int> v_;
    int i_;
};
```

A particular implementation idiom that is very swap-friendly is the so-called **pimpl idiom**, also known as the **handle-body** idiom. It is primarily used to minimize compilation dependencies and avoid exposing the implementation of the class in the header file. In this idiom, the entire declaration of a class in the header file consists of all the necessary public member functions, plus a single pointer that points to the actual implementation. The implementation and the body of the member functions are all in the `.c` file. The *pointer to implementation* data member is often called `p_impl` or `pimpl`, hence the name of the idiom. Swapping a pimpl-implemented class is as easy as swapping the two pointers:

```
// In the header C.h:
class C_impl;       // Forward declaration
class C {
    public:
    void swap(C& rhs) noexcept {
        swap(pimpl_, rhs.pimpl_);
    }
    void f(...);       // Declaration only
    ...
    private:
    C_impl* pimpl_;
```

```
};
// In the C file:
class C_impl {
    ... real implementation ...
};
void C::f(...) { pimpl_->f(...); } // Actual implementation of C::f()
```

This takes care of the member function `swap`. But what if someone calls a non-member `swap()` function on our custom types? As written, that call will invoke the default implementation of `std::swap()`, if it's visible (for example, due to a `using std::swap` declaration), that is, the one that uses the `copy` or `move` operations:

```
class C {
    public:
    void swap(C& rhs) noexcept;
};
...
C c1(...), c2(...);
swap(c1, c2);          // Either does not compile or calls std::swap
```

It is evident that we must also support a non-member `swap()` function. We can easily declare one, right after the class declaration. However, we should also consider what happens if the class is declared not in the global scope, but in a namespace:

```
namespace N {
class C {
    public:
    void swap(C& rhs) noexcept;
};
void swap(C& lhs, C& rhs) noexcept { lhs.swap(rhs); }
}
...
N::C c1(...), c2(...);
swap(c1, c2);          // Calls non-member N::swap()
```

The unqualified call to `swap()` calls the `swap()` non-member function inside the N namespace, which in turn calls the member function `swap()` on one of the arguments (the convention adopted by the standard library is to call `lhs.swap()`). Note, however, that we did not invoke `N::swap()`, only `swap()`. Outside of the N namespace and without a `using namespace N;` specification, an unqualified call would not normally resolve to a function inside a namespace. However, in this case, it does, due to the feature in the standard called the **Argument-Dependent Lookup (ADL)**, also known as the **Koenig lookup**. The ADL adds to the overload resolution all functions declared in the scopes where the arguments of the function are declared.

In our case, the compiler sees the c1 and c2 arguments of the swap(...) function and recognizes their type as N::C, even before it figures out what the swap name refers to. Since the arguments are in the N namespace, all functions declared in that namespace are added to the overload resolution, and thus, the N::swap function becomes visible.

If the type has a swap() member function, then the easiest way to implement the non-member swap() function is to call that. However, such a member function is not required; if the decision was made to not support a swap() member function, then the swap() non-member has to have access to the private data of the class. It would have to be declared a friend function:

```
class C {
    friend void swap(C& rhs) noexcept;
};
void swap(C& lhs, C& rhs) noexcept {
    ... swap data members of C ...
}
```

It is also possible to define the implementation of the swap() function inline, without a separate definition:

```
class C {
    friend void swap(C& lhs, C& rhs) noexcept {
        ... swap data members of C ...
    }
};
```

This is particularly handy when we have a class template, instead of a single class. We consider this pattern in more detail later, in Chapter 11, *Friend Factory*.

One often forgotten implementation detail is the self-swap—swap(x, x), or, in the case of a member function call, x.swap(x). Is it well-defined, but what does it do? The answer appears to be that it is, or should be, well-defined in both C++03 and C++11 (and later), but ends up doing nothing; that is, it does not change the object (although not necessarily at zero cost). A user-defined swap implementation should either be implicitly safe for self-swap or should explicitly test for it. If the swap is implemented in terms of copy or move assignments, it is important to note that the copy assignment is required by the standard to be safe against self-assignments, while the move assignment may change the object, but must leave it in a valid state, called a **moved-from** state (in this state, we can still assign something else to the object).

Using swap correctly

Up until now, we have switched between calling a `swap()` member function, a `swap()` non-member function, and the explicitly qualified `std::swap()` operation, without any pattern or reason. We should now bring some discipline to this matter.

First of all, it is always safe and appropriate to call the `swap()` member function as long as you know that it exists. The latter qualification usually comes up when writing template code—when dealing with concrete types, you typically know what interface they provide. This leaves us with just one question—when calling the `swap()` non-member function, should we use the `std::` prefix?

Consider what happens if we do, as shown here:

```
namespace N {
class C {
    public:
    void swap(C& rhs) noexcept;
};
void swap(C& lhs, C& rhs) noexcept { lhs.swap(rhs); }
}
...
N::C c1(...), c2(...);
std::swap(c1, c2);      // Calls std::swap()
swap(c1, c2);           // Calls N::swap()
```

Note that the argument-dependent lookup does not apply to qualified names, which is why the call to `std::swap()` still calls the instantiation of the template swap from the `<utility>` header file of the STL. For this reason, it is recommended never to call `std::swap()` explicitly, but to bring that overload into the current scope with a `using` declaration, then call the unqualified `swap`:

```
using std::swap;        // Makes std::swap() available
swap(c1, c2);           // Calls N::swap() if provided, otherwise
std::swap()
```

Unfortunately, the fully qualified invocation of `std::swap()` is often found in many programs. To protect yourself against such code and to ensure that your custom swap implementation is called no matter what, you can instantiate the `std::swap()` template for your own type:

```
namespace std {
    void swap(N::C& lhs, N::C& rhs) noexcept { lhs.swap(rhs); }
}
```

Generally, declaring your own functions or classes for the reserved `std::` namespace is not allowed by the standard. However, the standard makes an exception for explicit instantiations of certain template functions (`std::swap()` being among them). With such specialization in place, a call to `std::swap()` will invoke that instantiation, which forwards it to our custom swap implementation. Note that it is not sufficient to instantiate the `std::swap()` template, because such instantiations do not participate in the argument-dependent lookup. If the other non-member swap function is not provided, we have the reverse problem:

```
using std::swap;        // Makes std::swap() available
std::swap(c1, c2);      // Calls our std::swap() overload
swap(c1, c2);           // Calls default std::swap()
```

Now, the non-qualified call ends up calling the instantiation of the default `std::swap()` operation—the one with the move constructors and assignments. In order to ensure that every call to swap is correctly handled, both a non-member `swap()` function and the explicit `std::swap()` instantiation should be implemented (of course, they can, and should, all forward to the same implementation). Finally, note that the standard allows us to extend the `std::` namespace with template instantiations, but not with additional template overloads. Therefore, if, instead of a single type, we have a class template, we cannot specialize `std::swap` for it; such code will, in all likelihood, compile, but the standard does not guarantee that the desired overload will be selected (technically, the standard invokes the undefined behavior and guarantees nothing at all). For that reason alone, calling `std::swap` directly should be avoided.

Summary

The swap functionality in C++ is used to implement several important patterns. The most critical one is the copy-and-swap implementation of exception-safe transactions. All standard library containers, and most other STL objects, provide the swap member function that is fast and, when possible, does not throw exceptions. User-defined types that need to support swap should follow the same pattern. Note, however, that implementing a non-throwing swap function usually requires an extra indirection and goes against several optimization patterns. In addition to the member function swap, we have reviewed the use and the implementation of the non-member swap. Given that `std::swap` is always available, and can be called on any copyable or movable objects, the programmer should take care to implement a non-member swap function too, if a better way to swap exists for a given type (in particular, any type with a member function swap should also provide a non-member function overload that calls that member function).

Finally, while the preferred invocation of the non-member swap is without the `std::` prefix, the alternative use, although ill-advised, is common enough that an implicit instantiation of the `std::swap` template should be considered.

The next chapter takes us on a tour of one of the most popular, and powerful, C++ idioms—the C++ way of managing resources.

Questions

1. What does swap do?
2. How is swap used in exception-safe programs?
3. Why should a swap function be non-throwing?
4. Should a member or a non-member implementation of swap be preferred?
5. How do standard library objects implement swap?
6. Why should the non-member swap function be called without the `std::` qualifier?

A Comprehensive Look at RAII

5

Resource management is probably the second most frequent thing a program does, after computing. But just because it's frequently done does not mean it's visible—some languages hide most, or all, resource management from the user. And just because it is hidden, does not mean it's not there.

Every program needs to use some memory, and memory is a resource. A program would be of no use if it never interacted with the outside world in some way, at least to print the result, and input and output channels (files, sockets, and so on) are resources.

In this chapter, we will start by answering the following questions:

- What is considered a resource in a C++ program?
- What are the key concerns for managing resources in C++?

Then, we will introduce Resource Acquisition is Initialization (RAII) and explain how it helps in efficient resource management in C++ by answering these questions:

- What is the standard approach for managing resources in C++ (RAII)?
- How does RAII solve the problems of resource management?

We will end the chapter with a discussion about the implications and possible concerns of using RAII by providing the answers to these questions:

- What are the precautions that must be taken when writing RAII objects?
- What are the consequences of using RAII for resource management?

C++, with its zero-overhead abstraction philosophy, does not hide resources or their management at the core language level. But we would do well to not confuse hiding resources with managing them.

Technical requirements

- Google Test unit testing framework: `https://github.com/google/googletest`
- Google Benchmark library: `https://github.com/google/benchmark`
- Example code: `https://github.com/PacktPublishing/Hands-On-Design-Patterns-with-CPP/tree/master/Chapter05`

Resource management in C++

Every program operates on resources and needs to manage them. The most commonly used resource is memory, of course. Hence, you often read about **memory management** in C++. But really, resources can be just about anything. Many programs exist specifically to manage real, tangible physical resources, or the more ephemeral (but no less valuable) digital ones. Money in bank accounts, airline seats, car parts and assembled cars, or even crates of milk—in today's world, if it is something that needs to be counted and tracked, there is a piece of software somewhere that is doing it. But even in a program that does pure computations, there may be varied and complex resources, unless the program also eschews abstractions and operates at the level of bare numbers. For example, a physics simulation program may have particles as resources.

All of these resources have one thing in common—they need to be accounted for. They should not vanish without a trace, and a program should not just make up resources that don't really exist. Often, a specific instance of a resource is needed—you would not want someone else's purchase to be debited from your bank account; the specific instance of the resource matters. Thus, the most important consideration when evaluating different approaches to resource management is correctness—how well does the design ensure that resources are managed properly, how easy is it to make a mistake, and how hard would it be to find such a mistake? It should come as no surprise, then, that we use a testing framework to present the coding examples of resource management in this chapter.

Installing the microbenchmark library

In our case, we are interested in the efficiency of memory allocations and small fragments of code that may contain such allocations. The appropriate tool for measuring the performance of small fragments of code is a microbenchmark. There are many microbenchmark libraries and tools out there; in this book, we will use the Google Benchmark library. To follow along with the examples in this chapter, you must first download and install the library (follow the instructions in the `Readme.md` file). Then you can compile and run the examples. You can build the sample files included with the library to see how to build a benchmark on your particular system. For example, on a Linux machine, the command to build and run a benchmark program called `malloc1.C` might look something like this:

```
$CXX malloc1.C -I. -I$GBENCH_DIR/include -g -O4 -Wall -Wextra -Werror \
    -pedantic --std=c++14 $GBENCH_DIR/lib/libbenchmark.a -lpthread -lrt \
    -lm -o malloc1 && ./malloc1
```

Here, `$CXX` is your C++ compiler, such as `g++` or `g++-6`, and `$GBENCH_DIR` is the directory where the benchmark is installed.

Installing Google Test

We will be testing very small fragments of code for correctness. On the one hand, this is simply because each fragment illustrates a specific concept or idea. On the other hand, even in a large-scale software system, resource management is done by small building blocks of code. They may combine to form a quite complex resource manager, but each block performs a specific function and is testable. The appropriate testing system for this situation is a unit testing framework. There are many such frameworks to choose from; in this book, we will use the Google Test unit testing framework. To follow along with the examples in this chapter, you must first download and install the framework (follow the instructions in the `README` file). Once installed, you can compile and run the examples. You can build the sample tests included with the library to see how to build and link with Google Test on your particular system. For example, on a Linux machine, the command to build and run a `memory1.C` test might look something like this:

```
$CXX memory1.C -I. -I$GTEST_DIR/include -g -O0 -I. -Wall -Wextra -Werror \
    -pedantic --std=c++14 $GTEST_DIR/lib/libgtest.a \
    $GTEST_DIR/lib/libgtest_main.a -lpthread -lrt -lm -o memory1 && \
    ./memory1
```

Here, `$CXX` is your C++ compiler, such as `g++` or `g++-6`, and `$GTEST_DIR` is the directory where Google Test is installed.

Counting resources

A unit testing framework, such as Google Test, allows us to execute some code and verify that the results are what they should be. The results that we can look at include any variable or expression that we can access from the test program. That definition does not extend, for example, to the amount of memory that is currently in use. So, if we want to verify that resources are not disappearing, we have to count them.

In the following simple test fixture, we use a special resource class instead of, say, the `int` keyword. This class is instrumented to count how many objects of this type have been created, and how many are currently alive:

```
struct object_counter {
    static int count;
    static int all_count;
    object_counter() { ++count; ++all_count; }
    ~object_counter() { --count; }
};
```

Now we can test that our program manages resources correctly, as follows:

```
TEST(Scoped_ptr, Construct) {
    object_counter::all_count = object_counter::count = 0;
    object_counter* p = new object_counter;
    EXPECT_EQ(1, object_counter::count);
    EXPECT_EQ(1, object_counter::all_count);
    delete p;
    EXPECT_EQ(0, object_counter::count);
    EXPECT_EQ(1, object_counter::all_count);
}
```

In Google Test, every test is implemented as a **test fixture**. There are several types; the simplest one is a standalone test function, such as the one we use here. Running this simple test program tells us that the test has passed, as follows:

```
[----------] 1 test from Memory
[ RUN      ] Memory.AcquireRelease
[       OK ] Memory.AcquireRelease (0 ms)
[----------] 1 test from Memory (0 ms total)
```

The expected results are verified using one of the EXPECT_* macros and any test failures will be reported. This test verifies that, after creating and deleting an instance of the type object_counter, there are no such objects left, and that exactly one was constructed.

Dangers of manual resource management

C++ allows us to manage resources almost at the hardware level, and someone, somewhere, must indeed manage them at this level. The latter is actually true for every language, even the high-level ones that do not expose such details to the programmers. But the *somewhere* does not have to be in your program! Before we learn the C++ solutions and tools for resource management, let's first understand the problems that arise from not using any such tools.

Manual resource management is error-prone

The first and most obvious danger of managing every resource manually, with explicit calls to acquire and release each one, is that it is easy to forget the latter. For example see the following:

```
{
    object_counter* p = new object_counter;
        ... many more lines of code ...
} // Were we supposed to do something here? Can't remember now...
```

We are now leaking a resource (object_counter objects, in this case). If we did this in a unit test, it would fail, as follows:

```
TEST(Memory, Leak1) {
    object_counter::all_count = object_counter::count = 0;
    object_counter* p = new object_counter;
    EXPECT_EQ(1, object_counter::count);
    EXPECT_EQ(1, object_counter::all_count);
    //delete p;     // Forgot that
    EXPECT_EQ(0, object_counter::count);     // This test fails now!
    EXPECT_EQ(1, object_counter::all_count);
}
```

You can see the failing tests, and the location of the failures, as reported by the unit test framework:

```
[----------] 2 tests from Memory
[ RUN      ] Memory.AcquireRelease
[       OK ] Memory.AcquireRelease (0 ms)
[ RUN      ] Memory.Leak1
memory.C:33: Failure
Expected equality of these values:
  0
  object_counter::count
    Which is: 1
[  FAILED  ] Memory.Leak1 (0 ms)
[----------] 2 tests from Memory (0 ms total)
```

In a real program, finding such errors is much harder. Memory debuggers and sanitizers can help with memory leaks, but they require that the program actually execute the buggy code, so they depend on the test coverage.

The resource leaks can be much subtler and harder to find, too. Consider this code, where we did not forget to release the resource:

```
bool process(... some parameters ... ) {
    object_counter* p = new object_counter;
    ... many more lines of code ...
    delete p;          // A-ha, we remembered!
    return true;       // Success
}
```

During subsequent maintenance, a possible failure condition was discovered, and the appropriate test added:

```
bool process(... some parameters ... ) {
    object_counter* p = new object_counter;
    ... many more lines of code ...
    if (!success) return false;     // Failure, cannot continue
    ... even more lines of code ...
    delete p;          // Still here
    return true;       // Success
}
```

This change introduced a subtle bug—now, resources are leaked only if the intermediate computation has failed and triggered the early return. If the failure is rare enough, this mistake may escape all tests, even if the testing process employs regular memory sanitizer runs. This mistake is also all too easy to make, since the edit could be made in a place far removed from both the construction and deletion of the object, and nothing in the immediate context gives the programmer a hint that a resource needs to be released.

The alternative to leaking a resource, in this case, is to release it. Note that this leads to some code duplication:

```
bool process(... some parameters ... ) {
    object_counter* p = new object_counter;
    ... many more lines of code ...
    if (!success) { delete p; return false; }  // Failure, cannot continue
    ... even more lines of code ...
    delete p;        // Still here
    return true;     // Success
}
```

As with any code duplication, there comes the danger of code divergence. Let's say that the next round of code enhancements required more than one object_counter, and an array of them is now allocated as follows:

```
bool process(... some parameters ... ) {
    object_counter* p = new object_counter[10];    // Now an array
    ... many more lines of code ...
    if (!success) { delete p; return false; }   // Old scalar delete
    ... even more lines of code ...
    delete [] p;      // Matching array delete
    return true;      // Success
}
```

If we change new to the new array, we must change delete as well; the thought goes, there is probably one at the end of the function. Who knew that there was one more in the middle? Even if the programmer had not forgotten about the resources, the manual resource management gets disproportionately more error-prone as the program becomes more complex. And not all resources are as forgiving as a counter object. Consider the following code that performs some concurrent computation, and must acquire and release mutex locks. Note the very words **acquire** and **release**, the common terminology for locks, suggest that locks are treated as a kind of resource (the resource here is exclusive access to the data protected by the lock):

```
std::mutex m1, m2, m3;
bool process_concurrently(... some parameters ... ) {
    m1.lock();
    m2.lock();
    ... need both locks in this section ...
    if (!success) {
        m1.unlock();
        m2.unlock();
        return false;
    } // Both locks unlocked
    ... more code ...
```

```
    m2.unlock();      // Don't need exclusive access guarded by this mutex
                      // Still need m1
    m3.lock();
    if (!success) {
        m1.unlock();
        return false;
    } // No need to unlock m2 here
    ... more code ...
    m1.unlock(); m3.unlock();
    return true;
}
```

This code has both the duplication and the divergence. It also has a bug—see if you can find it (hint—count how many times m3 is unlocked, versus how many return statements there are after it's locked). As the resources become more numerous and complex to manage, such bugs are going to creep up more often.

Resource management and exception safety

Remember the code at the beginning of the previous section—the one we said is correct, where we did not forget to release the resource? Consider the following code:

```
bool process(... some parameters ... ) {
    object_counter* p = new object_counter;
        ... many more lines of code ...
    delete p;
    return true;     // Success
}
```

I have bad news for you—this code probably wasn't correct either. If any of the many more lines of code can throw an exception, then delete p is never going to be executed:

```
bool process(... some parameters ... ) {
    object_counter* p = new object_counter;
        ... many more lines of code ...
    if (!success) // Exceptional circumstances, cannot continue
        throw process_exception();
        ... even more lines of code ...
    delete p;       // Won't do anything if exception is thrown!
    return true;
}
```

This looks very similar to the early `return` problem, only worse—the exception can be thrown by any code that the `process()` function calls. The exception can even be added later to some code that the `process()` function calls, without any changes in the function itself. It used to work fine, then one day it does not.

Unless we change our approach to resource management, the only solution is to use `try...catch` blocks:

```
bool process(... some parameters ... ) {
    object_counter* p = new object_counter;
    try {
            ... many more lines of code ...
        if (!success) // Exceptional circumstances, cannot continue
            throw process_exception();
            ... even more lines of code ...
    } catch ( ... ) {
        delete p;    // For exceptional case
    }
    delete p;        // For normal case
    return true;
}
```

The obvious problem here is code duplication again, as well as the proliferation of the `try...catch` blocks literally everywhere. Worse than that, this approach does not scale should we need to manage multiple resources, or even just manage anything more complex than a single acquisition with a corresponding release:

```
std::mutex m;
bool process(... some parameters ... ) {
    m.lock();
    object_counter* p = new object_counter;
                        // Problem #1: constructor can throw
    try {
            ... many more lines of code ...
        m.unlock();     // Critical section ends here
            ... even more lines of code ...
    } catch ( ... ) {
        delete p;       // OK, always needed
        m.unlock();     // Do we need this? Maybe:
                        // Depends on where the exception was thrown!
        throw;          // Rethrow the exception for the client to handle
    }
    delete p;           // For normal case, no need to unlock mutex
    return true;
}
```

Now, we can't even decide whether the catch block should release the mutex or not—it depends on whether the exception was thrown before or after the `unlock()` operation that happens in the normal, non-exceptional control flow. Also, the `object_counter` constructor could throw an exception (not the simple one we had so far, but a more complex one that ours could evolve into). That would happen outside of the `try...catch` block, and the mutex would never get unlocked.

It should be clear to us by now that we need an entirely different solution for the resource management problem, not some patchwork. In the next section, we will discuss the pattern that became **golden standard** of resource management in C++.

The RAII idiom

We have seen in the previous section how the ad hoc attempts to manage resources become unreliable, then error-prone, and eventually fail. What we need is to make sure that resource acquisition is always paired up with resource release, and that these two actions happen before and after the section of code that uses the resource respectively. In C++, this kind of bracketing of a code sequence by a pair of actions is known as the Execute Around design pattern.

 For more information, see the article *C++ Patterns – Executing Around Sequences* by Kevlin Henney, available at `http://www.two-sdg.demon.co.uk/curbralan/papers/europlop/ExecutingAroundSequences.pdf`.

When specifically applied to resource management, this pattern is much more widely known as **Resource Acquisition is Initialization (RAII)**.

RAII in a nutshell

The basic idea behind RAII is very simple—there is one kind of function in C++ that is guaranteed to be called automatically, and that is the destructor of an object created on the stack, or the destructor of an object that is a data member of another object (in the latter case, the guarantee holds only if the containing class itself is destroyed). If we could hook up the release of the resource to the destructor of such an object, then the release could not be forgotten or skipped. It stands to reason that if releasing the resource is handled by the destructor, acquiring it should be handled by the constructor during the initialization of the object. Hence the full meaning of RAII as introduced in the title of this chapter—*A Comprehensive Look at RAII*.

Let's see how this works in the simplest case of memory allocation, via `operator new`. First, we need a class that can be initialized from a pointer to the newly allocated object, and whose destructor will delete that object:

```
template <typename T>
class raii {
    public:
    explicit raii(T* p) : p_(p) {}
    ~raii() { delete p_; }
    private:
    T* p_;
};
```

Now it is very easy to make sure that deletion is never omitted, and we can verify that it works as expected with a test that uses `object_counter`:

```
TEST(RAII, AcquireRelease) {
    object_counter::all_count = object_counter::count = 0;
    {
        raii<object_counter> p(new object_counter);
        EXPECT_EQ(1, object_counter::count);
        EXPECT_EQ(1, object_counter::all_count);
    } // No need to delete p, it's automatic
    EXPECT_EQ(0, object_counter::count);
    EXPECT_EQ(1, object_counter::all_count);
}
```

Note that in C++17, the class template type is deduced from the constructor and we can simply write the following:

```
raii p(new object_counter);
```

Of course, we probably want to use the new object for more than just creating and deleting it, so it would be nice to have access to the pointer stored inside the RAII object. There is no reason to grant such access in any way other than the standard pointer syntax, which makes our RAII object a kind of pointer itself:

```
template <typename T>
class scoped_ptr {
    public:
    explicit scoped_ptr(T* p) : p_(p) {}
    ~scoped_ptr() { delete p_; }
    T* operator->() { return p_; }
    const T* operator->() const { return p_; }
    T& operator*() { return *p_; }
    const T& operator*() const { return *p_; }
    private:
```

```
    T* p_;
};
```

This pointer can be used to automatically delete, at the end of the scope, the object that it points to (hence the name):

```
TEST(Scoped_ptr, AcquireRelease) {
    object_counter::all_count = object_counter::count = 0;
    {
        scoped_ptr<object_counter> p(new object_counter);
        EXPECT_EQ(1, object_counter::count);
        EXPECT_EQ(1, object_counter::all_count);
    }
    EXPECT_EQ(0, object_counter::count);
    EXPECT_EQ(1, object_counter::all_count);
}
```

The destructor is called when the scope containing the scoped_ptr object is exited. It does not matter how it is exited—an early return from a function, a break or continue statement in the loop, or an exception being thrown are all handled in exactly the same way, and without leaks. We can verify this with tests, of course:

```
TEST(Scoped_ptr, EarlyReturnNoLeak) {
    object_counter::all_count = object_counter::count = 0;
    do {
        scoped_ptr<object_counter> p(new object_counter);
        break;
    } while (false);
    EXPECT_EQ(0, object_counter::count);
    EXPECT_EQ(1, object_counter::all_count);
}

TEST(Scoped_ptr, ThrowNoLeak) {
    object_counter::all_count = object_counter::count = 0;
    try {
        scoped_ptr<object_counter> p(new object_counter);
        throw 1;
    } catch ( ... ) {
    }
    EXPECT_EQ(0, object_counter::count);
    EXPECT_EQ(1, object_counter::all_count);
}
```

All tests pass, confirming that there is no leak, as shown in the following screenshot:

```
[----------] 3 tests from Scoped_ptr
[ RUN      ] Scoped_ptr.AcquireRelease
[       OK ] Scoped_ptr.AcquireRelease (0 ms)
[ RUN      ] Scoped_ptr.EarlyReturnNoLeak
[       OK ] Scoped_ptr.EarlyReturnNoLeak (0 ms)
[ RUN      ] Scoped_ptr.ThrowNoLeak
[       OK ] Scoped_ptr.ThrowNoLeak (0 ms)
[----------] 3 tests from Scoped_ptr (0 ms total)
```

Similarly, we can use a scoped pointer as a data member in another class—a class that has secondary storage and must release it upon destruction:

```
class A {
    public:
    A(object_counter* p) : p_(p) {}
    private:
    scoped_ptr<object_counter> p_;
};
```

This way, we don't have to delete the object manually in the destructor of class A, and, in fact, if every data member of class A takes care of itself in a similar fashion, class A may not even need an explicit destructor.

Anyone familiar with C++11 should recognize our scoped_ptr as a very rudimentary version of std::unique_ptr, which can be used for the same purpose. As you might expect, the standard unique pointer's implementation has a lot more to it, and for good reason. We will review some of these reasons later in this chapter.

One last issue to consider is that of performance. C++ strives for zero-overhead abstractions whenever possible. In this case, we are wrapping a raw pointer into a smart pointer object. However, the compiler does not need to generate any additional machine instructions; the wrapper only forces the compiler to generate the code that, in a correct program, it would have done anyway. We can confirm with a simple benchmark that both the construction/deletion and the dereference of our scoped_ptr (or std::unique_ptr, for that matter) take exactly the same time as the corresponding operations on a raw pointer. For example, the following microbenchmark (using the Google benchmark library) compares the performance of all three pointer types for dereferencing:

```
void BM_rawptr_dereference(benchmark::State& state) {
    int* p = new int;
    for (auto _ : state) {
        REPEAT(benchmark::DoNotOptimize(*p);)
    }
    delete p;
```

```
        state.SetItemsProcessed(32*state.iterations());
    }
    void BM_scoped_ptr_dereference(benchmark::State& state) {
        scoped_ptr<int> p(new int);
        for (auto _ : state) {
            REPEAT(benchmark::DoNotOptimize(*p);)
        }
        state.SetItemsProcessed(32*state.iterations());
    }
    void BM_unique_ptr_dereference(benchmark::State& state) {
        std::unique_ptr<int> p(new int);
        for (auto _ : state) {
            REPEAT(benchmark::DoNotOptimize(*p);)
        }
        state.SetItemsProcessed(32*state.iterations());
    }
    BENCHMARK(BM_rawptr_dereference);
    BENCHMARK(BM_scoped_ptr_dereference);
    BENCHMARK(BM_unique_ptr_dereference);
    BENCHMARK_MAIN();
```

The benchmark shows that the smart pointers indeed incur no overhead:

Benchmark	Time	CPU	Iterations	
BM_rawptr_dereference	10 ns	10 ns	70042145	3.09321G items/s
BM_scoped_ptr_dereference	10 ns	10 ns	72095679	3.11026G items/s
BM_unique_ptr_dereference	10 ns	10 ns	71510079	3.04359G items/s

We have covered in enough details the applications of RAII for managing memory. But there are other resources that a C++ program needs to manage and keep track of, so we have to expand our view of RAII now.

RAII for other resources

The name, RAII, refers to *resources* and not *memory,* and indeed the same approach is applicable to other resources. For each resource type, we need a special object, although generic programming and lambda expressions may help us to write less code (we will learn more on this in Chapter 11, *ScopeGuard*). The resource is acquired in the constructor and released in the destructor. Note that there are two slightly different flavors of RAII. The first option is the one we have already seen—the actual acquisition of the resource is at initialization, but outside of the constructor of the RAII object.

The constructor merely captures the handle (such as a pointer) that resulted from this acquisition. This was the case with the scoped_ptr object that we just saw—memory allocation and object construction were both done outside of the constructor of the scoped_ptr object, but still during its initialization. The second option is for the constructor of the RAII object to actually acquire the resource. Let's see how this works, with the example of a RAII object that manages mutex locks:

```
class mutex_guard {
    public:
    explicit mutex_guard(std::mutex& m)  : m_(m) { m_.lock(); }
    ~mutex_guard() { m_.unlock(); }
    private:
    std::mutex& m_;
};
```

Here, the constructor of the mutex_guard class itself acquires the resource; in this case, exclusive access to the shared data protected by the mutex. The destructor releases that resource. Again, this pattern completely removes the possibility of **leaking** a lock (that is, exiting a scope without releasing the lock), for example, when an exception is thrown:

```
std::mutex m;
TEST(Scoped_ptr, ThrowNoLeak) {
    try {
        mutex_guard lg(m);
        EXPECT_FALSE(m.try_lock());    // Expect to be locked already
        throw 1;
    } catch ( ... ) {
    }
    EXPECT_TRUE(m.try_lock());         // Expect to be unlocked
    m.unlock();                        // try_lock() will lock, undo it
}
```

In this test, we check whether the mutex is locked or not by calling std::mutex::try_lock()—we cannot call lock() if the mutex is already locked, as it will deadlock. By calling try_lock(), we can check the state of the mutex without the risk of deadlock (but remember to unlock the mutex if try_lock() succeeds).

Again, the standard provides a RAII object for mutex locking, std::lock_guard. It is used in a similar manner, but can be applied to any mutex type that has lock() and unlock() member functions.

Releasing early

The scope of a function or a loop body does not always match the desired duration of the holding of the resource. If we do not want to acquire the resource at the very beginning of the scope, this is easy—the RAII object can be created anywhere, not just at the beginning of the scope. Resources are not acquired until the RAII object is constructed, as follows:

```
void process(...) {
    ... do work that does not need exclusive access ...
    mutex_guard lg(m);              // Now we lock
    ... work on shared data, now protected by mutex ...
} // lock is released here
```

However, the release still happens at the end of the function body scope. What if we only want to lock a short portion of code inside the function? The simplest answer is to create an additional scope:

```
void process(...) {
    ... do work that does not need exclusive access ...
    {
        mutex_guard lg(m);              // Now we lock
        ... work on shared data, now protected by mutex ...
    } // lock is released here
    ... more non-exclusive work ...
}
```

It may be surprising if you have never seen it before, but in C++, any sequence of statements can be enclosed in the curly braces, as { ... }. Doing so creates a new scope with its own local variables. Unlike the curly braces that come after loops or conditional statements, the only purpose of this scope is controlling the lifetime of these local variables. A program that uses RAII extensively often has many such scopes, enclosing variables with different lifetimes that are shorter than the overall function or loop body. This practice also improves readability by making it clear that some variables will not be used after a certain point, so the reader does not need to scan the rest of the code looking for possible references to these variables. Also, the user cannot accidentally add such a reference by mistake if the intent is to **expire** a variable and never use it again.

And what if a resource may be released early, but only if certain conditions are met? One possibility is, again, to contain the use of the resource in a scope, and exit that scope when the resource is no longer needed. It would be convenient to be able to use break to get out of a scope. A common way to do just that is to write a do...once loop:

```
void process(...) {
    ... do work that does not need exclusive access ...
    do {                                // Not really a loop
```

```
            mutex_guard lg(m);              // Now we lock
            ... work on shared data, now protected by mutex ...
            if (work_done) break;           // Exit the scope
            ... work on the shared data some more ...
        } while (false);                    // lock is released here
        ... more non-exclusive work ...
    }
```

However, this approach does not always work (we may want to release the resources, but not other local variables we defined in the same scope), and the readability of the code suffers as the control flow gets more complex. Resist the impulse to accomplish this by allocating the RAII object dynamically, with operator new! This completely defeats the whole point of RAII, since you now must remember to invoke operator delete. We can enhance our resource-managing objects by adding a client-triggered release, in addition to the automatic release by the destructor. We just have to make sure that the same resource is not released twice. Consider the following example, using scoped_ptr:

```
template <typename T>
class scoped_ptr {
    public:
    explicit scoped_ptr(T* p) : p_(p) {}
    ~scoped_ptr() { delete p_; }
        ...
    void reset() { delete p_; p_ = nullptr; }    // Releases resource early
    private:
    T* p_;
};
```

After calling reset(), the object managed by the scoped_ptr object is deleted, and the pointer data member of the scoped_ptr object is reset to null. Note that we did not need to add a condition check to the destructor, because calling delete on a null pointer is allowed by the standard—it does nothing. The resource is released only once, either explicitly by the reset() call, or implicitly at the end of the scope containing the scoped_ptr object.

For the mutex_guard class, we can't deduce from just the lock whether an early release was called or not, and we need an additional data member to keep track of that:

```
class mutex_guard {
    public:
    explicit mutex_guard(std::mutex& m) :
        m_(m), must_unlock_(true) { m_.lock(); }
    ~mutex_guard() { if (must_unlock_) m_.unlock(); }
    void reset() { m_.unlock(); must_unlock_ = false; }
    private:
    std::mutex& m_;
```

```
        bool must_unlock_;
    };
```

Now we can verify that the mutex is released only once, at the right time, with this test:

```
    TEST(mutex_guard, Reset) {
        {
            mutex_guard lg(m);
            EXPECT_FALSE(m.try_lock());
            lg.reset();
            EXPECT_TRUE(m.try_lock()); m.unlock();
        }
        EXPECT_TRUE(m.try_lock()); m.unlock();
    }
```

The standard `std::unique_ptr` pointer supports `reset()`, whereas `std::lock_guard` does not, so if you need to release a mutex early, you need to write your own guard object. Fortunately, a lock guard is a pretty simple class, but finish reading this chapter before you start writing, as there are a few *gotchas* to keep in mind.

Note that the `reset()` method of `std::unique_ptr` actually does more than just delete the object prematurely. It can also be used to **reset** the pointer by making it point to a new object while the old one is deleted. It works something like this (the actual implementation in the standard is a bit more complex, because of the additional functionality the unique pointer has):

```
    template <typename T>
    class scoped_ptr {
        public:
        explicit scoped_ptr(T* p) : p_(p) {}
        ~scoped_ptr() { delete p_; }
            ...
        void reset(T* p = nullptr) {
            delete p_; p_ = p;          // Reseat the pointer
        }
        private:
        T* p_;
    };
```

Note that this code breaks if a scoped pointer is reset to itself (for example, if `reset()` is called with the same value as that stored in `p_`). We could check for this condition and do nothing; it is worth noting that the standard does not require such a check for `std::unique_ptr`.

Careful implementation of Resource Acquisition is Initialization objects

It is obviously very important that the resource management objects do not mismanage the resources they are entrusted to guard. Unfortunately, the simple RAII objects we have been writing so far have several glaring holes.

The first problem arises when someone tries to copy these objects. Each of the RAII objects we have considered in this chapter is responsible for managing a unique instance of its resource, and yet, nothing prevents us from copying this object:

```
scoped_ptr<object_counter> p(new object_counter);
scoped_ptr<object_counter> p1(p);
```

This code invokes the default copy constructor, which simply copies the bits inside the object; in our case, the pointer is copied to the `object_counter`. Now we have two RAII objects that both control the same resource. Two destructors will be called, eventually, and both will attempt to delete the same object. The second deletion is undefined behavior (if we are very fortunate, the program will crash at that point).

Assignment of RAII objects is similarly problematic:

```
scoped_ptr<object_counter> p(new object_counter);
scoped_ptr<object_counter> p1(new object_counter);
p = p1;
```

The default assignment operator also copies the bits of the object. Again, we have two RAII objects that will delete the same managed object. Equally troublesome are the facts that we have no RAII objects that manage the second `object_counter`, the old pointer inside `p1` is gone, and there is no other reference to this object, so we have no way to delete it.

The `mutex_guard` does no better—an attempt to copy it results in two mutex guards that will unlock the same mutex. The second unlock will be done on a mutex that is not locked (at least not by the calling thread), which, according to the standard, is undefined behavior. Assignment of the `mutex_guard` object is not possible, though, because the default assignment operator is not generated for objects with reference data members.

As you may have probably noticed, the problem is created by the **default** copy constructor and default assignment operator. Does it mean that we should have implemented our own? What would they do? Only one destructor should be called for each object that was constructed; a mutex can only be unlocked once after it was locked. This suggests that a RAII object should not be copied at all, and we should disallow both copying and assignment:

```
template <typename T>
class scoped_ptr {
    public:
    explicit scoped_ptr(T* p) : p_(p) {}
    ~scoped_ptr() { delete p_; }
        ...
    private:
    T* p_;
    scoped_ptr(const scoped_ptr&) = delete;
    scoped_ptr& operator=(const scoped_ptr&) = delete;
};
```

Deleting default member functions is a C++11 feature; before that, we would have to declare, but not define, both functions as private:

```
template <typename T>
class scoped_ptr {
        ...
    private:
    scoped_ptr(const scoped_ptr&);                    // No {} - not defined!
    scoped_ptr& operator=(const scoped_ptr&);
};
```

There are some RAII objects that can be copied. These are reference-counted resource management objects; they keep track of how many copies of the RAII object exist for the same instance of the managed resource. The last of the RAII objects has to release the resource when it is deleted. We discuss shared management of resources in more detail in Chapter 3, *Memory Ownership*.

A different set of considerations exist for move constructor and assignment. Moving the object does not violate the assumption that there is only one RAII object that owns a particular resource. It merely changes which RAII object that is. In many cases, such as mutex guards, it does not make sense to move a RAII object (indeed, the standard does not make std::lock_guard movable). Moving a unique pointer is possible and makes sense in some contexts, which we also explore in Chapter 3, *Memory Ownership*.

However, for a scoped pointer, moving would be undesirable, as it allows the extension of the lifetime of the managed object beyond the scope where it was created. Note that we do not need to delete move constructor or move assignment operators if we already deleted the copying ones (although doing so does no harm). On the other hand, std::unique_ptr is a movable object, which means using it as a scope-guarding smart pointer does not offer the same protection because the resource could be moved out. However, if you need a scoped pointer, there is a very simple way to make std::unique_ptr do this job perfectly—all you have to do is to declare a const std::unique_ptr object:

```cpp
std::unique_ptr<int> p;
{
    // Can be moved out of the scope
    std::unique_ptr<int> q(new int);
    q = std::move(p);                       // and here it happens
    // True scoped pointer, cannot be moved anywhere
    const std::unique_ptr<int> r(new int);
    q = std::move(r);                       // Does not compile
}
```

So far, we have protected our RAII objects against duplicating or losing resources. But there is one more kind of resource management mistake that we have not yet considered. It seems obvious that a resource should be released in a way that matches its acquisition. And yet, nothing protects our scoped_ptr object from such a mismatch between construction and deletion:

```cpp
scoped_ptr<int> p(new int[10]);
```

The problem here is that we have allocated multiple objects using an array version of operator new; it should be deleted with the array version of operator delete—delete [] p_ must be called inside the scoped_ptr destructor, instead of delete p_ that we have there now.

More generally, a RAII object that accepts a resource handle during initialization, instead of acquiring the resource itself (like the mutex_guard does) must somehow ensure that the resource is released in the **right** way that matches the way it was acquired. Obviously, this is not possible, in general. In fact, it is impossible to do automatically, even for the simple case of mismatched new array and the delete scalar (std::unique_ptr does no better than our scoped_ptr here, although facilities such as std::make_unique make writing such code less error-prone).

In general, either the RAII class is designed to release resources in one particular way, or the caller must specify how the resource must be released. The former is certainly easier, and in many cases is quite sufficient. In particular, if the RAII class also acquires a resource, such as our `mutex_guard`, it certainly knows how to release it. Even for the `scoped_ptr`, it would not be too hard to create two versions, `scoped_ptr` and `scoped_array`; the second one is for objects allocated by the `operator new` array. A more general version of a RAII class is parameterized not just by the resource type, but also by a callable object used to release this type, usually known as the deleter. The deleter can be a function pointer, a member function pointer, or an object with `operator()` defined—basically, anything that can be called like a function. Note that the deleter has to be passed to the RAII object in its constructor, and stored inside the RAII object, which makes the object larger. Also, the type of the deleter is a template parameter of the RAII class, unless it is erased from the RAII type (this will be covered in `Chapter 6`, *Understanding Type Erasure*).

Downsides of RAII

Honestly, there aren't any significant downsides to RAII. It is by far the most widely used idiom for resource management in C++. The only issue of significance to be aware of has to do with exceptions. Releasing a resource can fail, like anything else. The usual way in C++ to signal a failure is to throw an exception. When that is undesirable, we fall back on returning error codes from functions. With RAII, we can do neither of these things.

It is easy to understand why error codes are not an option—the destructor does not return anything. Also, we cannot write the error code into some status data member of the object, since the object is being destroyed and its data members are gone, as are the other local variables from the scope containing the RAII object. The only way to save an error code for the future examination would be to write it into some sort of a global status variable, or at least a variable from the containing scope. This is possible in a bind, but such a solution is very inelegant and error-prone. This is exactly the problem that C++ was trying to solve when exceptions were introduced manually-propagated error codes are error-prone and unreliable.

So, if the exceptions are the answer to error reporting in C++, why not use them here? The usual answer is *because the destructors in C++ cannot throw*. This captures the gist of it, but the real restriction is a bit more nuanced. First of all, prior to C++11, the destructors technically could throw, but the exception would propagate and (hopefully) eventually get caught and processed. In C++11, all destructors are, by default, `noexcept`, unless explicitly specified as `noexcept(false)`. If a `noexcept` function throws, the program immediately terminates.

So indeed, in C++11, destructors cannot throw unless you specifically allow them to do so. But what's wrong with throwing an exception in the destructor? If the destructor is executed because the object was deleted, or because the control reached the end of the scope for a stack object, then nothing is wrong. The *wrong* happens if the control did not reach the end of the scope normally and the destructor is executed, because an exception was already thrown. In C++, two exceptions cannot propagate at the same time. If this happens, the program will immediately terminate (note that a destructor can throw and catch an exception, there is no problem with that, as long as that exception does not propagate out of the destructor). Of course, when writing a program, there is no way to know when some function called from something in a particular scope, could throw. If the resource release throws and the RAII object allows that exception to propagate out of its destructor, the program is going to terminate if that destructor was called during exception handling. The only safe way is never to allow exceptions to propagate from a destructor. This does not mean that the function that releases the resource itself cannot throw, but, if it does, a RAII destructor has to catch that exception:

```
class raii {
    ...
    ~raii() {
        try {
            release_resource();      // Might throw
        } catch ( ... ) {
            ... handle the exception, do NOT rethrow ...
        }
    }
};
```

This still leaves us with no way to signal that an error happened during resource release—an exception was thrown, and we had to catch it and not let it escape.

How much of a problem is this? Not that much, really. First of all, releasing memory—the most frequently managed resource—does not throw an exception. Usually, the memory is released not as just memory, but by deleting an object. But remember that the destructors should not throw an exception in order that the entire process of releasing memory by deleting an object doesn't throw an exception either. At this point, the reader might, in search of a counter-example, look up in the standard what happens if unlocking a mutex fails (that would force the destructor of `std::lock_guard` to deal with the error). The answer is both surprising and enlightening—unlocking a mutex cannot throw, but if it fails, undefined behavior results instead. This is no accident; the mutex was intended to work with a RAII object. Such is, in general, the C++ approach to releasing the resources: an exception should not be thrown if the release fails, or at least not allowed to propagate. It can be caught and logged, for example, but the calling program will, in general, remain unaware of the failure, possibly at the cost of undefined behavior.

Summary

After this chapter, the reader should be well aware of the dangers of an ad-hoc approach to resource management. Fortunately, we have learned the most widely used idiom for resource management in C++; the RAII idiom. With this idiom, each resource is owned by an object. Constructing (or initializing) the object acquires the resource, and deleting the object releases it. We saw how using RAII addresses the problems of resource management, such as leaking resources, accidentally sharing resources, and releasing resources incorrectly. We have also learned the basics of writing exception-safe code, at least as far as the leaking or otherwise mishandling resources is concerned. Writing RAII objects is simple enough, but there are several caveats to keep in mind. Finally, we reviewed the complications that arise when error handling has to be combined with RAII.

RAII is a resource management idiom, but it can also be viewed as an abstraction technique: the complex resources are hidden behind simple resource handles. The next chapter introduces another kind of abstraction idiom, type erasure: instead of complex objects, we will now hide complex types.

Questions

- What are the *resources* that a program can manage?
- What are the main considerations when managing resources in a C++ program?
- What is RAII?
- How does RAII address the problem of leaking resources?
- How does RAII address the problem of dangling resource handles?
- What RAII objects are provided by the C++ standard library?
- What precautions must be taken when writing RAII objects?
- What happens if releasing a resource fails?

Further reading

- https://www.packtpub.com/application-development/expert-c-programming
- https://www.packtpub.com/application-development/c-data-structures-and-algorithms
- https://www.packtpub.com/application-development/rapid-c-video

6
Understanding Type Erasure

Type erasure is often seen as a mysterious, enigmatic programming technique. It is not exclusive to C++ (most tutorials on type erasure use Java for their examples). The goal of this chapter is to lift the shroud of mystery and teach you what type erasure is and how to use it in C++.

The following topics will be covered in this chapter:

- What is type erasure?
- How can we implement type erasure?
- What design and performance considerations must be taken into account when deciding to use type erasure?

Technical requirements

- Example code: https://github.com/PacktPublishing/Hands-On-Design-Patterns-with-CPP/tree/master/Chapter06
- Google Benchmark library: https://github.com/google/benchmark (see Chapter 4, *Swap - From Simple to Subtle*)

What is type erasure?

Type erasure, in general, is a programming technique by which the explicit type information is removed from the program. It is a type of abstraction that ensures that the program does not explicitly depend on some of the data types.

This definition, while perfectly correct, also serves perfectly to surround type erasure in mystery. It does so by employing a sort of circular reasoning—it dangles before you the hope for something that, at first glance, appears impossible—a program written in a strongly typed language that does not use the actual types. How can this be? Why, by abstracting away the type, of course! And so, the hope and the mystery lives on.

It is hard to imagine a program that uses types without explicitly mentioning them (at least a C++ program; there are certainly languages where all types are not final until runtime). So, we begin by demonstrating what is meant by type erasure using an example. This should allow us to gain an intuitive understanding of type erasure, which, in the later sections of this chapter, we will develop and make more rigorous. The aim here is to increase the level of abstraction—instead of writing some type-specific code, perhaps several versions of it for different types, we can write just one version that is more abstract, expresses the concept—for example, instead of writing a function whose interface expresses the concept *sort an array of integers*, we want to write a more abstract function, *sort any array*.

Type erasure by example

We will go through a detailed explanation of what type erasure is and how it is accomplished in C++. But first, let's see what a program that had the explicit type information removed from it looks like.

We start with a very simple example of using a unique pointer, `std::unique_ptr`:

```
std::unique_ptr<int> p(new int(0));
```

This is an owning pointer (see `Chapter 3`, *Memory Ownership*)—the entity containing this pointer, such as an object or a functional scope, also controls the lifetime of the integer we allocated, and is responsible for its deletion. The deletion is not explicitly visible in the code and will happen when the `p` pointer is deleted (for example, when it goes out of scope). The way this deletion will be accomplished is also not explicitly visible—by default, `std::unique_ptr` deletes the object it owns using `operator delete`, or, more precisely, by invoking `std::default_delete`, which, in turn, calls `operator delete`. What if we do not want to use the regular standard `delete`? For example, we may have objects that are allocated on our own heap:

```
class MyHeap {
    public:
    ...
    void* allocate(size_t size);
    void deallocate(void* p);
    ...
```

```
    };
    void* operator new(size_t size, MyHeap* heap) {
        return heap->allocate(size);
    }
```

Allocation is no problem, with the help of the overloaded `operator new`:

```
    MyHeap heap;
    std::unique_ptr<int> p(new(&heap) int(0));
```

This syntax invokes the two-argument `operator new` function; the first argument is always the size and is added by the compiler, and the second argument is the heap pointer. Since we have such an overload declared, it will be invoked and will return the memory allocated from the heap. But we have not done anything to change the way the object is deleted. The regular operator `delete` function will be called and will attempt to return to the global heap some memory that wasn't allocated from there. The result is likely to be memory corruption, and probably a crash. We could define an `operator delete` function with the same additional argument, but it does us no good here—unlike `operator new`, there is no place to pass arguments to `delete` (you will often see such an `operator delete` function defined anyway, and it should behave as such, but it has nothing to do with any `delete` you see in the program; it is used in the stack unwinding if the constructor throws an exception).

Somehow, we need to tell the unique pointer that this particular object is to be deleted differently. It turns out that `std::unique_ptr` has a second `template` argument. You usually don't see it because it defaults to `std::default_delete`, but that can be changed and a custom `deleter` object can be defined to match the allocation mechanism. The `deleter` has a very simple interface—it needs to be callable:

```
    template <typename T> struct MyDeleter {
        void operator()(T* p);
    };
```

The `std::default_delete` policy is implemented pretty much like that, and simply calls `delete` on the p pointer. Our custom `deleter` will need a non-trivial constructor to store the pointer to the heap. Note that, while the `deleter` needs, in general, to be able to delete an object of any type that can be allocated, it does not have to be a template class. A non-template class with a template member function will do just as well, as long as the data members of the class do not depend on the deleted type. In our case, the data members depend only on the type of the heap, but not on what is being deleted:

```
    class MyDeleter {
        MyHeap* heap_;
        public:
```

```
        MyDeleter(MyHeap* heap) : heap_(heap) {}
        template <typename T> void operator()(T* p) {
                p->~T();
                heap_->deallocate(p);
        }
    };
```

The `deleter` has to perform the equivalent of both functions of the standard `operator delete` function—it has to invoke the destructor of the object being deleted, then it must deallocate the memory that was allocated for this object.

Now that we have the appropriate `deleter`, we can finally use `std::unique_ptr` with our own heap:

```
MyHeap heap;
MyDeleter deleter(&heap);
std::unique_ptr<int, MyDeleter> p(new(&heap) int(0), deleter);
```

Note that `deleter` objects are often created on demand, at the point of allocation:

```
MyHeap heap;
std::unique_ptr<int, MyDeleter> p(new(&heap) int(0), MyDeleter(&heap));
```

Either way, the `deleter` must be no-throw-copyable or no-throw-movable; that is, it must have a copy constructor or a move constructor, and the constructor must be declared `noexcept`. The built-in types, such as raw pointers, are, of course, copyable, and the default compiler-generated constructor does not throw. Any aggregate type combining one or more of these types as data members, such as our `deleter`, has a default constructor that also does not throw (unless it has been redefined, of course).

Note that the `deleter` is a part of the unique pointer's type. Two unique pointers that own objects of the same type, but have different deleters, are different types:

```
MyHeap heap;
std::unique_ptr<int, MyDeleter> p(new(&heap) int(0), MyDeleter(&heap));
std::unique_ptr<int> q(new int(0));
p = std::move(q);        // Does not compile, p and q are different types
```

Similarly, the unique pointer must be constructed with the `deleter` of the right type:

```
std::unique_ptr<int> p(new(&heap) int(0), MyDeleter(&heap));
                        // Does not compile
```

As an aside, while experimenting with unique pointers of different types, you might notice that the two pointers in the preceding code, p and q, while not assignable, are comparable—p == q compiles. This happens because the comparison operator is actually a template—it accepts two unique pointers of different types and compares the underlying raw pointers (if that type differs as well, the compilation error is likely to not mention the unique pointer at all, but instead, to say something about comparing pointers to distinct types without a cast).

Now let's do the same example, but with the shared pointer, std::shared_ptr. First, we point the shared pointer to an object constructed with the regular operator new function as follows:

```
std::shared_ptr<int> p(new int(0));
std::shared_ptr<int> q(new int(0));
```

For comparison, we left the unique pointer declaration there as well. The two smart pointers are declared and constructed in exactly the same way. And now, in the following code block, the shared pointer to an object allocated on our heap:

```
MyHeap heap;
std::unique_ptr<int, MyDeleter> p(new(&heap) int(0), MyDeleter(&heap));
std::shared_ptr<int> q(new(&heap) int(0), MyDeleter(&heap));
```

Now you see a difference—the shared pointer that was created with a custom deleter is, nonetheless, of the same type as the one that uses the default deleter! In fact, all shared pointers to int have the same type, std::shared_ptr<int>—the template does not have another argument. Think this through—the deleter is specified in the constructor but is used only in the destructor, therefore it must be stored inside the smart pointer object until needed. There is no way to recover it later if we lose the object that was given to us during construction. Both std::shared_ptr and std::unique_ptr must store the deleter object of an arbitrary type inside the pointer object itself. But only the std::unique_ptr class has the deleter information in its type. The std::shared_ptr class is the same for all deleter types. Going back to the very beginning of this section, the program that uses std::shared_ptr<int> does not have any explicit information about the deleter type. This type has been erased from the program. This, then, is what a type-erased program looks like:

```
MyHeap heap;
{
    std::shared_ptr<int> p(    // No deleter in the type
        new(&heap) int(0),
        MyDeleter(&heap)       // Deleter in constructor only
    );
    std::shared_ptr<int> q(p);// No deleter type anywhere
```

```
        // void some_function(std::shared_ptr<int>) - no deleter
    some_function(p);           // uses p, no deleter
}                                // Deletion happens, MyDeleter is invoked
```

Now that we know what type erasure does and what it looks like, there is only one more question—how does it work?

How is type erasure implemented in C++?

We have seen what type erasure looks like in C++. Now we understand what it means for a program to not explicitly depend on a type. But the mystery remains—the program makes no mention of the type, and yet, at the right time, invokes an operation on the type it knows nothing about. How? That is what we are about to see.

Very old type erasure

The idea of writing a program without explicit type information is certainly not new. In fact, it predates object-oriented programming and the notion of objects by a long time. Consider this C program (no C++ here) as an example:

```
int less(const void* a, const int* b) {
    return *(const int*)a - *(const int*)b;
}
int main() {
    int a[10] = { 1, 10, 2, 9, 3, 8, 4, 7, 5, 0 };
    qsort(a, sizeof(int), 10, less);
}
```

Now remember the function declaration for qsort from the standard C library:

```
void qsort(void *base, size_t nmemb, size_t size,
    int (*compar)(const void *, const void *));
```

Note that, while we are using it to sort an array of integers, the qsort function itself does not have any explicit types—it uses void* to pass in the array to be sorted. Similarly, the comparison function takes two void* pointers and has no explicit type information in its declaration. Of course, at some point, we need to know how to compare the real types. In our C program, the pointers that could, in theory, point to anything, are reinterpreted as pointers to integers. This action, which reverses the abstraction, is known as **reification**.

In C, restoring concrete types is entirely the responsibility of the programmer—our `less()` `comparison` function does, in fact, only compare integers, but it is impossible to deduce so from the interface. Neither it is possible to validate, at runtime, that the correct types are used throughout the program, and it is certainly not possible for the program to automatically select the right `comparison` operation for the actual type at runtime.

In object-oriented languages, we can lift some of these restrictions, but at a price.

Object-oriented type erasure

In object-oriented languages, we deal with abstracted types all the time. Any program that operates entirely on the pointers (or references) to the base class, while the concrete derived classes are not known until runtime, can be seen as a kind of type erasure. This approach is particularly popular in Java, but can be implemented in C++ as well (although, remember that just because you can do it, doesn't mean you should).

In order to use the object-oriented approach, our specific types must inherit from a known base class:

```
class Object {};
class Int : public Object {
    int i_;
    public:
    explicit Int(int i) : i_(i) {}
};
```

Immediately, we run into a problem—we want to sort an array of integers, but a built-in type is not a class and cannot inherit from anything. So, no more built-in types can be used, and the basic `int` type has to be wrapped in a class. But this isn't even the half of it; operating on base pointers only works if the types are polymorphic, meaning virtual functions must be used and our class now has to contain the v-pointer, in addition to the integer:

```
class Object {
    public:
    int less(const Object* rhs) const = 0;
};
class Int : public Object {
    int i_;
    public:
    explicit Int(int i) : i_(i) {}
    int less(const Object* rhs) const override {
        return i_ - dynamic_cast<const Int*>(rhs)->i_;
    }
```

```
};
```

Consider the following piece of code:

```
Object *p, *q;
p->less(q);
```

Now, whenever we write something like the preceding snippet, the program will, at runtime, automatically select the correct `less()` function to call, based on the type of one of the compared objects; in our case, `p`. The type of the second object is verified at runtime (a well-written program should not crash if the dynamic cast fails, but it may throw an exception). Of course, the `comparison` function is now embedded in the type itself. We could also provide an explicit `comparison` function:

```cpp
class Object {
    public:
    virtual ~Object() = 0;
};
inline Object::~Object() {};
class Int : public Object {
    int i_;
    public:
    explicit Int(int i) : i_(i) {}
    int Get() const { return i_; }
};
int less(const Object* a, const Object* b) {
    return dynamic_cast<const Int*>(a)->Get() -
            dynamic_cast<const Int*>(b)->Get();
}
```

The `comparison` function now converts the pointers to the expected type (again, a well-written program should check for `NULL` pointers after the dynamic cast). Since the `Get()` function is now not virtual (and cannot be virtual, since the base class cannot declare a *universal* return type), the object must be made polymorphic by some other means. The destructor of a polymorphic object often needs to be virtual anyway (but see the chapter on the non-virtual idiom for a more nuanced discussion of this issue). In our case, it is also a pure virtual, because we do not want any objects of the `Object` type to be created. The one unusual detail here is that a pure virtual function is actually implemented, too—it has to be, because the destructor of the derived class always calls the destructor of the base class at the end.

The programming error—invoking the `comparison` function on incorrect types—that would lead to undefined behavior in our earlier C program is now handled via a runtime exception. Alternatively, we could make the runtime system call the right comparison function for us, but at the cost of binding the `comparison` function and the object type together.

At this point, you might also wonder about the runtime performance cost. There is certainly a memory penalty, and in our case it is pretty heavy—our 4-byte integers have become objects containing a pointer and an integer, which, with padding, adds up to 16 bytes on a 64-bit system. Such an increase in the working memory set is likely to cause noticeable performance degradation, due to inefficient use of caches. There is also the cost of the virtual function call. However, in the case of the C program, the function was also called indirectly, via a function pointer. This is similar to how most compilers implement virtual function calls, and so the call to the `comparison` function is going to cost about the same. The dynamic cast and the `NULL` pointer check inside the `comparison` function will likely add some time.

But this is not the end of our problems. Remember that we wanted to sort an array of integers. While a pointer to an `Object` type can serve as an abstraction for a pointer to a derived class, such as our `Int`, an array of `Int` objects is not in any way an array of `Object` objects:

```
void sort(Object* a, ... );
Int a[10] = ...;
sort(a, ...);
```

This code can compile because the `a` type is `Int[]`, which decays to `Int*`, which itself can be implicitly converted to `Object*`, but it can't possibly do what we need—there is no way to advance the pointer to the next element of the array.

We have several options, but none of them are particularly attractive. The classic object-oriented way is to use an array of `Object*` pointers and sort that, as follows:

```
Int a[10] = ...;
Object* p[10];
for (int i = 0; i < 10;++i) p[i] = a + i;
```

The downside is that an additional array of pointers must be allocated, and it takes a double indirection to access the actual value.

We could add another virtual function to our class hierarchy, `Next()`, which would return the pointer to the next element of the array:

```
class Object {
    public:
    virtual Object* Next() const = 0;
};
class Int : public Object {
    ...
    Int* Next() const override { return this + 1; }
};
```

This makes iteration over the array that much more expensive, and on top of that, we have no way to verify, at compile time or runtime, that the object we called `Next()` on is actually an element of an array.

The opposite of the type erasure

We have gone so far down the rabbit hole of trying to erase every type in a C++ program, that we forgot why we started on this path in the first place. The original problem was that we did not want to write a new sort function for every type. C solved this problem by erasing the types and using `void*` pointers, but in doing so, it put all responsibility for the correctness of the code on the programmer—neither the compiler, nor the runtime system, can detect when the argument types do not match the function called.

Making every function virtual offers a very cumbersome solution to this problem. C++ has a much more elegant one—templates. A `template` function is, in a sense, the opposite of the erased type—on the one hand, the type is right there in the signature for all to see. On the other hand, the type can be anything, and the compiler will select the right type based on the arguments:

```
int a[10] = {...};
std::sort(a, a+10, std::less<void>());     // C++14
std::sort(a, a+10, std::less<int>());      // Before C++14
```

We can even provide our own `comparison` function, all without explicitly specifying the types:

```
int a[10] = {...};
std::sort(a, a+10, [](auto x, auto y) { return x < y; });     // C++14
```

Between the template type deduction and the type deduction done by `auto`, it may appear that this program has no explicit type information. This is only an illusion—the templates themselves are not types, template instantiations are types, and each one of those has the complete type information in its signature. Nothing is erased, the compiler knows exactly what is the type of every object or function, and, with some effort, so can the programmer.

In many cases, this kind of *out of sight, out of mind* pseudo-erasure of types is good enough. But it still does not solve the problem of different objects having different types when we may not want them to. We could hide the types of our unique pointers with different deleters:

```
template <typename T, typename D>
std::unique_ptr<T, D> make_unique_ptr(T* p, D d) {
    return std::unique_ptr<T, D>(p, d);
}
auto p(make_unique_ptr(new int, d));
```

Now, the `deleter` type is automatically deduced when the unique pointer is constructed, and not mentioned explicitly anywhere. Still, two unique pointers with deleters of different types remain different types in themselves:

```
struct deleter1 { ... };
struct deleter2 { ... };
deleter1 d1; deleter2 d2;
auto p(make_unique_ptr(new int, d1));
auto q(make_unique_ptr(new int, d2));
```

The types of the unique pointers may look to be the same, but they are not—`auto` is not the type; the actual type of the p pointer is `unique_ptr<int, deleter1>`, and the type of q is `unique_ptr<int, deleter2>`. So, we are back to where we started—we have a great way to write type-agnostic code, but if we need to actually erase types, and not just hide them, we still do not know how it is done. It is time we learned it.

Type erasure in C++

Let's finally see how `std::shared_ptr` does its magic. We will do it with a simplified example of a smart pointer that focuses specifically on the type erasure aspect. It should not surprise you to learn that this is done with a combination of generic and object-oriented programming:

```
template <typename T>
class smartptr {
    struct deleter_base {
```

```
        virtual void apply(void*) = 0;
        virtual ~deleter_base() {}
    };
    template <typename Deleter>
    struct deleter : public deleter_base {
        deleter(Deleter d) : d_(d) {}
        virtual void apply(void* p) { d_(static_cast<T*>(p)); }
        Deleter d_;
    };
    public:
    template <typename Deleter>
        smartptr(T* p, Deleter d) :
            p_(p), d_(new deleter<Deleter>(d)) {}
    ~smartptr() { d_->apply(p_); delete d_; }
    T* operator->() { return p_; }
    const T* operator->() const { return p_; }
    private:
    T* p_;
    deleter_base* d_;
};
```

The smartptr template has only one type parameter. Since the erased type is not part of the smart pointer's type, it has to be captured in some other object. In our case, this object is an instantiation of the nested smartptr<T>::deleter template. This object is created by the constructor, which is the last point in the code where the deleter type is explicitly present. But smartptr must refer to the deleter instance through a pointer whose type does not depend on deleter (since the smartptr object has the same type for all deleters). Therefore, all instances of the deleter template inherit from the same base class, deleter_base, and the actual deleter is invoked through a virtual function. The constructor is a template that deduces the type of deleter, but the type is only hidden, as it's a part of the actual declaration of the specific instantiation of this template. The smart pointer class itself, and, in particular, its destructor, where the deleter is actually used, really have the deleter type erased. The compile-time type detection is used to create a correct-by-construction polymorphic object that will rediscover the deleter type at runtime and perform the correct action. For that reason, we do not need a dynamic cast, and can use the static cast instead, which only works if we know the actual derived type (and we do).

This type erasure implementation is used in several other standard library features. The actual implementation varies in complexity but always uses the same approach. Let's start with `std::function`, which is a genetic function wrapper. The type of the `std::function` object tells us how the function is called, but that's it—it does not tell us whether this is a standalone function, a callable object, a lambda expression, or anything else that can be used with parentheses. For example, we can create a vector of callable objects as follows:

```
std::vector<std::function<void(int)>> v;
```

We can invoke any element of this vector as `v[i](5)`, but that is all we can deduce about these elements from the type signature. The actual type of what is being called has been erased.

Then there is the ultimate type-erased class, `std::any` (in C++17 and above). This is a class, not a template, but it can hold a value of any type:

```
std::any a(5);
int i = std::any_cast<int>(a);      // i == 5
std::any_cast<long>(a);             // throws bad_any_cast
```

Of course, without knowing the type, `std::any` cannot provide any interfaces. You can store any value in it, and get it back if you know the right type (or you can ask for the type and get back an `std::type_info` object).

While it may seem like type erasure and type-erased objects can greatly simplify our programs, in reality, type erasure should be used sparingly. The drawbacks of type erasure are discussed in the next section.

When to use type erasure, and when to avoid it

We have already seen an example where type erasure was used very successfully—the `std::shared_ptr` shared pointer. On the other hand, the standard library authors did not use this technique when they implemented `std::unique_ptr`, and not because it is any more difficult (our simple `smartptr` is, in fact, a lot closer to `std::unique_ptr` than `std::shared_ptr`, since it does not do any reference counting).

Then there was the unsuccessful attempt to type-erase the sort and related functions, which ended in a complex mess that was cleaned up once and for all by letting the compiler deduce the right types, instead of erasing them. We could do with some guidelines for when to consider type erasure. There are two types of issues to keep in mind—design considerations and performance considerations.

Type erasure and software design

As we saw in the ill-fated attempt at a fully type-erased sort, type erasure does not always make a program simpler. Even the introduction of standard type-erased classes, such as `std::any`, does not resolve the fundamental problem—at some point, we need to perform some action on the erased type. At this point, we have two choices—we either need to know the true type, so we can cast to it (using `dynamic_cast` or `any_cast`), or we have to operate on the object through a polymorphic interface (virtual functions), which requires that all involved types be derived from the same base class, and constrains the design to the interface of that class. The latter is just regular object-oriented programming, which is, of course, widely and successfully used, but extending it to a problem that is not a natural fit for object-oriented programming—doing this just so we can erase some types leads to very convoluted designs (as we have learned). The former is essentially a modern twist on the old C `void*` trick—the programmer still has to know the exact type and get the value out by using that type, and the program still will not run correctly if the programmer makes a mistake, but at least we can catch these mistakes at runtime and report them.

The *universal* type-erased objects, such as `std::any`, have their applications, usually as a safe replacement for `void*`. It is often used with tagged types, where the actual type can be identified by some runtime information. For example, `std::map<std::string, std::any>` can be used to add dynamic capabilities to a C++ program. The detailed description of such applications goes beyond the scope of this book. The common attribute of these applications is that, together with erased objects, the program stores some identifying information, and the programmer is responsible for mapping these *breadcrumbs* to the original types.

The *limited* type erasure, like that of `std::shared_ptr`, on the other hand, can be used whenever we can guarantee by construction, using templates and argument deduction, that all erased types are correctly restored. These implementations usually involve a single hierarchy that is used polymorphically—instead of asking the object, *what type are you really?*, or telling it, *I know your real type (I hope)*, we just tell it—*do this operation, you know how*. The *you know how* part is ensured because of the way the objects are constructed, completely under control of the implementation. Another distinction of this type erasure, from the design point of view, is that the type is erased only from the object the program directly interfaces with, such as `std::shared_ptr<int>`. The *greater* object, which is the shared pointer and all of its secondary objects, does capture the erased type somewhere in one of its parts. That's what allows the object to *do the right thing* automatically, without the programmer having to assert, or guess the actual type.

Clearly, not every software system can benefit from type erasure, even from the design point of view. Often, using the explicit types or letting the compiler deduce the right types is the simplest and the most direct way to solve a problem. Such is the case with `std::sort`. But there must be another reason why `std::unique_ptr` is not type-erased: after all, it is very similar to `std::shared_ptr`, which is. The second reason to not use type erasure is that it can adversely impact performance. But before we can reasonably discuss performance, we have to learn to measure it.

Installing the micro-benchmark library

In our case, we are interested in the efficiency of very small fragments of code that construct and delete objects using different kinds of smart pointers. The appropriate tool for measuring the performance of small fragments of code is a micro-benchmark. There are many micro-benchmark libraries and tools out there; in this book, we will use the Google Benchmark library. To follow along with the examples in this section, you must first download and install the library (to do this, follow the instructions in the `Readme.md` file). Then you can compile and run the examples. You can build the sample files included with the library to see how to build a benchmark on your particular system. For example, on a Linux machine, the command to build and run a `smartptr.C` benchmark program might look something like this:

```
$CXX smartptr.C smartptr_extra.C -I. -I$GBENCH_DIR/include -g -O4 -I. \
    -Wall -Wextra -Werror -pedantic --std=c++14 \
    $GBENCH_DIR/lib/libbenchmark.a -lpthread -lrt -lm -o smartptr && \
    ./smartptr
```

Here, `$CXX` is your C++ compiler, such as `g++` or `g++-6`, and `$GBENCH_DIR` is the directory where the benchmark is installed.

The overhead of type erasure

Every benchmark needs a baseline. In our case, the baseline is a raw pointer. We can reasonably assume that no smart pointer will be able to outperform a raw pointer, and the best smart pointer will have zero overhead. Thus, we begin by measuring how long it takes to construct and destroy a small object using a raw pointer:

```
struct deleter {
    template <typename T> void operator()(T* p) { delete p; }
};
void BM_rawptr(benchmark::State& state) {
    deleter d;
    for (auto _ : state) {
        int* p = new int(0);
        d(p);
    }
    state.SetItemsProcessed(state.iterations());
}
```

The actual numbers reported by the benchmark depend, of course, on the machine that it runs on. But we are interested in the relative changes, so any machine will do, as long as we stay with it for all measurements:

```
Benchmark            Time           CPU Iterations
-------------------------------------------------------------
BM_rawptr           21 ns         21 ns   31178493    46.2325M items/s
```

We can now verify that `std::unique_ptr` indeed has zero overhead (as long as we construct and delete objects the same way, of course):

```
void BM_uniqueptr(benchmark::State& state) {
    deleter d;
    for (auto _ : state) {
        std::unique_ptr<int, deleter> q(new int(0), d);
    }
    state.SetItemsProcessed(state.iterations());
}
```

The result is within the measurement noise from the raw pointer, as can be seen here:

```
Benchmark            Time           CPU Iterations
-------------------------------------------------------------
BM_uniqueptr        21 ns         21 ns   33681137    46.4407M items/s
```

We can similarly measure the performance of `std::shared_ptr` as follows:

```
void BM_sharedptr(benchmark::State& state) {
    deleter d;
    for (auto _ : state) {
        std::shared_ptr<int> p(new int(0), d);
    }
    state.SetItemsProcessed(state.iterations());
}
```

We can see that the shared pointer is indeed much slower in the following screenshot:

Benchmark	Time	CPU	Iterations	
BM_sharedptr	51 ns	51 ns	12689804	18.7263M items/s

Of course, there is more than one reason for that—`std::shared_ptr` is a reference-counting smart pointer, and maintaining reference count has its own overhead. To make sure that we measure only the overhead of type erasure, we should implement a type-erased unique pointer. But we already did—it's our `smartptr` that we saw in the *Type erasure in C++* section of this chapter. It has just enough functionality to measure the performance of the same benchmark that we used for all other pointers:

```
void BM_smartptr_te(benchmark::State& state) {
    deleter d;
    for (auto _ : state) {
        smartptr_te<int> p(new int(0), d);
    }
    state.SetItemsProcessed(state.iterations());
}
```

Here, `smartptr_te` stands for the type-erased version of the smart pointer. It is slightly faster than `std::shared_ptr`, proving our suspicion that the latter has more than one source of overhead. Nonetheless, we clearly see that type erasure makes our unique pointer approximately half as fast:

Benchmark	Time	CPU	Iterations	
BM_smartptr_te	42 ns	42 ns	13659133	22.6096M items/s

There are, however, ways to counteract this penalty and optimize the type-erased pointers (as well as any other type-erased data structures). The main reason for the slowdown is the additional memory allocation that happens when we construct the polymorphic `smartptr::deleter` object. We can avoid this allocation, at least sometimes, by pre-allocating a memory buffer for these objects. The details of this optimization, as well as its limitations, are discussed in the `Chapter 10` *Local Buffer Optimization*. Here we will just say that, when successful, the optimization can almost completely (but not quite) negate the overhead of type erasure, as seen here:

Benchmark	Time	CPU	Iterations	
BM_smartptr_te_lb	24 ns	24 ns	30539734	40.4705M items/s

We can conclude that using type erasure imposes additional overhead (the added virtual function call, if nothing else). Also, a type-erased implementation will almost always use more memory than the statically typed one. The overhead is particularly large when an additional memory allocation is required. It is sometimes possible to optimize the implementation and reduce this overhead, but there is always some performance penalty for using type erasure.

Summary

In this chapter, we have, hopefully, demystified the programming technique known as type erasure. We have shown how a program can be written without all of the type information being explicitly visible, and some of the reasons why this may be a desirable implementation. We have also demonstrated that not every problem, or every program, needs type erasure. For many applications, this is simply the wrong tool. Even when it simplifies the program, performance considerations may ultimately weigh against using type-erased constructs. However, when implemented efficiently and used wisely, it is a powerful technique that may lead to much simpler and flexible interfaces.

The next chapter is a change of direction—we are done with the abstraction idioms for some time and now move on to C++ idioms that facilitate binding of template components into complex interacting systems. We start with the SFINAE idiom.

Questions

1. What is type erasure, really?
2. How is type erasure implemented in C++?
3. What is the difference between hiding a type behind `auto` and erasing it?
4. How is the concrete type reified when the program needs to use it?
5. What is the performance overhead of type erasure?

7
SFINAE and Overload Resolution Management

The idiom we study in this chapter, **Substitution Failure Is Not An Error (SFINAE)**, is one of the more complex in terms of the language features it uses. Thus, it tends to get inordinate amounts of attention from C++ programmers. There is something in this feature that appeals to the mindset of a typical C++ programmer—a normal person thinks that, if it isn't broken, don't mess with it. A programmer, especially one writing in C++, tends to think that, if it isn't broken, you're not using it to its full potential. Let's just say that SFINAE has a lot of potential.

We will cover the following topics in this chapter:

- What are function overloading and overload resolution?
- What are type deduction and substitution?
- What is SFINAE, and why was it necessary in C++?
- How can SFINAE be used to write insanely complex, and sometimes useful, programs?

Technical requirements

Example code can be found at the following link: https://github.com/PacktPublishing/Hands-On-Design-Patterns-with-CPP/tree/master/Chapter07.

Overload resolution and overload sets

This section will test your knowledge of the latest and most advanced additions to the C++ standard. We will start with one of the most basic features of C++, functions and their overloads.

C++ function overloading

Function overloading is a very straightforward concept in C++; multiple different functions can have the same name. That's it, that is all there is to overloading—when the compiler sees syntax that indicates a function call, formatted as f(x), then there must be more than one function named f. If this happens, we are in an overload situation, and overload resolution must take place to find out which of these functions should be called.

Let's start with a simple example:

```
void f(int i) { std::cout << "f(int)" << std::endl; }        // 1
void f(long i) { std::cout << "f(long)" << std::endl; }      // 2
void f(double i) { std::cout << "f(double)" << std::endl; }  // 3

f(5);
f(51);
f(5.0);
```

Here, we have three function definitions for the same name, f, and three function calls. Note that the function signatures are all different (in that the parameter types are different). This is a requirement—overloaded functions must differ somehow in their parameters. It is not possible to have two overloads that take the exact same arguments, but differ in the return type or the function body. Also, note that, while the example is for a regular function, the exact same rules apply to the overloaded member functions, so we will not pay special attention to member functions exclusively.

Back to our example, which of the f() functions is called on each line? To understand that, we need to know how overloaded functions are resolved in C++. The exact rules for overload resolution are fairly complex and differ in subtle ways between different versions of the standard, but for the most part, they are designed so that the compiler does what you would expect it to do in the most commonly encountered cases. We would expect f(5) to call the overload that accepts an integer argument, since 5 is an int variable. And so it does. Similarly, 51 has the long type, and so f(51) calls the second overload. Finally, 5.0 is a floating-point number, and so the last overload is called.

That wasn't so hard, was it? But what happens if the argument does not match the parameter type exactly? Then, the compiler has to consider type conversions. For example, the type of the 5.0 literal is double. Let's see what happens if we call f() with an argument of the float type:

```
f(5.0f);
```

Now we have to convert the argument from the float type to one of the int, long, or double types. Again, the standard has the rules, but it should come as no surprise that the conversion to double is preferred and that the overload is called.

Let's see what happens with a different integer type, say, unsigned int:

```
f(5u);
```

Now we have two options; convert unsigned int to signed int, or to signed long. While it may be argued that the conversion to long is *safer*, and thus better, the two conversions are considered so close by the standard that the compiler cannot choose. This call does not compile because the overload resolution is considered ambiguous; the error message should say as much. If you encounter such a problem in your code, you have to help the compiler by casting the arguments to a type that makes the resolution unambiguous. Usually, the simplest way is to cast the type of the parameter for the overload you want to call:

```
unsigned int i = 5u;
f(static_cast<int>(i));
```

So far, we have dealt with the situation where the types of the parameters were different, but their number was the same. Of course, if the number of the parameters differs between different function declarations for the same name, only the functions that can accept the required number of arguments need to be considered. Here is an example of two functions with the same name but different number of arguments:

```
void f(int i) { std::cout << "f(int)" << std::endl; }              // 1
void f(long i, long j) { std::cout << "f(long, long)" << std::endl; } // 2

f(5.0, 7);
```

Here, the overload resolution is very simple—we need a function that can accept two arguments, and there is only one choice. Both arguments will have to be converted to `long`. But what if there is more than one function with the same number of parameters? Let's see what happens in the following example:

```
void f(int i, int j) { std::cout << "f(int, int)" << std::endl; }      // 1
void f(long i, long j) { std::cout << "f(long, long)" << std::endl; }  // 2
void f(double i) { std::cout << "f(double)" << std::endl; }            // 3

f(5, 5);        // 1
f(51, 51);      // 2
f(5, 5.0);      // 1
f(5, 51);       // ?
```

First of all, the obvious case—if the types of all arguments match exactly the types of the parameters for one of the overloads, that overload is called. Next, things start to get interesting—if there is no exact match, we can have conversions on each argument. Let's consider the third call, `f(5, 5.0)`. The first argument, `int`, matches the first overload exactly, but could be converted to `long` if necessary. The second argument, `double`, does not match either overload, but could be converted to match both. The first overload is a better match—it requires fewer argument conversions. Finally, what about the last line? The first overload can be called, with a conversion on the second argument. The second overload can also be made to work, with a conversion on the second argument. Again, this is an ambiguous overload, and this line will not compile. Note that it is not, in general, true that the overload with the fewer conversions always wins; in more complex cases, it is possible to have ambiguous overloads even if one requires fewer conversions (the general rule is, if there is an overload that has the best conversion on every argument, it wins; otherwise, the call is ambiguous).

Note how the third overload was completely left out because it has the wrong number of parameters for all function calls. It's not always that simple, though—functions can have default arguments, which means the number of arguments does not always have to match the number of parameters.

Consider the following code block:

```
void f(int i) { std::cout << "f(int)" << std::endl; }                  // 1
void f(long i, long j) { std::cout << "f(long, long)" << std::endl; }  // 2
void f(double i, double j = 0) {                                       // 3
    std::cout << "f(double, double = 0)" << std::endl;
}

f(5);         // 1
f(51, 5);     // 2
```

```
f(5, 5);      // ?
f(5.0);       // 3
f(5.0f);      // 3
f(5l);        // ?
```

We now have three overloads. The first and the second can never be confused, because they have a different number of parameters. The third overload, however, can be called with either one or two arguments; in the former case, the second argument is assumed to be zero. The first call is the simplest—one argument, where the type matches the parameter type of the first overload exactly. The second call reminds us of the case we have seen before—two arguments, where the first is an exact match to one of the overloads, but the second requires a conversion. The alternative overload needs conversions on both arguments, so the second function definition is the best match. The third call seems straightforward enough with its two integer arguments, but this simplicity is deceptive—there are two overloads that accept two arguments, and in both overload cases, both arguments need conversions. While the conversion from int to long may seem better than the one from int to double, C++ does not see it this way. This call is ambiguous. The next call, f(5.0), has only one argument, which can be converted to int, the type of the parameter in the one-argument overload. But it is still a better match for the third overload, where it needs no conversion at all. Change the argument type from double to float, and we get the next call. The conversion to double is better than that to int, and utilizing the default argument is not considered a conversion and so does not carry any other *penalty* when overloads are compared. The last call is again ambiguous—both conversions to double and to int are considered of equal weight, thus the first and third overloads are equally good. The second overload offers an exact match to the first parameter; however, there is no way to call that overload without the second argument, so it is not even considered.

So far, we have considered only ordinary C++ functions, although everything we have learned applies equally to member functions as well. Now, we need to add template functions to the mix.

Template functions

In addition to regular functions, for which the parameter types are known, C++ also has `template` functions. When these functions are called, the parameter types are deduced from the types of the arguments at the call site. The template functions can have the same name as the non-template functions, and several template functions can have the same name as well, so we need to learn about overload resolution in the presence of templates.

Consider the following example:

```cpp
void f(int i) { std::cout << "f(int)" << std::endl; }              // 1
void f(long i) { std::cout << "f(long)" << std::endl; }            // 2
template <typename T> void f(T i) { std::cout << "f(T)" << std::endl; }// 3

f(5);        // 1
f(5l);       // 2
f(5.0);      // 3
```

The `f` function name can refer to any of the three functions, one of which is a template. The best overload will be chosen from these three each time. The set of functions that are considered for the overload resolution of a particular function call is known as the **overload set**. The first call to `f()` matches exactly the first non-template function in the overload set—the argument type is `int`, and the first function is `f(int)`. If an exact match to a non-template function is found in the overload set, it is always considered the best overload. The template function can also be instantiated with an exact match—the process of replacing template parameters with concrete types is known as template argument substitution (or type substitution), and, if `int` is substituted for the T template parameter, then we arrive at another function that exactly matches the call. However, a non-template function that matches exactly is considered a better overload. The second call is processed similarly, but it is an exact match to the second function in the overload set, so that is the function that will be called. The last call has an argument of the `double` type that can be converted to `int` or `long`, or substituted for T to make the template instantiation an exact match. Since there is no exactly matching non-template function, the template function instantiated to an exact match is the next best overload and is selected.

But what happens when there are multiple template functions that can have their template parameters substituted to match the argument types of the call? Let's find out:

```
void f(int i) { std::cout << "f(int)" << std::endl; }    // 1
template <typename T> void f(T i) {                       // 2
    std::cout << "f(T)" << std::endl;
}
template <typename T> void f(T* i) {                       // 3
    std::cout << "f(T*)" << std::endl;
}

f(5);               // 1
f(5l);              // 2
int i = 0;
f(&i);              // 3
```

The first call is again an exact match to the non-template function, and so is resolved. The second call matches the first, non-template, overload, with a conversion, or the second overload exactly if the right type, `long`, is substituted for `T`. The last overload does not match either of these calls—there is no substitution that would make the `T*` parameter type match either `int` or `long`. The last call, however, can be matched to the third overload if `int` is substituted for `T`. The problem is that it could also match the second overload, if `int*` were substituted for `T`. So which template overload is chosen? The answer is the more specific one—the first overload, `f(T)`, can be made to match any one-argument function call, while the second overload, `f(T*)`, can only match calls with pointer arguments. The more specific, narrower overload is considered a better match and is selected. This is a new notion, specific to templates—instead of choosing better conversions (in general, *fewer* or *simpler* conversions), we select the overload that is *harder* to instantiate.

Finally, there is one more kind of function that can match just about any function call with the same name, and that is the function that takes variable arguments:

```
void f(int i) { std::cout << "f(int)" << std::endl; }     // 1
void f(...) { std::cout << "f(...)" << std::endl; }        // 2

f(5);        // 1
f(5l);       // 1
f(5.0);      // 1

struct A {};
A a;
f(a);        // 2
```

The first of the overloads can be used for the first three function calls—it is an exact match for the first call, and conversions exist to make the other two calls fit the signature of the first overload for `f()`. The second function in this example can be called with any number of arguments of any type. This is considered the choice of last resort—a function with specific arguments that can be made to match the call with the right conversions is preferred. This includes user-defined conversions, as follows:

```
struct B {
    operator int() const { return 0; }
};
B b;
f(b);    // 1
```

Only if there are no conversions that allow us to avoid calling the `f(...)` variadic function, then it has to be called.

Now we know the order of the overload resolution—first, a non-template function that matches the arguments exactly is chosen. If there is no such match in the overload set, then a template function is chosen if its parameters can be substituted with concrete types in a way that gives an exact match. If there is more than one option for such a template function, then a more specific overload is preferred over the more general one. If the attempt to match a template function in this manner also fails, then a non-template function is called if the arguments can be converted to its parameter types. Finally, if everything else fails, but a function with the right name that takes variable arguments is available, then that function is called. Note that certain conversions are considered *trivial* and are included in the notion of the *exact* match, for example, the conversion from `T` to `const T`. At every step, if there is more than one equally good option, the overload is considered ambiguous and the program is ill-formed.

The process of type substitution in a template function is what determines the final types of the template function parameters, and how good a match they are to the arguments of the function call. This process can lead to somewhat unexpected results and must be considered in more detail.

Type substitution in template functions

We must carefully differentiate between the two steps in instantiating a template function to match a particular call—first, the types of the template parameters are deduced from the argument types (a process referred to as type deduction). Once the types are deduced, the concrete types are substituted for all parameter types (this is a process called **type substitution**). The difference becomes more obvious when the function has multiple parameters.

Type deduction and substitution

Type deduction and substitution are closely related, but not exactly the same. Deduction is the process of *guessing*—What should the template type, or types, be in order to match the call? Of course, the compiler does not really guess, but applies a set of rules defined in the standard. Consider the following example:

```
template <typename T> void f(T i, T* p) {
    std::cout << "f(T, T8)" << std::endl;
}

int i;
f(5, &i);        // T == int
f(5l, &i);       // ?
```

When considering the first call, we can deduce from the first argument that the T template parameter should be int. Thus, int is substituted for T in both parameters of the function. The template is instantiated as f(int, int*) and is an exact match for the argument types. When considering the second call, we could deduce that T should be long from the first argument. Alternatively, we could deduce that T should be int from the second argument. This ambiguity leads to the failure of the type deduction process. If this is the only overload available, neither option is chosen, and the program does not compile. If more overloads exist, they are considered in turn, including possibly the overload of last resort, the f(...) variadic function. One important detail to note here is that conversions are not considered when deducing template types—the deduction of T as int would have yielded f(int, int*) for the second call, which is a viable option for calling f(long, int*) with the conversion of the first argument. However, this option is not considered at all, and instead, type deduction fails as ambiguous.

The ambiguous deduction can be resolved by explicitly specifying the template types, which removes the need for type deduction:

```
f<int>(5l, &i);      // T == int
```

Now, type deduction is not done at all: we know what T is from the function call, as it is explicitly specified. The type substitution, on the other hand, still has to happen—the first parameter is of the int type, and the second is of the int* type. The function call succeeds with a conversion on the first argument. We could also force deduction the other way:

```
f<long>(5l, &i);     // T == long
```

Again, the deduction is not necessary, as we know what T is. The substitution proceeds in a straightforward way, and we end up with f(long, long*). This function cannot be called with int* as the second argument, since there is no valid conversion from int* to long*. Thus, the program does not compile. Note that, by explicitly specifying the types, we have also specified that f() must be a template function. The non-template overloads for f() are no longer considered. On the other hand, if there is more than one f() template function, then these overloads are considered as usual, but this time with the results of the argument deduction forced by our explicit specification.

Template functions can have default arguments, just like non-template functions, however, the values of these arguments are not used to deduce types (in C++11, template functions can have default values for their type parameters, which provides an alternative). Consider the following example:

```
void f(int i, int j = 1) { std::cout << "f(int, int)" << std::endl; } // 1
template <typename T>
void f(T i, T* p = NULL) {std::cout << "f(T, T*)" << std::endl; }       // 2

int i;
f(5);          // 1
f(5l);         // 2
```

The first call is an exact match to the f(int, int) non-template function, with the default value 1 for the second argument. Note that it would have made no difference if we had declared the function as f(int i, int j = 1L), with the default value as long. The type of the default argument does not matter—if it can be converted to the specified parameter type, then that's the value that is used, otherwise, the program would not compile from line 1. The second call is an exact match to the f(T, T*) template function, with T == long and the default value of NULL for the second argument. Again, it does not matter at all that the type of that value is not long*.

We now understand the difference between type deduction and type substitution. Type deduction can be ambiguous when different concrete types can be deduced from different arguments. If this happens, it means we have failed to deduce the argument types and cannot use this template function. Type substitution is never ambiguous—once we know what T is, we simply substitute that type every time we see T in the function definition. This process can also fail, but in a different way.

Substitution failure

Once we have deduced the template parameter types, type substitution is a purely mechanical process:

```
template <typename T> T* f(T i, T& j) { j = 2*i; return new T(i); }
int i = 5, j = 7;
const int* p = f(i, j);
```

In this example, the T type can be deduced from the first argument as int. It can also be deduced from the second argument, also as int. Note that the return type is not used for the type deduction. Since there is only one possible deduction for T, we now proceed to substitute T with int every time we see T in the function definition:

```
int* f(int i, int& j) { j = 2*i; return new int(i); }
```

Not all types, however, are created equal, and some allow more liberties than others. Consider this code:

```
template <typename T> void f(T i, typename T::t& j) {
    std::cout << "f(T, T::t)" << std::endl;
}
template <typename T> void f(T i, T j) {
    std::cout << "f(T, T)" << std::endl;
}

struct A {
    struct t { int i; };
    t i;
};

A a{5};
f(a, a.i);      // T == A
f(5, 7);        // T == int
```

When considering the first call, the compiler deduces the T template parameter as being of the A type, from both the first and second argument—the first argument is a value of the A type, and the second one is a reference to the value of the A::t nested type, which matches T::t if we stick with our original deduction of T as A. The second overload yields conflicting values for T from the two arguments and, therefore, cannot be used. Thus, the first overload is called.

Now, look closely at the second call. The T type can be deduced as int from the first argument for both overloads. Substituting int for T, however, yields something strange in the second argument of the first overload—int::t. This, of course, would not compile—int is not a class and does not have any nested types. In fact, we could expect that the first template overload will fail to compile for every T type that is not a class, or that does not have a nested type called t. Indeed, the attempt to substitute int for T in the first template function fails with an invalid type for the second argument. However, this substitution failure does not mean that the entire program cannot compile. Instead, it is silently ignored, and the overload that would otherwise be ill-formed is removed from the overload set. The overload resolution then continues as usual. Of course, we could discover that none of the overloads match the function call, and the program will still not compile, but the error message will not mention anything about int::t being invalid; it'll just say that there are no functions that can be called.

Again, it is important to differentiate between type deduction failure and type substitution failure. We can remove the former from consideration entirely:

```
f<int>(5, 7);      // T == int
```

Now, the deduction is unnecessary, but the substitution of int for T must still take place, and this substitution yields an invalid expression in the first overload. Again, this substitution failure drops this candidate for f() from the overload set, and the overload resolution continues (in this case, successfully) with the remaining candidates. Ordinarily, this would be the end of our exercise in overloading: the template produces code that can't compile, so the entire program should not compile either. Fortunately, C++ is more forgiving in this one situation and has a special exception that we need to know about.

Substitution Failure Is Not An Error

The rule that a substitution failure arising from an expression that would be invalid with the specified or deduced types does not make the whole program invalid is known as **Substitution Failure Is Not An Error (SFINAE)**. This rule is essential for using template functions in C++; without SFINAE, it would be impossible to write many otherwise perfectly valid programs. Consider this template overload, which differentiates between regular pointers and member pointers:

```
template <typename T> void f(T* i) {          // 1
    std::cout << "f(T*)" << std::endl;
}
template <typename T> void f(int T::* p) {     // 2
    std::cout << "f(T::*)" << std::endl;
}

struct A {
    int i;
};

A a;
f(&a.i);      // 1
f(&A::i);     // 2
```

So far, so good—the first time, the function is called with a pointer to a specific variable, `a.i`, and the `T` type is deduced as `int`. The second call is with a pointer to a data member of the `A` class, where `T` is deduced as `A`. But now, let's call `f()` with a pointer to a different type:

```
int i;
f(&i);        // 1
```

The first overload still works fine and is what we want to call. But the second overload isn't just less suitable, it is altogether invalid—it would cause a syntax error if we tried to substitute `int` for `T`. This syntax error is observed by the compiler and silently ignored, together with the overload itself.

Note that the SFINAE rule is not limited to invalid types, such as references to non-existing class members. There are many ways in which substitution can fail:

```
template <size_t N> void f(char(*)[N % 2] = NULL) {      // 1
  std::cout << "N=" << N << " is odd" << std::endl;
}
template <size_t N> void f(char(*)[1 - N % 2] = NULL) { // 2
  std::cout << "N=" << N << " is even" << std::endl;
}
```

```
f<5>();
f<8>();
```

Here, the template parameter is a value, not a type. We have two template overloads that both take a pointer to an array of characters, and array size expressions are valid only for some values of N. Specifically, a zero-size array is invalid in C++. Therefore, the first overload is valid only if N % 2 is non-zero, that is, if N is odd. Similarly, the second overload is valid only if N is even. No arguments are given to the function, so we intend to use the default arguments. The two overloads would have been ambiguous in every way, were it not for the fact that, for both calls, one of the overloads fails during template argument substitution and is silently removed.

The preceding example is very condensed—in particular, the template parameter value deduction, the equivalent of type deduction for numeric parameters is disabled by the explicit specification. We can bring the deduction back and still have the substitution fail, or not, depending on whether an expression is valid:

```
template <typename T, size_t N = T::N>
void f(T t, char(*)[N % 2] = NULL) {
    std::cout << "N=" << N << " is odd" << std::endl;
}
template <typename T, size_t N = T::N>
void f(T t, char(*)[1 - N % 2] = NULL) {
    std::cout << "N=" << N << " is even" << std::endl;
}

struct A {
    enum {N = 5};
};
struct B {
    enum {N = 8};
};

A a;
B b;
f(a);
f(b);
```

Now, the compiler has to deduce the type from the first argument. For the first call, f(a), the A type is easily deduced. There is no way to deduce the second template parameter, N, so the default value is used (we are now in C++11 territory). Having deduced both template parameters, we now proceed to the substitution, where T is replaced by A, and N is replaced by 5. This substitution fails for the second overload but succeeds for the first one. With only one remaining candidate in the overload set, the overload resolution concludes. Similarly, the second call, f(b), ends up calling the second overload.

Note that SFINAE does not protect us from any and all syntax errors that might happen during template instantiation. For example, if the template parameters are deduced, and the template arguments are substituted, we may still end up with an ill-formed template function:

```
template <typename T> void f(T) { std::cout << sizeof(T::i) << std::endl; }
void f(...) { std::cout << "f(...)" << std::endl; }

f(0);
```

This code fragment is very similar to those we considered earlier, with one exception—we do not learn that the template overload presupposes that the `T` type is a class, and has a data member named `T::i`, until we examine the function body. By then, it is too late, as the overload resolution is done only on the basis of the function declaration—the parameters, the default arguments, and the return type (the latter is not used to deduce types or select a better overload, but still undergoes type substitution and is covered by SFINAE). Once the template is instantiated and chosen by the overload resolution, any syntax errors, such as an invalid expression in the body of the function, are not ignored—such a failure is very much an error. The exact list of contexts where a substitution failure is, or is not, ignored, is defined in the standard and is significantly expanded in C++11.

Now that we know why the SFINAE rule had to be added to C++, and how it applies to the overloaded template functions, we can attempt to intentionally cause a substitution failure to influence the overload resolution.

Taking control of overload resolution

The rule that a failure of the template argument substitution is not an error—the SFINAE rule—had to be added to the language simply to make certain narrowly defined template functions possible. But the ingenuity of a C++ programmer knows no bounds, and so SFINAE was repurposed and exploited to manually control the overload set by intentionally causing substitution failures.

Let's consider in detail how SFINAE can be used to knock out an undesirable overload from the overload set. Note that, for most of this chapter, we will lean heavily on C++11 and, later, C++14 features. You may want to review these recent additions to the language; if so, please refer to the *Further reading* section at the end of this chapter.

Basic SFINAE

Let's start with a very basic problem—we have some general code that we want to call for all objects, except for built-in types. For integers and other built-in types, we have a specialized version of our code. This problem can be solved by explicitly listing all built-in types in a set of overloaded functions. And let's not forget raw pointers; they are also built-in types. And references. And constant pointers. With care, this approach can be made to work. But perhaps it would be simpler to somehow test whether our type is a class or not. We just need to find something that classes have, and built-in types do not. The obvious distinction is member pointers. Any function declaration that uses the member pointer syntax will fail during substitution; we just need to provide an overload of last resort to catch these calls, and we already know how to do that:

```
template <typename T>
void f(int T::*) { std::cout << "T is a class" << std::endl; }
template <typename T>
void f(...) { std::cout << "T is not a class" << std::endl; }

struct A {
};

f<int>(0);
f<A>(0);
```

Note that we are not interested in type deduction here. We are asking the question—*Is* A *a class? Is* int *a class?* The first overload uses the member pointer syntax, the substitution fails for any non-class instance of the T type, and the failure is not an error (thanks to SFINAE!), but another overload has to be considered. Also, you may find the notion of the *doubly universal* `template f(...)` function curious—it takes any arguments of any type, even without the template, so why use the template? Of course, it is so a call with an explicitly specified type, like `f<int>()`, considers this function as a possible overload (remember that, by specifying the template parameter type, we also exclude all non-template functions from consideration).

If we often need to use this test for a type being a class often, we do not want to add SFINAE constructs to every function we call. A dedicated piece of code that checks whether something is a class and, perhaps, sets a compile-time constant value to `true` or `false`, would be preferable. We could then use any number of conditional compilation techniques with that value:

```
template <typename T> ??? test(int T::*); // selected if T is a class type
template <typename T> ??? test(...);       // selected otherwise
template <typename T>
struct is_class {
```

```
...
    static constexpr bool value = ???; // make this true if T is class
};
```

Now we just need to somehow make the value of the constant in our `is_class` helper class depend on the overload that would have been selected were we to call the `test<T>()` function, but without actually calling it (calling happens at runtime, but we need to know at compile time—note that we did not even bother to define the function bodies, since we do not plan on ever calling them).

The last piece to tie all of this together is a compile-time context, in which we can find out which functions would have been called. One such context is the `sizeof` operator—the compiler has to evaluate the `sizeof(T)` expression at compile time for any instance of `T`, and so, if we somehow made the two functions evaluate to different values inside a `sizeof()` expression, we would know which one was selected by the overload resolution. We can differentiate between the two functions based on their return types, so let's give them return types of different sizes and see which one we get:

```
template<typename T>
class is_class {
    // Selected if C is a class type
    template<typename C> static char test(int C::*);
    // Selected otherwise
    template<typename C> static int test(...);
    public:
    static constexpr bool value = sizeof(test<T>(0)) == 1;
};

struct A {
};
std::cout << is_class<int>::value << std::endl;
std::cout << is_class<A>::value << std::endl;
```

We have also hidden the test function inside the `is_class` class—no need to pollute the global scope with names of functions that nobody is supposed to call. Note that C++, strictly speaking, does not guarantee that the size of `int` is not the same as the size of `char`. We will deal with that, and other pedantic details, in the next section.

Before C++11 and `constexpr`, we would have had to use an `enum` specifier to achieve a similar effect, and you may still find such examples, so it is important to recognize them:

```
template <typename T>
struct is_class {
    ...
    enum { value = sizeof(test<T>(NULL)) == 1 };
};
```

If we work with C++11, however, we should note that it provides a standard type for this sort of compile-time constant object, in the form of `integral_constant`. This type has the value, `true` or `false`, but it also adds a few more details, and other STL classes expect to find them, so there is no reason to reinvent the wheel:

```
namespace implementation {
    // Selected if C is a class type
    template<typename C> static char test(int C::*);
    // Selected otherwise
    template<typename C> static int test(...);
}

template <class T>
struct is_class :
    std::integral_constant<bool, sizeof(implementation::test<T>(0)) ==
                          sizeof(char)> {};

struct A {
};

static_assert(!is_class<int>::value, "int is a class?");
static_assert(is_class<A>::value, "A is not a class?");
```

We don't have to wait until we can run the program to find out whether our implementation of is_class has worked either—the `static_assert` lets us test it at compile time, which is when we intend to use the result of is_class anyway.

Of course, in C++11, there is no reason to do any of that in the preceding code, since the standard provides the `std::is_class` type that is used in exactly the same way as the one we have just implemented, and works the same way (with the exception that unions are not considered classes in this sense). However, in re-implementing is_class, we have mastered the targeted application of SFINAE in the simplest possible context. Next, it gets harder.

Advanced SFINAE

Next, we consider a problem that is simply stated, although not as simply solved. We are writing generic code that operates on a container object of an arbitrary T type. At some point, we need to sort the data in this container. We assume that, if the container provides a T::sort() member function, then this is the best way to sort the data (the implementer of the container presumably knows how the data is organized). If there is no such member function, but the container is a sequence with the begin() and end() member functions, then we can call std::sort() on that sequence. Otherwise, we don't know how to sort the data and our code should not compile.

A naive attempt to solve the problem might look like this:

```
template <typename T> void best_sort(T& x, bool use_member_sort) {
    if (use_member_sort) x.sort();
    else std::sort(x.begin(), x.end());
}
```

The problem is that this code will not compile for any T type that does not have a sort() member function, even if we do not intend to use it. The situation may seem hopeless at this point: in order to call x.sort() for at least some types of x, we have to have the code x.sort() written somewhere in our program. But once we do, that code will not compile for any type of x that does not have this member function. But there is one possibility—in general, C++ templates do not produce syntax errors unless they are instantiated (this is a vast oversimplification, and the exact rules are quite complex, but it will do for now). For example, consider the following code:

```
class Base {
    public:
    Base() : i_() {}
    virtual void increment(long v) { i_ += v; }
    private:
    long i_;
};

template <typename T>
class Derived : public T {
    public:
    Derived() : T(), j_() {}
    void increment(long v) { j_ += v; T::increment(v); }
    void multiply(long v) { j_ *= v; T::multiply(v); }
    private:
    long j_;
};
```

```
int main() {
    Derived<Base> d;
    d.increment(5);
}
```

Here, we have the derived class that inherits from its template parameter. The `increment()` and `multiply()` member functions of the derived class call the corresponding member functions of the base class. But our base class has only the `increment()` member function! Nonetheless, this code compiles fine, unless we actually call `Derived::multiply()`. The potential syntax error does not become real, unless the template actually has to generate the invalid code.

Note that this only works as long as the potentially invalid code depends on the template type, and the compiler cannot check its validity until the template is instantiated (in our case, `Derived::multiply()` is never instantiated at all). If the possibly invalid code does not depend on the template parameter, then it's no longer *possibly invalid*, but just invalid, and is rejected:

```
template <typename T>
class Derived : public Base {
    public:
    Derived() : Base(), j_() {}
    void increment(long v) { j_ += v; Base::increment(v); }
    // multiply() is invalid for any T:
    void multiply(long v) { j_ *= v; Base::multiply(v); }
    private:
    T j_;
};
```

This example shows us a possible path to success—if we can hide the call to `x.sort()` in a template that is not instantiated unless we are absolutely sure that this code will compile, then the syntax error will never happen. One such place where we can hide code is class template specializations. What we need is something like the following:

```
template <typename T> struct fast_sort_helper;

template <typename T>
struct fast_sort_helper<???> {              // Specialization for member sort
    static void fast_sort(T& x) {
        std::cout << "Sorting with T::sort" << std::endl;
        x.sort();
    }
};

template <typename T>
struct fast_sort_helper<???> {              // Specialization for std::sort
```

```
        static void fast_sort(T& x) {
            std::cout << "Sorting with std::sort" << std::endl;
            std::sort(x.begin(), x.end());
        }
    };
```

Here, we have the general case template for a `fast_sort_helper` auxiliary type, and two specializations that we have not yet figured out how to instantiate. If we could instantiate only the right specialization, and not the other one, then the call to `fast_sort_helper::fast_sort(x)` would compile either to `x.sort()` or to `std::sort(x.begin(), x.end())`. If neither of the two specializations is instantiated, our program will fail to compile, because the `fast_sort_helper` type is incomplete.

But now we have a chicken-and-egg problem—in order to decide which specialization to instantiate, we have to try compiling `x.sort()` to see if it fails. If it does fail, then we must avoid instantiating the first specialization of `fast_sort_helper` precisely so we can avoid compiling `x.sort()`. We need to try compiling `x.sort()` in some context where the compilation failure would not be permanent. SFINAE provides us with just such a context—we need to declare a template function with an argument whose type is well defined only if the expression `x.sort()` is valid. In C++11, there is no reason to be oblique about it; if we need a certain type to be valid, we refer to this type using `decltype()`:

```
    template <typename T> ? test_sort(decltype(&T::sort));
```

We have just declared a template function that will cause a substitution failure, unless the deduced `T` type has a `sort()` member function (we refer to the type of the member function pointer to that function). We have no intention of actually calling this function; we only need it at compile time to generate the right template specialization for `fast_sort_helper`. If the substitution fails, we still need the entire overload resolution not to fail, so we need an overload that would not be preferred unless it's the only one left. We already know that `variadic` functions are the least preferred overloads. In order to know which overload was selected, we can again use `sizeof` on the return type of the function, as long as we give them return types of different sizes (since we don't plan to ever call any of these functions, we don't have to worry about actually returning an object, so we can use any return type we want). In the previous section, we used `char` and `int` and made the assumption that `sizeof(int)` is greater than `sizeof(char)`. While this is probably true on any real hardware, the standard does not guarantee it. With a little effort, we can create two types whose sizes are guaranteed to be different:

```
    struct yes { char c; };
    struct no { char c; yes c1; };
    static_assert(sizeof(yes) != sizeof(no),
                  "Do something else for yes/no types");
```

```
template <typename T> yes test_sort(decltype(&T::sort));
template <typename T> no test_sort(...);
```

Now, just like we did for our `is_class` test earlier, we can compare the size of the return type of the selected overload with the size of the `yes` type to determine whether an arbitrary `T` type has the `T::sort` member function. To select the right specialization of the `fast_sort_helper` object, we need to use this size as a template parameter, which means that, in addition to the `T` type parameter, our `fast_sort_helper` template needs to take an integer parameter. We are now ready to put it all together:

```
struct yes { char c; };
struct no { char c; yes c1; };
static_assert(sizeof(yes) != sizeof(no),
             "Do something else for yes/no types");
template <typename T> yes test_sort(decltype(&T::sort));
template <typename T> no test_sort(...);

template <typename T, size_t s>
struct fast_sort_helper;                 // General case is incomplete type
template <typename T>
struct fast_sort_helper<T, sizeof(yes)> {   // Specialized for yes
    static void fast_sort(T& x) {
        std::cout << "Sorting with T::sort" << std::endl;
        x.sort();                        // Isn't compiled unless selected
    }
};

template <typename T>
void fast_sort(T& x) {
    fast_sort_helper<T, sizeof(test_sort<T>(NULL))>::fast_sort(x);
}

class A {
    public:
    void sort() {}
};

class C {
    public:
    void f() {}
};

A a; fast_sort(a);    // Compiles, calls a.sort()
C c; fast_sort(c);    // Does not compile
```

We have combined a function template, `fast_sort(T&)`, which we need to use to deduce the type of the argument with a `fast_sort_helper<T, s>` class template. With this class template, we need to use partial specializations and hide potentially invalid code inside a template that does not get instantiated unless we are certain that it will compile.

So far, we have solved only half of our problem—we can decide whether to call the `sort()` member function, but not `std::sort`. For the latter, we need the container to have `begin()` and `end()` member functions. Of course, we also need the data type to be comparable via `operator<()`, but this is needed for any sort (we could also add support for an arbitrary `comparison` function, like `std::sort` does). We can handle the second half of the problem in the same way and test for the two `begin()` and `end()` member functions using two arguments of the member function pointer type:

```
template <typename T> ??? test_sort(decltype(&T::begin),
decltype(&T::end));
```

To make the other overload, which tests for the `sort()` member function, participate in the overload resolution with this one, we would have to change its number of parameters from one to two. The `variadic` function already takes any number of arguments. Finally, this is no longer a yes or no question—we need three return types to differentiate between containers that have `sort()`, containers that have `begin()` and `end()`, and containers that have neither:

```
struct have_sort { char c; };
struct have_range { char c; have_sort c1; };
struct have_nothing { char c; have_range c1; };
template <typename T> have_sort test_sort(decltype(&T::sort),
                                          decltype(&T::sort));
template <typename T> have_range test_sort(decltype(&T::begin),
                                           decltype(&T::end));
template <typename T> have_nothing test_sort(...);
template <typename T, size_t s> struct fast_sort_helper;

template <typename T>
struct fast_sort_helper<T, sizeof(have_sort)> {
    static void fast_sort(T& x) {
        std::cout << "Sorting with T::sort" << std::endl;
        x.sort();
    }
};

template <typename T>
struct fast_sort_helper<T, sizeof(have_range)> {
    static void fast_sort(T& x) {
        std::cout << "Sorting with std::sort" << std::endl;
```

```
            std::sort(x.begin(), x.end());
        }
};

template <typename T>
void fast_sort(T& x) {
    fast_sort_helper<T, sizeof(test_sort<T>(NULL, NULL))>::fast_sort(x);
}

class A {
    public:
    void sort() {}
};

class B {
    public:
    int* begin() { return i; }
    int* end() { return i + 10; }
    int i[10];
};

class C {
    public:
    void f() {}
};

A a; fast_sort(a);     // Compiles, uses a.sort()
B b; fast_sort(b);     // Compiles, uses std::sort(b.begin(), b.end())
C c; fast_sort(c);     // Does not compile
```

Calling `fast_sort()` on a container that cannot be sorted using either of these two approaches generates a somewhat cryptic error about `fast_sort_helper` being an incomplete type. We could make the error more explicit if we provided a specialization for the `have_nothing` result of the overload resolution, and used a static assert in it:

```
template <typename T>
struct fast_sort_helper<T, sizeof(have_nothing)> {
    static void fast_sort(T& x) {
        static_assert(sizeof(T) < 0, "No sort available");
    }
};
```

Note that we have to use a condition that depends on the template type. We cannot simply write the following:

```
static_assert(false, "No sort available");
```

This will fail unconditionally, even if the specialization of `fast_sort_helper` for the `have_nothing` result is never instantiated. Of course, the `sizeof(T) < 0` expression also fails every time, but the compiler is not allowed to make that determination in advance.

The solution we have just presented exposes the details of the implementation that uses SFINAE to check for compilation failures in a context where they are ignored, in order to avoid the same failures in a context where they would be fatal. It is a very revealing, and thus educational, way to write such code, but definitely not the most compact way. C++11 provides several utilities that make conditional compilation much easier. One of these utilities, in `std::enable_if`, is a class template parameterized by a Boolean value that triggers an SFINAE failure if that value is false (its implementation could be similar to our `fast_sort_helper` class template). A common way to use `std::enable_if` is in the return type of the overloaded function—if the expression is false, the return type substitution fails, and the function is removed from the overload set. With this utility, our solution can be simplified:

```
struct have_sort { char c; };
struct have_range { char c; have_sort c1; };
struct have_nothing { char c; have_range c1; };
template <typename T> have_sort test_sort(decltype(&T::sort),
                                          decltype(&T::sort));
template <typename T> have_range test_sort(decltype(&T::begin),
                                           decltype(&T::end));
template <typename T> have_nothing test_sort(...);

template <typename T>
typename std::enable_if<sizeof(test_sort<T>(NULL, NULL)) ==
                    sizeof(have_sort)>::type fast_sort(T& x) {
    std::cout << "Sorting with T::sort" << std::endl;
    x.sort();
}
template <typename T>
typename std::enable_if<sizeof(test_sort<T>(NULL, NULL)) ==
                    sizeof(have_range)>::type fast_sort(T& x) {
    std::cout << "Sorting with std::sort" << std::endl;
    std::sort(x.begin(), x.end());
}
```

Here, we got rid of the helper class and its specializations, and instead directly removed one or both `fast_sort()` overloads from the overload set. As before, if both overloads are removed, the error message is somewhat convoluted, and we could provide the third overload with the `static_assert` in it instead.

But we are not done yet. What happens if a container has both `sort()` and `begin()`/`end()`? Now we have two valid overloads for `test_sort()`, and the entire program fails to compile because of the ambiguity of the overload resolution. We could attempt to make one of the overloads preferred over the other, but it's tricky and does not generalize for a more complex case. Instead, we need to revisit the way we are asking the question: does the container have `sort()` or `begin()`/`end()`? Our problem lies in the way we formulated the test—the possibility of the answer *it has both* is not considered in this question, so it is no wonder we struggle with the answer. Instead of one either-or question, we need to ask two separate questions:

```
struct yes { char c; };
struct no { char c; yes c1; };
template <typename T> yes test_have_sort(decltype(&T::sort));
template <typename T> no test_have_sort(...);
template <typename T> yes test_have_range(decltype(&T::begin),
decltype(&T::end));
template <typename T> no test_have_range(...);
```

Now we should explicitly decide what to do in the event that the answer is *yes* to both questions. We can resolve the issue using `std::enable_if` and some moderately complex logical expressions, or go back to our helper class template that must now have two additional integer template parameters instead of one, and handle all four possible combinations of the yes/no answers to our two questions as follows:

```
template <typename T, bool have_sort, bool have_range> struct
fast_sort_helper;

template <typename T>
struct fast_sort_helper<T, true, true> {
    static void fast_sort(T& x) {
        std::cout << "Sorting with T::sort, ignoring std::sort"
                  << std::endl;
        x.sort();
    }
};

template <typename T>
struct fast_sort_helper<T, true, false> {
    static void fast_sort(T& x) {
        std::cout << "Sorting with T::sort" << std::endl;
        x.sort();
    }
};

template <typename T>
struct fast_sort_helper<T, false, true> {
```

```
        static void fast_sort(T& x) {
            std::cout << "Sorting with std::sort" << std::endl;
            std::sort(x.begin(), x.end());
        }
};

template <typename T>
struct fast_sort_helper<T, false, false> {
    static void fast_sort(T& x) {
        static_assert(sizeof(T) < 0, "No sort available");
    }
};

template <typename T>
void fast_sort(T& x) {
    fast_sort_helper<T,
        sizeof(test_have_sort<T>(NULL)) == sizeof(yes),
        sizeof(test_have_range<T>(NULL, NULL)) ==
            sizeof(yes)>::fast_sort(x);
}

class AB {
    public:
    void sort() {}
    int* begin() { return i; }
    int* end() { return i + 10; }
    int i[10];
};

AB ab; fast_sort(ab);    // Used ab.sort(), ignores the option of std::sort
```

Which method you use is largely a matter of personal preference—std::enable_if is a familiar idiom that clearly expresses the intent, but bugs in the logic expressions, which must be mutually exclusive and must cover all possible cases, may be difficult to debug. The verbosity and complexity of the code will vary depending on the problem.

Let's try using our fast_sort() function on some real containers. For example, std::list has both the sort() member function and begin()/end(), while std::vector does not have a sort() member function.

```
std::list<int> l; std::vector<int> v;
... store some data in the containers ...
fast_sort(l);    // l.sort() should be called
fast_soft(v);    // std::sort should be called
```

The result is rather unexpected—both calls to fast_sort() fail to compile. If we handle the *no to both* answer explicitly, we will get the static assert that we reserved for containers that have neither of the interfaces we need. But how can that be? We know, for sure, that std::list has a sort() member function, and the std::vector has begin() and end(). The problem is that they have too many of them. All these functions are overloaded. For example, std::list has two declarations of sort(): one is a regular void sort() member function that takes no arguments, and the other one is a void sort(Compare) template member function that takes a comparison object, to be used instead of operator<(). In our case, we intend to call sort() without any arguments, so what we really need to know is whether that call will compile or not. But we did not ask the right question we asked what is the type of T::sort?, regardless of its arguments. The answer we got was which sort do you mean?, which caused the substitution to fail because of the ambiguity (there are two possible answers, so the question cannot be answered definitively). We then misinterpreted the substitution failure as a sign that the type has no sort() member function at all. To remedy the situation, we have to ask a narrower question—does the type have a sort() member function with no arguments? To do this, we have to try to cast the &T::sort member function pointer to a specific type, such as void (T::*)(), which is a pointer to a member function that takes no arguments and returns void. If this cast succeeds, then the member function of the desired type exists among other possible overloads that we can safely ignore. We need only a small change to our SFINAE test functions:

```
template <typename T> yes test_have_sort(
    decltype(static_cast<void (T::*)()>(&T::sort)));
template <typename T> yes test_have_range(
    decltype(static_cast<typename T::iterator (T::*)()>(&T::begin)),
    decltype(static_cast<typename T::iterator (T::*)()>(&T::end)));
```

Note that, for begin() and end(), we also have to specify the return type (the same as for sort(), only void is easier to specify). Thus, we are really testing for begin() and end() functions that take no arguments and return a nested type, called T::iterator (the overload that was giving us trouble with the vector earlier returns T::const_iterator). Now fast_sort() can be used on a list, and calls the member function sort(), ignoring the option to call std:: sort on the begin() [...] end() sequence. It can also be called on the vector, where it will use the non-const version of begin() and end() with std::sort, as it should.

In all of the examples so far, we have taken full control of the overload resolution—after all failed substitutions were removed by SFINAE, only one overload was left. It is possible to (very carefully) combine manual and automatic overload resolution. For example, we could provide a `fast_sort` overload for regular C arrays, which can be sorted with `std::sort()` but do not have `begin()` and `end()`:

```
template <typename T, size_t N>
void fast_sort(T (&x)[N]) {
    std::sort(x, x + N);
}
```

This overload is preferred over all the other ones without any SFINAE involved, so we now have the regular, automatic overload resolution that handles arrays, and everything else needs the manual control of the overload set that is provided by SFINAE.

The problem is solved, and our tests produce the expected results. And yet, somehow, this complete and hard-fought victory feels unsatisfying. We can't help but have a nagging doubt—in the attempt to specifically exclude other overloads of the member functions—those we did not want to call in any case—did we make the solution too specific? What if the only `sort()` function that we have is one that does not return void? The return value can be ignored, so a call to `x.sort()` would still compile, but our code won't—we are checking only for the `sort()` member function that returns nothing. Perhaps we are asking the wrong question after all, and our approach to using SFINAE needs to be reconsidered?

Advanced SFINAE revisited

The problem we considered in the previous section, calling a `sort()` member function if one exists, naturally led us to ask the question *Does a* `sort()` *member function exist?* We came up with two ways to ask this question—first, we can ask *Does the class have a member function named* `sort`, *and what is the type of a pointer to it?* This question fails when the answer is *yes, it has two*, and the type of the pointer depends on which one you mean. The second way to ask was *Does the class have a* `void sort()` *member function?* This question fails when the answer is *No, but it has one that you can call anyway.* Perhaps the question we should have asked all along was, *If I write* `x.sort()`, *will it compile?*

To avoid falling into this trap again, let's consider a different problem, where we are forced to deal with such ambiguity head-on. We want to write a function that will multiply a value of any type by a given integer value, as follows:

```
template <typename T> ??? increase(const T& x, size_t n);
```

The T type is, in general, a user-defined type that has some arithmetic operators defined. There are many ways in which this operation can be accomplished. In the simplest case, there is an operator* that takes the arguments of the T type and size_t (and does not necessarily return T, so we do not yet know what the return type of our function should be). But even then, this operator could be a member function of the class T, or a non-member function. Barring such an operator, we could try to invoke x *= n, as maybe the T type has an operator*= that takes an integer? If that fails, we could try to compute x + x and repeat it n times, but only if the T type has an operator+ member function. Finally, what if none of those options work out, but the T type is convertible to another type, which can be multiplied by n? We want to use that path, then. It is, however, clear that it is futile to try to come up with a complete list of questions like *Does this operator or that member function exist?* There are just too many ways in which the desired functionality can be provided. Instead, what we should be asking is, *is x * n a valid expression?* Fortunately, in C++11, the decltype operator lets us do just that—decltype(x * n) will return the type of the result of the multiplication if the compiler can find a way to evaluate the expression. Otherwise, the expression is invalid, so the potential error must happen during type substitution, where it can be safely ignored in favor of some alternative way to compute the result. On the other hand, if the expression x * n is valid, then its type, whatever it is, should probably be the return type of the entire function. Fortunately, in C++11, we can have functions deduce their return type:

```
template <typename T>
auto increase(const T& x, size_t n) -> decltype(x * n)
{
    return x * n;
}
```

This function will compile fine if the x * n expression is valid, as the compiler will deduce its type and resolve the auto return type to that type. Then it will compile the body of the function. Here, a compilation error would be fatal and permanent, so it is fortunate that we have pre-tested the x * n expression and know that it will not generate any errors.

What happens if the substitution fails? We need another overload, then, or the entire program will be invalid. Let's try the operator*= function next:

```
template <typename T>
auto increase(const T& x, size_t n) -> decltype(T(x) *= n)
{
    T y(x);
    return y *= n;
}
```

Note that we can't just check whether x *= n is valid—first of all, x is passed by a constant reference, and operator*= always modifies its left-hand side. Second, it is not enough that the T type has operator*=. The body of our function needs to create a temporary object of the same type to have something on which we can call *=. Since we decided to create this object by a copy constructor, we need to make sure one is available. Overall, we need the entire T(x) *= n expression to be valid.

Between these two overloads, we have both multiplication scenarios covered—but not both at the same time! Again, we have the problem of an embarrassment of riches—if both overloads are valid, we cannot choose between them, and the compilation fails. Still, we have dealt with this before—we need a complex logic expression, or a helper class template that is specialized with multiple Boolean values:

```
struct yes { char c; };
struct no { char c; yes c1; };

template <typename T>
auto have_star_equal(const T& x, size_t n) -> decltype(T(x) *= n, yes());
no have_star_equal(...);

template <typename T>
auto have_star(const T& x, size_t n) -> decltype(x * n, yes());
no have_star(...);

template <typename T, bool have_star_equal, bool have_star> struct
increase_helper;

template <typename T> struct increase_helper<T, true, true> {
    static auto f(const T& x, size_t n) {
        std::cout << "T *= n, ignoring T * n" << std::endl;
        T y(x);
        return y *= n;
    }
};

template <typename T> struct increase_helper<T, true, false> {
    static auto f(const T& x, size_t n) {
        std::cout << "T *= n" << std::endl;
        T y(x);
        return y *= n;
    }
};

template <typename T> struct increase_helper<T, false, true> {
    static auto f(const T& x, size_t n) {
        std::cout << "T * n" << std::endl;
```

```
            return x * n;
    }
};

template <typename T> auto increase(const T& x, size_t n) {
    return increase_helper<T,
        sizeof(have_star_equal(x, n)) == sizeof(yes),
        sizeof(have_star(x, n)) == sizeof(yes)>::f(x, n);
}
```

Note that the ability to use auto return types without the help of an explicit `decltype` after the parameter list is a C++14 feature; in C++11, we would have to write the following:

```
static auto f(const T& x, size_t n) -> decltype(x * n) { ... }
```

This solution looks very similar to the one is the previous section, and indeed we are using the same tools (which is why you had to learn them there). The key difference is in the `have_star` and `have_star_equal` testing functions—instead of checking whether a particular type, such as `void T::sort()`, exists, we are checking whether the `x * n` expression is valid. Also note that, while we want to make sure the expression is valid, we don't want to actually return its type, we already have the intended return type, `struct yes`. That is why we have multiple expressions in the `decltype`, separated by commas:

```
auto have_star_equal(const T& x, size_t n) -> decltype(T(x) *= n, yes());
```

The type is deduced from the last expression, but all the preceding ones have to be valid too, otherwise, the substitution will fail (thankfully, in an SFINAE context).

So far, we have covered only two options to increment x. We can proceed to add more ways to do so, such as using addition several times as a last resort. We just need to keep adding Boolean parameters to the helper template. We also want a better way to deal with the ever-growing number of combinations—for example, if the simple `x * n` works, we don't really care whether `x + x` would also work. We can simplify our hierarchy of logical decisions by using partial template specializations:

```
// General case, incomplete type
template <typename T, bool have_star, bool have_star_equal>
struct increase_helper;
// Use this specialization if have_star is true
template <typename T, bool have_star_equal>
struct increase_helper<T, true, have_star_equal> {
    static auto f(const T& x, size_t n) {
        std::cout << "T * n" << std::endl;
        return x * n;
    }
};
```

Finally, enough with the homemade `yes` and `no` types already—C++11 has two special types, `std::true_type` and `std::false_type`. They are not meant to be compared for size (they actually have the same size), but they don't need to be—they have `constexpr` (compile-time constant) Boolean data members, named `value`, that have the values of `true` and `false`, respectively. Putting all of this together, we arrive at this solution:

```
template <typename T>
auto have_star(const T& x, size_t n) -> decltype(x * n, std::true_type());
std::false_type have_star(...);

template <typename T>
auto have_star_equal(const T& x, size_t n) -> decltype(T(x) *= n,
std::true_type());
std::false_type have_star_equal(...);

template <typename T>
auto have_plus(const T& x) -> decltype(x + x, std::true_type());
std::false_type have_plus(...);

template <typename T, bool have_star, bool have_star_equal, bool have_plus>
struct increase_helper;

template <typename T, bool have_star_equal, bool have_plus>
struct increase_helper<T, true, have_star, have_plus> {    // x * n works,
    static auto f(const T& x, size_t n) {       // don't care about the rest
        std::cout << "T * n" << std::endl;
        return x * n;
    }
};

template <typename T, bool have_plus>
struct increase_helper<T, false, true, have_plus> {  // x * n does not work
    static auto f(const T& x, size_t n) {            // but x *= n does,
        std::cout << "T *= n" << std::endl;          // don't care about +
        T y(x);
        return y *= n;
    }
};

template <typename T>
struct increase_helper<T, false, false, true> {         // nothing works
except x + x
    static auto f(const T& x, size_t n) {
        std::cout << "T + T + ... + T" << std::endl;
        T y(x);
        for (size_t i = 1; i < n; ++i) y = y + y;
```

```
                return y;
        }
};

template <typename T> auto increase(const T& x, size_t n) {
        return increase_helper<T,
                                decltype(have_star_equal(x, n))::value,
                                decltype(have_star(x, n))::value,
                                decltype(have_plus(x))::value
                        >::f(x, n);
}
```

This code works for any combination of operators that provides *, *=, and + operations and accepts the arguments of the necessary types, possibly with type conversions. It is also notably similar to the code we studied in the previous section, even though we were solving an entirely different problem. Confronted with such boilerplate code that is repeated over and over, we must look for a more universal, reusable solution next.

The ultimate SFINAE

Our goal now is to make a reusable framework that we could use to test any expression for validity, without creating a syntax error if our expression is not valid. Just as in the previous section, we don't want to actually specify how the expression is evaluated, whether by a specific function, or using conversions, or in some other way. We just want to precompile the expression we are about to use in the body of the function, to make sure that the real compilation will not fail, or to instantiate some other template function if it does fail. We need a general is_valid feature that we can apply to any expression.

To accomplish this goal, we need to use all the template programming tricks we have studied so far, including SFINAE, decltype, and the return type deduction. We also need to use one of the more advanced features added in C++14—polymorphic lambdas, which we will use as a convenient way to hold an arbitrary expression. If you are not familiar with any of these features, now is the time to consult the *Further reading* section of this chapter.

For this solution, we have entirely eschewed homemade props, such as yes/no types, and are fully taking advantage of the facilities provided by C++14. With that and the terse language of lambda expressions, the solution is surprisingly compact:

```
template <typename Lambda> struct is_valid_helper {
        template <typename LambdaArgs>
        constexpr auto test(int) ->
                decltype(std::declval<Lambda>()(std::declval<LambdaArgs>()),
                                                std::true_type())
        {
```

```
        return std::true_type();
    }

    template <typename LambdaArgs> constexpr std::false_type test(...) {
        return std::false_type();
    }

    template <typename LambdaArgs>
    constexpr auto operator()(const LambdaArgs&) {
        return this->test<LambdaArgs>(0);
    }
};

template <typename Lambda> constexpr auto is_valid(const Lambda&) {
    return is_valid_helper<Lambda>();
}
```

Before we explain how it works, it is helpful to see how to use this is_valid. It is used to declare *verification objects* with arbitrary embedded expressions, such as the following example:

```
auto is_assignable = is_valid([](auto&& x) -> decltype(x = x) {});
void my_function( const A& a ) {
    static_assert(decltype(is_assignable(a))::value,
                  "A is not assignable");
}
```

The expression we are testing here is x = x; that is, the assignment of an object to another object of the same type (the fact that the actual expression is a self-assignment makes no difference whatsoever—we just want to see whether an assignment operator exists that takes two arguments of the same type as x). The is_assignable object that we have defined using is_valid is an std::integral_constant, so it has a constexpr member named value that can be true or false, depending on whether the expression is valid. We can use this compile-time constant in a compile-time assert, or to specialize a template, or to conditionally enable a function using std::enable_if, or in any other way that a compile-time constant can be used.

A detailed explanation of the `is_valid` code would require a tour of C++14 and is beyond the scope of this book. We can, however, highlight some details that connect this code with the solutions we studied previously. Start with the two `test()` overloads that are now hidden inside the `struct` helper, instead of being standalone non-member functions. Aside from better encapsulation, it makes no difference. Instead of any arguments specific to the problem at hand, the overloaded test functions take a dummy integer argument, zero, which is not used, but is needed to establish the precedence of the overloads (the variadic version is the overload of the last resort). The SFINAE test that may fail during the substitution is, as before, in the first expression inside the `decltype` operator of the *yes* (or *true*) `test()` overload. That expression is now

`std::declval<Lambda>()(std::declval<LambdaArgs>())`, so it uses `declval` and attempts to construct a reference to the specified `Lambda` and `LambdaArgs` types (without using the default constructor, which may or may not exist). `Lambda` is the type that comes from the template parameter of the `struct` helper. `LambdaArgs` is deduced by the `operator()` template member from its argument. Where is the call to that operator? Hold that thought, we'll get there. The `is_valid()` template function default-constructs and returns a callable object (an object with the `operator()` member function); that callable object is of type `is_valid_helper<Lambda>` where `Lambda` is the type of the lambda expression in the particular call to `is_valid()`; in our case it is `[](auto&& x) -> decltype(x = x) {}`. That type of the lambda expression is captured and used to instantiate the helper template, and it's the same `Lambda` type that ends up in the first overload of the `test()` function. The callable object is finally called with the variable; we want to test whether or not it is assignable. In our case, it's the `a` argument of the `my_function()` function—that's the `operator()` function finally getting called, which deduces the type of `a` and passes it to the `test()` overload to construct a reference to that type, so that it can be tested with the expression inside the specified lambda; in our case `x + x`, where `x` is substituted with `a`. Because of the overabundance of parentheses, it may help to better understand that last bit of code if we temporarily change the name of the member function from `operator()` to `f()`, and see where that `f()` comes out:

```
template <typename Lambda> struct is_valid_helper {
    ...
    // The callable
    template <typename LambdaArgs> constexpr auto f(const LambdaArgs&) {
        return this->test<LambdaArgs>(0);
    }
};
    ...
// And the call
static_assert(decltype(is_assignable.f(a))::value, "A is not assignable");
```

While there is nothing wrong with just keeping the name as `f()`, it serves no purpose, and callable objects are a very common C++ idiom.

Now that we have a very general hammer at our disposal, all conditional compilation problems start to look like nails. We can, for example, check if an object can be added:

```
auto is_addable = is_valid([](auto&& x) -> decltype(x + x) {});
```

We can also check whether it is a pointer-like object as follows:

```
auto is_pointer = is_valid([](auto&& x) -> decltype(*x) {});
```

The latter example is very instructive. It actually checks whether the `*p` expression is valid. The `p` object could be just a pointer, but it could also be any kind of smart pointer, for example, `std::shared_ptr`.

We can check if an object has a default constructor that we can call, although with some difficulty—we cannot declare a variable of the same type as x in the expression. We can test, for example, whether the `new X` expression is valid, where X is the type of x that we can get with `decltype`, except that `decltype` faithfully preserves every detail of the type, including the reference (the type of x captured by the lambda includes the `&&`). The reference has to be stripped as follows:

```
auto is_default_constructible =
    is_valid([](auto&& x) ->
        decltype(new typename std::remove_reference<decltype(x)>::type)
        {});

auto is_destructible =
    is_valid([](auto&& x) -> d
        decltype(delete (&x)) {});
```

The destruction test is easier—we can just invoke operator delete on the address of the object (note that actually running such code is highly inadvisable, as it is likely to deallocate some memory we didn't get from a `new` expression in the first place, but nothing is getting executed here—all of it is happening at compile time).

There is one last limitation to overcome—so far, our lambda expressions have only one argument. We can, of course, define a lambda with multiple arguments:

```
auto is_addable2 = is_valid([](auto&& x, auto&&y) -> decltype(x + y) {});
```

But this is not enough since we are going to call this lambda with one argument in our `struct` helper—we only have space for one, `LambdaArgs`. In case you did not get your fill of C++14, we now bring the last of the heavy guns to bear on the problem—`variadic` templates are in!

```
template <typename Lambda> struct is_valid_helper {
    template <typename... LambdaArgs>
    constexpr auto test(int) ->
        decltype(std::declval<Lambda>()(std::declval<LambdaArgs>()...),
                std::true_type())
    {
        return std::true_type();
    }

    template <typename... LambdaArgs>
    constexpr std::false_type test(...) {
        return std::false_type();
    }

    template <typename... LambdaArgs>
    constexpr auto operator()(const LambdaArgs& ...) {
        return this->test<LambdaArgs...>(0);
    }
};

template <typename Lambda> constexpr auto is_valid(const Lambda&) {
    return is_valid_helper<Lambda>();
}
```

We can now declare feature-checking objects with any number of arguments, such as our `is_addable2` argument in the preceding example.

In C++17, we don't need to explicitly specify the type of the helper template parameter inside `is_valid`:

```
template <typename Lambda> constexpr auto is_valid(const Lambda&) {
    return is_valid_helper();    // C++17 constructor type deduction here
}
```

Those of us who are still stuck in the dark ages before C++11 must feel pretty left out at this point. No lambdas, no variadic templates, no `decltype`—is there anything we can do to still use SFINAE? It turns out that there is, although the lack of variadic templates is hard to overcome and forces us to explicitly declare `is_valid` for one argument, two arguments, and so on. Also, without the convenient context to use SFINAE on the return type, and with the much shorter list of SFINAE contexts in C++03 to begin with, we have to find a safe place to try out our expressions without generating compilation errors. There is one such context, in the default arguments of template functions, but it has to be something that is evaluated at compile time. First, we show how an SFINAE test can be constructed without using any C++11 features:

```cpp
struct valid_check_passes { char c; };
struct valid_check_fails { valid_check_passes c; char c1; };

struct addable2 {
    // Unused last argument, triggers SFINAE
    template <typename T1, typename T2>
    valid_check_passes operator()(
        const T1& x1,
        const T2& x2,
        char (*a)[sizeof(x1 + x2)] = NULL);
    // Variadic overload
    template <typename T1, typename T2>
    valid_check_fails operator()(const T1& x1, const T2& x2, ...);
};

sizeof(addable2()(i, x, 0)) ==      // compile-time constant
    sizeof(valid_check_passes)
```

The compile-time `sizeof(addable2()(i, x, 0)) == sizeof(valid_check_passes)` constant expression can be used in any context where a compile-time constant is required; for example, in a template integer parameter for conditional compilation using template specializations.

To package this facility into something more or less reusable, we have to use macros:

```cpp
namespace IsValid {
struct check_passes { char c; };
struct check_fails { check_passes c; char c1; };
} // namespace IsValid

#define DEFINE_TEST2(NAME, EXPR) \
struct NAME { \
    template <typename T1, typename T2> \
    IsValid::check_passes operator()( \
        const T1& x1, \
```

```
        const T2& x2, \
        char (*a)[sizeof(EXPR)] = NULL); \
    template <typename T1, typename T2> \
    IsValid::check_fails operator()(const T1& x1, const T2& x2, ...); \
}

#define IS_VALID2(TEST, X1, X2) \
    sizeof(TEST()(X1, X2, 0)) == sizeof(IsValid::check_passes)
```

Note that the number of the arguments, 2, as well as their names, x1 and x2, are hard-coded into the macros. Now we can use these macros to define a compile-time check for addition:

```
DEFINE_TEST2(addable2, x1 + x2);
int i, j;
IS_VALID2(addable2, i, j)      // Evaluates to true at compile time
IS_VALID2(addable2, &i, &j)    // Evaluates to false at compile time
```

We have to define these macros for any number of arguments we wish to handle. Prior to C++11, this was the best we could do.

Summary

SFINAE is a somewhat esoteric feature of the C++ standard—it is complex and has many subtle details. While it is usually mentioned in the context of *manual control of the overload resolution*, its main purpose is actually not to enable very elaborate guru-level code, but to make the regular (automatic) overload resolution work the way the programmer intended. In this role, it usually works exactly as desired and with no additional effort—in fact, the programmer usually does not need to even be aware of this feature. Most of the time, when you write a generic overload and a special overload for the pointers, you expect the latter not to be called for types that are not pointers. Most of the time, you probably don't even pause to notice that the rejected overload would be ill-formed—who cares, it's not supposed to be used. But to find out that it's not supposed to be used, the type has to be substituted, which would result in invalid code. SFINAE breaks this chicken-and-egg problem—to find out that the overload should be rejected, we have to substitute types, but that would create code that should not compile, which should not be a problem, because the overload should be rejected in the first place, but we do not know that until we substitute the types, and so on.

Of course, we did not go through a few dozen pages just to learn that the compiler magically does the right thing and you don't have to worry about it. The more elaborate use of SFINAE is to create an artificial substitution failure, and thus take control of the overload resolution by removing some of the overloads. In this chapter, we learned the *safe* contexts for these *temporary* errors that are eventually suppressed by SFINAE. With careful application, this technique can be used to inspect and differentiate, at compile time, anything from the simple features of different types (*is this a class?*) to complex behaviors that can be provided by any number of C++ language features (*is there any way to add these two types?*).

The next chapter we will introduce another advanced template pattern that is used to greatly increase the power of class hierarchies in C++: class inheritance lets us pass information from the base class to the derived, and the Curiously Recurring Template Pattern does the opposite, it makes the base class aware of the derived.

Questions

1. What is overload set?
2. What is overload resolution?
3. What are type deduction and type substitution?
4. What is SFINAE?
5. In what contexts can potentially invalid code be present and not trigger a compilation error, unless that code is actually needed?
6. How can we determine which overload was chosen without actually calling it?
7. How is SFINAE used to control conditional compilation?

Further reading

- https://www.packtpub.com/application-development/c17-example
- https://www.packtpub.com/application-development/getting-started-c17-programming-video
- https://www.packtpub.com/application-development/mastering-c17-stl
- https://www.packtpub.com/application-development/c17-stl-cookbook

8
The Curiously Recurring Template Pattern

We are already familiar with the concepts of inheritance, polymorphism, and virtual functions. A derived class inherits from the base class and customizes the behavior of the base class by overriding its virtual functions. All operations are done on an instance of the base class, polymorphically. When the base object is actually an instance of the derived class, the right customized overrides are called. The base class knows nothing about the derived class, which may not even have been written when the base class code was written and compiled. The **Curiously Recurring Template Pattern (CRTP)** turns this well-ordered picture on its head, and inside out.

The following topics will be covered in this chapter:

- What is CRTP?
- What is static polymorphism and how does it differ from the dynamic polymorphism?
- What are the downsides of virtual function calls, and why may it be preferable to resolve such calls at compile time?
- What are other uses of CRTP?

Technical requirements

Google Benchmark library: `https://github.com/google/benchmark`

Example code: `https://github.com/PacktPublishing/Hands-On-Design-Patterns-with-CPP/tree/master/Chapter08`

Wrapping your head around CRTP

CRTP was first introduced, under this name, by James Coplien in 1995, in his article in *C++ Report*. It is a particular form of a more general bounded polymorphism (Peter S. Canning et al., *F-bounded polymorphism for object-oriented programming, Conference on Functional Programming Languages and Computer Architecture, 1989*). While not a general replacement for virtual functions, it provides the C++ programmer with a similar tool that, under the right circumstances, offers several advantages.

What is wrong with a virtual function?

Before we can talk about a *better* alternative to a virtual function, we should consider why we would want to have an alternative at all. What is not to like about virtual functions?

The problem is the performance overhead. A virtual function call can be several times more expensive than a non-virtual call, more for very simple functions that would have been inlined were they not virtual (recall that a virtual function can never be inlined). We can measure this difference with a microbenchmark, the ideal tool for measuring the performance of small fragments of code. There are many microbenchmark libraries and tools out there; in this book, we will use `Google Benchmark library`. To follow along with the examples in this chapter, you must first download and install the library (the detailed instructions can be found in `Chapter 5`, *A Comprehensive Look at RAII*). Then, you can compile and run the examples.

Now that we have the microbenchmark library ready, we can measure the overhead of a virtual function call. We are going to compare a very simple virtual function, with the minimum amount of code, against a non-virtual function doing the same thing. Here is our virtual function:

```
class B {
    public:
    B() : i_(0) {}
    virtual ~B() {}
    virtual void f(int i) = 0;
```

```
        int get() const { return i_; }
    protected:
        int i_;
};
class D : public B {
    public:
        void f(int i) { i_ += i; }
};
```

And, here is the equivalent non-virtual one:

```
class A {
    public:
        A() : i_(0) {}
        void f(int i) { i_ += i; }
        int get() const { return i_; }
    protected:
        int i_;
};
```

We can now call both of them in a micro-benchmark fixture and measure how long each call takes:

```
void BM_none(benchmark::State& state) {
    A* a = new A;
    int i = 0;
    for (auto _ : state) {
        a->f(++i);
    }
    benchmark::DoNotOptimize(a->get());
    delete a;
}

void BM_dynamic(benchmark::State& state) {
    B* b = new D;
    int i = 0;
    for (auto _ : state) {
        b->f(++i);
    }
    benchmark::DoNotOptimize(b->get());
    delete b;
}
```

The benchmark::DoNotOptimize wrapper prevents the compiler from optimizing away the unused object, and, along with it, renders the entire set of function calls as unnecessary. Note that there is a subtlety in measuring the virtual function call time; a simpler way to write the code would be to avoid new and delete operators and simply construct the derived object on the stack:

```
void BM_dynamic(benchmark::State& state) {
    D d;
    int i = 0;
    for (auto _ : state) {
        d.f(++i);
    }
    benchmark::DoNotOptimize(b->get());
}
```

However, this benchmark is likely to yield the same time as the non-virtual function call. The reason is not that a virtual function call has no overhead. Rather, in this code, the compiler is able to deduce that the call to the virtual function, f(), is always a call to D::f() (it helps that the call is not done through the base class pointer, but rather the derived class reference, so it could hardly be anything else). A decent optimizing compiler will de-virtualize such a call, for instance, generating a direct call to D::f() without the indirection and the reference to the *v-table*. Such a call can even be inlined.

Another possible complication is that both microbenchmarks, especially the non-virtual call, may be too fast—the body of the benchmark loop is likely to take less time than the overhead of the loop. We can remedy that by making several calls inside the body of the loop. This can be accomplished with the copy-paste feature of your editor, or with the C++ preprocessor macros:

```
#define REPEAT2(x) x x
#define REPEAT4(x)  REPEAT2(x)  REPEAT2(x)
#define REPEAT8(x)  REPEAT4(x)  REPEAT4(x)
#define REPEAT16(x)  REPEAT8(x)  REPEAT8(x)
#define REPEAT32(x)  REPEAT16(x)  REPEAT16(x)
#define REPEAT(x)  REPEAT32(x)
```

Now, inside the benchmark loop, we can write the following:

```
REPEAT(b->f(++i);)
```

The per-iteration time reported by the benchmark now refers to `32` function calls. While this does not matter for comparing the two calls, it may be convenient to make the benchmark itself report the true number of calls per second by adding this line to the end of the benchmark fixture, after the loop:

```
state.SetItemsProcessed(32*state.iterations());
```

We can now compare the results of the two benchmarks:

```
---------------------------------------------------------------
Benchmark              Time           CPU Iterations
---------------------------------------------------------------
BM_none                6 ns         6 ns  112876558    5.2072G items/s
BM_dynamic            52 ns        52 ns   13330215  592.541M items/s
```

We see that the virtual function call is almost 10 times more expensive than the non-virtual one. Note that this is not exactly a fair comparison; the virtual call provides additional functionality. However, some of this functionality can be implemented in other ways, without paying the performance overhead.

Introducing CRTP

Now, we will introduce CRTP, which turns inheritance on its head:

```
template <typename D> class B {
    ...
};
class D : public B<D> {
    ...
};
```

The first change that jumps out is that the base class is now a `class` template. The derived class still inherits from the base class, but now from the specific instantiation of the base class template—on its own! Class `B` is instantiated on class `D`, and class `D` inherits from that instantiation of class `B`, which is instantiated on class `D`, which inherits from class `B`, which... that's recursion in action. Get used to it because you will see it often in this chapter.

What is the motivation for this mind-twisting pattern? Consider that now the base class has compile-time information about the derived class. Therefore, what used to be a virtual function call can now be bound to the right function at compile time:

```
template <typename D> class B {
    public:
    B() : i_(0) {}
    void f(int i) { static_cast<D*>(this)->f(i); }
    int get() const { return i_; }
    protected:
    int i_;
};
class D : public B<D> {
    public:
    void f(int i) { i_ += i; }
};
```

The call itself can still be done on the base class pointer:

```
B<D>* b = ...;
b->f(5);
```

There is no indirection and no overhead for the virtual call. The compiler can, at compile time, track the call all the way to the actual function called, and even inline it:

```
void BM_static(benchmark::State& state) {
    B<D>* b = new D;
    int i = 0;
    for (auto _ : state) {
        REPEAT(b->f(++i);)
    }
    benchmark::DoNotOptimize(b->get());
    state.SetItemsProcessed(32*state.iterations());
}
```

The benchmark shows that the function call made through the CRTP takes exactly as much time as a regular function call:

Benchmark	Time	CPU	Iterations	
BM_none	6 ns	6 ns	114162238	5.26757G items/s
BM_dynamic	52 ns	52 ns	13353176	587.244M items/s
BM_static	6 ns	6 ns	119104189	5.16101G items/s

The main restriction on the CRTP is that the size of the base class, B, cannot depend on its template parameter, D. More generally, the template for class B has to instantiate with type D being an incomplete type. For example, this will not compile:

```
template <typename D> class B {
    typedef typename D::T T;
    T* p_;
};
class D : public B<D> {
    typedef int T;
};
```

The realization that this code will not compile may come somewhat as a surprise, given how similar it is to many widely used templates that refer to the nested types of their template parameters. For example, consider this template, which converts any sequence container with push_back() and pop_back() functions to a stack:

```
template <typename C> class stack {
    C c_;
    public:
    typedef typename C::value_type value_type;
    void push(const valuetype& v) { c.push_back(v); }
    value_type pop() { value_type v = c.back(); c.pop_back(); return v; }
};
stack<std::vector<int>> s;
```

Note that typedef for value_type looks exactly the same as the preceding one, in our attempt to declare class B. So, what is wrong with the one in B? Actually, nothing is wrong with class B itself. It would compile just fine in a context similar to that of our stack class:

```
class A {
    public:
    typedef int T;
    T x_;
};
B<A> b;          // Compiles with no problems
```

The problem lies not with class B itself, but with our intended use of it:

```
class D : public B<D> ...
```

At the point where B<D> has to be known, type D has not been declared yet. It cannot be—the declaration of class D requires us to know exactly what the base class B<D> is. So, if class D has not been declared yet, how does the compiler know that the identified D even refers to a type? After all, you cannot instantiate a template on a completely unknown type. The answer lies somewhere in between—class D is forward-declared, the same as if we had this code:

```
class A;
B<A> b;          // Now does not compile
```

Some templates can be instantiated on forward-declared types, while others cannot. The exact rules can be painstakingly gathered from the standard, but the gist is this—anything that might affect the size of the class has to be fully declared. A reference to a type declared inside an incomplete type, such as our `typedef typename D::T T`, would be a forward declaration of a nested class, and those are not allowed either.

On the other hand, the body of a member function of a class template is not instantiated until it's called. In fact, for a given template parameter, a member function does not even have to compile, as long as it's not called. Therefore, references to the derived class, its nested types, and its member functions, inside the member functions of the base class are perfectly fine. Also, since the derived class type is considered forward-declared inside the base class, we can declare pointers and references to it. Here is a very common refactoring of the CRTP base class that consolidates the uses of the static cast in one place:

```
template <typename D> class B {
    ...
    void f(int i) { derived()->f(i); }
    D* derived() { return static_cast<D*>(this); }
};
class D : public B<D> {
    ...
    void f(int i) { i_ += i; }
};
```

The base class declaration owns a pointer to the incomplete (forward-declared) type D. It works like any other pointer to an incomplete type; by the time the pointer is de-referenced, the type has to be complete. In our case, this happens inside the body of the member function; B::f(), which, as we discussed, is not compiled until it's called by the client code.

CRTP and static polymorphism

Since CRTP allows us to override base class functions with those of the derived class, it implements polymorphic behavior. The key difference is that polymorphism happens at compile time, not at runtime.

Compile-time polymorphism

As we have just seen, CRTP can be used to allow the derived class to customize the behavior of the base class:

```
template <typename D> class B {
    public:
    ...
    void f(int i) { static_cast<D*>(this)->f(i); }
    protected:
    int i_;
};
class D : public B<D> {
    public:
    void f(int i) { i_ += i; }
};
```

If the base class B::f() method is called, it dispatches the call to the derived class method for the real derived class, just like a virtual function does. Of course, in order to fully take advantage of this polymorphism, we have to be able to call the methods of the base class through the base class pointer. Without this ability, we are simply calling methods of the derived class whose type we already know:

```
D* d = ...;         // Get an object of type D
d->f(5);
B<D>* b = ...;      // Also has to be an object of type D
b->f(5);
```

Note that the function call looks exactly like any virtual function class, with the base class pointer. The actual function, f(), that is called comes from the derived class, D::f(). There is, however, a significant difference—the actual type of the derived class, D, has to be known at compile time—the base class pointer is not B* but rather B<D>*, which implies that the derived object is of type D. There does not seem to be much point to such *polymorphism* if the programmer has to know the actual type. But, that is because we have not fully thought through what *compile-time polymorphism* really means. Just as the benefit of the virtual function is that we can call member functions of a type we don't even know exists, the same has to be true for the *static polymorphism* to be useful.

How do we write a function that has to compile for parameters of an unknown type? With a function template, of course:

```
template <typename D> void apply(B<D>* b, int& i) {
    b->f(++i);
}
```

This is a template function that can be called on any base class pointer, and it automatically deduces the type of the derived class, D. Now, we can write what looks like regular polymorphic code:

```
B<D>* b = new D;          // 1
apply(b);                 // 2
```

Note that, on line one, the object has to be constructed with the knowledge of the actual type. This is always the case; the same is true for regular runtime polymorphism with virtual functions:

```
void apply(B* b) { ... }
B* b = new D;             // 1
apply(b);                // 2
```

In both cases, on line two, we invoke some code that was written only with the knowledge of the base class.

The compile-time pure virtual function

What would be the equivalent of the pure virtual function in this scenario? A pure virtual function must be implemented in all derived classes; a class that declares a pure virtual function, or inherits one and does not override it, is an abstract class; it can be further derived from, but it cannot be instantiated.

When we contemplate the equivalent of a pure virtual function for static polymorphism, we realize that our CRTP implementation suffers from a major vulnerability. What happens if we forget to override the *compile-time virtual function,* f(), in one of the derived classes?

```
template <typename D> class B {
    public:
    ...
    void f(int i) { static_cast<D*>(this)->f(i); }
};
class D : public B<D> {
    // no f() here!
};
...
```

```
B<D>* b = ...;
b->f(5);                    // 1
```

This code compiles with no errors or warnings—on line one, we call `B::f()`, which, in turn, calls `D::f()`. Class `D` does not declare its own version of the member `f()`, so the one inherited from the base class is the one that is called. That is, of course, the member function, `B::f()`, that we have already seen, which again calls `D::f()`, which is really `B::f()` ... and we have an infinite loop.

The problem here is that nothing requires us to override the member function `f()` in the derived class, but the program is malformed if we don't. The root of the problem is that we are mixing together the interface and the implementation—the public member function declaration in the base class says that all derived classes must have a function, `void f(int)`, as a part of their public interface. The derived class's version of the same function provides the actual implementation. We have covered the separating of interface and the implementation in Chapter 14, *The Template Method Pattern and the Non-Virtual Idiom*, but for now, suffice it to say that our life would be a lot easier if these functions had different names:

```
template <typename D> class B {
    public:
    ...
    void f(int i) { static_cast<D*>(this)->f_impl(i); }
};
class D : public B<D> {
    void f_impl(int i) { i_ += i; }
};
...
B<D>* b = ...;
b->f(5);
```

What happens now if we forget to implement `D::f_impl()`? The code does not compile, because there is no such member function in class `D`, either directly or through inheritance. So, we have implemented a compile-time pure virtual function! Note that the virtual function is actually `f_impl()`, not `f()`.

With that accomplished, how would we implement a regular virtual function, with a default implementation that can be optionally overridden? If we follow the same pattern of separating the interface and the implementation, we only have to provide the default implementation for `B::f_impl()`:

```
template <typename D> class B {
    public:
    ...
    void f(int i) { static_cast<D*>(this)->f_impl(i); }
```

```
        void f_impl(int i) {}
};
class D : public B<D> {
    void f_impl(int i) { i_ += i; }
};
class D1 : public B<D1> {
    // No f() here
};
...
B<D>* b = ...;
b->f(5);        // Calls D::f()
B<D1>* b1 = ...;
b1->f(5);       // Calls B::f() by default
```

Destructors and polymorphic deletion

So far, we have willfully avoided tackling the issue of deleting objects implemented with CRTP in some sort of polymorphic fashion. In fact, if you go back and re-read the examples that presented complete code, such as the benchmark fixture, BM_static, in the *Introducing CRTP* section, we either avoided deleting the object altogether or constructed a derived object on the stack. This is because polymorphic deletion presents an additional complication that we are finally ready to deal with.

First of all, let's note that, in many cases, polymorphic deletion is not a concern. All objects are created with their actual types known. If the code that constructs the objects also owns and eventually deletes them, the question *What is the type of the deleted object?* is never really asked. Similarly, if the objects are stored in a container, they are not deleted through the base class pointer or reference:

```
template <typename D> void apply(B<D>& b) { ... operate on b ... }
{
    std::vector<D> v;
    v.push_back(D(...));        // Objects created as D
    ...
    apply(v[0]);                // Objects processed as B&
}                               // Objects deleted as D
```

In many cases, as in the preceding example, the objects are constructed and deleted with their actual type known and no polymorphism involved, but the code that works on them in between is universal, written to work on the base type and, therefore, any class derived from that base type.

But, what if we need to actually delete the object through the base class pointer? Well, that is not easy. First of all, the simple call to the `delete` operator will do the wrong thing:

```
B<D>* b = new D;
...
delete b;
```

This code compiles. Worse, even the compilers that normally warn when a class has a virtual function but a non-virtual destructor do not generate any warnings in this case, because there are no virtual functions, and CRTP polymorphism is not recognized by the compiler as a potential source of trouble. However, the trouble there is that only the destructor of the base class, `B<D>`, itself is called; the destructor of `D` is never called!

You may be tempted to resolve this problem the same way as we deal with other *compile-time virtual* functions, by casting to the known derived type and calling the indented member function of the derived class:

```
template <typename D> class B {
    public:
    ~B() { static_cast<D*>(this)->~D(); }
};
```

Unlike the regular functions, this attempt at polymorphism is badly broken, for not one but two reasons—first of all, in the destructor of the base class, the actual object is not of the derived type anymore, and calling any member functions of the derived class on it results in undefined behavior. Secondly, even if this somehow worked, the destructor of the derived class is going to do its work and then call the destructor of the base class, which results in an infinite loop.

There are two solutions to this problem. One option is to extend the compile-time polymorphism to the act of deletion in the same way as we do for any other operation, with a function template:

```
template <typename D> void destroy(B<D>* b) { delete static_cast<D*>(b); }
```

This is well-defined. The `delete` operator is called on the pointer of the actual type, `D`, and the right destructor is called. However, you must take care to always delete these objects using this `destroy()` function, instead of calling the `delete` operator.

The second option is to actually make the destructor virtual. This does bring back the overhead of the virtual function call, but only for the destructor. It also increases the object size by the size of the virtual pointer. If neither of these two sources of overhead is a concern, you could use this hybrid static-dynamic polymorphism, where all virtual function calls are bound at compile time and with no overhead, except the destructor.

CRTP and access control

When implementing CRTP classes, you do have to worry about access—any method you want to call has to be accessible. Either the method has to be public, or the caller has to have special access. This is a little different from the way virtual functions are called—when calling a virtual function, the caller must have access to the member function that is named in the call. For example, a call to the base class function, B::f(), requires that either B::f() is public or the caller has access to non-public member functions (another member function of class B can call B::f() even if it's private). Then, if B::f() is virtual and overridden by the derived class, D, the override, D::f(), is actually called at **runtime**. There is no requirement that D::f() be accessible from the original call site; for example, D::f() can be private.

The situation with CRTP polymorphic calls is somewhat different. All calls are explicit in the code, and the callers must have access to the functions they call. Usually, it means that the base class must have access to the member functions of the derived class. Consider the following example from an earlier section, but now with explicit access control:

```
template <typename D> class B {
    public:
    ...
    void f(int i) { static_cast<D*>(this)->f_impl(i); }
    private:
    void f_impl(int i) {}
};
class D : public B<D> {
    private:
    void f_impl(int i) { i_ += i; }
    friend class B<D>;
};
```

Here, both functions, `B::f_impl()` and `D::f_impl()`, are private in their respective classes. The base class has no special access to the derived class, and cannot call its private member functions. Unless we want to change the member function, `D::f_impl()`, from private to public and allow any caller access to it, we have to declare the base class to be a friend of the derived class.

There is also some benefit in doing the reverse. Let's create a new derived class, `D1`, with a different override of the implementation function, `f_impl()`:

```
class D1 : public B<D> {
    private:
    void f_impl(int i) { i_ -= i; }
    friend class B<D1>;
};
```

This class has a subtle error—it is not actually derived from `D1` but from the old class, `D`; a mistake that is easy to make when creating a new class from an old template. This mistake will be found if we attempt to use the class polymorphically:

```
B<D1>* b = new D1;
```

This does not compile because `B<D1>` is not a base class of `D1`. However, not all uses of CRTP involve a polymorphic call. In any case, it would be better if the error was caught when class `D1` was first declared. We can accomplish that by making class `B` into a sort of abstract class, only in the sense of static polymorphism. All it takes is to make the constructor of class `B` private and to declare the derived class to be a friend:

```
template <typename D> class B {
    int i_;
    B() : i_(0) {}
    friend D;
    public:
    void f(int i) { static_cast<D*>(this)->f_impl(i); }
    private:
    void f_impl(int i) {}
};
```

Note the somewhat unusual form of the friend declaration—`friend D` and not `friend class D`. This is how you write a friend declaration for the template parameter. Now, the only type that can construct an instance of class `B<D>` is that specific derived class, `D`, which is used as the template parameter, and the erroneous code, `class D1 : public B<D>`, does not compile any longer.

CRTP as a delegation pattern

So far, we have used CRTP as a compile-time equivalent of dynamic polymorphism, including virtual-like calls through the base pointer (compile-time, of course, with a template function). This is not the only way CRTP can be used. In fact, more often than not, the function is called directly on the derived class. This is a very fundamental difference—typically, public inheritance expresses the *is-a* relationship—the derived object is a kind of a base object. The interface and the generic code are in the base class, while the derived class overrides the specific implementation. This relation continues to hold when a CRTP object is accessed through the base class pointer or reference. Such use of CRTP is sometimes also called **static interface**.

When the derived object is used directly, the situation is quite different—the base class is no longer the interface, and the derived class is not just the implementation. The derived class expands the interface of the base class, and the base class delegates some of its behavior to the derived class.

Expanding the interface

Let's consider several examples where CRTP is used to delegate behavior from the base class to the derived one.

The first example is a very simple one—for any class that provides `operator==()`, we want to generate `operator!=()` automatically as the inverse of the former:

```
template <typename D> struct not_equal {
    bool operator!=(const D& rhs) const {
        return !static_cast<const D*>(this)->operator==(rhs);
    }
};

class C : public not_equal<C> {
    int i_;
    public:
    C(int i) : i_(i) {}
    bool operator==(const C& rhs) const { return i_ == rhs.i_; }
};
```

Any class that inherits from `not_equal` in this manner automatically acquires the *not equal* operator that is guaranteed to match the provided operator, *equal*. An observant reader might point out that the way we have declared the operators `==` and `!=` here is, well, strange. Aren't they supposed to be non-member functions? Indeed, they usually are. Nothing in the standard requires them to be, and the preceding code is technically valid. The reason binary operators such as `==`, `+`, and so on are usually declared as non-member functions has to do with implicit conversions—if we have a comparison, `x == y`, and the intended `operator==` is a member function, it has to be a member function of the x object. Not any object implicitly convertible to the type of x, but x itself—it's a member function call on x. In contrast, the y object has to be implicitly convertible to the type of the argument of that member `operator==`, usually, the same type as x. To restore the symmetry and allow implicit conversions (if any are provided) on both the left-and right-hand side of the `==` sign, we have to declare `operator==` as a non-member function. Usually, such a function needs to have access to the private data members of the class, as in the example previously, so it has to be declared a friend. Putting all of the above together, we arrive at this alternative implementation:

```
template <typename D> struct not_equal {
    friend bool operator!=(const D& lhs, const D& rhs) {
        return !(lhs == rhs);
    }
};

class C : public not_equal<C> {
    int i_;
    public:
    C(int i) : i_(i) {}
    friend bool operator==(const C& lhs, const C& rhs) {
        return lhs.i_ == rhs.i_;
    }
};
```

Note that this implementation of `not_equal` will work fine even if the derived class provides the `operator==` as a member function (with the preceding clarification of the difference in implicit conversions in mind).

There is a significant difference between this use of CRTP and the one we saw earlier—the object that is going to be used in the program is of type C, and it will never be accessed through a pointer to `not_equal<C>`. The latter isn't a complete interface for anything but is really an implementation that makes use of the interface provided by the derived class.

A similar but slightly more complete example is an object registry. It may be desirable, often for debugging purposes, to know how many objects of a certain type are currently in existence, and perhaps even to maintain a list of such objects. We definitely do not want to instrument every class with the registry mechanism, so we want to move it to the base class. But, now we have a problem—if we have two derived classes, C and D, both inherit from the same base class, B, and the count of instances of B will be the total for both C and D. The problem is not that the base class can't determine what the real type of the derived class is—it can, if we're willing to pay the cost of runtime polymorphism. The problem is that the base class has only one counter (or however many are coded in the class), while the number of different derived classes is unlimited. We could implement a very complex, expensive, and non-portable solution that uses **Run-Time Type Information (RTTI)**, such as typeid, to determine the class name and maintain a map of names and counters. But, what we really need is one counter per derived type, and the only way to do it is to make the base class aware of the derived class type at compile time. This brings us back to CRTP:

```
template <typename D> class registry {
    public:
    static size_t count;
    static D* head;
    D* prev;
    D* next;
    protected:
    registry() {
        ++count;
        prev = nullptr;
        next = head;
        head = static_cast<D*>(this);
        if (next) next->prev = head;
    }
    registry(const registry&) {
        ++count;
        prev = nullptr;
        next = head;
        head = static_cast<D*>(this);
        if (next) next->prev = head;
    }
    ~registry() {
        --count;
        if (prev) prev->next = next;
        if (next) next->prev = prev;
        if (head == this) head = next;
    }

};
template <typename D> size_t registry<D>::count(0);
template <typename D> D* registry<D>::head(nullptr);
```

We have declared the constructor, and the destructor protected because we don't want any registry objects created, except by the derived classes. It is also important to not forget the copy constructor, otherwise the default one is generated by the compiler, and it does not increment the counter or update the list (but the destructor does, so the counter will go negative and overflow). For each derived class, D, the base class is registry<D>, which is a separate type with its own static data members, count and head (the latter is the head of the list of currently active objects). Any type that needs to maintain the runtime registry of active objects now only needs to inherit from registry:

```
class C : public registry<C> {
    int i_;
    public:
    C(int i) : i_(i) {}
};
```

A similar example, where the base class needs to know the type of the derived class and use it to declare its own members, can be found in Chapter 9, *Named Arguments and Method Chaining*.

Another scenario where it is often necessary to delegate behavior to derived classes is the problem of visitation. Visitors, in a general sense, are objects that are invoked to process a collection of data objects and execute a function on each one in turn. Often, there are hierarchies of visitors, where the derived classes customize or alter some aspect of the behavior of the base classes. While the most common implementation of visitors uses dynamic polymorphism and virtual function calls, a static visitor offers the same sort of performance benefits we saw earlier. Visitors are not usually invoked polymorphically; you create the visitor you want and run it. The base visitor class, however, does call the member functions that may be dispatched, at compile time, to the derived classes if they have the right overrides. Consider this generic visitor for a collection of animals:

```
struct Animal {
    public:
    enum Type { CAT, DOG, RAT };
    Animal(Type t, const char* n) : type(t), name(n) {}
    const Type type;
    const char* const name;
};

template <typename D> class GenericVisitor {
    public:
    template <typename it> void visit(it from, it to) {
        for (it i = from; i != to; ++i) {
            this->visit(*i);
        }
    }
}
```

```
    private:
    D& derived() { return *static_cast<D*>(this); }
    void visit(const Animal& animal) {
        switch (animal.type) {
            case Animal::CAT:
                derived().visit_cat(animal);
                break;
            case Animal::DOG:
                derived().visit_dog(animal);
                break;
            case Animal::RAT:
                derived().visit_rat(animal);
                break;
        }
    }
    void visit_cat(const Animal& animal) {
        std::cout << "Feed the cat " << animal.name << std::endl;
    }
    void visit_dog(const Animal& animal) {
        std::cout << "Wash the dog " << animal.name << std::endl;
    }
    void visit_rat(const Animal& animal) {
        std::cout << "Eeek!" << std::endl;
    }
    friend D;
    GenericVisitor() {}
};
```

Note that the main visitation method is a template member function (a template within a template!), and it accepts any kind of iterator that can iterate over a sequence of `Animal` objects. Also, by declaring a private default constructor at the bottom of the class, we are protecting ourselves from making a mistake where the derived class incorrectly specifies its own type for the inheritance. Now, we can start creating some visitors. The default visitor simply accepts the default actions provided by the generic visitor:

```
class DefaultVisitor : public GenericVisitor<DefaultVisitor> {
};
```

We can visit any sequence of `Animal` objects, for example, a vector:

```
std::vector<Animal> animals {{Animal::CAT, "Fluffy"},
                             {Animal::DOG, "Fido"},
                             {Animal::RAT, "Stinky"}};
DefaultVisitor().visit(animals.begin(), animals.end());
```

The visitation yields the expected result:

```
Feed the cat Fluffy
Wash the dog Fido
Eeek!
```

But, we don't have to constrain ourselves to the default actions—we can override the visitation actions for one or more animal types:

```cpp
class TrainerVisitor : public GenericVisitor<TrainerVisitor> {
    friend class GenericVisitor<TrainerVisitor>;
    void visit_dog(const Animal& animal) {
        std::cout << "Train the dog " << animal.name << std::endl;
    }
};

class FelineVisitor : public GenericVisitor<FelineVisitor> {
    friend class GenericVisitor<FelineVisitor>;
    void visit_cat(const Animal& animal) {
        std::cout << "Hiss at the cat " << animal.name << std::endl;
    }
    void visit_dog(const Animal& animal) {
        std::cout << "Hiss at the dog " << animal.name << std::endl;
    }
    void visit_rat(const Animal& animal) {
        std::cout << "Eat the rat " << animal.name << std::endl;
    }
};
```

When a dog trainer chooses to visit our animals, we use `TrainerVisitor`:

```
Feed the cat Fluffy
Train the dog Fido
Eeek!
```

Finally, a visiting cat would have a set of actions all of its own:

```
Hiss at the cat Fluffy
Hiss at the dog Fido
Eat the rat Stinky
```

We will learn a lot more about different kinds of Visitors later, in `Chapter 18`, *The Visitor Pattern and Multiple Dispatch*.

Summary

We have examined a rather convoluted design pattern that combines both sides of C++—generic programming (templates) and object-oriented programming (inheritance). True to its name, the Curiously Recurring Template Pattern creates a circular loop, where the derived class inherits the interface and the implementation from the base class, while the base class has access to the interface of the derived class through the template parameters. CRTP has two main use modes—true static polymorphism, or *static interface*, where the object is primarily accessed as the base type, and expanding the interface, or delegation, where the derived class is accessed directly but the implementation uses CRTP to provide common functionality.

The next chapter introduces an idiom that makes use of the pattern we have just learned. This idiom also changes the standard way we pass arguments to functions, in order of the parameters, and lets us have order-independent named arguments instead. Read on to find out how!

Questions

- How expensive is a virtual function call, and why?
- Why does a similar function call, resolved at compile time, have no such performance overhead?
- How would you make compile-time polymorphic function calls?
- How would you use CRTP to expand the interface of the base class?

Named Arguments and Method Chaining

In this chapter, we are going to examine a solution to a very common C++ problem, too many arguments. No, we are not talking about the arguments between C++ programmers, such as whether to put curly braces at the end of the line or at the start of the next one (we have no solution to that problem). This is the problem of C++ functions with too many arguments. If you have maintained a large C++ system long enough, you have seen it—functions start with simple declarations and, over time, grow additional arguments, often defaulted, to support new features.

The following topics will be covered in this chapter:

- What are the problems with long function declarations?
- What is the alternative?
- What are the downsides of using the named arguments idiom?
- How can the named arguments idiom be generalized?

Technical requirements

Here is the example code: https://github.com/PacktPublishing/Hands-On-Design-Patterns-with-CPP/tree/master/Chapter09.

Here is the Google Benchmark library: https://github.com/google/benchmark (see Chapter 4, *Swap – From Simple to Subtle*, for installation instructions).

The problem with arguments

Everyone who has worked on a sufficiently large C++ system at some point has had to add arguments to a function. To avoid breaking the existing code, the new argument is often given a default value's which usually retains the old functionality. That works great the first time, is OK the second time, and then one has to start counting arguments on every function call. There are other problems with long function declarations as well, and if we want a better solution, it is worth our time to understand what they are before trying to solve them. We begin this section with a more in-depth analysis of the problem before moving on to the solution.

What's wrong with many arguments

Whether the code that passes around a lot of arguments was written this way from the start or has grown *organically*, it is fragile and vulnerable to programmer mistakes. The main problem is that there are, usually, many arguments of the same type, and they can be miscounted. Consider designing a civilization-building game—when a player creates a new city, a corresponding object is constructed. The player gets to choose what facilities to build in the city, and the game sets the options for available resources:

```cpp
class City {
    public:
    enum center_t { KEEP, PALACE, CITADEL };
    City(size_t number_of_buildings,
         size_t number_of_towers,
         size_t guard_strength,
         center_t center,
         bool with_forge,
         bool with_granary,
         bool has_fresh_water,
         bool is_coastal,
         bool has_forest);
    ...
};
```

It looks like we have taken care of everything. To start the game, let's give each player a city with a keep, a guard tower, two buildings, and a guard company:

```cpp
City Capital(2, 1, 1, City::KEEP, false, false, false, false);
```

Can you see the mistake? The compiler, fortunately, can—not enough arguments. Since the compiler won't let us make a mistake here, this is no big deal, we just need to add the argument for `has_forest`. Also, let's say the game placed the city near a river, so it has water now:

```
City Capital(2, 1, 1, City::KEEP, false, true, false, false, false);
```

That was easy ... oops. We now have the city on the river but without fresh water (just what is in that river?). At least the townsfolk won't starve, thanks to the free granary they accidentally received. That error—where the `true` value was passed to the wrong parameter—will have to be found during debugging. Also, this code is quite verbose, and we may find ourselves typing the same values over and over. Maybe the game tries to place cities near the rivers and forests by default? OK then:

```
class City {
    public:
    enum center_t { KEEP, PALACE, CITADEL };
    City(size_t number_of_buildings,
         size_t number_of_towers,
         size_t guard_strength,
         center_t center,
         bool with_forge,
         bool with_granary,
         bool has_fresh_water = true,
         bool is_coastal = false,
         bool has_forest = true);
    ...
};
```

Now, let's go back to our first attempt to create a city—it now compiles, one argument short, and we are none the wiser that we miscounted the arguments. The game is a great success, and, in the next update, we get an exciting new building—a temple! We need to add a new argument to the constructor, of course. It makes sense to add it after `with_granary`, with all the other buildings and before the terrain features. But then we have to edit every call to the `City` constructor. What is worse, it is very easy to make a mistake since the `false` for *no temple* looks, to both the programmer and the compiler, exactly like the `false` for *no fresh water*. The new argument has to be inserted in the right place, in a long line of very similarly-looking values.

Of course, the existing game code works without temples, so they are only needed in the new updated code. There is some value in not disturbing existing code unless necessary. We could do that if we added the new argument at the end and gave it the default value, so any constructor call that was not changed still creates the exact same city as before:

```cpp
class City {
    public:
    enum center_t { KEEP, PALACE, CITADEL };
    City(size_t number_of_buildings,
        size_t number_of_towers,
        size_t guard_strength,
        center_t center,
        bool with_forge,
        bool with_granary,
        bool has_fresh_water = true,
        bool is_coastal = false,
        bool has_forest = true,
        bool with_temple = false);
    ...
};
```

But now, we let short-term convenience dictate our long-term interface design. The parameters no longer have at least a logical grouping, and in the long run, mistakes are even more likely. Also, we did not fully solve the problem of not updating the code that does not need to change—the next release adds a new terrain, desert, and with it, another argument:

```cpp
class City {
    public:
    enum center_t { KEEP, PALACE, CITADEL };
    City(size_t number_of_buildings,
        size_t number_of_towers,
        size_t guard_strength,
        center_t center,
        bool with_forge,
        bool with_granary,
        bool has_fresh_water = true,
        bool is_coastal = false,
        bool has_forest = true,
        bool with_temple = false,
        bool is_desert = false);
    ...
};
```

Once started, we have to give default values to all new arguments added at the end. Also, in order to create a city in the desert, we also have to specify whether it has the temple. There is no logical reason why it has to be this way, but we are bound by the process in which the interface evolved. The situation gets even worse when you consider that many types we used are convertible to each other:

```
City Capital(2, 1, false, City::KEEP, false, true, false, false, false);
```

This creates a city with zero guard companies and not whatever the programmer expected to disable when he set the third argument to `false`. Even `enum` types do not offer full protection. You probably noticed that all new cities usually start as a keep, so it would make sense to have that as default as well:

```cpp
class City {
    public:
    enum center_t { KEEP, PALACE, CITADEL };
    City(size_t number_of_buildings,
         size_t number_of_towers,
         size_t guard_strength,
         center_t center = KEEP,
         bool with_forge = false,
         bool with_granary = false,
         bool has_fresh_water = true,
         bool is_coastal = false,
         bool has_forest = true,
         bool with_temple = false,
         bool is_desert = false);
    ...
};
```

Now, we don't have to type as many arguments and might even avoid some mistakes (if you don't write arguments, you can't write them in the wrong order). But, we can make new ones:

```
City Capital(2, 1, City::CITADEL);
```

The two guard companies we just hired (because the numerical value of `CITADEL` is 2) will find themselves quite short on space in the lowly keep (which we intended to change but did not). The `enum class` of C++11 offers better protection since each one is a different type without conversions to integers, but the overall problem remains. As we have seen, there are two problems with passing a lot of values to C++ functions as separate arguments. First, it creates very long declarations and function calls that are error-prone. Second, if we need to add a value or change the type of a parameter, there is a lot of code to be edited. The solution to both problems existed even before C++ was created; it comes from C—use aggregates—that is, structs—to combine many values into one parameter.

Aggregate parameters

With aggregate parameters, we create a struct or a class that contains all the values, instead of adding one parameter per value. We don't have to be limited to one aggregate; for example, our city may take several structs, one for all terrain-related features that the game sets, and another for all features that the player controls directly:

```cpp
struct city_features_t {
    size_t number_of_buildings;
    size_t number_of_towers;
    size_t guard_strength;
    enum center_t { KEEP, PALACE, CITADEL };
    center_t center = KEEP;
    bool with_forge = false;
    bool with_granary = false;
    bool with_temple;
};
struct terrain_features_t {
    bool has_fresh_water;
    bool is_coastal;
    bool has_forest;
    bool is_desert;
};
class City {
    public:
    City(city_features_t city_features, terrain_features_t
terrain_features);
    ...
};
```

This solution has many advantages. First of all, assigning values to the arguments has to be done explicitly, by name, and is very visible:

```cpp
city_features_t city_features;
city_features.number_of_buildings = 2;
city_features.center = city_features::KEEP;
...
terrain_features_t terrain_features;
terrain_features.has_fresh_water = true;
...
City Capital(city_features, terrain_features);
```

It is much easier to see what each argument's value is, and mistakes are much less likely. If we need to add a new feature, most of the time we just have to add a new data member to one of the aggregate types. Only the code that actually deals with the new argument has to be updated; all the functions and classes that simply pass the arguments and forward them do not need to change at all. We can even give the aggregate types default constructors to provide default values for all arguments:

```
struct terrain_features_t {
    bool has_fresh_water;
    bool is_coastal;
    bool has_forest;
    bool is_desert;
    terrain_features_t() :
        has_fresh_water(true),
        is_coastal(false),
        has_forest(true),
        is_desert(false)
    {}
};
```

This is, overall, an excellent solution to the problem of functions with many parameters. However, it has one drawback: the aggregates have to be explicitly created and initialized, line by line. This works out fine for many cases, especially when these classes and structs represent state variables that we are going to keep for a long time. But, when used purely as parameter containers, they create unnecessarily verbose code, starting from the fact that the aggregate variable must have a name. We don't really need that name, as we are going to use it only once to call the function, but we have to make one up. It would be tempting just to use a temporary variable:

```
City Capital(city_features_t() ... arguments somehow go here? ... );
```

This would work if we could assign the values to the data members. We could do it with a constructor:

```
struct terrain_features_t {
    bool has_fresh_water;
    bool is_coastal;
    bool has_forest;
    bool is_desert;
    terrain_features_t(
        bool has_fresh_water,
        bool is_coastal,
        bool has_forest,
        bool is_desert
    ) :
        has_fresh_water(has_fresh_water),
```

```
            is_coastal(is_coastal),
            has_forest(has_forest),
            is_desert(is_desert)
        {}
    };

    City Capital(city_features_t(...),
                 terrain_features_t(true, false, false, true));
```

This works, but it brings us full circle, right to where we started; a function with a long list of easily mixed Boolean arguments. The fundamental problem we encounter is that C++ functions have positional arguments, and we are trying to come up with something that would let us specify arguments by name. Aggregate objects resolve this problem mostly as a side effect, and if the overall design benefits from collecting a group of values into one class, you should certainly do it. However, as a solution specifically for the problem of named arguments, with no other, more permanent reason to group the values together, they fall short. We will now see how this deficiency can be addressed.

Named arguments in C++

We have seen how collecting logically related values into aggregate objects gives us the side benefit; we can pass these values to functions and access them by name instead of by their order in a long list. The key is *logically related,* though; aggregating values for no reason other than they happen to be used together in one function call creates unnecessary objects with names we would rather not have to invent. We need a way to create temporary aggregates, preferably without explicit names or declarations. We have a solution to this problem, and had it for a long time in C++; all it needs is a fresh look from a different perspective, which we are about to take now.

Method chaining

Method chaining is a borrowed C++ technique; it originates in **Smalltalk**. Its main purpose is to eliminate unnecessary local variables. You have used method chaining already, although you may not have realized it. Consider this code that you have probably written many times:

```
int i, j;
std::cout << i << j;
```

The last line invoked the inserter operator << twice. The first time it is invoked on the object on the left-hand side of the operator, `std::cout`. What object is the second call on? In general, the operator syntax is just a way to call a function named `operator<<()`. Usually, this particular operator is a non-member function, but the `std::ostream` class has several member function overloads as well, and one of them is for `int` values. So, the last line really is this:

```
std::cout.operator(i).operator<<(j);
```

The second call to `operator<<()` is done on the result of the first one. The equivalent C++ code is this:

```
auto& out1 = std::cout.operator(i);
out1.operator<<(j);
```

This is the method chaining—the call to one method function returns the object on which the next method should be called. In the case of `std::cout`, the member `operator<<()` returns a reference to the object itself. By the way, the non-member `operator<<()` does the same, only instead of the implicit argument `this`, it has the stream object as an explicit first argument (the difference will become much less visible in C++20 because of the universal calling syntax).

Now, we can use method chaining to eliminate the explicitly named argument object.

Method chaining and named arguments

As we have seen before, the aggregate argument objects work well when they are not used mainly to hold arguments; if we need an object to hold the state of the system, and we build it over time and keep it for a long time, we can also pass this object as a single argument to any function that needs this state. It's creating aggregates for just one function call that we have a problem with. On the other hand, we do not like to write functions with many arguments either. This is particularly true for functions that usually have most arguments left as default, with only a few changes. Going back to our game, let's say that each day, game time, is processed by a function call.

The function is called, once per game day, to advance the city through the day and process the consequences of various random events the game can generate:

```
class City {
    ...
    void day(bool flood = false, bool fire = false,
            bool revolt = false, bool exotic_caravan = false,
            bool holy_vision = false, bool festival = false, ... );
    ...
};
```

A lot of different events can happen over time, but rarely more than one happens on any particular day. We set all arguments to false by default, but this does not really help; there is no particular order to these events, and if the festival happens, all the previous arguments must be specified even though they are still equal to their default values.

An aggregate object helps a lot, but we need to create and name it:

```
class City {
    ...
    struct DayEvents {
        bool flood;
        bool fire;
        ...
        DayEvents() : flood(false), fire(false) ,,, {}
    };
    void day(DayEvents events);
    ...
};

City capital(...);
City::DayEvents events;
events.fire = true;
capital.day(events);
```

We would like to create a temporary `DayEvents` object just for the call to `City::day()`, but we need a way to set its data members. This is where method chaining comes in:

```
class City {
    ...
    class DayEvents {
        public:
        DayEvents() : flood(false), fire(false) ,,, {}
        DayEvents& SetFlood() { flood = true; return *this; }
        DayEvents& SetFire() { fire = true; return *this; }
        ...
        private:
```

```
        friend City;
        bool flood;
        bool fire;
        ...
    };
    void day(DayEvents events);
    ...
};

City capital(...);
capital.day(City::DayEvents().SetFire());
```

The default constructor constructs an unnamed temporary object. On that object, we invoke the SetFire() method. It modifies the object and returns a reference to itself. We pass the created and modified temporary object to the day() function, which processes the events of the day, displays the updated graphics of the city in flames, plays the sound of fire, and updates the status of the city to reflect that some buildings were damaged by fire.

Since each of the Set() methods return a reference to the same object, we can invoke more than one in a method chain, to specify multiple events. Also, the Set() methods can take arguments, of course; for example, instead of SetFire() that always changes the fire event to true from its default false, we could have a method that can set the event flag either way:

```
DayEvents& SetFire(bool value = true) { fire = value; return *this; }
```

Today is the market day in our city, which coincides with a major festival, so the king hired an extra guard company in addition to the two already stationed in the city:

```
City capital(...);
capital.day(City::DayEvents().SetMarket().SetFestival().SetGuard(3));
```

Note that we did not have to specify anything for all the events that did not happen. We now have true named arguments; when we call a function, we pass the arguments in any order, by name, and we do not need to explicitly mention any arguments we wish to leave at their default values. This is the C++ named arguments idiom. A call with named arguments is, of course, more verbose than a call with positional arguments; each argument must have the name explicitly written. That was the point of the exercise. On the other hand, we come out ahead if there is a long list of default arguments we did not have to change. One question that could be asked is that of performance—we have a lot of extra function calls, the constructor, and a Set() call for every named argument, and that must cost something. Let's find out exactly what it costs.

Performance of the named arguments idiom

There is definitely more going on with the named argument call, as more functions are called. On the other hand, the function calls are really simple and, if they are defined in the header file, and the entire implementation is visible to the compiler, there is no reason for the compiler not to inline all the Set() calls and eliminate the unnecessary temporary variables. With good optimization, we could expect similar performance from the named arguments idiom and the explicitly named aggregate object.

The appropriate tool to measure the performance of a single function call is the microbenchmark. We use the Google microbenchmark library for this purpose. While the benchmarks are usually written in one file, we need another source file if we want the function we call to be external, not inlined. On the other hand, the Set() methods should definitely be inlined, so they should be defined in the header file. The second source file should contain the definition of the function we are calling with named or positional arguments. Both files are combined at link time:

```
$CXX named_args.C named_args_extra.C -I$GBENCH_DIR/include -g -O4 -I. \
    -Wall -Wextra -Werror -pedantic --std=c++14 \
    $GBENCH_DIR/lib/libbenchmark.a -lpthread -lrt -lm -o named_args
```

We can compare the positional arguments, the named arguments, and the arguments aggregate. The result will depend on the type and number of arguments. For example, for a function with four Boolean arguments, we can compare these calls:

```
Positional p(true, false, true, false);          // Positional arguments

Named n(Named::Options().SetA(true).SetC(true));  // Named arguments idiom

Aggregate::Options options;
options.a = true;
options.c = true;
Aggregate a(options));                            // Aggregate object
```

The performance measured by the benchmark will depend greatly on the compiler and on the options that control optimization. For example, these numbers were collected on GCC6 with -O3:

Benchmark	Time	CPU	Iterations	
BM_positional_const	47 ns	47 ns	13459657	642.531M items/s
BM_named_const	40 ns	40 ns	17145954	767.657M items/s
BM_aggregate_const	182 ns	182 ns	3872255	167.293M items/s

There is a performance hit for the explicitly named aggregate object that the compiler was unable to optimize away (since the object is not used elsewhere, such optimization is, in theory, possible). The named and positional arguments perform similarly, with the named arguments even slightly ahead in this case (do not try to make too much out of this; the performance of the function calls depends greatly on what else is going on in the program at the same time, since the arguments are passed on registers, and register availability is affected by the context).

In our benchmark, we have used compile-time constants as argument values. This is not uncommon, especially for arguments that specify certain options—very often, at each call site many of the options will be static, unchanging (the values are different in other places in the code where the same function is called, but on this line many of the values are fixed at compile time). For example, if we have a special code branch to process natural disasters in our game, the ordinary branch will always call our day simulation with flood, fire, and other disaster flags set to `false`. But, just as often the arguments are computed at runtime. How does this affect the performance? Let's create another benchmark where the values of the arguments are retrieved, for example, from a vector:

```cpp
std::vector<int> v;                      // Fill v with random values

size_t i = 0;
// ... Benchmark loop ...
const bool a = v[i++];
const bool b = v[i++];
const bool c = v[i++];
const bool d = v[i++];
if (i == v.size()) i = 0;                // Assume v.size() % 4 == 0

Positional p(a, b, c, d);                // Positional arguments

Named n(Named::Options().SetA(a).SetC(b)
                 .SetC(c).SetD(d));      // Named arguments idiom

Aggregate::Options options;
options.a = a;
options.b = b;
options.c = c;
options.d = d;
Aggregate a(options));                   // Aggregate object
```

By the way, it would be ill-advised to shorten the preceding code in this manner:

```
Positional p(v[i++], v[i++], v[i++], v[i++]);
```

The reason is that the order in which the arguments are evaluated is undefined, so it is arbitrary which of the i++ calls is executed first. If i starts from 0, this call may end up calling Positional(v[0], v[1], v[2], v[3]) or Positional(v[3], v[2], v[1], v[0]) or any other permutation.

On the same compiler and hardware, we now get different numbers:

Benchmark	Time	CPU	Iterations	
BM_positional_var	77 ns	77 ns	8873908	396.065M items/s
BM_named_var	211 ns	211 ns	2929368	144.322M items/s
BM_aggregate_var	200 ns	200 ns	3391551	152.224M items/s

We can guess from the results that the compiler did not fully eliminate the unnamed temporary object this time, and generated the code similar to what we get for an explicitly named local argument object. In general, the result of the compiler optimizations is difficult to predict. For example, we can test a slightly different case, with a function that takes more arguments, and only the last one is different from the default value:

Benchmark	Time	CPU	Iterations	
BM_positional_const	115 ns	115 ns	5921750	265.832M items/s
BM_named_const	42 ns	42 ns	16754061	727.64M items/s
BM_aggregate_const	220 ns	220 ns	3147659	138.592M items/s
BM_positional_var	142 ns	142 ns	5894532	214.538M items/s
BM_named_var	49 ns	49 ns	13096441	623.279M items/s
BM_aggregate_var	258 ns	257 ns	3058525	118.651M items/s

Calling a function with a lot of positional arguments, in general, takes more time, and our positional argument tests reflect that. The time to construct the aggregate object is essentially the same, at least for small objects, but the change that jumps out is that in this case, the compiler was able to optimize away the unnamed temporary options object.

The benchmark did not yield any conclusive results. We can say that the named arguments idiom performs no worse than an explicitly named aggregate object. If the compiler were able to eliminate the unnamed temporary, the result would likely be comparable or even faster than calling with positional arguments, especially if there are many arguments. If the optimization does not happen, the call may be a bit slower. On the other hand, in many cases the performance of the function call itself is not critical; for example, our cities are constructed only when the player builds one, a few times during the game. The day events are processed once per game day, which probably takes more than a few seconds of real time, not least so the player can enjoy interacting with the game. On the other hand, the functions that are repeatedly called in performance-critical code should be inlined whenever possible, and we can expect better optimizations for argument passing in this case as well. Overall, we can conclude that, unless the performance of the particular function call is critical for program performance, one should not be concerned with the overhead of named arguments. For performance-critical calls, performance should be measured on a case-by-case basis, and it is possible for named arguments to be faster than positional ones.

General method chaining

Applications of method chaining in C++ are not limited to argument passing (we have already seen another application, although a well-hidden one, in the form of streaming I/O). For use in other contexts, it is helpful to consider some more general forms of method chaining.

Method chaining versus method cascading

The term *method cascading* is not often found in the context of C++, and for a good reason—C++ does not really support it. Method cascading refers to calling a sequence of methods on the same object. For example, in *Dart*, where method cascading is supported explicitly, we can write the following:

```
var opt = Options();
opt.SetA()..SetB();
```

This code first calls SetA() on the opt object, then calls SetB() on the same object. The equivalent code is this:

```
var opt = Options();
opt.SetA()
opt.SetB();
```

But wait, did we not just do the same with C++ and our options object? We did, but we skimmed over an important difference. In method chaining, the next method is applied to the result of the previous one. This is a chained call in C++:

```
Options opt;
opt.SetA().SetB();
```

This chained call is equivalent to the following code:

```
Options opt;
Options& opt1 = opt.SetA();
Options& opt2 = opt1.SetB();
```

C++ does not have the cascading syntax, but the code equivalent to a cascade would be this:

```
Options opt;
opt.SetA();
opt.SetB();
```

But this is exactly what we did earlier, and the short form was the same:

```
Options opt;
opt.SetA().SetB();
```

What makes the C++ cascading possible in this case is that the methods return the reference to the same object. We can still say that the equivalent code is this:

```
Options opt;
Options& opt1 = opt.SetA();
Options& opt2 = opt1.SetB();
```

And, it's technically true. But, because of the way the methods are written, we have the additional guarantee that opt, opt1, and opt2 all refer to the same object. Method cascading can always be implemented through method chaining, but it restricts the interfaces because all calls must return a reference to this. This implementation technique is sometimes called by the somewhat unwieldy name **cascading-by-chaining by returning self**. The method chaining, in general, is not restricted to return *self*, or the reference to the object itself (*this in C++). What can be accomplished with the more general chaining? Let's see.

General method chaining

If the chained method does not return a reference to the object itself, it should return a new object. Usually, this object is of the same type, or at least a type from the same class hierarchy, if the methods are polymorphic. For example, let's consider a class that implements data collection. It has a method to filter the data using a predicate (a callable object, an object with the `operator()` that returns `true` or `false`). It also has a method to sort the collection. Each of these methods creates a new collection object and leaves the original object intact. Now, if we want to filter all valid data in our collection, and assuming that we have an `is_valid` predicate object, we can create a sorted collection of valid data:

```
Collection c;
... store data in the collection ...
Collection valid_c = c.filter(is_valid);
Collection sorted_valid_c = valid_c.sort();
```

The intermediate object can be eliminated using method chaining:

```
Collection c;
...
Collection sorted_valid_c = c.filter(is_valid).sort();
```

It should be clear after reading the last section that this is an example of method chaining, and a more general one than what we saw earlier—each method returns an object of the same type, but not the same object. The difference between chaining and cascading is very clear in this example—a cascade of methods would filter and sort the original collection (assuming we decided to support such operations).

Method chaining in class hierarchies

When applied to class hierarchies, method chaining runs into a particular problem; let's say that our `sort()` method returns a sorted data collection that is an object of a different type, `SortedCollection`, which is derived from the `Collection` class. The reason it is a derived class is that after sorting we can support efficient search, and so the `SortedCollection` class has a `search()` method that the base class does not have. We can still use method chaining, and even call the base class methods on the derived class, but doing so breaks the chain:

```
class SortedCollection;
class Collection {
    public:
    Collection filter();
    SortedCollection sort();    // Converts Collection to SortedCollection
```

```
};

class SortedCollection : public Collection {
    public:
    SortedCollection search();
    SortedCollection median();
};

SortedCollection Collection::sort() {
    SortedCollection sc;
    ... sort the collection ...
    return sc;
}

Collection c;
auto c1 = c.sort()                    // Now SortedCollection
            .search()                 // Needs SortedCollection, gets it
            .filter()                 // Invokes but returns Collection
            .median();                // Needs SortedCollection, got Collection
}
```

Polymorphism, or virtual functions, does not help here; first of all, we would need to define virtual functions for search() and median() in the base class, even though we don't intend to support this functionality there, as only the derived class supports them. We cannot declare them pure virtual because we use the Collection as a concrete class, and any class with a pure virtual function is an abstract class, so objects of this class cannot be instantiated. We can make these functions abort at runtime, but at the very least we have moved the detection of a programming error—searching in an unsorted collection—from compile time to runtime. Worse, it does not even help:

```
class SortedCollection;
class Collection {
    public:
    Collection filter();
    SortedCollection sort();     // Converts Collection to SortedCollection
    virtual SortedCollection median();
};

class SortedCollection : public Collection {
    public:
    SortedCollection search();
    SortedCollection median();
};

SortedCollection Collection::sort() {
    SortedCollection sc;
    ... sort the collection ...
```

```
        return sc;
    }
    SortedCollection Collection::median() {
        cout << "Collection::median called!!!" << endl;
        abort();
        SortedCollection dummy;
        return dummy;                    // Still need to return something
    }

    Collection c;
    auto c1 = c.sort()                   // Now SortedCollection
                .search()                // Needs SortedCollection, gets it
                .filter()                // Invokes but returns Collection
                .median();               // Collection::median is called!
    }
```

This is not going to work because `Collection::filter` returns a copy of the object, not a reference to it. The object it returns is the base class, `Collection`. If called on a `SortedCollection` object, it rips out the base class portion from the derived object and returns that. If you think that making `filter()` virtual as well, and overriding it in the derived class, solves this problem at the expense of overriding every function in the base class, you have another surprise coming—virtual functions must have identical return types, except for the *covariant return types*. References to the base and derived classes are covariant return types. Classes themselves, returned by value, are not.

Note that this problem would not have happened if we were returning object references. However, we can only return references to the object we are called on; if we create a new object in the body of a method function and return a reference to it, it's a dangling reference to a temporary object that is deleted the moment the function returns. The result is undefined behavior (the program is likely to crash). On the other hand, if we always return the reference to the original object, we cannot change its type from based to derived in the first place.

The C++ solution to this problem involves the use of templates and a curious design pattern. In fact, it is so mind-twisting that the word *curious* is even in its name—the Curiously Recurring Template Pattern. We have a whole chapter on the CRTP pattern in this book. The application of the pattern to our case is relatively straightforward—the base class needs to return the right type from its functions, but can't because it does not know what the type is. The solution—pass the right type into the base class as the template argument. Of course, the base class would have to be a base class template for this to work:

```
template <typename T>
class Collection {
    public:
    Collection() {}
    T filter();                        // "*this" is really a T, not an A
    T sort() { T sc; ... return sc; } // Create new sorted collection
};

class SortedCollection : public Collection<SortedCollection> {
    public:
    SortedCollection search();
    SortedCollection median();
};

Collection<SortedCollection> c;
auto c1 = c.sort()                 // Now SortedCollection
            .search()              // Needs SortedCollection, gets it
            .filter()              // Invokes, preserves SortedCollection
            .median();             // SortedCollection::median is called
}
```

This is a complex solution. While it works, its complexity suggests that method chaining should be used sparingly, if at all, if the object type has to change in the middle of the chain. There is a good reason for that—changing the object type is fundamentally different than calling a sequence of methods. It is a more significant event that perhaps should be made explicit, and the new object should get its own name.

Summary

Yet again, we have seen the power of C++ to essentially create a new language out of the existing one; C++ does not have named function arguments, only positional ones. That is part of the core language. And yet, we were able to extend the language and add support for named arguments in a reasonable-looking way, using the method chaining technique. We have also explored the other applications of method chaining beyond the named arguments idiom.

The next chapter introduces the only purely performance-oriented idiom in this book. We have discussed in several chapters the performance cost of memory allocation, and its impact on the implementation of several patterns. The next idiom, local buffer optimization, attacks the problem head-on, by avoiding the memory allocation altogether.

Questions

- Why do functions with many arguments of the same or related types lead to fragile code?
- How do aggregate argument objects improve code maintainability and robustness?
- What is the named argument idiom and how does it differ from aggregate arguments?
- What is the difference between method chaining and cascading?

10
Local Buffer Optimization

Not all design patterns are concerned with designing class hierarchies. For commonly occurring problems, a software design pattern is the most general and reusable solution and, for those programming in C++, one of the most commonly occurring problems is inadequate performance. One of the most common causes of such poor performance is inefficient memory management. Patterns were developed to deal with these problems. In this chapter, we will explore one such pattern that addresses, in particular, the overhead of small, frequent memory allocations.

The following topics will be covered in this chapter:

- What is the overhead of small memory allocations, and how can it be measured?
- What is the local buffer optimization, how does it improve performance, and how can the improvements be measured?
- When can the local buffer optimization pattern be used effectively?
- What are the possible downsides of, and restrictions on, the use of the local buffer optimization pattern?

Technical requirements

You will need the Google Benchmark library installed and configured, details for which can be found here: https://github.com/google/benchmark (see Chapter 4, *Swap – From Simple to Subtle* for installation instructions).

Example code can be found at the following link: https://github.com/PacktPublishing/Hands-On-Design-Patterns-with-CPP/tree/master/Chapter10.

The overhead of small memory allocations

The local buffer optimization is just that—an optimization. It is a performance-oriented pattern, and we must, therefore, keep in mind the first rule of performance—never guess anything about performance. Performance, and the effect of any optimization, must be measured.

The cost of memory allocations

Since we are exploring the overhead of memory allocations and the ways to reduce it, the first question we must answer is how expensive a memory allocation is. After all, nobody wants to optimize something so fast that it needs no optimization. We can use Google Benchmark (or any other microbenchmark, if you prefer) to answer this question. The simplest benchmark to measure the cost of memory allocation might look like this:

```
void BM_malloc(benchmark::State& state) {
    for (auto _ : state) {
        void* p = malloc(64);
        benchmark::DoNotOptimize(p);
    }
    state.SetItemsProcessed(state.iterations());
}
BENCHMARK(BM_malloc_free);
```

The `benchmark::DoNotOptimize` wrapper prevents the compiler from optimizing away the unused variable. Alas, this experiment is probably not going to end well; the microbenchmark library needs to run the test many times, often millions of times, to accumulate a sufficiently accurate average runtime. It is highly likely that the machine will run out of memory before the benchmark is complete. The fix is easy enough, we must also free the memory we allocated:

```
void BM_malloc_free(benchmark::State& state) {
    const size_t S = state.range(0);
    for (auto _ : state) {
        void* p = malloc(S);
        benchmark::DoNotOptimize(p);
        free(p);
    }
    state.SetItemsProcessed(state.iterations());
}
BENCHMARK(BM_malloc_free)->Arg(64);
```

We must note that we now measure the cost of both allocation and deallocation, which is reflected in the changed name of the function. This is not an unreasonable change; any allocated memory will need to be deallocated some time later, so the cost must be paid at some point. We have also changed the benchmark to be parameterized by the allocation size. If you run this benchmark, you should get something like this:

Benchmark	Time	CPU	Iterations	
BM_malloc_free/64	18 ns	18 ns	39155519	54.0953M items/s

This tells us that the allocation and deallocation of 64 bytes of memory costs about 18 nanoseconds on this particular machine, which adds up to million allocations/deallocations per second. If you're curious whether the *64 bytes* size is special in some way, you can change the size value in the argument of the benchmark, or run the benchmark for a whole range of sizes:

```
void BM_malloc_free(benchmark::State& state) {
    const size_t S = state.range(0);
    for (auto _ : state) {
        void* p = malloc(S);
        benchmark::DoNotOptimize(p);
        free(p);
    }
    state.SetItemsProcessed(state.iterations());
}
BENCHMARK(BM_malloc_free)->RangeMultiplier(2)->Range(32, 256);
```

You might also note that, so far, we have measured the time it takes to make the very first memory allocation in the program since we have not allocated anything else. The C++ runtime system probably did some dynamic allocations at the startup of the program, but still, this is not a very realistic benchmark. We can make the measurement more relevant by reallocating some amount of memory:

```
#define REPEAT2(x)  x x
#define REPEAT4(x)  REPEAT2(x) REPEAT2(x)
#define REPEAT8(x)  REPEAT4(x) REPEAT4(x)
#define REPEAT16(x)  REPEAT8(x) REPEAT8(x)
#define REPEAT32(x)  REPEAT16(x) REPEAT16(x)
#define REPEAT(x)  REPEAT32(x)

void BM_malloc_free(benchmark::State& state) {
    const size_t S = state.range(0);
    const size_t N = state.range(1);
    std::vector<void*> v(N);
    for (size_t i = 0; i < N; ++i) v[i] = malloc(S);
```

```
      for (auto _ : state) {
          REPEAT({
          void* p = malloc(S);
          benchmark::DoNotOptimize(p);
          free(p);
          });
      }
      state.SetItemsProcessed(32*state.iterations());
      for (size_t i = 0; i < N; ++i) free(v[i]);
  }
  BENCHMARK(BM_malloc_free)->RangeMultiplier(2)
                          ->Ranges({{32, 256}, {1<<15, 1<<15}});
```

Here, we make N calls to malloc before starting the benchmark. Further improvements can be achieved by varying the allocation size during the reallocations. We have also replicated the body of the benchmark loop 32 times (using the C preprocessor macro) to reduce the overhead of the loop itself on the measurement. The time reported by the benchmark is now the time it takes to do 32 allocations and deallocations, which is not very convenient, but the allocation rate remains valid, since we have accounted for the loop unrolling, and multiplied the number of iterations by 32 when setting the number of processed items (in Google Benchmark, an item is whatever you want it to be, and the number of items per second is reported at the end of the benchmark, so we have declared one allocation/deallocation to be an item).

Even with all these modifications and improvements, the final result is going to be pretty close to our initial measurement of 54 million allocations per second. This seems very fast, just 18 nanoseconds. Remember, however, that a modern CPU can do dozens of instructions in this time. As we are dealing with small allocations, it is highly likely that the processing time spent on each allocated memory fragment is also small, and the overhead of allocation is non-trivial. This, of course, represents guessing about performance and is something I warned you against, and so we will confirm this claim via direct experiments.

First, however, I want to show you another reason why small memory allocations are particularly inefficient. So far, we have explored the cost of memory allocations on only one thread. Today, most programs that have any performance requirements at all are concurrent, and C++ supports concurrency and multi-threading. Let's take a look at how the cost of memory allocations changes when we do it on several threads at once:

```
  void BM_malloc_free(benchmark::State& state) {
      const size_t S = state.range(0);
      const size_t N = state.range(1);
      std::vector<void*> v(N);
      for (size_t i = 0; i < N; ++i) v[i] = malloc(S);
      for (auto _ : state) {
          REPEAT({
```

```
            void* p = malloc(S);
            benchmark::DoNotOptimize(p);
            free(p);
            });
    }
    state.SetItemsProcessed(32*state.iterations());
    for (size_t i = 0; i < N; ++i) free(v[i]);
}
BENCHMARK(BM_malloc_free)->RangeMultiplier(2)
                        ->Ranges({{32, 256}, {1<<15, 1<<15}})
                        ->ThreadRange(1, 2);
```

The result greatly depends on the hardware and the version of `malloc` used by the system. Also, on large machines with many CPUs, you can have many more than two threads. Nonetheless, the overall trend should look something like this:

Benchmark	Time	CPU	Iterations	
BM_malloc_free/32/32768/threads:1	649 ns	648 ns	1044207	47.1165M items/s
BM_malloc_free/32/32768/threads:2	1077 ns	2153 ns	327732	14.1718M items/s

This is quite dismal; the cost of allocations increased several times when we went from one thread to two (on a larger machine, a similar increase is going to happen, but probably with more than two threads). The system memory allocator appears to be the bane of effective concurrency. There are better allocators that can be used to replace the default `malloc()` allocator, but they have their own downsides. Plus, it would be better if our C++ program did not depend on a particular, non-standard, system library replacement for its performance. We need a better way to allocate memory. Let's have a look at it.

Introducing local buffer optimization

The least amount of work a program can do to accomplish a certain task is no work at all. Free stuff is great. Similarly, the fastest way to allocate and deallocate memory is this—don't. Local buffer optimization is a way to get something for nothing; in this case, to get some memory for no additional computing cost.

The main idea

To understand local buffer optimization, you have to remember that memory allocations do not happen in isolation. Usually, if a small amount of memory is needed, the allocated memory is used as a part of some data structure. For example, let's consider a very simple character string:

```
class simple_string {
    public:
    simple_string() : s_() {}
    explicit simple_string(const char* s) : s_(strdup(s)) {}
    simple_string(const simple_string& s) : s_(strdup(s.s_)) {}
    simple_string& operator=(const char* s) {
        free(s_); s_ = strdup(s); return *this;
    }
    simple_string& operator=(const simple_string& s)
    {
        free(s_); s_ = strdup(s.s_); return *this;
    }
    bool operator==(const simple_string& rhs)
    const {
            return strcmp(s_, rhs.s_) == 0;
        }
    ~simple_string() { free(s_); }
    private:
    char* s_;
};
```

The string allocates its memory from `malloc()` via a `strdup()` call, and returns it by calling `free()`. To be in any way useful, the string would need many more member functions, but these are sufficient for now to explore the overhead of memory allocation. Speaking of allocation, every time a string is constructed, copied, or assigned, an allocation happens. To be more precise, every time a string is constructed, an additional allocation happens; the string object itself has to be allocated somewhere, which may be on the stack for a local variable, or on the heap if the string is a part of some dynamically allocated data structure. In addition to that, an allocation for the string data happens, and the memory is always taken from `malloc()`.

This, then, is the idea of the local buffer optimization—why don't we make the string object larger so it can contain its own data? That really would be getting something for nothing; the memory for the string object has to be allocated anyway, but the additional memory for the string data we would get at no extra cost. Of course, a string can be arbitrarily long, and so we do not know in advance how much larger we need to make the string object to store any string the program will encounter. Even if we did, it would be a tremendous waste of memory to always allocate the object of that large size, even for very short strings.

We can, however, make an observation—the longer the string is, the longer it takes to process it (copy, search, convert, or whatever we need to do with it).

For very long strings, the cost of allocations is going to be small compared to the cost of processing. For short strings, on the other hand, the cost of the allocation could be significant. Therefore, the most performance benefit can be obtained by storing short strings in the object itself, while any string that is too long to fit in the object will be stored in allocated memory as before. This is, in a nutshell, local buffer optimization, which for strings is also known as **short string optimization**; the object (string) contains a local buffer of a certain size, and any string that fits into that buffer is stored directly inside the object:

```
class small_string {
    public:
    small_string() : s_() {}
    explicit small_string(const char* s)
        : s_((strlen(s) + 1 < sizeof(buf_)) ? buf_ : strdup(s))
    {
        if (s_ == buf_) strncpy(buf_, s, sizeof(buf_));
    }
    small_string(const small_string& s)
        : s_((s.s_ == s.buf_) ? buf_ : strdup(s.s_))
    {
        if (s_ == buf_) memcpy(buf_, s.buf_, sizeof(buf_));
    }
    small_string& operator=(const char* s) {
        if (s_ != buf_) free(s_);
        s_ = (strlen(s) + 1 < sizeof(buf_)) ? buf_ : strdup(s);
        if (s_ == buf_) strncpy(buf_, s, sizeof(buf_));
        return *this;
    }
    small_string& operator=(const small_string& s) {
        if (s_ != buf_) free(s_);
        s_ = (s.s_ == s.buf_) ? buf_ : strdup(s.s_);
        if (s_ == buf_) memcpy(buf_, s.buf_, sizeof(buf_));
        return *this;
    }
    bool operator==(const small_string& rhs) const {
        return strcmp(s_, rhs.s_) == 0;
    }
    ~small_string() {
        if (s_ != buf_) free(s_);
    }
    private:
    char* s_;
    char buf_[16];
};
```

In the preceding code example, the buffer size is set statically at 16 characters, including the null character used to terminate the string. Any string that is longer than 16 is allocated from malloc(). When assigning or destroying a string object, we must check whether the allocation was done or the internal buffer was used, in order to appropriately release the memory used by the string.

Effect of local buffer optimization

How much faster is the small_string compared to the simple_string? That depends, of course, on what you need to do with it. Let's start with just creating and deleting the strings. To avoid typing the same benchmark code twice, we can use the template benchmark, as follows:

```
template <typename T>
void BM_string_create_short(benchmark::State& state) {
    const char* s = "Simple string";
    for (auto _ : state) {
        REPEAT({ T S(s); benchmark::DoNotOptimize(S); })
    }
    state.SetItemsProcessed(32*state.iterations());
}
BENCHMARK_TEMPLATE1(BM_string_create_short, simple_string);
BENCHMARK_TEMPLATE1(BM_string_create_short, small_string);
```

The result is quite impressive:

Benchmark	Time	CPU	Iterations	
BM_string_create_short<simple_string>	726 ns	726 ns	928017	42.0364M items/s
BM_string_create_short<small_string>	29 ns	29 ns	24449910	1067.15M items/s

It gets even better when we try the same test on multiple threads:

Benchmark	Time	CPU	Iterations	
BM_string_create_short<simple_string>/threads:2	1117 ns	2233 ns	312608	13.6656M items/s
BM_string_create_short<small_string>/threads:2	15 ns	31 ns	22646526	997.64M items/s

While regular string creation is much slower on multiple threads, the small string shows no such penalty and, in fact, scales almost perfectly. Of course, this is pretty much the best case scenario for small string optimization—firstly because all we do is create and delete strings, which is the very part we optimized, and secondly because the string is a local variable its memory is allocated as a part of the stack frame, so there is no additional allocation cost.

However, this is not an unreasonable case; after all, local variables are not rare at all, and if the string is a part of some larger data structure, the allocation cost for that structure has to be paid anyway, so allocating anything else at the same time and without additional cost is effectively free.

Nonetheless, it is unlikely that we only allocate the strings to immediately deallocate them, so we should consider the cost of other operations. We can expect similar improvements for copying or assigning strings, as long as they stay short, of course:

```
template <typename T>
void BM_string_copy_short(benchmark::State& state) {
    const T s("Simple string");
    for (auto _ : state) {
        REPEAT({ T S(s); benchmark::DoNotOptimize(S); })
    }
    state.SetItemsProcessed(32*state.iterations());
}

template <typename T>
void BM_string_assign_short(benchmark::State& state) {
    const T s("Simple string");
    T S;
    for (auto _ : state) {
        REPEAT({ benchmark::DoNotOptimize(S = s); })
    }
    state.SetItemsProcessed(32*state.iterations());
}

BENCHMARK_TEMPLATE1(BM_string_copy_short, simple_string);
BENCHMARK_TEMPLATE1(BM_string_copy_short, small_string);
BENCHMARK_TEMPLATE1(BM_string_assign_short, simple_string);
BENCHMARK_TEMPLATE1(BM_string_assign_short, small_string);
```

Indeed, a similar dramatic performance gain is observed:

Benchmark	Time	CPU	Iterations	
BM_string_copy_short<simple_string>	706 ns	706 ns	971142	43.2178M items/s
BM_string_copy_short<small_string>	45 ns	45 ns	15621788	672.256M items/s
BM_string_assign_short<simple_string>	754 ns	753 ns	924908	40.5313M items/s
BM_string_assign_short<small_string>	51 ns	51 ns	13281364	596.836M items/s

We are also likely to need to read the data in the strings at least once, to compare them or search for a specific string or character, or compute some derived value. We do not expect improvements of a similar scale for these operations, of course, since none of them involves any allocations or deallocations. You might ask why, then, should we expect any improvements at all?

Indeed, a simple test of string comparison, for example, shows no difference between the two versions of the string. In order to see any benefit, we have to create many string objects and compare them:

```
template <typename T>
void BM_string_compare_short(benchmark::State& state) {
    const size_t N = state.range(0);
    const T s("Simple string");
    std::vector<T> v1, v2;
    ... populate the vectors with strings ...
    for (auto _ : state) {
        for (size_t i = 0; i < N; ++i) {
            benchmark::DoNotOptimize(v1[i] == v2[i]);
        }
    }
    state.SetItemsProcessed(N*state.iterations());
}
#define ARG Arg(1<<22)
BENCHMARK_TEMPLATE1(BM_string_compare_short, simple_string)->ARG;
BENCHMARK_TEMPLATE1(BM_string_compare_short, small_string)->ARG;
```

For small values of N (a small total number of strings), there won't be any significant benefit from the optimization. But when we have to process many strings, comparing strings with the small string optimization can be approximately twice as fast:

Benchmark	Time	CPU	Iterations	
BM_string_compare_short<simple_string>/4194304	36388678 ns	36385972 ns	19	109.932M items/s
BM_string_compare_short<small_string>/4194304	14640789 ns	14639702 ns	55	273.23M items/s

Why is that happening, if there are no allocations at all? This experiment shows the second, very important, benefit of the local buffer optimization—improved cache locality. The string object itself has to be accessed before the string data can be read; it contains the pointer to the data. For the regular string, accessing the string characters involves two memory accesses at different, generally unrelated addresses. If the total amount of data is large, then the second access, to the string data, is likely to miss the cache and wait for the data to be brought from the main memory. On the other hand, the optimized string keeps the data close to the string object, so that once the string itself is in the cache, so is the data. The reason that we need a sufficient amount of different strings to see this benefit is that with few strings, all string objects and their data can reside in the cache permanently. Only when the total size of the strings exceeds the size of the cache will the performance benefits manifest themselves. Now, let's dive deeper with some additional optimizations.

Additional optimizations

The `simple_string` class we have implemented has an obvious inefficiency—when the string is stored in the local buffer, we do not really need the pointer to the data. We know exactly where the data is, in the local buffer. We do need to know, somehow, whether the data is in the local buffer or in the externally allocated memory, but we don't need to use 8 bytes (on a 64-bit machine) just to store that. Of course, we still need the pointer for storing longer strings, but we could reuse that memory for the buffer when the string is short:

```
class small_string {
    ...
    private:
    union {
    char* s_;
    struct {
        char buf[15];
        char tag;
    } b_;
    };
};
```

Here, we use the last byte as a `tag` to indicate whether the string is stored locally (`tag == 0`) or in a separate allocation (`tag == 1`). Note that the total buffer size is still 16 characters, 15 for the string itself and 1 for the tag, which also doubles at the trailing zero if the string needs all 16 bytes (this is why we have to use `tag == 0` to indicate local storage, as it would cost us an extra byte to do otherwise). The pointer is overlaid in memory with the first 8 bytes of the character buffer. In this example, we have chosen to optimize the total memory occupied by the string; this string still has a 16-character local buffer, just like the previous version, but the object itself is now only 16 bytes, not 24. If we were willing to keep the object size the same, we could have used a larger buffer and stored longer strings locally. The benefit of the small string optimization does, generally, diminish as the strings become longer. The optimal crossover point from local to remote strings depends on the particular application and must of course be determined by benchmark measurements.

Local buffer optimization beyond strings

The local buffer optimization can be used effectively for much more than just short strings. In fact, any time a small dynamic allocation of a size that is determined at runtime is needed, this optimization should be considered. In this section, we will consider several such data structures.

Small vector

Another very common data structure that often benefits from local buffer optimization is vectors. Vectors are essentially dynamic contiguous arrays of data elements of the specified type (in this sense, a string is a vector of bytes, although null termination gives strings their own specifics). A basic vector, such as the `std::vector` found in the C++ standard library, needs two data members, data pointer and data size:

```
class simple_vector {
    public:
    simple_vector() : n_(), p_() {}
    simple_vector(std::initializer_list<int> il)
        : n_(il.size()), p_(static_cast<int*>(malloc(sizeof(int)*n_)))
    {
        int* p = p_;
        for (auto x : il) *p++ = x;
    }
    ~simple_vector()
    {
        free(p_);
    }
    size_t size() const { return n_; }
    private:
    size_t n_;
    int* p_;
};
```

Vectors are usually templates, like the standard `std::vector`, but we have simplified this example to show a vector of integers (converting this vector class to a template is left as an exercise to the reader, and does not in any way alter the application of the local buffer optimization pattern). We can apply *small vector optimization* and store the vector data in the body of the vector object as long as it is small enough:

```
class small_vector {
    public:
    small_vector() : n_(), p_() {}
    small_vector(std::initializer_list<int> il)
        : n_(il.size()),
          p_((n_ < sizeof(buf_)/sizeof(buf_[0])) ?
                    buf_ :
                    static_cast<int*>(malloc(sizeof(int)*n_)))
    {
        int* p = p_;
        for (auto x : il) *p++ = x;
    }
    ~small_vector() {
```

```
                if (p_ != buf_) free(p_);
        }
        private:
        size_t n_;
        int* p_;
        int buf_[16];
    };
```

We can further optimize the vector in a similar manner to the string, and overlay the local buffer with the pointer. We cannot use the last byte as a `tag`, as we did before, since any element of the vector can have any value, and the value of zero is, in general, not special. However, we need to store the size of the vector anyway, so we can use it at any time to determine whether the local buffer is used or not. We can take further advantage of the fact that if the local buffer optimization is used, the size of the vector cannot be very large, so we do not need a field of the `size_t` type to store it:

```cpp
class small_vector {
    public:
    small_vector() { short_.n = 0; }
    small_vector(std::initializer_list<int> il) {
        int* p;
        if (il.size() < sizeof(short_.buf)/sizeof(short_.buf[0])) {
            short_.n = il.size();
            p = short_.buf;
        } else {
            short_.n = UCHAR_MAX;
            long_.n = il.size();
            p = long_.p = static_cast<int*>(malloc(sizeof(int)*long_.n));
        }
        for (auto x : il) *p++ = x;
    }
    ~small_vector() {
        if (short_.n == UCHAR_MAX) free(long_.p);
    }
    private:
    union {
        struct {
            size_t n;
            int* p;
        } long_;
        struct {
            int buf[15];
            unsigned char n;
        } short_;
    };
};
```

Here, we store the vector size either in `size_t long_.n` or in `unsigned char short_.n`, depending on whether or not the local buffer is used. A remote buffer is indicated by storing `UCHAR_MAX` (that is, 255) in the short size. Since this value is larger than the size of the local buffer, this `tag` is unambiguous (were the local buffer increased to store more than 255 elements, the type of `short_.n` would need to be changed to a longer integer).

We can measure the performance gains from small vector optimization using a benchmark similar to the one we used for the strings. Depending on the actual size of the vector, gains of about 10x can be expected in creating and copying the vectors, and more if the benchmark runs on multiple threads. Of course, other data structures can be optimized in a similar manner when they store small amounts of dynamically allocated data.

Type-erased and callable objects

There is another, very different, type of application where the local buffer optimization can be used very effectively—storing callable objects, which are objects that can be invoked as functions. Many template classes provide an option to customize some part of their behavior using a callable object. For example, `std::shared_ptr`, the standard shared pointer in C++, allows the user to specify a custom deleter. This deleter will be called with the address of the object to be deleted, so it is a callable with one argument of the `void*` type. It could be a function pointer, a member function pointer, or a functor object (an object with an `operator()` defined)—any type that can be called on a `p` pointer; that is, any type that compiles in the `callable(p)` function call syntax can be used. The deleter, however, is more than a type; it is an object and is specified at runtime, and so it needs to be stored someplace where the shared pointer can get to it. Were the deleter a part of the shared pointer type, we could simply declare a data member of that type in the shared pointer object (or, in the case of the C++ shared pointer, in its reference object that is shared between all copies of the shared pointer). You could consider it a trivial application of the local buffer optimization, as in the following smart pointer that automatically deletes the object when the pointer goes out of scope (just like `std::unique_ptr`):

```
template <typename T, typename Deleter>
class smartptr {
    public:
    smartptr(T* p, Deleter d) : p_(p), d_(d) {}
    ~smartptr() { d_(p_); }
    T* operator->() { return p_; }
    const T* operator->() const { return p_; }
    private:
```

```
    T* p_;
    Deleter d_;
};
```

We are after more interesting things, however, and one such thing can be found when we deal with type-erased objects. The details of such objects were considered in the chapter dedicated to type erasure, but in a nutshell, they are objects where the callable is not a part of the type itself (as in, it is *erased* from the type of the containing object). The callable is instead stored in a polymorphic object, and a virtual function is used to call the object of the right type at runtime. The polymorphic object, in turn, is manipulated through the base class pointer.

Now, we have a problem that is, in a sense, similar to the preceding small vector—we need to store some data, in our case the callable object, whose type, and therefore size, is not statically known. The general solution is to dynamically allocate such objects and access them through the base class pointer. In the case of a smart pointer deleter, we could do it like this:

```
template <typename T>
class smartptr_te {
    struct deleter_base {
        virtual void apply(void*) = 0;
        virtual ~deleter_base() {}
    };
    template <typename Deleter> struct deleter : public deleter_base {
        deleter(Deleter d) : d_(d) {}
        virtual void apply(void* p) { d_(static_cast<T*>(p)); }
        Deleter d_;
    };
    public:
    template <typename Deleter> smartptr_te(T* p, Deleter d)
        : p_(p), d_(new deleter<Deleter>(d))
    {}
    ~smartptr_te() { d_->apply(p_); delete d_; }
    T* operator->() { return p_; }
    const T* operator->() const { return p_; }
    private:
    T* p_;
    deleter_base* d_;
};
```

Note that the `Deleter` type is no longer a part of the smart pointer type; it was *erased*. All smart pointers for the same `T` object type have the same type, `smartptr_te<T>` (here, `te` stands for *type-erased*). However, we have to pay a steep price for this syntactic convenience—every time a smart pointer is created, there is an additional memory allocation. How steep? The first rule of performance must again be remembered—*steep* is only a guess until confirmed by an experiment, such as the following benchmark:

```
struct deleter {     // Very simple deleter, matches operator new
    template <typename T> void operator()(T* p) { delete p; }
};

void BM_smartptr(benchmark::State& state) {
    deleter d;
    for (auto _ : state) {
        smartptr<int, deleter> p(new int, d);
    }
    state.SetItemsProcessed(state.iterations());
}

void BM_smartptr_te(benchmark::State& state) {
    deleter d;
    for (auto _ : state) {
        smartptr_te<int> p(new int, d);
    }
    state.SetItemsProcessed(state.iterations());
}
BENCHMARK(BM_smartptr);
BENCHMARK(BM_smartptr_te);
```

For a smart pointer with a statically defined deleter, we can expect the cost of each iteration to be very similar to the cost of calling `malloc()` and `free()`, which we measured earlier:

```
--------------------------------------------------------------------
Benchmark                    Time           CPU Iterations
--------------------------------------------------------------------
BM_smartptr                 21 ns          21 ns   34069972   45.7846M items/s
BM_smartptr_te              42 ns          42 ns   16832659   22.7958M items/s
```

For a type-erased smart pointer, there are two allocations instead of one, and so the time it takes to create the pointer object is doubled. By the way, we can also measure the performance of a raw pointer, and it should be the same as the smart pointer within the accuracy of the measurements (this was, in fact, a stated design goal for the `std::unique_ptr` standard).

We can apply the same idea of local buffer optimization here, and it is likely to be even more effective than it was for strings; after all, most callable objects are small. We can't completely count on that, however, and must handle the case of a callable object that is larger than the local buffer:

```
template <typename T>
class smartptr_te_lb {
    struct deleter_base {
        virtual void apply(void*) = 0;
        virtual ~deleter_base() {}
    };
    template <typename Deleter> struct deleter : public deleter_base {
        deleter(Deleter d) : d_(d) {}
        virtual void apply(void* p) { d_(static_cast<T*>(p)); }
        Deleter d_;
    };
    public:
    template <typename Deleter> smartptr_te_lb(T* p, Deleter d) :
        p_(p),
        d_((sizeof(Deleter) > sizeof(buf_)) ? new deleter<Deleter>(d) :
                                        new (buf_)
deleter<Deleter>(d))
    {}
    ~smartptr_te_lb() {
        d_->apply(p_);
        if (static_cast<void*>(d_) == static_cast<void*>(buf_)) {
            d_->~deleter_base();
        } else {
            delete d_;
        }
    }
    T* operator->() { return p_; }
    const T* operator->() const { return p_; }
    private:
    T* p_;
    deleter_base* d_;
    char buf_[16];
};
```

Using the same benchmark as before, we can measure the performance of the type-erased smart pointer with the local buffer optimization. While the construction and deletion of a smart pointer without type erasure took 21 nanoseconds, and 42 nanoseconds with type erasure, the optimized type-erased shared pointer test takes 23 nanoseconds on the same machine. The slight overhead comes from checking whether the deleter is stored locally or remotely.

Local buffer optimization in the C++ library

We should note that the last application of local buffer optimization, storing callables for type-erased objects, is widely used in the C++ standard template library. For example, `std::shared_ptr` has a type-erased deleter, and most implementations use the local buffer optimization; the deleter is stored with the reference object and not with each copy of the shared pointer, of course. The `std::unique_pointer` standard, on the other hand, is not type-erased at all, to avoid even a small overhead, or potentially a much larger overhead should the deleter not fit into the local buffer.

The *ultimate type-erased* object of the C++ standard library, `std::function`, is also typically implemented with a local buffer for storing small callable objects without the expense of an additional allocation. The universal container object for any type, `std::any` (since C++17), is also typically implemented without a dynamic allocation when possible.

Downsides of local buffer optimization

Local buffer optimization is not without its downsides. The most obvious one is that all objects with a local buffer are larger than they would be without one. If the typical data stored in the buffer is smaller than the chosen buffer size, then every object is wasting some memory, but at least the optimization is paying off. Worse, if our choice of the buffer size is badly off and most data is, in fact, larger than the local buffer, the data is stored remotely but the local buffers are still created inside every object, and all that memory is wasted. There is an obvious trade-off between the amount of memory we are willing to waste and the range of data sizes where the optimization is effective. The size of the local buffer should be carefully chosen with the application in mind.

The more subtle complication is this—the data that used to be external to the object is now stored inside the object. This has several consequences, in addition to the performance benefits we were so focused on. First of all, every copy of the object contains its own copy of the data as long as it fits into the local buffer. This prevents designs such as the reference counting of data; for example, a **Copy-On-Write (COW)** string, where the data is not copied as long as all string copies remain the same, cannot use the small string optimization.

Secondly, the data must be moved if the object itself is moved. Contrast this with the `std::vector`, which is moved or swapped, essentially like a pointer—the pointer to the data is moved but the data remains in place. As similar consideration exists for the object contained inside `std::any`. You could dismiss this concern as trivial; after all, local buffer optimization is used primarily for small amounts of data, and the cost of moving them should be comparable to the cost of copying the pointer. However, more than performance is at stake here—moving an instance of `std::vector` (or `std::any`, for that matter) is guaranteed not to throw an exception. However, no such guarantees are offered when moving an arbitrary object. Therefore, `std::any` can be implemented with a local buffer optimization only if the object it contains is `std::is_nothrow_move_constructible`. Even such a guarantee does not suffice for the case of `std::vector`, however; the standard explicitly states that moving, or swapping, a vector does not invalidate iterators pointing to any element of the vector. Obviously, this requirement is incompatible with local buffer optimization, since moving a small vector would relocate all its elements to a different region of memory. For that reason, many high-efficiency libraries offer a custom vector-like container that supports small vector optimization, at the expense of the standard iterator invalidation guarantees.

Summary

We have just introduced a design pattern aimed solely at improved performance. Efficiency is an important consideration for the C++ language; thus, the C++ community developed patterns to address the most common inefficiencies. Repeated or wasteful memory allocation is perhaps the most common of all. The design pattern we have just seen—local buffer optimization—is a powerful tool that can greatly reduce such allocations. We have seen how it can be applied to compact data structures, as well as to store small objects, such as callables. We have also reviewed the possible downsides of using this pattern.

With the next `Chapter 11`, *ScopeGuard,* we move on to study more complex patterns that address broader design issues. The idioms we have learned so far are often used in the implementation of these patterns.

Questions

1. How can we measure the performance of a small fragment of code?
2. Why are small and frequent memory allocations particularly bad for performance?
3. What is local buffer optimization, and how does it work?
4. Why is an allocation of an additional buffer inside an object effectively *free*?
5. What is short string optimization?
6. What is small vector optimization?
7. Why is local buffer optimization particularly effective for callable objects?
8. What are the trade-offs to consider when using local buffer optimization?
9. When should an object not be placed in a local buffer?

Further reading

- *C++ High Performance* by Viktor Sehr and Björn Andrist: https://www.packtpub.com/application-development/c-high-performance
- *C++ Data Structures and Algorithms* by Wisnu Anggoro: https://www.packtpub.com/application-development/c-data-structures-and-algorithms
- *High Performance Applications with C++* [Video] by Jeganathan Swaminathan: https://www.packtpub.com/application-development/high-performance-applications-c-video

11
ScopeGuard

This chapter covers a pattern that can be seen as a generalization of the RAII idiom we studied earlier. In its earliest form, it is an old and established C++ pattern, however, it is also one that has particularly benefited from the language additions in C++11, C++14, and C++17. We will witness the evolution of this pattern as the language becomes more powerful. The ScopeGuard pattern exists at the intersection of the declarative programming (say what you want to happen, not how you want it done) and error-safe programs (especially exception safety). We will have to learn a bit about both before we fully understand the ScopeGuard.

The following topics will be covered in this chapter:

- How can we write error-safe and exception-safe code?
- How does RAII make error handling easier?
- What is composability as applied to error handling?
- Why is RAII not powerful enough for error handling, and how is it generalized?
- How can we implement declarative error handling in C++?

Technical requirements

Here is the example code: `https://github.com/PacktPublishing/Hands-On-Design-Patterns-with-CPP/tree/master/Chapter11`.

You will also need the Google Benchmark library installed and configured: `https://github.com/google/benchmark` (see `Chapter 4`, *Swap – From Simple to Subtle*, for installation instructions).

This chapter is rather heavy on advanced C++ features, so keep a C++ reference nearby (https://en.cppreference.com unless you want to dig through the standard itself).

Finally, a very thorough and complete implementation of the ScopeGuard can be found in the Folly library: https://github.com/facebook/folly/blob/master/folly/ScopeGuard.h ; it includes C++ library programming details beyond those covered in this book.

Error handling and Resource Acquisition Is Initialization

We begin by reviewing the concepts of error handling, and, in particular, writing exception-safe code in C++. The **Resource Acquisition Is Initialization (RAII)** idiom is one of the primary methods of error handling in C++. We already dedicated an entire chapter to it, and you will need it here to make sense of what we are about to do. Let's first recognize the problem we are facing.

Error safety and exception safety

For the rest of this chapter, we will consider the following problem—suppose we are implementing a database of records. The records are stored on disk, but there is also an in-memory index for fast access to the records. The database API offers a method to insert records into the database:

```
class Record { ... };
class Database {
    public:
    void insert(const Record& r);
    ...
};
```

If the insertion succeeds, both the index and the disk storage are updated and are consistent with each other. If something goes wrong, an exception is thrown.

While it appears to the clients of the database that the insertion is a single transaction, the implementation has to deal with the fact that it is done in multiple steps—we need to insert the record into the index and write it to disk. To facilitate this, the database contains two classes, each responsible for its type of storage:

```
class Database {
    class Storage { ... };     // Disk storage
    Storage S;
```

```
    class Index { ... };       // Memory index
    Index I;
    public:
    void insert(const Record& r);
    ...
};
```

The implementation of the insert() function must insert the record into both the storage and the index, there is no way around it:

```
void Database::insert(const Record& r) {
    S.insert(r);
    I.insert(r);
}
```

Unfortunately, either of these operations can fail. Let's see first what happens if the storage insertion fails. Let's assume that all failures in the program are signaled by throwing exceptions. If the storage insertion fails, the storage remains unchanged, the index insertion is not attempted at all, and the exception is propagated out of the Database::insert() function. That is exactly what we want—the insertion failed, the database is unchanged, and an exception is thrown.

So, what happens if the storage insertion succeeds but the index fails? Things are not looking so good this time—the disk is altered successfully, then the index insertion fails, the exception propagates to the caller of Database::insert() to signal the insertion failure, but the truth is the insertion did not completely fail. It did not completely succeed either. The database is left in an inconsistent state; there is a record on disk that is not accessible from the index. This is a failure to handle an error condition, exception-unsafe code, and it just won't do.

The impulsive attempt to change the order of the sub-operations does not help:

```
void Database::insert(const Record& r) {
    I.insert(r);
    S.insert(r);
}
```

Sure, everything is now fine if the index fails. But we have the same problem if the storage insertion throws an exception—we now have an entry in the index that is pointing to nowhere, since the record was never written to disk.

Obviously, we cannot just ignore the exceptions thrown by `Index` or `Storage`; we have to somehow deal with them to maintain the consistency of the database. We know how to handle exceptions, that's what the try-catch block is for:

```
void Database::insert(const Record& r) {
    S.insert(r);
    try {
        I.insert(r);
    } catch (...) {
        S.undo();
        throw;          // Rethrow
    }
}
```

Again, if the storage fails, we don't need to do anything special. If the index fails, we have to undo the last operation on the storage (let's assume that it has the API to do that). Now the database is again consistent, as if the insertion never happened. Even though we caught the exception thrown by the index, we still need to signal to the caller that the insertion fails, and so we re-throw the exception. So far, so good.

The situation is not much different if we choose to use error codes instead of exceptions; let's consider the variant where all `insert()` functions return `true` if they succeed and `false` if they fail:

```
bool Database::insert(const Record& r) {
    if (!S.insert(r)) return false;
    if (!I.insert(r)) {
        S.undo();
        return false;
    }
    return true;
}
```

We have to check the return value of every function, undo the first action if the second one fails, and return `true` only if both actions succeed.

So far, so good; we were able to fix the simplest two-stage problem, so the code is error-safe. Now, it is time to up the complexity. Suppose that our storage needs some cleanup to be performed at the end of the transaction, for example, the inserted record is not in its final state until we call the `Storage::finalize()` method (maybe this is done so `Storage::undo()` can work, and after the insertion is finalized it can no longer be undone). Note the difference between `undo()` and `finalize()`; the former must be called only if we want to roll back the transaction, while the latter must be called if the storage insertion succeeded, regardless of what happens after.

Our requirements are met with this flow of control:

```
void Database::insert(const Record& r) {
    S.insert(r);
    try {
        I.insert(r);
    } catch (...) {
        S.undo();
        S.finalize();
        throw;
    }
    S.finalize();
}
```

Or we have something similar in the case of returning error codes (for the rest of this chapter, we will use exceptions in all our examples, but conversion to error codes is not hard).

This is already getting ugly, particularly the part about getting the cleanup code (in our case, `S.finalize()`) to run in every execution path. It's only going to get worse if we have a more complex sequence of actions that must all be undone unless the entire operation succeeds. Here is the control flow for three actions, each with their own rollback and cleanup:

```
if (action1() == SUCCESS) {
    if (action2() == SUCCESS) {
        if (action3() == FAIL) {
            rollback2();
            rollback1();
        }
        cleanup2();
    } else {
        rollback1();
    }
    cleanup1();
}
```

The obvious problem is the explicit tests for success, either as conditionals or as try-catch blocks. The more serious problem is that this way of error handling is not composable. The solution for N+1 actions is not the code for N actions with some bits added to it; no, we have to go deep inside the code and add the right pieces there. But we have already seen the C++ idiom for solving this very problem.

Resource Acquisition Is Initialization

The RAII idiom binds resources to objects. The object is constructed when the resource is acquired, and the resource is deleted when the object is destroyed. In our case, we are interested only in the second half, the destruction. The advantage of the RAII idiom is that the destructors of all local objects must be called when the control reaches the end of the scope, regardless of how it happens (return, throw, break, and so on). Since we struggled with the cleanup, let's hand that off to an RAII object:

```
class StorageFinalizer {
    public:
    StorageFinalizer(Storage& S) : S_(S) {}
    ~StorageFinalizer() { S_.finalize(); }
    private:
    Storage& S_;
};
void Database::insert(const Record& r) {
    S.insert(r);
    StorageFinalizer SF(S);
    try {
        I.insert(r);
    } catch (...) {
        S.undo();
        throw;
    }
}
```

The StorageFinalizer object binds to the Storage object when it is constructed and calls finalize() when it is destroyed. Since there is no way to exit the scope in which the StorageFinalizer object is defined without calling its destructor, we do not need to worry about the control flow, at least for the cleanup; it is going to happen. Note that the StorageFinalizer is properly constructed after the storage insertion succeeds; if the first insertion fails, there is nothing to finalize.

This code works, but it looks somehow half-done; we have two actions that are performed at the end of the function, and the first one (cleanup, or finalize()) is automated while the second one (rollback, or undo()) is not. Also, the technique is still not composable; here is the flow of control for three actions:

```
class Cleanup1() {
    ~Cleanup1() { cleanup1(); }
    ...
};
class Cleanup2() {
    ~Cleanup2() { cleanup2(); }
```

```
    . . .
};

action1();
Cleanup1 c1;
try {
    action2();
    Cleanup2 c2;
    try {
        action3();
    } catch (...) {
        rollback2();
        throw;
    }
} catch (...) {
    rollback1();
}
```

Again, to add another action, we have to add a try-catch block deep in the code. On the other hand, the cleanup part by itself is perfectly composable. Consider what the previous code looks like if we don't need to do a rollback:

```
action1();
Cleanup1 c1;
action2();
Cleanup2 c2;
```

If we need one more action, we simply add two lines at the end of the function, and the cleanup happens in the right order. If we could do the same for the rollback, we would be all set.

We cannot simply move the call to undo() into a destructor of another object; the destructors are always called, but the rollback happens only in the case of an error. But we can make the destructor call the rollback conditionally:

```
class StorageGuard {
    public:
    StorageGuard(Storage& S) : S_(S), commit_(false) {}
    ~StorageGuard() { if (!commit_) S_.undo(); }
    void commit() noexcept { commit_ = true; }
    private:
    Storage& S_;
    bool commit_;
};
void Database::insert(const Record& r) {
    S.insert(r);
    StorageFinalizer SF(S);
```

```
        StorageGuard SG(S);
        I.insert(r);
        SG.commit();
    }
```

Examine the code now; if the storage insertion fails, the exception is thrown and the database is unchanged. If it succeeds, two RAII objects are constructed. The first one will unconditionally call `S.finalize()` at the end of the scope. The second one will call `S.undo()` unless we commit the change first by calling the `commit()` method on the `StorageGuard` object. That will happen unless the index insertion fails, in which case an exception is thrown, the rest of the code in the scope is bypassed, and the control jumps straight to the end of the scope (the closing `}`) where the destructors of all local objects are called. Since we never called `commit()` in this scenario, the `StorageGuard` is still active and will undo the insertion.

The destructors of the local objects are called in the reverse construction order. This is important; if we have to undo the insertion, this can be done only until the action is finalized, so the rollback has to happen before the cleanup. Therefore, we construct the RAII objects in the correct order—first, the cleanup (to be done last), then the rollback guard (to be done first, if necessary).

The code now looks very nice, no try-catch blocks at all. In some ways, it does not look like regular C++. This programming style is called **declarative programming**; it is a programming paradigm in which the program logic is expressed without explicitly stating the flow of control (the opposite, and the more common in C++, is **imperative programming**, where the program describes which steps to do and in what order, but not necessarily why). There are declarative programming languages (the prime example is SQL), but C++ is not one of them. Nonetheless, C++ is very good at implementing constructs that allow the creation of higher-order languages on top of C++, and so we have implemented a declarative error handling language. Our program now says that after the record was inserted into storage, two actions are pending—the cleanup and the rollback. The rollback is disarmed if the entire function succeeds. The code looks linear, without the explicit flow of control, in other words, declarative.

Nice as it is, it is also far from perfect. The obvious problem is that we have to write a guard or a finalizer class for every action in our program. The less obvious one is that writing these classes correctly is not easy, and we have not done a particularly good job so far. Take a moment to figure out what is missing before looking at the fixed version here:

```
    class StorageGuard {
        public:
        StorageGuard(Storage& S) : S_(S), commit_(false) {}
        ~StorageGuard() { if (!commit_) S_.undo(); }
```

```
    void commit() noexcept { commit_ = true; }
    private:
    Storage& S_;
    bool commit_;
    // Important: really bad things happen if this guard is copied!
    StorageGuard(const StorageGuard&) = delete;
    StorageGuard& operator=(const StorageGuard&) = delete;
};
void Database::insert(const Record& r) {
    S.insert(r);
    StorageFinalizer SF(S);
    StorageGuard SG(S);
    I.insert(r);
    SG.commit();
}
```

What we need is a general framework that lets us schedule an arbitrary action to be executed at the end of the scope, unconditionally or conditionally. The next section presents the pattern that provides such a framework, the ScopeGuard.

The ScopeGuard pattern

In this section, we learn how to write the on-exit action RAII classes like the ones we implemented in the previous section, but without all the boilerplate code. This can be done in C++03 but is much improved in C++14, and again in C++17.

ScopeGuard basics

Let's start with the more difficult problem—how to implement a generic rollback class, a generic version of StorageGuard from the last section. The only difference between that and the cleanup class is that the cleanup is always active, but the rollback is canceled after the action is committed. If we have the conditional rollback version, we can always take out the condition check, and we get the cleanup version, so let's not worry about that for now.

In our example, the rollback is a call to the S.undo() method. To simplify the example, let's start with a rollback that calls a regular function, not a member function:

```
void undo(Storage& S) { S.undo(); }
```

Once the implementation is finished, the program should look something like this:

```
{
    S.insert(r);
    ScopeGuard SG(undo, S);      // Sample desired syntax (approximate)
    ...
    SG.commit();                 // Disarm the scope guard
}
```

This code tells us (in a declarative manner!) that if the insert action succeeded, we schedule the rollback to be done upon exiting the scope. The rollback will call the undo() function with the argument S, which in turn will undo the insertion. If we made it to the end of the function, we disarm the guard and disable the rollback call, which commits the insertion and makes it permanent.

A much more general and reusable solution was proposed by Andrei Alexandrescu in the *Dr. Dobbs article* in 2000 (http://www.drdobbs.com/cpp/generic-change-the-way-you-write-excepti/184403758?). Let's look at the implementation and analyze it:

```
class ScopeGuardImplBase {
    public:
    ScopeGuardImplBase() : commit_(false) {}
    void commit() const throw() { commit_ = true; }

    protected:
    ScopeGuardImplBase(const ScopeGuardImplBase& other)
        : commit_(other.commit_) { other.commit(); }
    ~ScopeGuardImplBase() {}
    mutable bool commit_;

    private:
    ScopeGuardImplBase& operator=(const ScopeGuardImplBase&);
};

template <typename Func, typename Arg>
class ScopeGuardImpl : public ScopeGuardImplBase {
    public:
    ScopeGuardImpl(const Func& func, Arg& arg) : func_(func), arg_(arg) {}
    ~ScopeGuardImpl() { if (!commit_) func_(arg_); }
    private:
    const Func& func_;
    Arg& arg_;
};

template <typename Func, typename Arg>
ScopeGuardImpl<Func, Arg> MakeGuard(const Func& func, Arg& arg) {
    return ScopeGuardImpl<Func, Arg>(func, arg);
```

```
}
```

From the top, we have the base class for all the scope guards, `ScopeGuardImplBase`. The base class holds the commit flag and the code to manipulate it; the constructor initially creates the guard in the armed state, so the deferred action will happen in the destructor. The call to `commit()` will prevent that from happening and make the destructor do nothing. Finally, there is a copy constructor that creates a new guard in the same state as the original but then disarms the original guard. This is so the rollback does not happen twice, from the destructors of both objects. The object is copyable but not assignable. We use C++03 features for everything here, including the disabled assignment operator. This implementation is fundamentally C++03, the few C++11 twists are just icing on the cake (that is about to change in the next section).

There are several details of the implementation of `ScopeGuardImplBase` that may seem odd and need elaboration. First of all, the destructor is not virtual; this is not a typo or a bug, this is intentional, as we will see later. Second, the `commit_` flag is declared `mutable`. This is, of course, so that it can be changed by the `commit()` method, which we declared `const`. So, why is `commit()` declared `const`? One reason is so we can call it on the source object from the copy constructor, to transfer the responsibility for the rollback from the other object to this one. In this sense, the copy constructor really does a move and will be officially declared as such later. The second reason for the `const` will become obvious later (it is related to the non-virtual destructor, of all things).

Let's now turn to the derived class, `ScopeGuardImpl`. This is a class template with two type parameters—the first is the type of the function or any other callable object we are going to call for the rollback, and the second is the type of the argument. Our rollback function is restricted, for now, to having only one argument. That function is called in the destructor of the `ScopeGuard` object unless the guard was disarmed by calling `commit()`.

Finally, we have a factory function template, `MakeGuard`. This is a very common idiom in C++; if you need to create an instantiation of a class template from the constructor arguments, use a template function that can deduce the type of the parameters and that of the return value from the arguments (in C++17 class templates can do that too, as we will see later).

How is this all used to create a guard object that will call `undo(S)` for us? Like this:

```
void Database::insert(const Record& r) {
    S.insert(r);
    const ScopeGuardImplBase& SG = MakeGuard(undo, S);
```

```
        I.insert(r);
        SG.commit();
}
```

The `MakeGaurd` function deduces the types of the `undo()` function and the argument `s` and returns a `ScopeGuard` object of the corresponding type. The return is by value, so there is a copy involved (the compiler may choose to elide the copy as an optimization, but is not required to). The returned object is a temporary variable, it has no name, and binds it to the base class reference `SG` (casting from the derived class to the base class is implicit for both pointers and references). The lifetime of the temporary variable is until the closing semicolon of the statement that created it, as everyone knows. But then, what does the `SG` reference point to after the end of the statement? It has to be bound to something, as references cannot be unbound, they are not like `NULL` pointers. The truth is, *everyone* knows wrong, or rather only mostly right—usually the temporaries indeed live until the end of the statement. However, binding a temporary to a `const` reference extends its lifetime to coincide with the lifetime of the reference itself. In other words, the unnamed temporary `ScopeGuard` object created by `MakeGuard` will not be destroyed until the `SG` reference goes out of scope. Const-ness is important here, but do not worry, you can't forget it; the language does not permit binding non-`const` references to temporary variables, so the compiler will let you know. So this explains the `commit()` method; it has to be `const` since we are going to call it on the `const` reference (and, therefore, the `commit_` flag has to be `mutable`).

But what about the destructor? At the end of the scope, the destructor of the `ScopeGuardImplBase` class will be called, since that is the type of the reference that goes out of scope. The base class destructor itself does nothing, it's the derived class that has the destructor we want. A polymorphic class with a virtual destructor would have served us right, but we did not take that route. Instead, we availed ourselves of yet another special rule in the C++ standard concerning `const` references and temporary variables—not only is the lifetime of the temporary variable extended, but also the destructor of the derived class, that is the actual class that was constructed, is going to be called at the end of the scope. Note that this rule applies only to destructors; you still cannot call derived class methods on the base class `SG` reference . Also, the lifetime extension works only when the temporary variable is directly bound to a `const` reference. It does not work if, for example, we initialize another `const` reference from the first one. This is why we had to return the `ScopeGuard` object from the `MakeGuard` function by value; if we tried to return it by reference, the temporary would be bound to that reference, which is going to go away at the end of the statement. The second reference, `SG`, initialized from the first one, would not have extended the lifetime of the object.

The function implementation we just saw comes very close to the original goal, it is just a bit more verbose (and it mentions `ScopeGuardImplBase` instead of the promised `ScopeGuard`). Fear not, for the last step is merely syntactic sugar:

```
typedef const ScopeGuardImplBase& ScopeGuard;
```

Now, we can write this:

```
void Database::insert(const Record& r) {
    S.insert(r);
    ScopeGuard SG = MakeGuard(undo, S);
    I.insert(r);
    SG.commit();
}
```

This is as far as we are going to get with the language tools we've used so far. Ideally, the desired syntax would be as follows (and we are not very far off):

```
ScopeGuard SG(undo, S);
```

We can tidy up our ScopeGuard a bit by making use of the C++11 features. First of all, we can properly disable the assignment operator. Second, we can stop pretending that our copy constructor is anything other than a move constructor. Finally, the no-throw declaration is changed from `throw()` to `noexcept`:

```
class ScopeGuardImplBase {
    public:
    ScopeGuardImplBase() : commit_(false) {}
    void commit() const noexcept { commit_ = true; }

    protected:
    ScopeGuardImplBase(ScopeGuardImplBase&& other)
        : commit_(other.commit_) { other.commit(); }
    ~ScopeGuardImplBase() {}
    mutable bool commit_;

    private:
    ScopeGuardImplBase& operator=(const ScopeGuardImplBase&) = delete;
};
typedef const ScopeGuardImplBase& ScopeGuard;

template <typename Func, typename Arg>
class ScopeGuardImpl : public ScopeGuardImplBase {
    public:
    ScopeGuardImpl(const Func& func, Arg& arg)
        : func_(func), arg_(arg) {}
    ~ScopeGuardImpl() { if (!commit_) func_(arg_); }
```

```
        ScopeGuardImpl(ScopeGuardImpl&& other)
            : ScopeGuardImplBase(std::move(other)),
              func_(other.func_),
              arg_(other.arg_) {}
    private:
    const Func& func_;
    Arg& arg_;
};

template <typename Func, typename Arg>
ScopeGuardImpl<Func, Arg> MakeGuard(const Func& func, Arg& arg) {
    return ScopeGuardImpl<Func, Arg>(func, arg);
}
```

Moving to C++14, we can make one more simplification and deduce the return type of the `MakeGuard` function:

```
template <typename Func, typename Arg>
auto MakeGuard(const Func& func, Arg& arg) {
    return ScopeGuardImpl<Func, Arg>(func, arg);
}
```

There is still one concession we had to make—we did not really need the `undo(S)` function what we really wanted was to call `S.undo()`. This is done just as easily with a member function variant of the `ScopeGuard`. In fact, the only reason we have not done so from the beginning is to make the example easier to follow; the member function pointer syntax is not the most straightforward aspect of C++:

```
template <typename MemFunc, typename Obj>
class ScopeGuardImpl : public ScopeGuardImplBase {
    public:
    ScopeGuardImpl(const MemFunc& memfunc, Obj& obj)
        : memfunc_(memfunc), obj_(obj) {}
    ~ScopeGuardImpl() { if (!commit_) (obj_.*memfunc_)(); }
    ScopeGuardImpl(ScopeGuardImpl&& other)
        : ScopeGuardImplBase(std::move(other)),
          memfunc_(other.memfunc_),
          obj_(other.obj_) {}
    private:
    const MemFunc& memfunc_;
    Obj& obj_;
};

template <typename MemFunc, typename Obj>
auto MakeGuard(const MemFunc& memfunc, Obj& obj) {      // C++14
    return ScopeGuardImpl<MemFunc, Obj>(memfunc, obj);
}
```

Of course, if both versions of the ScopeGuard template are used in the same program, we have to rename one of them. Also, our function guard is limited to calling functions with only one argument, while our member function guard can call only member functions with no arguments. In C++03, this problem is solved in a tedious but reliable way—we have to create versions of the implementation, `ScopeGuardImpl0`, `ScopeGuardImpl1`, `ScopeGuardImpl2`, and so on, for functions with zero, one, two, and so on arguments. We then create `ScopeObjGuardImpl0`, `ScopeObjGuardImpl1`, and so on, for member functions with zero, one, two, and so on arguments. If we do not create enough, the compiler will let's know. The base class remains the same for all these variants of the derived class, and so is the `ScopeGuard` typedef.

In C++11, we have variadic templates that are designed to address this exact problem, but we're not going to see such an implementation here. There is no reason for it; we can do so much better than that, as you are about to see.

Generic ScopeGuard

We are now firmly in C++11 territory, nothing that you are about to see has a C++03 equivalent of any practical worth.

Our `ScopeGuard` has, so far, allowed us to all arbitrary functions as rollback for any action. Just like the hand-crafted guard objects, the scope guards are composable and guarantee exception safety. But our implementation, so far, is somewhat limited in what exactly we can call to implement the rollback; it has to be a function or a member function. While this seems to cover a lot, we may want to call, for example, two functions to do a single rollback. We could, of course, write a wrapper function for that, but that sets us back on the path toward single-purpose hand-crafted rollback objects.

There is, in truth, another problem with our implementation. We decided to capture the function argument by reference:

```
ScopeGuardImpl(const Func& func, Arg& arg);
```

This mostly works, unless the argument is a constant or a temporary variable; then, our code will not compile.

C++11 gives us another way to create arbitrary callable objects, lambda expressions. Lambdas are actually classes, but they behave like functions in that they can be called with parentheses. They can take arguments, but they can also capture any arguments from the containing scope, and that often obviates the need to pass arguments to the function call itself. We can also write arbitrary code and package it in a lambda expression. This sounds ideal for the scope guard; we could just write something that says *at the end of the scope run this code.*

Let's see what a lambda expression ScopeGuard looks like:

```
class ScopeGuardBase {
    public:
    ScopeGuardBase() : commit_(false) {}
    void commit() const noexcept { commit_ = true; }

    protected:
    ScopeGuardBase(ScopeGuardBase&& other)
        : commit_(other.commit_) { other.commit(); }
    ~ScopeGuardBase() {}
    mutable bool commit_;

    private:
    ScopeGuardBase& operator=(const ScopeGuardBase&) = delete;
};

template <typename Func>
class ScopeGuard : public ScopeGuardBase {
    public:
    ScopeGuard(Func&& func) : func_(func) {}
    ScopeGuard(const Func& func) : func_(func) {}
    ~ScopeGuard() { if (!commit_) func_(); }
    ScopeGuard(ScopeGuard&& other)
        : ScopeGuardBase(std::move(other)),
          func_(other.func_) {}
    private:
    Func func_;
};

template <typename Func>
ScopeGuard<Func> MakeGuard(Func&& func) {
    return ScopeGuard<Func>(std::forward<Func>(func));
}
```

The base class is essentially the same as before, except we are not going to use the const reference trick anymore, and so the `Impl` suffix is gone; what you see is not an implementation aid but the base of the guard class itself.

The derived class, on the other hand, is much different. First of all, there is only one class for all types of rollback, and the argument type parameter is gone; instead, we have a functional object that is going to be a lambda, and it'll contain all the arguments that it needs. The destructor is the same as before (except for the missing argument to the callable func_), so is the move constructor. But the primary constructor of the object is quite different; the callable object is stored by value, and initialized from either a `const` reference or an r-value reference, with a suitable overload selected automatically by the compiler.

The `MakeGuard` function is largely unchanged, and we do not need two of them; we can use perfect forwarding (`std::forward`) to forward the argument of any type to one of the constructors of `ScopeGuard`.

Here is how this ScopeGuard is used:

```
void Database::insert(const Record& r) {
    S.insert(r);
    auto SG = MakeGuard([&] { S.undo(); });
    I.insert(r);
    SG.commit();
}
```

The punctuation-rich construct that is used as an argument to `MakeGuard` is the lambda expression. It creates a callable object, and calling this object will run the code in the body of the lambda, in our case `S.undo()`. There is no `S` variable declared in the lambda object itself, so it has to be captured from the containing scope. All captures are done by reference (`[&]`). Finally, the object is called with no arguments; the parentheses can be omitted, although `MakeGuard([&]() { S.undo(); });` is also valid. The function does not return anything, that is, the return type is `void`; it does not have to be explicitly declared. Note that, so far, we have used C++11 lambdas and have not taken advantage of the more powerful C++14 lambdas. This will usually be the case with the ScopeGuard, although in practice one would probably use C++14 just for auto-deduced return types if nothing else.

We have, until now, intentionally set aside the matter of the regular cleanup and focused on the error handling and the rollback. Now that we have a decent working ScopeGuard, we can tie up loose ends quite easily:

```
void Database::insert(const Record& r) {
    S.insert(r);
    auto SF = MakeGuard([&] { S.finalize(); });
    auto SG = MakeGuard([&] { S.undo(); });
    I.insert(r);
    SG.commit();
}
```

As you can see, nothing special needs to be added to our framework to support the cleanup. We simply create another ScopeGuard that we never disarm.

We should also point out that, in C++17, we no longer need the `MakeGuard` function since the compiler can deduce the template arguments from the constructor:

```
void Database::insert(const Record& r) {
    S.insert(r);
    auto SF = ScopeGuard([&] { S.finalize(); });    // C++17 only
    auto SG = ScopeGuard([&] { S.undo(); });
    I.insert(r);
    SG.commit();
}
```

As long as we are on the subject of making ScopeGuard use prettier, we should consider some helpful macros. We can easily write a macro for the cleanup guard, the one that is always executed. We would like the resulting syntax to look something like this (if this isn't declarative enough, I don't know what is):

```
ON_SCOPE_EXIT { S.finalize(); };
```

We can, infact, get that very syntax. First of all, we need to generate a name for the guard, what used to be called `SF`, and we need it to be something unique. From the cutting edge of the modern C++, we are now reaching decades back, to the classic C and its preprocessor tricks, to generate a unique name for an anonymous variable:

```
#define CONCAT2(x, y) x##y
#define CONCAT(x, y) CONCAT2(x, y)
#ifdef __COUNTER__
#define ANON_VAR(x) CONCAT(x, __COUNTER__)
#else
#define ANON_VAR(x) CONCAT(x, __LINE__)
#endif
```

The `CONCAT` macros are how you concatenate two tokens in the preprocessor (and yes, you need two of them, that's the way the preprocessor works). The first token will be a user-specified prefix, and the second one is something unique. Many compilers support a preprocessor variable, `__COUNTER__`, that is incremented every time it's used, so it's never the same. However, it is not in the standard. If `__COUNTER__` is not available, we have to use the line number `__LINE__` as a unique identifier. Of course, it is only unique if we don't put two guards on the same line, so don't.

Now that we have a way to generate an anonymous variable name, we can implement the `ON_SCOPE_EXIT` macro. It would be trivial to implement one where the code is passed as a macro argument, but it would not give us the syntax we want; the argument has to be in parentheses, so at best we could get `ON_SCOPE_EXIT(S.finalize();)`. Also, commas in the code confuse the preprocessor, since it interprets them as a separator between the macro arguments. If you look carefully at the syntax we requested, `ON_SCOPE_EXIT {` `S.finalize(); };`, you will realize that this macro has no arguments at all, and the body of the lambda expression is just typed after the no-argument macro. The macro expansion, therefore, ends on something that can be followed by an opening curly brace. Here is how this is done:

```
struct ScopeGuardOnExit {};
template <typename Func>
ScopeGuard<Func> operator+(ScopeGuardOnExit, Func&& func) {
    return ScopeGuard<Func>(std::forward<Func>(func));
}
#define ON_SCOPE_EXIT \
    auto ANON_VAR(SCOPE_EXIT_STATE) = ScopeGuardOnExit() + [&]()
```

The macro expansion declares an anonymous variable that starts with `SCOPE_EXIT_STATE`, followed by a unique number, and it ends on the incomplete lambda expression, `[&]()`, that is completed by the code in the curly braces. In order to not have a closing parenthesis of the former `MakeGuard` function, which the macro cannot generate (the macro is expanded before the lambda body, so it cannot generate any code after that), we have to replace the `MakeGuard` function (or the `ScopeGuard` constructor in C++17) with an operator. The choice of the operator does not matter; we use +, but we could use any binary operator. The first argument to the operator is a temporary object of a unique type, it limits the overload resolution only to the `operator+()` defined previously (the object itself is not used at all, we only need its type). The `operator+()` itself is exactly what `MakeGuard` used to be, it deduces the type of the lambda expression and creates the corresponding `ScopeGuard` object. The only downside of this technique is that the closing semicolon at the end of the `ON_SCOPE_EXIT` statement is required, and should you forget it, the compiler will remind you in the most obscure and opaque way possible.

Our program code can now be further tidied up:

```
void Database::insert(const Record& r) {
    S.insert(r);
    ON_SCOPE_EXIT { S.finalize(); };
    auto SG = ScopeGuard([&] { S.undo(); });
    I.insert(r);
    SG.commit();
}
```

It is tempting to apply the same technique to the second guard. Unfortunately, this is not so simple; we have to know the name of this variable so we can call `commit()` on it. We can define a similar macro that does not use an anonymous variable but instead takes the user-specified name:

```
#define ON_SCOPE_EXIT_ROLLBACK(NAME) \
    auto NAME = ScopeGuardOnExit() + [&]()
```

We can use it to complete the conversion of our code:

```
void Database::insert(const Record& r) {
    S.insert(r);
    ON_SCOPE_EXIT { S.finalize(); };
    ON_SCOPE_EXIT_ROLLBACK(SG){ S.undo(); };
    I.insert(r);
    SG.commit();
}
```

At this point, we should revisit the issue of composability. For three actions, each with their own rollback and cleanup, we now have the following:

```
action1();
ON_SCOPE_EXIT { cleanup1; };
ON_SCOPE_EXIT_ROLLBACK(g2){ rollback1(); };
action2();
ON_SCOPE_EXIT { cleanup2; };
ON_SCOPE_EXIT_ROLLBACK(g4){ rollback2(); };
action3();
g2.commit();
g4.commit();
```

One can see how this pattern is trivially extended to any number of actions. An observant reader might wonder whether they have noticed a bug in the code, though—should not the rollback guards be dismissed in reverse construction order? This is not a bug, although neither is the reverse order of `commit()` calls. The reason is that `commit()` cannot throw an exception, it was declared `noexcept`, and indeed its implementation is such that no exception can be thrown. This is vitally important for the ScopeGuard pattern to work; if `commit()` could throw, then there would be no way to guarantee that all rollback guards are properly disarmed. At the end of the scope, some actions would be rolled back and others would not, leaving the system in an inconsistent state.

While the ScopeGuard was primarily designed to make exception-safe code easier to write, the interaction of the ScopeGuard pattern with exceptions is far from trivial, and we should spend more time on it.

ScopeGuard and exceptions

The ScopeGuard pattern is designed to correctly run various cleanup and rollback operations automatically upon exiting a scope, no matter what caused the exit—normal completion by reaching the end of the scope, an early return, or an exception. This makes writing error-safe code in general, and exception-safe code in particular, much easier; as long as we queued up the right guards after every action, the correct cleanup and error handling will automatically happen. That is, of course, assuming that the ScopeGuard itself is functioning correctly in the presence of exceptions. We are going to learn how to make sure it does, and how to use it to make the rest of the code error-safe.

What must not throw an exception

We have already seen that the `commit()` function that is used to commit an action and disarm the rollback guard must never throw an exception. Fortunately, that is easy to guarantee since all this function does is set a flag. But what happens if the rollback function also fails, and throws an exception?

```
void Database::insert(const Record& r) {
    S.insert(r);
    auto SF = MakeGuard([&] { S.finalize(); });
    auto SG = MakeGuard([&] { S.undo(); });      // What if undo() can throw?
    I.insert(r);                                 // Let's say this fails
    SG.commit();                                 // Commit never happens
}                                                // Control jumps here and
undo() throws
```

The short answer is *nothing good*. In general, we have a conundrum—we cannot allow the action, in our case the storage insertion, to remain, but we also cannot undo it, since that also fails. Specifically, in C++, two exceptions cannot propagate at the same time. For that reason, the destructors are not allowed to throw exceptions; a destructor may be called when an exception is thrown, and if that destructor also throws, we now have two exceptions propagating at the same time. If this happens, the program immediately terminates. This is not so much a shortcoming of the language as a reflection on the unsolvable nature of the problem in general; we cannot let things stay the way they are, but we also failed in an attempt to change something. There aren't any good options left.

In general, there are three ways a C++ program can handle this situation. The best option is not to fall into this trap—if the rollback cannot throw, none of this will happen. A well-written exception-safe program thus goes to great lengths to provide non-throwing rollback and cleanup. For example, the main action can produce the new data and have it ready, then making the data available to the callers is as simple as swapping a pointer, definitely a non-throwing operation. The rollback involves only swapping the pointer back and maybe deleting something (as we already said, destructors should not throw exceptions; if they do, the program behavior is undefined).

The second option is to suppress the exception in the rollback. We tried to undo the operation, it didn't work, there is nothing else we can do about it, so let's push on. The danger here is that the program may be in an undefined state, and every operation from this point forward may be incorrect. This is, however, the worst case scenario. In practice, consequences may be less severe. For example, for our database, we may know that if the rollback fails, there is a chunk of disk space that is claimed by the record but is unreachable from the index. The caller will be correctly informed that the insertion failed, but we have wasted some disk space. This may be preferable to terminating the program outright. If this is what we want, we have to catch any exceptions that might be thrown by the ScopeGuard action:

```
template <typename Func>
class ScopeGuard : public ScopeGuardBase {
    public:
    ...
    ~ScopeGuard() {
        if (!commit_) try { func_(); } catch (...) {}
    }
    ...
};
```

The catch clause is empty; we catch everything, but do nothing. This implementation is sometimes called a *shielded ScopeGuard*.

The final option is to allow the program to fail. That will happen with no effort on our part if we just let two exceptions happen, but we could also print a message or otherwise signal to the user what is about to happen and why. If we want to insert our own dying action before the program terminates, we have to write code that is very similar to previously:

```
template <typename Func>
class ScopeGuard : public ScopeGuardBase {
    public:
    ...
    ~ScopeGuard() {
        if (!commit_) try { func_(); } catch (...) {
            std::cout << "Rollback failed" << std::endl;
```

```
            throw;              // Rethrow
        }
    }
    ...
};
```

The key difference is the `throw;` statement without any arguments. This re-throws the exception we caught and allows it to continue propagating.

The difference between the last two code fragments highlights a subtle detail that we have glossed over earlier, but one that will become important later. It is imprecise to say that in C++ the destructors should not throw exceptions. The correct statement is that an exception should not propagate out of the destructor. The destructor can throw anything it wants as long as it also catches it:

```
class LivingDangerously {
    public:
    ~LivingDangerously() {
        try {
            if (cleanup() != SUCCESS) throw 0;
            more_cleanup();
        } catch (...) {
            std::cout << "Cleanup failed, proceeding anyway" << std::endl;
            // No rethrow - this is critical!
        }
    }
};
```

Up until now, we have dealt with exceptions mostly as a nuisance; the program has to remain in a well-defined state if something somewhere throws something, but other than that, we have no use for these exceptions, we just pass them on. On the other hand, our code could work with any type of error handling, be it exceptions or error codes. If we knew for sure that errors are always signaled by exceptions and that any return from a function other than an exception thrown is a success, we could take advantage of that to automate the detection of success or failure, and therefore allow a commit or rollback to happen as needed.

Exception-driven ScopeGuard

We are now going to assume that if a function returns without throwing an exception, the operation has succeeded. If the function throws, it obviously failed. The objective now is to get rid of the explicit call to `commit()` and instead detect whether the destructor of a ScopeGuard is executed because an exception was thrown, or because the function returned normally.

There are two parts to this implementation. The first part is specifying when we want the action to be taken. The cleanup guard must be executed regardless of how we exit the scope. The rollback guard is executed only in case of a failure. For completeness, we can also have a guard that is executed only if the function has succeeded. The second part is determining what actually happened.

We will start with the second part. Our ScopeGuard now needs two additional parameters that will tell us whether it should be executed on success and whether it should be executed on failure (both can be enabled at the same time). Only the destructor of the ScopeGuard needs to be modified:

```
template <typename Func, bool on_success, bool on_failure>
class ScopeGuard {
    public:
    ...
    ~ScopeGuard() {
        if ((on_success && is_success()) ||
            (on_failure && is_failure())) func_();
    }
    ...
};
```

We still need to figure out how to implement the pseudo-functions is_success() and is_failure(). Remember that failure means that an exception was thrown. In C++, we have a function for that: std::uncaught_exception(). It returns true if an exception is currently propagating, and false otherwise. Armed with this knowledge, we can implement our guard:

```
template <typename Func, bool on_success, bool on_failure>
class ScopeGuard {
    public:
    ...
    ~ScopeGuard() {
        if ((on_success && !std::uncaught_exception()) ||
            (on_failure && std::uncaught_exception())) func_();
    }
    ...
};
```

Now, back to the first part: the ScopeGuard will execute the delayed action if the conditions are right, so how do we tell it what conditions are right? Using the macro approach we developed earlier, we can define three versions of the guard—ON_SCOPE_EXIT is always executed, ON_SCOPE_SUCCESS is executed only if no exceptions were thrown, and ON_SCOPE_FAILURE is executed if an exception was thrown. The latter replaces our ON_SCOPE_EXIT_ROLLBACK macro, only now it too can use an anonymous variable name, since there are no explicit calls to commit(). The three macros are defined in a very similar way, we just need three different unique types instead of one ScopeGuardOnExit, so we can decide which operator+() to call:

```
struct ScopeGuardOnExit {};
template <typename Func>
auto operator+(ScopeGuardOnExit, Func&& func) {
    return ScopeGuard<Func, true, true>(std::forward<Func>(func));
}
#define ON_SCOPE_EXIT \
    auto ANON_VAR(SCOPE_EXIT_STATE) = ScopeGuardOnExit() + [&]()

struct ScopeGuardOnSuccess {};
template <typename Func>
auto operator+(ScopeGuardOnSuccess, Func&& func) {
    return ScopeGuard<Func, true, false>(std::forward<Func>(func));
}
#define ON_SCOPE_SUCCESS \
    auto ANON_VAR(SCOPE_EXIT_STATE) = ScopeGuardOnSuccess() + [&]()

struct ScopeGuardOnFailure {};
template <typename Func>
auto operator+(ScopeGuardOnFailure, Func&& func) {
    return ScopeGuard<Func, false, true>(std::forward<Func>(func));
}
#define ON_SCOPE_FAILURE \
    auto ANON_VAR(SCOPE_EXIT_STATE) = ScopeGuardOnFailure() + [&]()
```

Each overload of the operator+() constructs a ScopeGuard object with different Boolean arguments that control when it does and does not execute. Each macro directs the lambda expression to the desired overload by specifying the type of the first argument to the operator+() using one of the unique tree types we defined just for this purpose: ScopeGuardOnExit, ScopeGuardOnSuccess, and ScopeGuardOnFailure.

This implementation can pass simple and even fairly elaborate tests and appears to work. Unfortunately, it has a fatal flaw—it does not correctly detect success or failure. To be sure, it works fine if our `Database::insert()` function was called from the normal control flow, where it may or may not succeed. The problem is we may call `Database::insert()` from a destructor of some other object, and that object may be used in a scope where an exception is thrown:

```
class ComplexOperation {
    Database db_;
    public:
    ...
    ~ComplexOperation() {
        try {
            db_.insert(some_record);
        } catch (...) {}      // Shield any exceptions insert() may throw
    }
};

{
    ComplexOperation OP;
    throw 1;
}                                // OP.~ComplexOperation() runs here
```

Now, `db_.insert()` runs in the presence of an uncaught exception, and so `std::uncaught_exception()` will return `true`. The problem is this is not the exception we were looking for. This exception does not indicate that `insert()` failed, but it will be treated as such and the database insertion will be undone.

What we really need is to know how many exceptions are currently propagating. This may seem a strange statement since C++ does not allow multiple exceptions to propagate at the same time. However, we have already seen that this is an oversimplification; the second exception can propagate just fine as long as it does not escape the destructor. In the same manner, three or more exceptions can propagate if we have nested destructor calls, we just have to catch them all in time. To solve this problem correctly, we need to know how many exceptions were propagating when the `Database::insert()` function was called. Then, we can compare it with the number of exceptions propagating at the end of the function, however we got there. If these numbers are the same, `insert()` did not throw any exceptions, and any preexisting ones are not our concern. If a new exception was added, `insert()` has failed and the exit handling must change accordingly.

C++17 lets us implement this detection; in addition to the
previous `std::uncaught_exception()`, which is deprecated (and removed in C++20), we
now have a new function, `std::uncaught_exceptions()`, which returns the number of
currently propagating exceptions. We can now implement
this `UncaughtExceptionDetector` to detect new exceptions:

```
class UncaughtExceptionDetector {
    public:
    UncaughtExceptionDetector()
        : count_(std::uncaught_exceptions()) {}
    operator bool() const noexcept {
        return std::uncaught_exceptions() > count_;
    }
    private:
    const int count_;
};
```

With this detector, we can finally implement the automatic `ScopeGuard`:

```
template <typename Func, bool on_success, bool on_failure>
class ScopeGuard {
    public:
    ...
    ~ScopeGuard() {
        if ((on_success && !detector_) ||
            (on_failure && detector_)) func_();
    }
    ...
    private:
    UncaughtExceptionDetector detector_;
    ...
};
```

The need to use C++17 may present a (hopefully short-term) obstacle to using this
technique. While there is no other standard-compliant, portable way to solve this problem,
most modern compilers have ways to get to the uncaught exception counter. This is how it
is done in GCC or Clang (the names starting with __ are GCC internal types and functions):

```
namespace __cxxabiv1 {
    struct __cxa_eh_globals;
    extern "C" __cxa_eh_globals* __cxa_get_globals() noexcept;
}
class UncaughtExceptionDetector {
    public:
    UncaughtExceptionDetector()
        : count_(uncaught_exceptions()) {}
    operator bool() const noexcept {
```

```
            return uncaught_exceptions() > count_;
    }
    private:
    const int count_;
    int uncaught_exceptions() const noexcept {
            return *(reinterpret_cast<int*>(
                    static_cast<char*>(
                    static_cast<void*>(
                    __cxxabiv1::__cxa_get_globals())) + sizeof(void*)));
    }
};
```

Whether we use the exception-driven ScopeGuard or the explicitly named ScopeGuard (perhaps to handle error codes as well as exceptions), we have accomplished our goals—we now can specify deferred actions that must be taken at the end of a function or any other scope.

At the end of this chapter, we will show another implementation of the ScopeGuard that can be found in several sources on the web. This implementation deserves some consideration, but the reader should be aware of the downsides as well.

Type-erased ScopeGuard

If you search online for a ScopeGuard example, you may chance upon an implementation that uses std::function instead of a class template. The implementation itself is quite simple:

```
class ScopeGuard {
    public:
    template <typename Func> ScopeGuard(Func&& func)
        : commit_(false), func_(func) {}
    template <typename Func> ScopeGuard(const Func& func)
        : commit_(false), func_(func) {}
    ~ScopeGuard() { if (!commit_) func_(); }
    void commit() const noexcept { commit_ = true; }
    ScopeGuard(ScopeGuard&& other)
        : commit_(other.commit_),
          func_(other.func_)
        { other.commit(); }
    private:
    mutable bool commit_;
    std::function<void()> func_;
    ScopeGuard& operator=(const ScopeGuard&) = delete;
};
```

Note that this ScopeGuard is a class, not a class template. It has template constructors that can accept the same lambda expression or another callable object as the other guard. But the variable used to store that expression has the same type no matter what the type of the callable is. That type is `std::function<void()>`, a wrapper for any function that takes no arguments and returns nothing. How can a value of any type be stored in an object of some fixed type? That is the magic of type erasure, and we have a whole chapter dedicated to it. This non-template ScopeGuard makes the code that uses it simpler because there are no types to deduce:

```
void Database::insert(const Record& r) {
    S.insert(r);
    ScopeGuard SF([&] { S.finalize(); });
    ScopeGuard SG([&] { S.undo(); });
    I.insert(r);
    SG.commit();
}
```

There is, however, a serious downside to this approach—a type-erased object has to do a non-trivial amount of computation to achieve its magic. As a minimum, it involves a virtual function call, and often some memory is allocated and deallocated as well.

We can compare the runtime cost of the type-erased ScopeGuard versus the template ScopeGuard using the Google Benchmark library. The results will depend on what operation we are guarding. The most extreme case is an empty guard that does nothing (we are using a REPEAT macro to replicate the benchmarked code 32 times to reduce the overhead of the loop):

```
void BM_type_erased_noop(benchmark::State& state) {
    for (auto _ : state) {
        REPEAT({ScopeGuardTypeErased::ScopeGuard SG([&] { noop(); });})
    }
    state.SetItemsProcessed(32*state.iterations());
}

void BM_template_noop(benchmark::State& state) {
    for (auto _ : state) {
        REPEAT({auto SG = ScopeGuardTemplate::MakeGuard([&] { noop(); });})
    }
    state.SetItemsProcessed(32*state.iterations());
}
```

The result looks rather dramatic:

```
--------------------------------------------------------------------
Benchmark                    Time              CPU Iterations
--------------------------------------------------------------------
BM_type_erased_noop          55 ns          55 ns   12658705   559.464M items/s
BM_template_noop              0 ns           0 ns 1000000000   61.6523P items/s
```

The type-erased version takes some time, just under 2 nanoseconds per call, but the template version appears to be infinitely fast. That is because the code was entirely optimized away; the compiler recognized that there is nothing to be done at the end of the scope, and removed the entire ScopeGuard machinery as dead code.

For a more realistic example, we can use the ScopeGuard to release some memory we allocated (in a real program, this task is better handled by std::unique_ptr, but it provides a useful benchmark):

```
void BM_free(benchmark::State& state) {
    void* p = NULL;
    for (auto _ : state) {
        benchmark::DoNotOptimize(p = malloc(8));
        free(p);
    }
    state.SetItemsProcessed(state.iterations());
}

void BM_type_erased_free(benchmark::State& state) {
    void* p = NULL;
    for (auto _ : state) {
        benchmark::DoNotOptimize(p = malloc(8));
        ScopeGuardTypeErased::ScopeGuard SG([&] { free(p); });
    }
    state.SetItemsProcessed(state.iterations());
}

void BM_template_free(benchmark::State& state) {
    void* p = NULL;
    for (auto _ : state) {
        benchmark::DoNotOptimize(p = malloc(8));
        auto SG = ScopeGuardTemplate::MakeGuard([&] { free(p); });
    }
    state.SetItemsProcessed(state.iterations());
}
```

Just to set a baseline and the expectations for what is *fast* here, we also benchmark the allocation-deallocation sequence without any guards:

```
Benchmark                     Time            CPU Iterations
------------------------------------------------------------
BM_free                       18 ns           18 ns  39010078    53.1427M items/s
BM_type_erased_free           27 ns           27 ns  25172157    34.7562M items/s
BM_template_free              18 ns           18 ns  40311482    52.6061M items/s
```

The result is much more applicable to a real program, if less spectacular. The template ScopeGuard adds no significant overhead, while the type-erased guard nearly doubles the execution time.

Summary

In this chapter, we have studied, in detail, one of the best C++ patterns for writing exception-safe and error-safe code. The ScopeGuard pattern allows us to schedule an arbitrary action, a fragment of C++ code, to be executed upon completion of a scope. The scope may be a function, the body of a loop, or just a scope inserted into the program to manage the lifetime of local variables. The actions that are executed to the end may be conditional on the successful completion of the scope, however that is defined. The ScopeGuard pattern works equally well when success or failure are indicated by return codes or exceptions, although in the latter case we can automatically detect the failure (with return codes, the programmer has to explicitly specify which return values mean success and which do not). We have observed the evolution of the ScopeGuard pattern as more recent language features are used. In its optimal form, the ScopeGuard provides a simple declarative way to specify post-conditions and deferred actions, such as cleanup or rollback, in a manner that is trivially composable for any number of actions that need to be committed or undone.

The next chapter describes another very C++-specific pattern, the Friends Factory, which is a kind of Factory, only instead of objects during the execution of a program, it manufactures functions during its compilation.

Questions

1. What is an error-safe, or exception-safe, program?
2. How can we make a routine that performs several related actions be error-safe?
3. How does RAII assist in writing error-safe programs?
4. How does the ScopeGuard pattern generalize the RAII idiom?
5. How can the program automatically detect when a function exits successfully and when it fails?
6. What are the advantages and drawbacks of a type-erased ScopeGuard?

12
Friend Factory

n this chapter, we are going to talk about making friends. We mean the C++ friends here, not friends of C++ (you find those in your local C++ users group). In C++, friends of classes are functions or other classes that are granted special access to the class. In that way, they are not so different from your friends. But C++ can just manufacture friends as needed, on demand!

The following topics will be covered in this chapter:

- How do friend functions work in C++ and what do they do?
- When should you use friend functions versus class member functions?
- How to combine friends and templates
- How to generate friend functions from templates

Technical requirements

The example code for this chapter can be found at the following GitHub link: `https://github.com/PacktPublishing/Hands-On-Design-Patterns-with-CPP/tree/master/Chapter12`.

Friends in C++

Let's start by reviewing the way in which C++ grants friendship to classes, and the effects of this action, as well as when and for what reasons the friendship should be used (*my code does not compile until I add friend everywhere* is not a valid reason, but an indication of a poorly designed interface—redesign your classes instead).

How to grant friendship in C++

Friend is a C++ concept that applies to classes and affects the access to class members (*access* is what *public* and *private* control). Usually, public member functions and data members are accessible to anyone, and private ones are only accessible to other member functions of the class itself. The following code does not compile because the data member `C:x_` is private:

```
class C {
    int x_;
    public:
    C(int x) : x_(x) {}
};
C increase(C c, int dx) { return C(c.x_ + dx); }    // Does not compile
```

The easiest way to solve this particular problem is to make `increase()` a member function, but let's stay with this version for a moment. The other option is to relax access and make `C::x_` public. That is a bad idea because it exposes `x_`—not just to `increase()`, but to any other code out there that wants to directly modify an object of type `C`. What we need is to make `x_` public, or at least accessible, to `increase()` and to nobody else. This is done with a friend declaration:

```
class C {
    int x_;
    public:
    C(int x) : x_(x) {}
    friend C increase(C c, int dx);
};
C increase(C c, int dx) { return C(c.x_ + dx); }    // Now it compiles
```

The friend declaration does nothing more than give the specified function the same access as the class member functions get. There is also a form of friend declaration that grants friendship, not to a function, but to a class; this is just a way to grant friendship to all member functions of that class.

Friends versus member functions

We do have to come back to the question, why not just make `increase()` a member function of the `C` class? In the example given in the preceding section, there's no reason to, really—`increase()` is clearly meant to be a part of the public interface of the `C` class, since it's one of the operations `C` supports. It needs special access to do its work, so it should be a member function. There are, however, cases where member functions come with limitations, or even cannot be used at all.

Let's consider an addition operator for the same C class—it's what is needed to make an expression like c1 + c2 compile if both variables are of type C. The addition, or operator+(), can be declared as a member function:

```
class C {
    int x_;
    public:
    C(int x) : x_(x) {}
    C operator+(const C& rhs) const { return C(x_ + rhs.x_); }
};
...
C x(1), y(2);
C z = x + y;
```

This code compiles and does exactly what we want; there does not seem to be anything obviously wrong with it. That's because there isn't—so far. But we can add more than just objects of type C:

```
C x(1);
C z = x + 2;
```

This also compiles, and points to a subtle detail in the declaration of the C class—we did not make the C(int) constructor explicit. This constructor now introduces an implicit conversion from int to C, and that is how the expression x + 2 compiles—first, 2 is converted into a temporary object, C(2), using the constructor we provided, and second the member function, x.operator+(const C&), is called—the right-hand side is the temporary object we just created. The temporary object itself is deleted right after the expression is evaluated. The implicit conversion from integers is rather broad and might have been an oversight. Let's assume that it wasn't and that we really want the expression like x + 2 to compile. What's not to like, then? Again, nothing so far. The objectionable feature of our design is what comes next:

```
C x(1);
C z = 2 + x;          // Does NOT compile
```

If x + 2 compiles, you would reasonably expect 2 + x to compile and give the same result (there are areas of math where the addition is not commutative, but let's stick with the arithmetic here). The reason it does not compile is that the compiler cannot get to the operator+() in the C class from here, and no other operator+() is available for these arguments. The x + y expression, when used with member function operators, is just syntactic sugar for the equivalent, if verbose, call to x.operator+(y). The same is true for any other binary operator such as multiplication or comparison.

The point is, the member function operator is invoked on the first argument of the expression (so technically, x + y and y + x are not identical; the member function is called on different objects, but the implementation is so that both give the same result). In our case, the member function would have to be invoked on the number 2, which is an integer and has no member functions at all. So, how did the expression x + 2 compiled? Quite simple, really: x + by itself implies x.operator+(), and the argument is whatever comes after +. In our case, it's 2. So, either x.operator+(2) compiles, or it does not, but in either case, the search for the operator+ to the call is over. The implicit conversion from int in our C class makes this call compile. So, why doesn't the compiler attempt a conversion on the first argument? The answer is, it never does, because it has no guidance on what to convert it into—there may be any number of other types that have the operator+() member function, and some of them may accept the C class as their argument, or something C can be converted to. The compiler does not attempt to explore the almost infinite number of such possible conversions.

If we want to use plus in expressions where the first type may be a built-in type or any other type that does not have or cannot have a member function of operator+(), then we have to use a non-member function. No problem; we know how to write those:

```
C operator+(const C& lhs, const C& rhs) {
    return C(lhs.x_ + rhs.x_);
}
```

But now we have lost access to the private data member C::x_, so our non-member operator+() does not compile either. We have seen the solution to that problem in the previous section—we need to make it a friend:

```
class C {
    int x_;
    public:
    C(int x) : x_(x) {}
    friend C operator+(const C& lhs, const C& rhs);
};
C operator+(const C& lhs, const C& rhs) {
    return C(lhs.x_ + rhs.x_);
}
C x(1), y(2);
C z1 = x + y;
C z2 = x + 2;
C z3 = 1 + y;
```

Now, everything compiles and works as intended—the non-member function
`operator+()` is simply a non-member function with two arguments of type `const C&`.
The rules for it are the same as for any other such function.

We can avoid typing the declaration of the `operator+()` twice if we define its body *in-situ* (immediately following the declaration, inside the class):

```
class C {
    int x_;
    public:
    C(int x) : x_(x) {}
    friend C operator+(const C& lhs, const C& rhs) {
        return C(lhs.x_ + rhs.x_);
    }
};
```

The latter example does not do anything different from the previous one, so it is simply a
matter of style—moving the body of the function into the object makes the object itself
longer, but defining the function outside of the class is more typing (as well as a possible
divergence between the friend declaration and the actual function, if the code is ever
changed).

Either way, the friend function is really a part of the class public interface, but, for technical
reasons, we prefer a non-member function in this case. There is even a case when the non-
member function is the only choice. Consider the C++ input/output operators, such as the
inserter, or `operator<<()`, which are used to write objects out into a stream (for example,
`std::cout`). We want to be able to print an object of type `C` like so:

```
C c1(5);
std::cout << c1;
```

There is no standard `operator<<()` for our type C, so we have to declare our own. The
inserter is a binary operator, just like plus (it has parameters on either side), so, were it a
member function, it would have to be one on the left-hand side object. Look at the
preceding statement—the left-hand side object in the `std::cout << c1` expression is not
our object, c1, but the standard out stream, `std::cout`. That's the object we would have to
add a member function to, but we cannot—`std::cout` is declared somewhere in the C++
standard library headers, and there is no way to extend its interface, at least not in a direct
manner. Member functions on the C class can be declared by us, but this does not
help—only the member functions of the left-hand side object are considered.

The only alternative is a non-member function. The first argument has to be
`std::ostream&`:

```
std::ostream& operator<<(std::ostream& out, const C& c) {
    out << c.x_;
    return out;
}
```

This function has to be declared as a friend since it also needs access to the private data of
the C class. It can also be defined *in-situ*:

```
class C {
    int x_;
    public:
    C(int x) : x_(x) {}
    friend std::ostream& operator<<(std::ostream& out, const C& c) {
        out << c.x_;
        return out;
    }
};
```

By convention, the return value is the same stream object, so the inserter operators can be
chained:

```
C c1(5), c2(7);
std::cout << c1 << c2;
```

The way the last statement is interpreted is `(std::cout << c1) << c2`, which boils
down to `operator<<(operator<< (std::cout, c1), c2)`. The outer `operator<<()`
is called on the return value of the inner `operator<<()`, which is the same: `std::cout`.
Again, the inserter is part of the public interface of the C class—it makes the objects of type
C printable. However, it has to be a non-member function.

So far, our classes are just regular classes, not templates, and our non-member functions
have declared friends that were just regular non-template functions. Now, let's consider
what, if anything, needs to change if the class becomes a template.

Friends and templates

Both classes and functions in C++ can be templates, and we can have several different combinations—a class template can grant friendship to a non-template function if its parameter types don't depend on the template parameters; this is not a particularly interesting case and certainly does not solve any of the problems we're dealing with now. When the friend function needs to operate on the template parameter types, making the right friends becomes trickier.

Friends of template classes

Let's start by making our C class into a template:

```
template <typename T> class C {
    T x_;
    public:
    C(T x) : x_(x) {}
};
```

We still want to add objects of type C and print them out. We have already considered reasons why the former is better accomplished with a non-member function, and the latter cannot be done in any other way. These reasons remain valid for class templates as well.

No problem—we can declare template functions to go with our template classes and do the work that the non-template functions used to do in the previous section. Let's start with operator+():

```
template <typename T>
C<T> operator+(const C<T>& lhs, const C<T>& rhs) {
    return C<T>(lhs.x_ + rhs.x_);
}
```

This is the same function that we saw previously, only made into a template that can accept any instantiation of the class template C. Note that we parameterized this template on the type T, that is, the template parameter of C. We could, of course, simply declare the following:

```
template <typename C>
C operator+(const C& lhs, const C& rhs) {     // NEVER do this!
    return C<T>(lhs.x_ + rhs.x_);
}
```

However, this introduces—into the global scope no less—an `operator+()` that claims to accept two arguments of any type. Of course, it really only handles types that have an `x_` data member. So, what are we going to do when we have a template class, `D`, that is also addable but has a `y_` data member instead?

The earlier version of the template is at least restricted to all possible instantiations of the class template `C`. Of course, it suffers from the same problem as our very first attempt at a non-member function—it does not have access to the private data member `C<T>::x_`. No problem—this chapter is about friends, after all. But friends to what? The entire class template, `C`, is going to have a friend declaration, just one for all `T` types, and that has to work for every instantiation of the template function `operator+()`. It appears that we have to grant friendship to the entire template function:

```
template <typename T> class C {
    int x_;
    public:
    C(int x) : x_(x) {}
    template <typename U>
    friend C<U> operator+(const C<U>& lhs, const C<U>& rhs);
};
template <typename T>
C<T> operator+(const C<T>& lhs, const C<T>& rhs) {
    return C<T>(lhs.x_ + rhs.x_);
}
```

Note the correct syntax—the keyword `friend` appears after the template and its parameters but before the return type of the function. Also note that we had to rename the template parameter of the nested friend declaration—the `T` identifier is already used for the class template parameter. Similarly, we could rename the template parameter `T` in the definition of the function itself, but we don't have to—just like in function declarations and definitions, the parameter is just a name; it is only meaningful within each declaration—two declarations for the same function can use different names for the same parameter. What we can do instead is move the function body inline, into the class:

```
template <typename T> class C {
    int x_;
    public:
    C(int x) : x_(x) {}
    template <typename U>
    friend C<U> operator+(const C<U>& lhs, const C<U>& rhs) {
        return C<U>(lhs.x_ + rhs.x_);
    }
};
```

The reader might point out that we have blown a rather wide hole in the encapsulation of the template class C—by granting friendship of any instantiation of C<T> to the entire template function, we have, for example, made the operator+(const C&<double>, const C&<double>) instantiation a friend of C<int>. This is clearly not necessary, although it may not be immediately obvious where the harm is in that (an example that shows actual harm would be rather convoluted, as necessary). But this misses a much more serious problem with our design, which becomes apparent as soon as we start using it to add something. It works, up to a point:

```
C<int> x(1), y(2);
C<int> z = x + y;          // So far so good...
```

But only up to a point:

```
C<int> x(1), y(2);
C<int> z1 = x + 2;         // This does not compile!
C<int> z2 = 1 + 2;         // Neither does this!
```

But was this not the very reason to use a non-member function? What happened to our implicit conversions? This used to work! The answer is in the details—it used to work, but for a non-template function, operator+(). The conversion rules for a template function are very different. The exact technical details can be gleaned from the standard, with great diligence and effort, but this is the gist of it—when considering non-member, non-template functions, the compiler will look for all functions with the given name (operator+, in our case), then check if they accept the right number of parameters (possibly considering default arguments), then check if, for each such function, for each of its parameters, a conversion from the supplied argument to the specified parameter type exists (the rules on which conversions, exactly, are considered, and again fairly complex, but let's say that both user-given implicit conversions and built-in conversions such as non-const to const are considered). If this process yields only one function, that function is called (otherwise the compiler either selects the *best* overload or complains that several candidates are equally possible and the call is ambiguous).

For template functions, this process would again yield an almost unlimited number of candidates—every template function with the name operator+() would have to be instantiated on every known type just to check if enough type conversions are available to make it work. Instead, a much simpler process is attempted—in addition to all non-template functions described in the previous paragraph (in our case, none), the compiler also considers instantiations of template functions with the given name (again, operator+) and the types of all parameters equal to the types of the function arguments at the call site (so-called trivial conversions, like adding a const, are allowed).

In our case, the argument types in the x + 2 expression are C<int> and int, respectively. The compiler looks for an instantiation of the template function, operator+, that accepts two arguments of this type, and the user-given conversions are not considered. There is no such function, of course, and so the call to operator+() cannot be resolved.

The root of the problem is that we really want the user-given conversions to be used by the compiler automatically, but this is not going to happen as long as we are trying to instantiate a template function. We could declare a non-template function for operator+(const C<int>&, const C<int>&), but, with a C template class, we would have to declare one for every T type that the C class might be instantiated on.

The template friend factory

What we need is to automatically generate a non-template function for every T type that's used to instantiate the class template C. Of course, it is impossible to generate all of these functions in advance—there is a nearly unlimited number of T types that could, in theory, be used with the template class C. Fortunately, we do not need to generate an operator+() for every one of such types—we only need them for the types that were actually used with this template in our program.

Generating friends on demand

The pattern that we are about to see is a very old one, and was introduced by John Barton and Lee Nackman in 1994 for a completely different purpose—they used it to work around certain limitations of the compilers that existed at the time. The inventors proposed the name *Restricted Template Expansion*, which was never widely used. Years later, Dan Sacks coined the name *Friends Factory*, but the pattern is also sometimes referred to simply as the *Barton-Nackman trick*.

The pattern looks very simple and very similar to the code we wrote earlier, throughout this chapter:

```
template <typename T> class C {
    int x_;
    public:
    C(int x) : x_(x) {}
    friend C operator+(const C& lhs, const C& rhs) {
        return C(lhs.x_ + rhs.x_);
    }
};
```

We are taking advantage of a very specific C++ feature, and so the code must be written precisely. A non-template friend function is defined inside the class template. This function must be defined inline; it cannot be declared a friend and then defined later, except as an explicit template instantiation—we could have declared the friend function inside the class and then defined `operator+<const C<int>>&, const C<int>&)`, which would work for `C<int>` but not `C<double>` (since we do not know what types the callers may instantiate later, this is not very useful). It may have the parameters of the `T` type, the template parameter, the `C<T>` type (which, inside the class template, can be referred to as simply `C`), and any other type that is either fixed or depends only on the template parameters, but it may not be a template itself. Every instantiation of the `C` class template, with any combination of template parameter types, generates exactly one non-template, non-member function with the specified name. Note that the generated functions are non-template functions; they are regular functions, and the usual conversion rules apply to them. We are now back to the non-template `operator+()`, and all conversions work exactly the way we want them to:

```
C<int> x(1), y(2);
C<int> z1 = x + y;        // This works
C<int> z2 = x + 2;        // and this too
C<int> z3 = 1 + 2;        // so does this
```

This is it—this is the whole pattern. There are a few details we must note. First of all, the keyword `friend` cannot be omitted. A class cannot normally generate a non-member function, except for declaring a friend. Even if the function does not need access to any private data, in order to automatically generate non-template functions from instantiations of class templates, these functions have to be declared friends (static non-member functions can be generated in a similar manner, but the binary operators cannot be static functions—the standard explicitly forbids it). Second, the generated function is placed in the scope containing the class. For example, let's define the inserter operator for our `C` template class, but not before wrapping the entire class in a namespace:

```
namespace NS {
template <typename T> class C {
    int x_;
    public:
    C(int x) : x_(x) {}
    friend C operator+(const C& lhs, const C& rhs) {
        return C(lhs.x_ + rhs.x_);
    }
    friend std::ostream& operator<<(std::ostream& out, const C& c) {
        out << c.x_;
        return out;
```

```
        }
    };
    }
```

We can now both add and print the objects of the C type:

```
    NS::C<int> x(1), y(2);
    std::cout << (x + y) << std::endl;
```

Note that, even though the C class template is now in the namespace NS, and has to be used as such (NS::C<int>), we did not need to do anything special to invoke either operator+() or operator<<(). This does not mean that they were generated in the global scope. No, they are still in the namespace NS, but what we see is the argument-dependent lookup in action—when looking for a function named operator+(), for example, the compiler considers the candidates in the current scope (that is, the global scope, and there aren't any), as well as the scope in which the arguments to the function are defined. In our case, at least one of the arguments to the operator+() is of type NS::C<int>, which automatically brings all functions declared in the NS namespace into play. The friend factory generates its functions in the scope containing the class template, which is, of course, also the NS namespace. Thus, the lookup finds the definition, and both the + and << operations are resolved exactly the way we would want them to be. Rest assured that this is by design and is no accident; the argument lookup rules are fine-tuned to produce this desired and expected result.

Also note that, even though friend functions are generated in the scope containing the class, in our case namespace, NS, they can only be found by the argument-dependent lookup (again, a special provision in the standard). A straightforward attempt to find the function without using an argument-dependent lookup will fail:

```
    auto p = &NS::C<int>::operator+;          // Does not compile
```

The friend factory and the Curiously Recurring Template Pattern

The friend factory is a pattern that synthesizes a non-template, non-member function from every instantiation of a class template—every time the template is instantiated on a new type, a new function is generated. For its parameters, this function can use any types we can declare in that instantiation of the class template. Usually, this is the class itself, but it can be any type the template knows about.

In this manner, the friend factory can be employed together with the **Curiously Recurring Template Pattern (CRTP)** that we studied in an Chapter 7, *The Curiously Recurring Template Pattern*. Recall that the main idea of the CRTP is that a class inherits from an instantiation of a base class template that is parameterized by the derived class type. Consider what we have here—a template for a base class that is automatically instantiated with every class derived from it, and it knows what that type is. This seems like an ideal place to put a friend factory. Of course, the operators generated by the base class have to not only know what the type of the object is that they operate on, but also what to do with it (for example, how to print it). Sometimes, the necessary data actually resides in the base class, and then the base class can provide complete implementations. But it is rare that the derived class adds so little to the base class. The more common use of CRTP, together with the friend factory, is to implement some operators in a standard way through some other functionality. For example, operator!=() can be implemented through operator==():

```
template <typename D> class B {
    public:
    friend bool operator!=(const D& lhs, const D& rhs) {
        return !(lhs == rhs);
    }
};
template <typename T> class C : public B<C<T>> {
    T x_;
    public:
    C(T x) : x_(x) {}
    friend bool operator==(const C& lhs, const C& rhs) {
        return lhs.x_ == rhs.x_;
    }
};
```

Here, the derived class, C, uses the friend factory pattern to generate a non-template function for the binary operator==() directly from the instantiation of the class template. It also inherits from the base class B, which triggers an instantiation of that template as well, which in turn generates a non-template function for the operator!=() for every type for which we have generated operator==().

The second use of CRTP is to convert member functions to non-member functions. For example, the binary `operator+()` is sometimes implemented in terms of the `operator+=()`, which is always a member function (it acts on its first operand). To implement the binary `operator+()`, someone has to take care of the conversions to that object's type, and then the `operator+=()` can be called. These conversions are provided by the binary operators that are generated by the common CRTP base class when using the friend factory. Similarly, the inserter operator can be generated if we establish the convention that our classes have a `print()` member function:

```cpp
template <typename D> class B {
    public:
    friend D operator+(const D& lhs, const D& rhs) {
        D res(lhs);
        res += rhs;                  // Convert += to +
        return res;
    }
    friend std::ostream& operator<<(std::ostream& out, const D& d) {
        d.print(out);
        return out;
    }
};

template <typename T> class C : public B<C<T>> {
    T x_;
    public:
    C(T x) : x_(x) {}
    C operator+=(const C& incr) {
        x_ += incr.x_;
        return *this;
    }
    void print(std::ostream& out) const {
        out << x_;
    }
};
```

In this fashion, CRTP can be used to add boilerplate interfaces while delegating the implementation to the derived classes. It is, after all, a static (compile-time) delegation pattern.

Summary

In this chapter, we have learned about a very C++-specific pattern that was originally introduced as a workaround for the buggy early C++ compilers but found new use years later. The friend factory is used to generate non-template functions from instantiations of class templates. As non-template functions, these generated friends have much more flexible rules with regards to argument conversions compared to template functions. We have also learned how the argument-dependent lookup, type conversions, and the friend factory work together to deliver a result that looks very natural, by a process that is far from intuitive.

The next chapter describes a totally different kind of Factory—a C++ pattern that's based on the classic Factory pattern and addresses a certain asymmetry in the language—all member functions, even destructors, can be virtual, except the constructors.

Questions

1. What is the effect of declaring a function as a *friend*?
2. What is the difference between granting friendship to a function versus a function template?
3. Why are binary operators usually implemented as non-member functions?
4. Why is the inserter operator always implemented as a non-member function?
5. What is the main difference between argument conversions for template and non-template functions?
6. How can we make the act of instantiating the template also generate a unique non-template, non-member function?

13
Virtual Constructors and Factories

In C++, any member function of any class, including its destructor, can be made virtual—any member function except one—the constructor. Without virtual functions, the exact type of the object on which the member function is invoked is known at compile time. Therefore, the type of the object that is constructed is always known at compile time, at the point of the constructor call. Nonetheless, we often need to construct objects whose type is not known until runtime. This chapter describes several related patterns and idioms that address this design problem in various ways, including the Factory pattern.

The following topics will be covered in this chapter:

- Why there is no way to make a constructor virtual

- How to use the Factory pattern to defer the choice of the constructed object type until compile time

- Using C++ idioms to construct and copy objects polymorphically

Technical requirements

The example code for this chapter can be found at the following GitHub link: https://github.com/PacktPublishing/Hands-On-Design-Patterns-with-CPP/tree/master/Chapter13.

Why constructors cannot be virtual

We already understand how polymorphism works—when a virtual function is called through a pointer or a reference to the base class, that pointer or reference is used to access the v-pointer in the class. The v-pointer is used to identify the true type of the object, that is, the type that the object was created with. It could be the base class itself, or any one of the derived classes. The member function on that object is actually called. So, why can't the same be done for constructors? Let's investigate this.

When does an object get its type?

It is pretty easy to understand why the process that we described previously cannot work for creating *virtual constructors*. First of all, it is evident from the description of the preceding process—as a part of it, we *identify the type that the object was created with*. That can only happen after the object is constructed—before construction, we don't have an object of this type yet, just some uninitialized memory. Another way to look at it is this—before the virtual function is dispatched to the correct type, the v-pointer needs to be looked up. Who puts the right value into the v-pointer? Considering that the v-pointer uniquely identifies the type of the object, it can only be initialized during construction. This implies that it wasn't initialized before construction. But if it wasn't initialized, it can't be used to dispatch virtual function calls. And so again, we realize that constructors cannot be virtual.

For derived classes in the hierarchy, the process of establishing the type is even more complex. We can try to observe the type of an object as it's being constructed. The easiest way to do this is to use the `typeid` operator, which returns information about the object's type, including the name of the type:

```
class A {
    public:
    A() { std::cout << "A::A(): " << typeid(*this).name() << std::endl; }
    virtual ~A() {
        std::cout << "A::~A(): " << typeid(*this).name() << std::endl;
    }
};
class B : public A {
    public:
    B() { std::cout << "B::B(): " << typeid(*this).name() << std::endl; }
    ~B() { std::cout << "B::~B(): " << typeid(*this).name() << std::endl; }
};
class C : public B {
    public:
    C() { std::cout << "C::C(): " << typeid(*this).name() << std::endl; }
    ~C() { std::cout << "C::~C(): " << typeid(*this).name() << std::endl; }
```

```
};

int main() {
    C c;
}
```

Running this program produces the following result:

```
A::A():  1A
B::B():  1B
C::C():  1C
C::~C(): 1C
B::~B(): 1B
A::~A(): 1A
```

The type name returned by the `std::typeinfo::name()` call is the so-called mangled type name—it's the internal name that the compiler uses to identify types, instead of human-readable names like `class A`. How many objects were constructed in this example? The source code says just one, the `c` object of type `C`. The runtime output says three, that is, one of each type. Both answers are correct—when an object of type `C` is constructed, the base class, `A`, has to be constructed first, and so its constructor is called. Then, the intermediate base class, `B`, is constructed, and only then will `C` be. The destructors are executed in reverse order. The type of the object inside its constructor or destructor, as reported by the `typeid` operator, is the same as the type of the object whose constructor or destructor is running.

It appears that the type, as indicated by the virtual pointer, is changing during the construction! That is, of course, assuming that the `typeid` operator returns the dynamic type, the type indicated by the virtual pointer, and not the static type that can be determined at compile time. The standard says that this is, indeed, the case. Does this mean that, if we called the same virtual method from each constructor, we would really be calling three different overrides of this method? It's easy enough to find out:

```
class A {
    public:
    A() { whoami(); }
    virtual ~A() { whoami(); }
    virtual void whoami() const { std::cout << "A::whoami" << std::endl; }
};
class B : public A {
    public:
    B() { whoami(); }
    ~B() { whoami(); }
    void whoami() const { std::cout << "B::whoami" << std::endl; }
};
```

```cpp
class C : public B {
    public:
    C() { whoami(); }
    ~C() { whoami(); }
    void whoami() const { std::cout << "C::whoami" << std::endl; }
};

int main() {
    C c;
    c.whoami();
}
```

Now, we will create the object of type C, and the call to whoami() after the creation confirms it—the dynamic type of the object is C. That was true from the beginning of the construction process; we asked the compiler to construct one object of type C, but the dynamic type of the object has changed during construction:

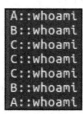

It is clear that the virtual pointer value has changed as the construction of the object progressed. In the beginning, it was identifying the object type as A, even though the final type is C. Is this because we created the object on the stack? Would it be any different if the object was created on the heap? We can easily find out:

```cpp
C* c = new C;
c->whoami();
delete c;
```

Running the modified program produces exactly the same results as the original.

Another reason that the constructor cannot be virtual, or, more generally, why the type of the object being constructed has to be known at compile time at the point of construction, is that the compiler has to know how much memory to allocate for the object. The amount of memory is determined by the size of the type, that is, by the sizeof operator. The result of sizeof(C) is a compile-time constant, so the amount of memory allocated for the new object is always known at compile time. This is true whether we create the object on the stack or on the heap.

The bottom line is this—if the program creates an object of the T type, somewhere in the code there is an explicit call to the T::T constructor. After that, we can hide the T type in the rest of the program, for example, by accessing the object through a base class pointer, or by erasing the type (see Chapter 6, *Understanding Type Erasure*). But there has to be at least one explicit mention of the T type in the code, and that is at the point of construction.

On the one hand, we now have a very reasonable explanation of why constructing objects can never be polymorphic. On the other hand, this does nothing to address a design challenge that may require constructing an object whose type is not known at compile time. Consider designing a game—a player can recruit or summon any number of adventurers for his/her party and build settlements and cities. It would be reasonable to have a separate class for each creature kind and each building type, but then we have to construct an object of one of these types when an adventurer joins the party, or a building is erected, and until the player selects it, the game cannot know which object to construct.

As usual in software, the solution involves adding another level of indirection.

The Factory pattern

The problem we are faced with, that is, how to decide at runtime to create an object of a particular type, is obviously a very common design problem. Design patterns are the solutions for just such problems, and there is a pattern for this problem as well—it's called the Factory pattern. The Factory pattern is a creational pattern, and it provides solutions for several related problems—how to delegate the decision of which object to create to a derived class, how to create objects using a separate factory method, and so on. We will review these variations of the Factory pattern one by one, starting with the basic factory method.

The basics of the Factory method

In its simplest form, the factory method constructs an object of a type that's specified at runtime:

```
class Base { ... };
class Derived : public Base { ... };
Base* p = ClassFactory( some_type_identifier, ... arguments );
```

How do we identify at runtime which object to create? We need some runtime identifier for each type that the factory can create. In the simplest case, the list of these types is known at compile time. Consider a game design where the player selects the type of building to construct from a menu. The program has the list of buildings that can be constructed, each represented by an object, with an identifier for each one:

```
enum Buildings {
    FARM, FORGE, MILL, GUARDHOUSE, KEEP, CASTLE
};
class Building {
    virtual ~Building() {}
};
class Farm : public Building { ... };
class Forge : public Building { ... };
```

When the player selects the building type, the corresponding identifier value is also selected by the game program. Now, the program can construct the building using the factory method:

```
Building* new_building = MakeBuilding(Buildings building_type);
```

Note that the factory takes the type identifier argument and returns the pointer to the base class. The returned object should have the type that corresponds to the type identifier. How is the factory implemented? Remember the conclusion of the last section—somewhere in the program, every object has to be explicitly constructed with its true type. The Factory pattern does not remove this requirement; it merely hides the place where the construction happens:

```
Building* MakeBuilding(Buildings building_type) {
    switch (building_type) {
        case FARM: return new Farm;
        case FORGE: return new Forge;
        ...
    }
}
```

The correspondence between the type identifier and the object type is encoded in the `switch` statement inside the factory. The return type has to be the same for all types that are constructed by the factory since there is only one factory method, and its type is declared at compile time. In the simplest case, it is the base class pointer, although if you follow the modern memory ownership idioms described in Chapter 3, *Memory Ownership*, of this book, the factory may return a unique pointer, `std::unique_ptr<Base>`, if the object has a clear owner, or, in rare cases when the shared ownership is really needed, the shared pointer, `std::shared_ptr<Base>`, should be constructed with `std::make_shared()` and returned.

This is the basic form of the factory method. There are many variations that make it more suitable for a particular problem. We will review some of these variations here.

Arguments for factory methods

In our simple example, the constructor took no arguments. Passing arguments to the constructor presents a bit of a problem if the constructors of different types have different parameters—after all, the `MakeBuilding()` function has to be declared with some specific parameters. One option that appears straightforward is to use functions with a variable number of arguments, or parameter packs—if you need a variable type and a number of arguments, use a function with variable arguments. It's a complex solution that looks much less attractive once you start implementing it. The simpler option is to create a parameter object with the hierarchy matching the hierarchy of the objects to create. Let's assume that, in our game, the player can select upgrades for each building to be constructed. The user interface will have to offer building-specific options, of course, and the results of the user selections are stored in a building-specific object:

```
struct BuildingSpec {
    virtual Buildings building_type() const = 0;
};
struct FarmSpec : public BuildingSpec {
   Buildings building_type() const { return FARM; }
   bool with_pasture;
   int number_of_stalls;
};
struct ForgeSpec : public BuildingSpec {
   Buildings building_type() const { return FORGE; }
   bool magic_forge;
   int number_of_apprentices;
};
```

Note that we included the type identifier with the argument object—there is no reason to call the factory method with two arguments that must always correctly match each other; it only creates the possibility of an error occurring. This way, we are guaranteed that the type identifier and the arguments match in every factory call:

```
Building* MakeBuilding(const BuildingSpec* building_spec) {
    switch (building_spec->building_type()) {
        case FARM: return new Farm(static_cast<const
FarmSpec*>(building_spec));
        case FORGE: return new Forge(static_cast<const
ForgeSpec*>(building_spec));
```

```
            . . .
        }
    }
```

This technique can be combined with some of the other factory variations that are shown in the following sections so that we can pass arguments when the constructors require them.

Dynamic type registry

So far, we have assumed that the complete list of the types is known at compile time and can be encoded in the type identifier correspondence table (implemented with a switch statement, in our example). The former requirement is unavoidable in the scope of the entire program: since every constructor call is explicit somewhere, the total list of types that can be constructed is known at compile time. However, our solution is more constrained than that—we have the list of all types that are hard-coded in the factory method. No additional derived classes can be created without also adding them to the factory. Sometimes, this restriction is not as bad as it appears—for example, the list of buildings in the game may not change very often, and even when it does, there is a complete list that must be manually updated for the right menu to be generated, the pictures and sounds to appear in the right places, and so on.

Nonetheless, one of the advantages of the hierarchical designs is that derived classes can be added later and without modifying any of the code written to operate on the hierarchy. The new virtual function simply plugs into the existing control flow and provides the necessary customized behavior. We can implement the same idea for the factory constructor.

First of all, each derived class has to be responsible for constructing itself. This is necessary because, as we have already learned, the explicit call to the constructor has to be written somewhere. If it's not in the generic code, it has to be a part of the code that is added when a new derived class is created:

```
class Farm : public Building {
    public:
    static Building* MakeBuilding() { return new Farm; }
};
class Forge : public Building {
    public:
    static Building* MakeBuilding() { return new Forge; }
};
```

Second, the list of the types has to be extensible at runtime instead of being fixed at compile time. We could still use an `enum`, but then it would have to be updated every time a new derived class is added. Alternatively, we could assign each derived class an integer identifier at runtime, making sure that the identifiers are unique. Either way, we need a map of these identifiers to the factory functions, and it cannot be a `switch` statement or anything else that is fixed at compile time. The map has to be extensible. We could use a table of function pointers as a registry of all building types in the program, stored in, for example, a vector:

```
class Building;
typedef Building* (*BuildingFactory)();

int building_type_count = 0;

std::vector<std::pair<int, BuildingFactory>> building_registry;
void RegisterBuilding(BuildingFactory factory) {
    building_registry.push_back(std::make_pair(building_type_count++,
                                factory));
}
```

This table is a global object in the program, a singleton. It could simply be a global object, as in the preceding example, or we could use one of the singleton patterns that will be described in `Chapter 15`, *Singleton – A Classic OOP Pattern*, in this book. To make sure that each building gets a unique identifier, we maintain a global count of building types that is incremented every time a new type is added to the registry.

Now, we just need to add every new building type to the registry. This is done in two steps—first, we need to add a registration method to every building class, like so:

```
class Farm : public Building {
    public:
    static void Register() {
        RegisterBuilding(Farm::MakeBuilding);
    }
};
class Forge : public Building {
    public:
    static void Register() {
        RegisterBuilding(Forge::MakeBuilding);
    }
};
```

Second, we need to arrange for all `Register()` methods to be called before the game begins. There are several ways to do this. We could register all types during static initialization, before `main()`, but such designs are prone to errors because the static initialization order is undefined between different compilation units. On the other hand, the game must have a place where the user interface elements for every building that the player can create are initialized and drawn, so it is also natural to register the factory methods there:

```
Farm::Register();       // Farm gets ID 0
Forge::Register();      // Forge gets ID 1
```

Note that, if the same singleton registry is used for other purposes, such as building graphics, it really should be encapsulated into its own class.

With all the types and their factory constructors registered, we can implement the main factory method by simply forwarding the call to the right type-specific factory constructor:

```
class Building {
    public:
    static Building* MakeBuilding(int building_type) {
        BuildingFactory factory = building_registry[building_type].second;
        return factory();
    }
};
Building* b0 = Building::MakeBuilding(0);    // A Farm actually
Building* b1 = Building::MakeBuilding(1);    // Really this is a Forge
```

Now, a call to `Building::MakeBuilding(i)` will construct an object of the type that's registered with the identifier `i`. In our solution, the correspondence between the identifier values and the types is not known until runtime—we cannot say what building has the ID of 5 until we run the program. If this is undesirable, we can assign static identifier values to each type, but then we would have to make sure that they are unique. Alternatively, we could make sure that the registration calls always happen in the same order.

Note that this implementation is very similar to the code that the compilers generate for true virtual functions—virtual function calls are done through function pointers that are stored in tables and accessed by means of a unique identifier (the virtual pointer). The main difference is that the unique identifier cannot be in the class since we need to use it before the object is constructed. Nonetheless, this is as close to a *virtual constructor* as you can get.

In a well-written C++ program, the ownership of all objects is clearly evident. The most common case is when an object has one clearly identified owner, which can be both enforced and expressed by using an owning pointer such as `std::unique_ptr`. The factory should return an owning pointer, and the client should store the result in one:

```
class Building {
    public:
    static std::unique_ptr<Building> MakeBuilding(int building_type) {
        BuildingFactory factory = building_registry[building_type].second;
        return std::unique_ptr<Building>(factory());
    }
};
std::unique_ptr<Building> b0 = Building::MakeBuilding(0);
std::unique_ptr<Building> b1 = Building::MakeBuilding(1);
```

In all of our factory constructors so far, the decision about which object to construct was driven by the external input to the program, and the construction was done by the same factory method (possibly using delegation to the derived classes). We will now see a different variant of the factory, which is used to address a slightly different scenario.

Polymorphic factory

Consider a slightly different problem—imagine that, in our game, each building produces a unit of some kind, and the type of the unit is uniquely associated with the type of the building. The Castle recruits knights, the Wizard Tower trains mages, and the Spider Mound produces giant spiders. Now, our generic code not only constructs a building of the type that is selected at runtime, but also creates new units whose types are also not known at compile time. We already have the building factory. We could implement the Unit factory in a similar way, where every building has a unique unit identifier associated with it. But this design exposes the correspondence between the units and the buildings to the rest of the program, and that is really not necessary—each building knows how to build the *right* unit; there is no reason for the rest of the program to know it too.

This design challenge calls for a slightly different factory—the factory method determines that a unit is created, but exactly which unit is decided by the building. This is the Template pattern in action, combined with the Factory pattern—the overall design is the Factory, but the unit type is customized by the derived classes:

```
class Unit {};
class Knight : public Unit { ... };
class Mage : public Unit { ... };
class Spider : public Unit { ... };
```

```
class Building {
    public:
    virtual Unit* MakeUnit() const = 0;
};
class Castle : public Building {
    public:
    Knight* MakeUnit() const { return new Knight; }
};
class Tower : public Building {
    public:
    Mage* MakeUnit() const { return new Mage; }
};
class Mound : public Building {
    public:
    Spider* MakeUnit() const { return new Spider; }
};

Building* building = MakeBuilding(identifier);
Unit* unit = building->MakeUnit();
```

The factory methods for the buildings themselves are not shown in this example—the Unit factory can coexist with any of the building factory implementations we have learned. The generic code at the bottom of the listing is written once and does not need to change when new derived classes for buildings and units are added.

Note that the return types of all `MakeUnit()` functions are different. Nonetheless, they are all overrides of the same virtual `Building::MakeUnit()` function. These are known as the *covariant return types*—the return type of the override method may be a derived class of the return type of the overridden method. In our case, return types match the class types, but in general, this is not required. Any base and derived classes can be used as covariant types, even if they come from a different hierarchy. However, only such types can be covariant, and, other than that exception, the return type of the override must match the base class virtual function.

The strict rules for covariant return types present some problems when we try and make factories return anything other than a raw pointer. For example, let's assume that we want to return `std::unique_ptr` instead of the raw pointer. But, unlike `Unit*` and `Knight*`, `std::unique_ptr<Unit>` and `std::unique_ptr<Knight>` are not covariant types and cannot be used as return types for a virtual method and its override.

We will consider solutions for this, and several other C++; specific problems related to factory methods, in the next section.

Factory-like patterns in C++

There are many variations of the basic Factory patterns used in C++ to address specific design needs and constraints. In this section, we will consider several of them. This is by no means an exclusive list of factory-like patterns in C++, but understanding these variants should prepare the reader for combining the techniques that they have learned from this book to address various design challenges related to object factories.

Polymorphic copy

So far, we have considered factory alternatives to the object constructor—either the default constructor or one of the constructors with arguments. However, a similar pattern can be applied to the copy constructor—we have an object, and we want to make a copy.

This is a similar problem in many ways—we have an object that's accessed through the base class pointer, and we want to call its copy constructor. For the reasons we discussed earlier, not the least of which is that the compiler needs to know how much memory to allocate, the actual constructor call has to be done on the statically determined type. However, the control flow that gets us to a particular constructor call can be determined at runtime, and that, again, calls for an application of the Factory pattern.

The factory method we will use to implement polymorphic copy is somewhat similar to the Unit factory example from the previous section—the actual construction has to be done by each derived class, and the derived class knows what type of the object to construct. The base class implements the control flow that dictates that someone's copy will be constructed, and the derived class customizes the construction part:

```cpp
class Base {
    public:
    virtual Base* clone() const = 0;
};
class Derived : public Base {
    public:
    Derived* clone() const { return new Derived(*this); }
};

Base* b = ... get an object somewhere ...
Base* b1 = b->clone();
```

Again, we are using covariant return types, and, therefore, are limited to the raw pointers.

Let's say that we want to return unique pointers instead. Since only the raw pointers to the base and derived types are considered covariant, we have to always return the unique pointer to the base class:

```
class Base {
    public:
    virtual std::unique_ptr<Base> clone() const = 0;
};
class Derived : public Base {
    public:
    std::unique_ptr<Base> clone() const {        // Not unique_ptr<Derived>
        return std::unique_ptr<Base>(new Derived(*this));
    }
};

std::unique_ptr<Base> b(...);
std::unique_ptr<Base> b1 = b->clone();
```

In many cases, this is not a significant limitation. Sometimes, however, it can lead to unnecessary conversions and casts. If returning a smart pointer to the exact type is important, there is another version of this pattern that we will consider next.

CRTP Factory and return types

The only way we could return `std::unique_ptr<Derived>` from the factory copy constructor of the derived class is to make the virtual `clone()` method of the base class return the same type. But this is impossible, at least if we have more than one derived class—for each derived class, we would need the return type of `Base::clone()` to be that class. But there is only one `Base::clone()`! Or is there? Fortunately, in C++, we have an easy way of making many out of one—the templates. If we template the base class, we could make the base of each derived class return the right type. But to do this, we need the base class to somehow know the type of the class that will be derived from it. Of course, there is a pattern for that, too—in C++, it is called the Curiously Recurring Template Pattern, which we looked at in Chapter 8, *The Curiously Recurring Template Pattern*. Now, we can combine the CRTP and the Factory patterns:

```
template <typename Derived> class Base {
    public:
    virtual std::unique_ptr<Derived> clone() const = 0;
};
class Derived : public Base<Derived> { // CRTP makes Base aware of Derived
    public:
    std::unique_ptr<Derived> clone() const {
        return std::unique_ptr<Derived>(new Derived(*this));
```

```
        }
    };

    std::unique_ptr<Derived> b0(new Derived);
    std::unique_ptr<Derived> b1 = b0->clone();
```

`auto` return types make writing code like this significantly less verbose. In this book, we don't use them to make it clear which function returns what. Note that, since the `Base` class now knows the type of the derived class, we don't even need the `clone()` method to be virtual:

```
    template <typename Derived> class Base {
        public:
        std::unique_ptr<Derived> clone() const {
            return std::unique_ptr<Derived>(
                new Derived(*static_cast<const Derived*>(this)));
        }
    };
    class Derived : public Base<Derived> { // CRTP makes Base aware of Derived
        ...
    };
```

There are significant downsides to this method, at least regarding the way we have implemented it so far. First of all, we had to make the base class a template, which means that we no longer have a common pointer type to use in our general code (or we have to make an even wider use of templates). Second, this approach only works if no more classes are derived from the `Derived` class, because the type of the base class does not track the second derivation—only the one that instantiated the `Base` template. Overall, except for the specific cases where it is very important to return the exact type instead of the base type, this approach cannot be recommended.

On the other hand, there are some attractive features of this implementation that we may want to preserve. Specifically, we got rid of the multiple copies of the `clone()` function, one per each derived class, and got a template to generate them for us automatically. In the next section, we will show you how to retain that useful feature of the CRTP implementation, even if we have to give up on extending the notion of the *covariant return types* to cover smart pointers by playing template tricks.

CRTP Factory with less copy-paste

We will now focus on using CRTP to avoid writing the clone() function in every derived class. This is not just done to reduce typing—the more code is written—especially the very similar code that gets copied and modified—the more likely you are to make an error. We have already seen how to use CRTP to generate a version of clone() for every derived class automatically. We just don't want to give up the common (non-template) base class to do so. We don't really have to do so if we delegate the cloning to the special base class that handles only that:

```
class Base {
    public:
    virtual Base* clone() const = 0;
};
template <typename Derived> class Cloner : public Base {
    public:
    Base* clone() const {
        return new Derived(*static_cast<const Derived*>(this));
    }
};
class Derived : public Cloner<Derived> {
    ...
};

Base* b0(new Derived);
Base* b1 = b0->clone();
```

Here, for simplicity, we went back to returning raw pointers, although we could also return std::unique_ptr<Base>. What we cannot do is return Derived* since, at the time when the template for the Cloner is parsed, it is not known that Derived is always derived from Base.

This design allows us to derive any number of classes from Base, indirectly through Cloner, and not have to write another clone() function ever again. It still has the limitation that, if we derive another class from Derived, it will not be copied correctly. In many designs, this is not an issue—enlightened self-interest should guide you to avoid deep hierarchies and make all classes be one of two kinds: abstract base classes that are never instantiated, and concrete classes that are derived from one of these base classes, but never from another concrete class. However, should the enlightened self-interest prove insufficient to the cause, another variant of the CRTP factory can be employed to reduce copy-pasting, even in deep hierarchies:

```
class Base {
    public:
```

```
        virtual ~Base() {}
        Base* clone() const;
};

class ClonerBase {
    public:
    virtual Base* clone() const = 0;
};

Base* Base::clone() const {
    dynamic_cast<const ClonerBase*>(this)->clone();    // Cross-cast
};

template <typename Derived> class Cloner : public ClonerBase {
    public:
    Base* clone() const {
        return new Derived(*static_cast<const Derived*>(this));
    }
};

class Derived : public Base,
                public Cloner<Derived> {    // Multiple inheritance
    ...
};

Base* b0(new Derived);
Base* b1 = b0->clone();
```

This is a clear case of *in for a penny, in for a pound*—once we decided to dabble in complexity and use deep hierarchies, we also had to employ multiple inheritance and complex dynamic casting. Any derived class, whether it is derived directly from Base or not, also derives from Cloner<Derived>, which, in turn, is derived from the ClonerBase. Thus, every Derived class gets a corresponding base class with a customized clone() virtual method, courtesy of CRTP. All of these clone() methods override the same method of the ClonerBase base class, so we have to get from Base to ClonerBase, even though they are not in the same hierarchy. The strange dynamic_cast that accomplishes that is known as a *cross-cast*—it casts from one base class of an object to the other base class of the same object. If it turns out, at runtime, that the actual derived object is of a type that does not combine both base classes, the dynamic_cast will fail and return NULL (or throw an exception if we cast references instead of pointers). A robust program should check that the cross-cast have succeeded, and handle the possible errors.

Summary

In this chapter, we have learned why constructors cannot be made virtual, and what to do when we really want a virtual constructor anyway. We have learned how to construct and copy objects whose type becomes known at runtime by using the Factory pattern and one of its variations. We also explored several implementations of the Factory constructor that differ in the way that the code is organized and that the behavior is delegated to different components of the system, and compared their advantages and trade-offs. We have also seen how multiple design patterns interact with each other.

While in C++, the constructor has to be invoked with the true type of the object to construct—always—this does not mean that the application code has to specify the complete type. The Factory pattern allows us to write code that specifies the type indirectly, using an identifier that is associated with the type elsewhere (*create an object of the third kind*), or an associated object type (*create a unit that goes with this building type*), or even the same type (*make me a copy of this, whatever it is*).

The next design pattern we will study in the following chapter is the Template Method pattern, one of the classic object-oriented patterns that, in C++, has additional implications for the way we design class hierarchies.

Questions

1. Why does C++ not allow a virtual constructor?
2. What is the Factory pattern?
3. How do you use the Factory pattern to achieve the effect of a virtual constructor?
4. How do you achieve the effect of a virtual copy constructor?
5. How do you use the Template and Factory patterns together?

The Template Method Pattern and the Non-Virtual Idiom **14**

The Template Method is one of the classic *Gang of Four* design patterns, or, more formally, one of the 24 patterns described in the book *Design Patterns – Elements of Reusable Object-Oriented Software* by Erich Gamma, Richard Helm, Ralph Johnson, and John Vlissides. It is a behavioral design pattern, meaning that it describes a way for communicating between different objects. As an object-oriented language, C++, of course, fully supports the Template Method pattern. There are some implementation details that are specific or unique to C++ that this chapter will elucidate.

The following topics will be covered in this chapter:

- What is the Template Method pattern, and what problems does it solve?
- What is the non-virtual interface?
- Should you make virtual functions public, private, or protected by default?
- Should you always make destructors virtual and public in polymorphic classes?

Technical requirements

No special tools or other technical knowledge is required for this chapter.

The Template Method pattern

The Template Method pattern is a common way to implement an algorithm whose overall structure is pre-determined, but some of the details of the implementation need to be customized. If you are thinking about a solution that goes something like this—first, we do X, then Y, then Z, but how exactly we do Y depends on the data we process—you are thinking about the Template Method. As a pattern that allows the behavior of the program to change dynamically, the Template Method is somewhat similar to the strategy pattern. The key difference is that the strategy changes the entire algorithm at runtime, while the Template Method lets us customize specific parts of the algorithm. This section deals with the latter, while we have a separate Chapter 16, *Policy-Based Design*, dedicated to the former.

The Template Method in C++

The Template Method pattern is easily implemented in any object-oriented language. The C++ implementation uses inheritance and virtual functions. Note that this has nothing to do with C++ templates, as in generic programming. The *template* here is the skeleton implementation of the algorithm:

```
class Base {
    public:
    bool TheAlgorithm() {
        if (!Step1()) return false;        // Step 1 failed
        Step2();
        return true;
    }
};
```

The *template* here is the structure of the algorithm—all implementations must first do Step one, which may fail. If this happens, the entire algorithm is considered to have failed, and nothing more is done. If Step one succeeded, we must do Step two. By design, Step two cannot fail, and the overall algorithm computation is considered a success once Step two is completed.

Note that the TheAlgorithm() method is public, but not virtual—any class derived from Base has it as a part of its interface, but cannot override what it does. What the derived classes can override are the implementations of Step one and Step two, within the restrictions of the algorithm template—Step one may fail and must signal the failure by returning false, and Step two may not fail:

```
class Base {
```

```
    public:
    ...
    virtual bool Step1() { return true };
    virtual void Step2() = 0;
};
class Derived1 : public Base {
    public:
    void Step2() { ... do the work ... }
};
class Derived2 : public Base {
    public:
    bool Step1() { ... check preconditions ... }
    void Step2() { ... do the work ... }
};
```

In the preceding example, overriding the potentially failing Step 1 is optional, and the default implementation is trivial; it does nothing and never fails. Step 2 must be implemented by every derived class—there is no default, and it is declared as a pure virtual function.

You can see that the overall flow of control—the framework—remains invariant, but it has *placeholders* for customizable options, possibly with a default offered by the framework itself. Such a flow is known as inversion of control. In a traditional control flow, its specific implementation determines the flow of computation and sequence of operations and makes calls to library functions or other lower-level functions to implement the necessary general algorithms. In the Template Method, it is the framework that calls specific implementations in the custom code.

Applications of the Template Method

There are many reasons to use the Template Method. In general, it is used to control what can and cannot be sub-classed—as opposed to a general polymorphic override, where the entire virtual function can be replaced, the base class here determines what can and cannot be overridden. Another common use of the Template Method is to avoid code duplication, and in this context, you can arrive to use the Template Method as follows. Suppose that you start with the regular polymorphism—a virtual function—and it overrides. For example, let's consider this toy design for a turn-based combat system for a game:

```
class Character {
    public:
    virtual void CombatTurn() = 0;
    protected:
    int health_;
};
```

```
class Swordsman : public Character {
    bool wielded_sword_;
    public:
    void CombatTurn() {
        if (health_ < 5) {              // Critically injured
            Flee();
            return;
        }
        if (!wielded_sword_) {
            Wield();
            return;                     // Wielding takes a full turn
        }
        Attack();
    }
};
class Wizard : public Character {
    int mana_;
    bool scroll_ready_;
    public:
    void CombatTurn() {
        if (health_ < 2 ||
            mana_ == 0) {               // Critically injured or out of mana
            Flee();
            return;
        }
        if (!scroll_ready_) {
            ReadScroll();
            return;                     // Reading takes a full turn
        }
        CastSpell();
    }
};
```

Note how this code is highly repetitive—all characters may be forced to disengage from combat on their turn, then they must take a turn to get ready for combat, and only then, if they are ready and strong enough, can they use their offensive capabilities. If you see this pattern repeating over and over, it is a strong hint that the Template Method may be called for. With the Template Method, the overall sequence of the combat turn is fixed, but how each character advances to the next step and what he/she does once he/she gets there remains character-specific:

```
class Character {
    public:
    void CombatTurn() {
        if (MustFlee()) {
            Flee();
            return;
```

```
        }
        if (!Ready()) {
            GetReady();
            return;                     // Getting ready takes a full turn
        }
        CombatAction();
    }
    virtual bool MustFlee() const = 0;
    virtual bool Ready() const = 0;
    virtual void GetReady() = 0;
    virtual void CombatAction() = 0;
    protected:
    int health_;
};
class Swordsman : public Character {
    bool wielded_sword_;
    public:
    bool MustFlee() const { return health_ < 5; }    // Critically injured
    bool Ready() const { return wielded_sword_; }
    void GetReady() { Wield(); }
    void CombatAction() { Attack(); }
};
class Wizard : public Character {
    int mana_;
    bool scroll_ready_;
    public:
    bool MustFlee() const { return health_ < 2 ||    // Critically injured
                                   mana_ == 0; }      // Out of mana
    bool Ready() const { return scroll_ready_; }
    void GetReady() { ReadScroll(); }
    void CombatAction() { CastSpell(); }
};
```

Note how this code is much less repetitive. The advantage of the Template Method goes beyond good looks, though. Let's say that in the next revision of the game that we have added healing potions, and, at the beginning of the turn, each character may drink a potion. Now, imagine going through every derived class and adding code like if (health_ < ... some class-specific value ... && potion_count_ > 0) .... If the design already used the Template Method, the logic of potion-quaffing needs to be coded only once, and different classes implement their specific conditions for using a potion, as well as the consequences of drinking one. However, don't rush to implement this solution until you get to the end of this chapter, as this is not the best C++ code you can do.

Pre-and post-conditions and actions

Another common use of the Template Method is dealing with pre-and post-conditions, or actions. In a class hierarchy, pre-and post-conditions generally verify that the design invariants of the abstraction provided by the interface are not violated by any specific implementation at any point during execution. Such verification naturally submits to the Template Method's design:

```
class Base {
    public:
    void VerifiedAction() {
        assert(StateIsValid());
        ActionImpl();
        assert(StateIsValid());
    }
    virtual void ActionImpl() = 0;
};
class Derived : public Base {
    public:
    void ActionImpl() { ... }
};
```

Of course, in software design, one man's invariants are another's customization points. Sometimes, it is the main code that remains the same, but what happens right before and right after depends on the specific application. In this case, we probably wouldn't be verifying any invariants, but executing initial and final actions:

```
class FileWriter {
    public:
    void Write(const char* data) {
        Preamble(data);
        ... write data to a file ...
        Postscript(data);
    }
    virtual void Preamble(const char* data) {}
    virtual void Postscript(const char* data) {}
};
class LoggingFileWriter : public FileWriter {
    void Preamble(const char* data) {
        std::cout << "Writing " << data << " to the file" << std::endl;
    }
};
```

The Non-Virtual Interface

The implementation of the dynamically customizable parts of the templated algorithm is usually done with virtual functions. For a general Template Method pattern, this is not a requirement, but in C++, we rarely need another way. Now, we are going to focus specifically on using the virtual functions and improve on what we have learned.

Virtual functions and access

Let's start with a general question—should virtual functions be public or private? The textbook object-oriented design style uses public virtual functions, so we often make them public without a second thought. Within the Template Method, this practice needs to be reevaluated—a public function is part of the class interface. In our case, the class interface includes the entire algorithm, and the framework we put in place in the base class. This function should be public, but it is also non-virtual. The customized implementations of some parts of the algorithm were never meant to be called directly by the clients of the class hierarchy. They are used in one place only—in the non-virtual public function, where they replace the placeholders we put in the template of the algorithm.

This idea may seem trivial, but it comes as a surprise to many programmers. I've had this question asked more than once—*does C++ even allow virtual functions to be anything other than public?* In fact, the language itself makes no restrictions on the access to virtual functions; they can be private, protected, or public, just like any other class member functions. This takes some time to wrap your mind around; perhaps an example would help:

```
class Base {
    public:
    void method1() { method2(); }
    private:
    virtual void method2() { ... }
};
class Derived : public Base {
    private:
    virtual void method2() { ... }
};
```

Here, `Derived::method2()` is private. Can the base class even call private methods of its derived classes? The answer is, it doesn't have to—`Base::method1()` only calls `Base::method2()`, which is its own private member function; there is no problem with calling private member functions of the same class. But if the actual class type is `Derived`, the virtual override of `method2()` is called at runtime instead. These two decisions, *can I call* `method2()`*?* and *which* `method2()`*?*, happen at totally different times—the former happens when the module containing the `Base` class is compiled (and the `Derived` class may not have even been written yet), while the latter happens when the program is executed (and the words *private* or *public* don't mean anything at that point).

There is another, more fundamental reason, to avoid public virtual functions. A public method is a part of the class interface. Virtual function override is a customization of the implementation. A public virtual function inherently does both of these, at once. The same entity performs two very different functions that should not be coupled—declaring the public interface and providing an alternative implementation. Each of these functions have different constraints—the implementation can be altered in any way, as long as the hierarchy invariants hold. But the interface cannot be actually changed by the virtual function (except for returning covariant types, but even that does not really change the interface). All the public virtual function does is restate that yes, indeed, the public interface still looks like what the base class has declared. Such mixing of two very distinct roles calls for a better separation of concerns. The Template Method pattern is an answer to that design problem, and in C++, it takes the form of the **Non-Virtual Interface (NVI)**.

The NVI idiom in C++

The tension between the two roles of a public virtual function, and the unnecessary exposure of the customization points created by such functions, lead us to the idea of making the implementation-specific virtual functions private. Herb Sutter in his article, *Virtuality* (`http://www.gotw.ca/publications/mill18.htm`), suggests that most, if not all, virtual functions should be private.

For the Template Method, moving virtual functions from public to private comes with no consequences (other than the initial shock of seeing a private virtual function, if you have never realized that C++ allows them):

```
class Base {
    public:
    bool TheAlgorithm() {
        if (!Step1()) return false; // Step 1 failed
        Step2();
        return true;
```

```
    }
    private:
    virtual bool Step1() { return true };
    virtual void Step2() = 0;
};
class Derived1 : public Base {
    private:
    void Step2() { ... do the work ... }
};
class Derived2 : public Base {
    private:
    bool Step1() { ... check preconditions ... }
    void Step2() { ... do the work ... }
};
```

This design nicely separates the interface and the implementation—the client interface is, and always was, the one call to run the entire algorithm. The possibility to change parts of the algorithm's implementation is not reflected in the interface, but the user of this class hierarchy who only accesses it through the public interface and does not need to extend the hierarchy (write more derived classes), which does not need to know about that.

The NVI gives complete control of the interface to the base class. The derived classes can only customize the implementation of this interface. The base class can determine and verify the invariants, impose the overall structure of the implementation, and specify which parts can, must, and cannot be customized. The NVI also separates the interface from the implementation explicitly. The implementers of the derived classes do not need to be concerned with exposing part of their implementation to the callers unintentionally—the implementation-only private methods cannot be called by anyone except the base class.

So far, we have made all virtual functions that customize the implementation private. That, however, is not exactly the main point of the NVI—this idiom, and the more general Template Method, focus on making the public interface non-virtual. It follows, by extension, that the implementation-specific overrides should not be public since they are not part of the interface. It does not necessarily follow that they should be private. That leaves *protected*. So, should the virtual functions that provide customization's for the algorithm be private or protected? The Template Method allows both—the client of the hierarchy cannot directly call either one, so the framework of the algorithm remains unaffected. The answer depends on whether the derived classes may need to sub-invoke the implementations provided by the base class. For an example of the latter, consider a class hierarchy that can be serialized and sent to a remote machine through a socket:

```
class Base {
    public:
    void Send() {      // Template Method used here
        ... open connection ...
```

```
            SendData();
            ... close connection ...
    }
    protected:
    virtual void SendData() { ... send base class data ... }
    private:
    ... data ...
};
class Derived : public Base {
    protected:
    void SendData() {
            ... send derived class data ...
            Base::SendData();
    }
};
```

Here, the framework is provided by the public non-virtual method `Base::Send()`, which handles the connection protocol and, at the right time, sends the data across the network. Of course, it can only send the data that the base class knows about. That is why `SendData` is a customization point and is made virtual. The derived class must send its own data, of course, but someone must still send the base class data, and so the derived class makes a call to the protected virtual function in the base class.

A note about destructors

The entire discussion of the NVI is an elaboration on a simple guideline—make virtual functions private (or protected), and present the public interface through non-virtual base class functions. This sounds fine until it runs head-on into another well-known guideline—if the class has at least one virtual function, its destructor must also be made virtual. Since the two are in conflict, some clarification is needed.

The reason to make destructors virtual is this—if the object is deleted polymorphically, for example, a derived class object is deleted through a pointer to the base class, the destructor must be virtual, otherwise only the base part of the class will be destructed (the usual result is *slicing* of the class, partial deletion, although the standard simply states that the results are undefined). So, if the objects are deleted through the base class pointers, the destructors must be virtual; there is no way around it. But that is the only reason. If the objects are always deleted with the correct derived type, then this reason does not apply. This situation is not uncommon: for example, if derived class objects are stored in a container, they will be deleted as their true type.

The container has to know how much memory to allocate for the object, so it can't store a mix of base and derived objects, or delete them as base (note that a container of pointers to the base class object is a different construct altogether, and is usually created specifically so that we can store and delete objects polymorphically).

Now, if the derived class has to be deleted as itself, its destructor does not need to be virtual. However, bad things will still happen if someone calls the destructor of the base class when the actual object is of the derived class type. To safely prevent that from happening, we can declare the non-virtual base class destructor as protected instead of public. Of course, if the base class is not abstract, and there are objects of both base and derived types around, then both destructors must be made public, and the safer option is to make them virtual (a runtime check can be implemented to verify that the base class destructor is not called to destroy a derived class object).

We must also caution the reader against trying to employ the Template Method, or the non-virtual interface idiom, for class destructors. It may be tempting to do something like this:

```
class Base {
    public:
    ~Base() {                  // Non-virtual interface!
        std::cout << "Deleting now" << std::endl;
        clear();          // Employing Template Method here
        std::cout << "Deleting done" << std::endl;
    }
    protected:
    virtual void clear() { ... }     // Customizable part
};
class Derived : public Base {
    private:
    void clear() { ... }
        ...
        Base::clear();
    }
};
```

However, this is not going to work (if the base class has a pure virtual `Base::clear()` instead of a default implementation, it is not going to work in a rather spectacular fashion). The reason for this is that, inside the destructor of the base class, `Base::~Base()`, the actual, real, true type of the object is not `Derived` anymore. It's `Base`. That's right—when the `Derived::~Derived()` destructor is done with its work and the control is transferred to the base class destructor, the dynamic type of the object changes to `Base`.

The only other class member that works this way is the constructor—the type of the object is `Base` as long as the base constructor is running, and then changes to `Derived` when the derived constructor has started. For all other member functions, the type of the object is always the type it was created with. If the object was created as `Derived`, then that is the type, even if a method of the base class is called. So, what happens if, in the preceding example, `Base::clear()` is pure virtual? It's called anyway! The result depends on the compiler; most compilers will generate code that aborts the program with some diagnostic that *a pure virtual function was called*.

Drawbacks of the Non-Virtual Interface

There aren't many drawbacks regarding the use of the NVI. That is why the guideline to always make virtual functions private, and use NVI to call them, is widely accepted. However, there are some considerations that you must be aware of when deciding whether the Template Method is the right design pattern to follow. Use of the template pattern may lead to fragile hierarchies. Also, there is some overlap between design problems that can be solved using the template pattern and the ones better served by the strategy pattern, or, in C++, policies. We will review both considerations in this section.

Composability

Consider the earlier design for the `LoggingFileWriter`. Now, suppose that we want to also have a `CountingFileWriter` that counts how many characters were written into the file:

```
class CountingFileWriter : public FileWriter {
    size_t count_;
    void Preamble(const char* data) {
        count_ += strlen(data);
    }
};
```

That was easy. But there is no reason a counting file writer cannot also log. How would we implement a `CountingLoggingFileWriter`? No problem, we have the technology—change the private virtual functions to protected and call the base class version from the derived class:

```
class CountingLoggingFileWriter : public LoggingFileWriter {
    size_t count_;
    void Preamble(const char* data) {
        count_ += strlen(data);
```

```
        LoggingFileWriter::Preamble(data);
    }
};
```

Or should it be `LoggingCountingFileWriter` that inherits from `CountingFileWriter`?
Note that, either way, some code is duplicated—in our case, the counting code is present in
both `CountingLoggingFileWriter` and `CountingFileWriter`. This duplication is only
going to get worse as we add more variations. The Template Method just isn't the right
pattern if you need composable customizations. For that, you should read `Chapter 16`,
Policy-Based Design.

The Fragile Base Class problem

The Fragile Base Class problem is not limited to the Template Method, but is, to some
degree, inherent in all object-oriented languages. The problem arises when changes to the
base class break the derived class. To see how this can happen, specifically when using the
non-virtual interface, let's go back to the file writer and add the ability to write many
strings at once:

```cpp
class FileWriter {
    public:
    void Write(const char* data) {
        Preamble(data);
        ... write data to a file ...
        Postscript(data);
    }
    void Write(std::vector<const char*> huge_data) {
        Preamble(huge_data);
        for (auto data: huge_data) { ... write data to file ... }
        Postscript(huge_data);
    }
    private:
    virtual void Preamble(std::vector<const char*> huge_data) {}
    virtual void Postscript(std::vector<const char*> huge_data) {}
    virtual void Preamble(const char* data) {}
    virtual void Postscript(const char* data) {}
};
```

The counting writer is kept up to date with the changes:

```
class CountingFileWriter : public FileWriter {
    size_t count_;
    void Preamble(std::vector<const char*> huge_data) {
        or (auto data: huge_data) count_ += strlen(data);
    }
    void Preamble(const char* data) {
        count_ += strlen(data);
    }
};
```

So far, so good. Later, a well-intentioned programmer notices that the base class suffers from some code duplication and decides to refactor it:

```
class FileWriter {
    public:
    void Write(const char* data) { ... no changes here ... }
    void Write(std::vector<const char*> huge_data) {
        Preamble(huge_data);
        for (auto data: huge_data) Write(data); // Code reuse!
        Postscript(huge_data);
    }
    private:
    ... no changes here ...
};
```

Now, the derived class is broken—the counting customizations of both versions of `Write` are called when a vector of strings is written, and the data size is counted twice.

While there is no general solution to the Fragile Base Class problem as long as inheritance is used at all, the guideline that helps to avoid it when using the Template Method is straightforward—when changing the base class and the structure of the algorithms, or the framework, avoid changing which customization points are invoked. Specifically, do not skip any customization options that were already invoked and do not add new calls to already existing ones (it's OK to add new customization points, as long as the default implementation is sensible). If such a change cannot be avoided, you will need to review every derived class to see whether it relied on the implementation override that is now removed or replaced, and what the consequences of such a change are.

Summary

In this chapter, we have reviewed a classic object-oriented design pattern, the Template Method, as it applies to C++ programs. This pattern works in C++ as well as in any other object-oriented language, but C++ also has its own flavor of the Template Method—the non-virtual interface idiom. The advantages of this design pattern lead to a rather broad guideline—make all virtual functions private or protected. Be mindful, however, of the specifics of the destructors with regard to polymorphism.

The next chapter introduces a somewhat controversial pattern, the Singleton. Learn about the valid applications of this pattern as well as the misuse that gives it a bad reputation.

Questions

1. What is a behavioral design pattern?
2. What is the Template Method pattern?
3. Why is the Template Method considered a behavioral pattern?
4. What is the inversion of control, and how does it apply to the Template Method?
5. What is the non-virtual interface?
6. Why is it recommended to make all virtual functions in C++ private?
7. When should virtual functions be protected?
8. Why can't the Template Method be used for destructors?
9. What is the Fragile Base class problem, and how can we avoid it when employing the Template Method?

Further reading

https://www.packtpub.com/application-development/learn-example-c-programming-75-solved-problems-video

https://www.packtpub.com/application-development/c-data-structures-and-algorithms

15
Singleton - A Classic OOP Pattern

In this chapter, we are going to cover one of the simplest classic C++ object-oriented patterns—the singleton. It is also one of the most misused ones. With its apparent simplicity comes an unusual danger—everyone likes to implement their own singleton, and these implementations often have subtle bugs.

The following topics will be covered in this chapter:

- What is the singleton pattern?
- When should the singleton pattern be used?
- How can singletons be implemented in C++?
- What are the downsides and trade-offs of different implementations of the singleton?

Technical requirements

The example code for this chapter can be found at the following link: `https://github.com/PacktPublishing/Hands-On-Design-Patterns-with-CPP/tree/master/Chapter15`.

You will also need the Google Benchmark library installed and configured, the details for which can be found here: `https://github.com/google/benchmark`.

The singleton pattern – what is it and what is it for?

Let's start by reviewing what the singleton pattern is, what it does, and when it should be used. Each pattern is a commonly accepted solution to a frequently occurring design problem, so what problem does the singleton pattern solve?

The singleton is a pattern that's used to restrict the number of class instantiations to exactly one. It should be considered when, by design, there should only be one object of a certain type in the entire system. A frequent criticism of the singleton is that it is a global variable in disguise, and global variables are bad. As a supposed downside of the singleton pattern itself, this critique misses the point: the pattern is a solution to the design challenge. You can argue that having a single global object in the entire system is a sign of bad design, but that is an argument against the problem itself, not against its particular solution. Assuming that the design need is legitimate, the singleton pattern is the canonical solution to address it.

We will, at first, set aside the question of whether good design can have global objects, which is to be revisited later. Let's start with a demonstration of a basic singleton.

What is a singleton?

Let's suppose that, in our program, we want to have a class for logging all debug, information, and error messages. The message logger will ensure that, even if multiple threads or processes print messages at the same time, the messages are printed in order, not garbled or interleaved. We also maintain a count of errors and warnings of different types, and some messages we want to store so they can be reported later, perhaps as a summary of all errors at the end of the run. There is only one set of message counts for the entire program, and, to ensure synchronization across multiple threads, one lock that must be used for printing all messages.

While there are other ways to solve this problem, the most straightforward one is a class that can be instantiated only once. There are multiple implementations, but here is one of the simpler ones:

```
// In the header logger.h:
class Logger {
    public:
    static Logger&amp; instance() {
        return instance_;
    }
}
```

```
    // Logger API here:
    void LogError(const char* msg) {
        std::lockguard<std::mutex> guard(lock_);
        std::cerr << "ERROR: " << msg << std::endl;
        ++error_count_;
        ... count and log the error ...
    }
    ... The rest of Logger API ...

    private:
    Logger() : error_count_(0) {}
    ~Logger() {}
    Logger(const Logger&) = delete;
    Logger& operator=(const Logger&) = delete;

    private:
    static Logger instance_;
    std::mutex lock_;
    size_t error_count_;
};

// In the implementation file logger.C:
Logger Logger::instance_;
```

There is only one instance of the `Logger` class in the entire program, that is, the static
`Logger::instance_` data member of the `Logger` class itself. No other instance can be
created, because we made the constructor private and deleted all copy operations. The
unique instance of the `Logger` class can be accessed anywhere in the program by calling
the `Logger::instance()` static function, which returns a reference to the singleton object
itself:

```
void func(int* p) {
    if (!p) Logger::instance().LogError("Unexpected NULL pointer");
}
```

The only way to access a `Logger` object is through this static function, and without an
object, we cannot call the `Logger` API methods. This guarantees that all logging in the
entire program is done using one `Logger` object, which, in turn, ensures that all I/O is
protected by the same lock, that only one set of counts is used, and so on. We wanted all
logging to be channeled though one object, and that is exactly what we got with the
singleton pattern.

There are several subtle complications that may arise when using this singleton. Before we
review them in detail, let's address the question of whether this problem should be solved
at all.

When to use the singleton

The superficial answer to the question of when to use a singleton is very simple—when you need to have only one object of some type in the entire program. This answer, of course, simply kicks the can down the road—OK, so when, if ever, is it a good design principle to have only one object of some type in the entire program? There isn't an easy universal answer to this, which gives rise to the argument that, like any other global object, a singleton is a sign of bad design.

There are two general categories of design problems that can be addressed with a singleton, or, more generally, with a unique global object. The first category is objects that represent some physical object or resource, where the corresponding physical object is unique, at least within the context of the program. The latter qualification is very important—there are millions of cars in the world, and yet, from the point of view of the software that runs on a car and controls its engine, electronics, and other systems, there is only *the car*, that is, the one that the software is running on (other cars may enter into the picture as obstacles to avoid, but they are fundamentally different from *the car*). In the entire software suite running on various microprocessors and microcomputers embedded in the car, the *car object* should refer to the same entity—it would be bad, for example, if one component of the software applied the brakes, and another component tried to accelerate because its check for braking refers to a different car object.

Similarly, the software that simulates the solar system and computes trajectory for a solar probe or a Mars orbiter can reasonably assume that there is only one star in the system, and only one object of the *star* type to represent it. You could argue, pedantically, that this limits the applicability of the software to star systems with only one star, thus excluding binary stars. A programmer can be excused, however, for deferring this generalization and creating a technical debt, to be paid at the time when the interstellar flight becomes commonplace enough to worry about such things (perhaps with an expectation that the program will no longer be in use when such a time arrives).

The second category of global objects are the objects that are global by design, without any physical entity standing behind them. For example, resource managers are often implemented as singletons. Sometimes, this reflects the nature of the resource itself, such as memory—there is only so much of it, physically, so whether there is one manager or many, they must all count their use toward the same single limit. At other times, there is no physical reason—for example, in a parallel system, we can design a single manager object for all processors and all work to be done by the system—the clients submit the work and the global manager assigns it to the processors.

Again, the programmer can say that there is no reason to over complicate the program—a single resource manager is sufficient for every need we can anticipate, and thus defer the generalization until such a time as it is really needed (with luck, the program will be completely rewritten or replaced before this happens).

The line between absurdly general and absurdly short-sighted is, unfortunately, never quite clear. The general principle of agile programming, known as **You Aren't Gonna Need It (YAGNI)**, dictates that an implementation that is sufficient for the needs of today should be preferred over a more general one. You should be careful when applying this rule to the design, especially when the design decision limits future extensibility and is difficult to reverse. Programs tend to live and remain in use much longer than the original author anticipates. While it would be hard to blame any programmer for saying *we will handle multiple suns in a thousand years when we can reach one, until then one sun is enough,* we can imagine similar argument made over keyboards and monitors some 30 years ago—there is only one keyboard connected to the computer, and every program that does keyboard input should read from it, so naturally the keyboard should be a singleton. In fact, a keyboard object used to be a classic example of the singleton application: if this book was written at the end of the last century, the preceding example would probably feature a `Keyboard` instead of the `Logger`, because that's what everyone did. Today, we have USB keyboards, laptop docking station keyboards, wireless and wired keyboards, plug-and-play multiple keyboards, but we also have *headless* servers with no keyboards. Rewriting the I/O drivers that were written in the assumption that the operating system must handle only one and exactly one keyboard, and which produce a hard error on boot if the keyboard is not connected, must have been painful. On the other hand, we survived, and the effort must be weighed against all the time that was saved by all the programmers not handling the general case of multiple keyboards for a few decades.

In general, considering whether to use the singleton pattern is putting the cart before the horse. You should instead consider whether the design should enforce that a certain object is unique. The singleton pattern is only a solution to this design problem. It is such a common and preferred solution that it is often seen as equivalent, and programmers say *I decided to use a singleton* when they mean *I decided to use a design with a global object, and implement it as a singleton* (if anything in this sentence is objectionable, it is the first part). So, when should designs rely on a unique object? Or, as it is more commonly, if not entirely correctly, said, when should we use a singleton?

The first case for which a singleton object should be considered is when there is a physical reason for having only one object. Sometimes, it is a universal reason—there is only one speed of light, for instance. Sometimes, the physical reason exists only in the context of a particular problem—any program that models or controls spaceflight in our solar system will have only one star to deal with; any program that manages a car or a plane has only one such vehicle to control. Every decision to use a singleton does, in theory, limit the generalizability of the code and restricts how widely it can be reused. The question that should be asked is, firstly, *how likely are we to encounter this limitation?*, and secondly, *how difficult would the redesign be compared to the effort needed to design, implement, and maintain the code that is not currently used?* The maintenance consideration is arguably the most important of all—while we can envision a software system that controls multiple cars (in a way less trivial than cars alerting each other to avoid collisions), we are still far away from any practical use of such a system. Even if we refuse to make the car a singleton, and choose to support multiple engines in the engine control software, for many years this code will remain unused and untested. Chances are, it will be broken by the time we actually need it and will need to be rewritten anyway. The few obvious cases aside, the decision to use a singleton is a judgment decision that trades generalizability for expediency.

With this discussion behind us, the reader is, hopefully, convinced that there are legitimate use cases for the singleton pattern. We can now return to the question of the preferred implementation.

Types of singletons

The implementation of the singleton in the previous section works, at least as far as enforcing a unique single global object and providing access to it for the entire program. There are, however, other considerations that may influence the choice of the implementation. We should also point out that, over the years, there have been a wide variety of implementations created. At the time, many of them were valid implementations that dealt with specific challenges in various ways. However, today, most are obsolete and should not be considered.

When it comes to the implementation of the singleton, there are several different types of implementations to choose from. First of all, we can classify implementations by how the singleton is accessed in the program—while there is definitely only one instance of the singleton object itself, or at least of the data that must be unique and global, there are several ways to provide access to this unique data. The most straightforward way is to have a single global object:

```
// In the header:
extern Singleton SingletonInstance;
```

```
// In the C file:
Singleton SingletonInstance;
```

This is really just a global object, and the singleton nature of it is not enforced by the compiler, but is maintained by convention. Nothing stops an incorrect program from creating another `Singleton` object (it is possible to verify the uniqueness of this object at runtime). When used correctly, there is only one instance of the object that is used to access the global data, in this case, the `Singleton` object itself. We can also imagine an implementation that allows the user to create an arbitrary number of *singleton* objects, all of which are identical and refer to the same data. The client program may look like this:

```
void f() {
    Singleton Sf;
    S.do_operation();
}
void g() {
    Singleton Sg;          // Refers to the same data as Sf above
    S.do_operation();
}
```

We will see a possible implementation in the next subsection, but for now, it is important to notice the distinction—in this design, there are multiple *singleton handle* objects corresponding to one real singleton. There are no restrictions on constructing the handles, but they are interchangeable, and all refer to the same singleton. The uniqueness of the latter is, thus, enforced at compile time. By comparison, the previous design had only one *singleton handle* (in our example, the handle was the singleton itself).

Finally, there is the third option—the user cannot construct the singleton object at all, so there are zero handle objects:

```
// In the header:
extern Singleton&amp; SingletonInstance();
// In the C file:
Singleton instance;
Singleton&amp; SingletonInstance() { return instance; }
```

In this design, the program does not construct or use any handle objects to get access to the singleton, so there are zero handles. Again, the uniqueness of the singleton can be enforced at compile time.

The implementation that relies on programming discipline to enforce the uniqueness of the singleton is clearly not ideal. Between the other two, the choice of the implementations is largely a matter of style, as there is no significant difference between the two.

An entirely independent classification of singleton implementations can be achieved by using the lifetime of the singleton—the singleton can be initialized when the object is used for the first time, or it can be initialized sometime earlier, usually when the program starts. It may be destroyed at some point at the end of the program, or not destroyed at all (leaked). We will now see examples of each of these implementations and discuss their advantages and disadvantages.

Static singleton

One of the simplest implementations of the singleton pattern is a static singleton. In this implementation, the object has only static data members:

```
class Singleton {
    public:
    Singleton() {}
    int&amp; get() { return value_; }
    private:
    static int value_;
};
int Singleton::value_ = 0;
```

For the rest of this section, we will consider a singleton with one integer data member, and the member functions that provide access to it. We do this only for the sake of a concrete example—the real-life implementation can have an arbitrary number of data members of different types, and an arbitrarily complex API that's provided by the member functions.

The member functions may be static or not. If the member functions are not static, the implementation may be classified as a *multiple handle objects, one data* type, because to access the singleton, the programmer simply constructs a Singleton object as many times as needed:

```
Singleton S;
int i = S.get();
++S.get();
```

The object may even be constructed on the fly, as a temporary variable:

```
int i = Singleton().get();
++Singleton().get();
```

There is no actual construction, that is, no code is generated or executed at runtime to construct this object—after all, there is nothing to construct, as all data is static. We can expect this singleton to be very fast—an expectation that is confirmed by the benchmark:

```
#define REPEAT(X) ... repeat X 32 times
void BM_singleton(benchmark::State& state) {
    Singleton S;
    for (auto _ : state) {
        REPEAT(benchmark::DoNotOptimize(++S.get());)
    }
    state.SetItemsProcessed(32*state.iterations());
}
```

In this benchmark, we use the REPEAT macro to generate 32 copies of the benchmarked code inside the loop; this is done to reduce the overhead of the loop, since each iteration is very short:

Benchmark	Time	CPU	Iterations	
BM_singleton/threads:1	10 ns	10 ns	66071182	2.85622G items/s

The alternative use of the singleton, where a temporary object is created every time, can be benchmarked just as easily:

```
void BM_singletons(benchmark::State& state) {
    for (auto _ : state) {
        REPEAT(benchmark::DoNotOptimize(++Singleton().get());)
    }
    state.SetItemsProcessed(32*state.iterations());
}
```

We expect it to be equally fast—an expectation that is confirmed by the following measurements:

Benchmark	Time	CPU	Iterations	
BM_singletons/threads:1	11 ns	11 ns	66099954	2.82814G items/s

As far as the lifetime of the singleton goes (not the handle object, the data itself), it is initialized together with all the static data in the program, some time before main() is called. It is destroyed at some point at the end of the program, after main() exits.

An alternative way is to declare not just data members, as static, but also function members, as shown here:

```
class Singleton {
    public:
    static int& get() { return value_; }
    private:
    Singleton() = delete;
    static int value_;
};
int Singleton::value_ = 0;
```

In this approach, we never have to construct the `Singleton` object at all:

```
int i = Singleton::get();
++Singleton::get();
```

This implementation can be classified as a *zero handle objects, one data* type. However, in every way that matters, it is identical to the previous one—the exact syntax of the function calls is different, but what they do is the same, and so is the performance.

An important consideration is the thread safety of the singleton implementation, as well as the performance in a concurrent program. The static singleton itself is obviously thread-safe—it is initialized and destroyed by the C++ runtime system, together with the rest of the static data, and no user threads can be running at that time. The thread-safe use of the singleton is always the responsibility of the programmer, of course—if the singleton provides access to modify its data, it must be protected by a mutex, or implemented in a thread-safe way. When we discuss thread safety of the singleton implementation, we focus on the initialization, destruction, and provision of access to the singleton object—these operations are part of the implementation of the pattern; the rest is specific to the program.

The thread safety of the static singleton is trivially assured, but what about performance? In this case, to access the singleton the program, all that needs to be read is the static data, so there is no overhead. Of course, there may be overhead if the program needs to synchronize modifications of this data, but that is no different from any other shared data in a concurrent program.

There are two potential downsides to this implementation. First of all, this singleton cannot be extended through inheritance. This is the less important of the two problems—singleton objects are, or should be, rare enough in a good design, so code reuse is not a significant concern.

The more important problem has to do with the object's lifetime—the singleton is initialized as a static object before the program itself is started. The order of initialization of the static objects is, in general, undefined and left to the implementation—the standard guarantees that all objects defined in one file are initialized in the order of their definitions, but for objects initialized in different files, there are no guarantees at all with regard to the order.

This is not a problem if the singleton is going to be used by the program when it executes; that is, used for anything that is called from `main()`—the singleton will definitely be constructed before the program starts and will not be destroyed until after it ends. It is, however, a problem for any code in any other static object that uses this singleton. Such dependencies between static objects are not uncommon—for example, if our singleton is the memory manager, and there is only one instance of such in the program, then any static object that allocates memory has to get it from the memory manager. However, unless the whole program is contained in one file, there is no way to guarantee that the singleton memory manager is initialized before its first use. The next implementation attempts to address this problem.

Meyers' Singleton

This implementation is named after its inventor, Scott Meyers. If the main problem with the static singleton is that it can be initialized later than its first use, then the solution must be to initialize the singleton when it is needed for the first time:

```
class Singleton {
    public:
    static Singleton& instance() {
        static Singleton inst;
        return inst;
    }

    int& get() { return value_; }

    private:
    Singleton() : value_(0) {
        std::cout << "Singleton::Singleton()" << std::endl;
    }
    Singleton(const Singleton&) = delete;
    Singleton& operator=(const Singleton&) = delete;
    ~Singleton() {
        std::cout << "Singleton::~Singleton()" << std::endl;
    }
```

```
        private:
        int value_;
};
```

The Meyers' Singleton has a private constructor, so it cannot be constructed by the program directly (in our example, we added a printout to the constructor, only to see when the singleton is initialized). Nor can the program make copies of the singleton object. Since the Meyers' Singleton cannot be directly constructed by the program, it is again a *zero handle objects* implementation. The only way to access this singleton is through the `Singleton::instance()` static member function:

```
int i = Singleton::instance().get();
++Singleton::instance().get();
```

The `Singleton::instance()` function returns a reference to the singleton object, but which one, and when is it created? We can see from the preceding code that the return value is a reference to a local object defined in the body of the `instance()` function itself. Ordinarily, returning references to local objects is a serious programming error—these objects don't exist once the function completes. But the Meyers' Singleton doesn't use an ordinary local object, but a local static object. Just like file-static objects, only one instance of the static object exists in the entire program. Unlike the file static objects, the function static objects are initialized the first time they are used; in our case, the first time the function is called. In pseudo-code, you can think of the function-static object like this:

```
static bool initialized = false;       // Hidden compiler-generated variable
// Memory for the static object, uninitialized at first
char memory[sizeof(Singleton)];
class Singleton {
    public:
    static Singleton& instance() {
        if (!initialized) {             // Happens only once
            initialized = true;
            new (memory) Singleton;     // Placement new
                                        // Calls Singleton constructor
        }
        // memory now contains a Singleton object
        return *(Singleton*)(memory);
    }
    ...
};
```

This initialization of the singleton may occur after the program starts, or possibly long after, if the singleton is not used for a while. On the other hand, if another static object (not necessarily a singleton) uses our singleton object and requests a reference to it, the initialization is guaranteed to happen before the object can be used. This implementation is an example of lazy initialization—the initialization is deferred until it's needed (if the singleton object is not used at all in a particular run of the program, it will not be initialized at any point).

One possible concern about Meyers' Singleton is its performance. While the initialization occurs only once, every call to `Singleton::instance()` must check whether the object is already initialized. We can measure the cost of this check by comparing the time it takes to access the instance for some operations, compared to the time it takes to call the same operations on an instance already stored in a reference:

```
void BM_singleton(benchmark::State& state) {
    Singleton& S = Singleton::instance();
    for (auto _ : state) {
        REPEAT(benchmark::DoNotOptimize(++S.get());)
    }
    state.SetItemsProcessed(32*state.iterations());
}

void BM_singletons(benchmark::State& state) {
    for (auto _ : state) {
        REPEAT(benchmark::DoNotOptimize(++Singleton::instance().get());)
    }
    state.SetItemsProcessed(32*state.iterations());
}
```

Here, the first benchmark calls `Singleton::instance()` every time, while the second one calls the same member functions on the singleton, but accesses the instance only once. The difference between the two invocations shows us the cost of checking whether the singleton has to be initialized (the cost of the initialization itself is irrelevant, since the benchmark is executed many times, while the initialization happens only once):

```
Running ./singleton_meyers
Run on (4 X 3400 MHz CPU s)
Singleton::Singleton()
------------------------------------------------------
Benchmark              Time           CPU Iterations
------------------------------------------------------
BM_singleton          11 ns        11 ns   64858630   2.62924G items/s
BM_singletons         70 ns        70 ns    9945667   437.73M items/s
Singleton::~Singleton()                       _
```

We can see that the cost of the implementation of the function static variable is considerable, significantly greater than the cost of a simple operation on the singleton object (an integer increment, in our case). Therefore, if the singleton object is to be used extensively, it may be beneficial to store a reference to it, instead of requesting one every time. We can also see, thanks to the debug printouts we put in place earlier, that the singleton is indeed initialized the first time it is used—if the messages *Running...* and *Run on...* are printed by the program (by the `main()` function provided by the Google Benchmark library, to be exact), then the singleton is initialized. If the singleton used a file static object, the constructor would have been called before the program has a chance to print anything.

Not to be confused with Meyers' singleton is the following implementation:

```cpp
class Singleton {
    public:
    static Singleton& instance() {
        return instance_;
    }

    int& get() { return value_; }

    private:
    Singleton() : value_(0) {
        std::cout << "Singleton::Singleton()" << std::endl;
    }
    ~Singleton() {
        std::cout << "Singleton::~Singleton()" << std::endl;
    }
    Singleton(const Singleton&) = delete;
    Singleton& operator=(const Singleton&) = delete;

    private:
    static Singleton instance_;
    int value_;
};
Singleton Singleton::instance_;
```

While superficially similar, this implementation differs in the most important aspect—the time of initialization. The static instance is not a function static object, and is initialized with other static objects, regardless of whether it is used or not (eager initialization, as opposed to lazy initialization). The access to the singleton instance looks exactly the same as for Meyers' Singleton, but there, the similarities end. In fact, this is just another variant of the static singleton, only instead of declaring every data member as static, we created a static instance of the object.

We can expect the performance to be similar to that of the static singleton, or that of the Meyers' Singleton if we were to optimize the code to avoid repeated initialization checks:

```
Singleton::Singleton()
2018-09-01 15:17:01
Running ./singleton_eager
Run on (4 X 3400 MHz CPU s)
----------------------------------------------------------------------
Benchmark                        Time          CPU Iterations
----------------------------------------------------------------------
BM_singleton/threads:1          11 ns        11 ns   65362522   2.80485G items/s
Singleton::~Singleton()
```

We call the reader's attention to the timing of the construction again—this time, the constructor of the static singleton instance is called before the program has started to print its own messages.

An interesting variant of this implementation is a combination of the Meyers' Singleton with the *pimpl idiom*, where the header file contains only the interface declarations, and the actual implementation, including the data members, is moved to a different class and hidden in the C file, with only a pointer to this implementation object declared in the header (hence the name, *pointer to impl*, or *pimpl* for short). This idiom is often used to reduce the compilation dependencies—if the implementation of the object changes, but the public API remains the same, then the header file remains unchanged and all files that depend on it do not need to be recompiled. In the case of the singleton, the combination of these two patterns looks like this:

```cpp
// In the header file:
struct SingletonImpl;      // Forward declaration
class Singleton {
    public:                // Public API
    int& get();
    private:
    static SingletonImpl& impl();
};

// In the C file:
struct SingletonImpl {     // Client code does not care if this changes
    SingletonImpl() : value_(0) {}
    int value_;
};

int& Singleton::get() { return impl().value_; }

SingletonImpl& Singleton::impl() {
    static SingletonImpl inst;
```

```
        return inst;
    }
```

In this implementation, the program can create any number of `Singleton` objects, but they all operate on the same implementation, accessed by the `impl()` method (in our case, this method returns a reference to the implementation, and not a pointer; nonetheless, we call it **pimpl** since it is fundamentally the same pattern). Note that we did not put any protection on the implementation class—since it is limited to one `C` file and is not used directly, only being used through the methods of the `Singleton` class, it is quite common to rely on the programmer's discipline instead.

The advantage of this implementation is a better separation between the interface and the implementation, which is the reason for any use of the *pimpl* idiom. The disadvantage is the extra level of indirection, and the performance overhead it adds. Also, note that it is no longer possible for the program to avoid the test for lazy initialization, since it is now hidden inside the implementation of the `Singleton` methods. It is possible to optimize the `Singleton` class to avoid the repeated initialization checks by storing a reference to the implementation in every object:

```cpp
// In the header file:
struct SingletonImpl;
class Singleton {
    public:
    Singleton();
    int& get();
    private:
    static SingletonImpl& impl();
    SingletonImpl& impl_;              // Cached reference
};

// In the C file:
struct SingletonImpl {
    SingletonImpl() : value_(0) {}
    int value_;
};

Singleton::Singleton() : impl_(impl()) {}

int& Singleton::get() { return impl_.value_; }

SingletonImpl& Singleton::impl() {    // Called once per object now
    static SingletonImpl inst;
    return inst;
}
```

The singleton instance is now created the first time a `Singleton` object is constructed, instead of the first time its member function is called. Also, each `Singleton` object now has a reference data member, so we are using a bit more memory as a trade-off for increased performance:

```
Benchmark                      Time          CPU Iterations
BM_singleton_pimpl            70 ns        70 ns   9918408   438.475M items/s
BM_singleton_pimpl_opt        11 ns        11 ns  64369401   2.80543G items/s
```

We can see that the optimized implementation is on par with any of the lightweight implementations we considered earlier, while the straightforward *pimpl* implementation is significantly slower.

Another important consideration in modern programs is thread safety. In the case of the Meyers' Singleton, the question of thread safety is non-trivial. The issue boils down to this: is the initialization of a local static variable thread-safe? The focus of our attention is this code:

```
static Singleton&amp; instance() {
    static Singleton inst;
    return inst;
}
```

The actual code behind this C++ construct is fairly complex—there is a conditional check to see if the variable is already constructed, and a flag that is set when this code is executed for the first time. What happens if multiple threads call the `instance()` function at the same time? Do we have a guarantee that, for all threads, only one instance of the static object will be created? In C++11 and later standards, the answer is a definite yes. Prior to C++11, the standard did not guarantee any thread safety at all. This led to the proliferation of various alternative implementations that can still be found in examples online and in print. Such alternatives are many, and in general, they look something like this, with various combinations of locking thrown in:

```
static bool initialized - false;
static Singleton&amp; instance() {
    if (!initialized) { ... initialize the instance under lock ... }
    return ... reference to the singleton instance ...
}
```

At this point in time, such implementations are thoroughly obsolete and are, at most, of historical interest. We will not spend time explaining how they work, and whether they work correctly (many don't). There is no reason to do anything more than simply declare a local static variable and return a reference to it.

As we have explained before, the Meyers' Singleton solves the problem of initialization order by initializing, on demand, the first time the object is used. Even if we have multiple singletons (of different types, of course) and they refer to one another, the objects will be initialized no later than they are needed. The problem of the initialization order is indeed solved. But that is not the only problem, as we will see next.

Leaky singletons

We have just seen how Meyers' singleton solves the problem of the order of static initializations. The problem of the destruction order, on the other hand, is a different matter altogether. The order of destruction is well-defined by the standard—the static variables—the ones at the function scope, as well as the ones at the file scope—are destroyed after the program itself terminates (after the return from `main()`). The destruction is done in the opposite order to that of construction; that is, the object that was constructed last is destroyed first. Why is this a concern?

First of all, we can say with certainty that any references to a singleton object in the program itself (and not in other static objects) are definitely safe, since `main()` returns before any such destruction occurs. So our only concern is with other static objects; specifically, with their destructors. At first glance, there is no problem: the objects are destroyed in the reverse construction order, so any object that was constructed later and can depend on the preceding objects will be destroyed first. But that's not the only kind of dependency that can happen. Let's consider a concrete example—in our program, we have two singleton objects. The first one is the `MemoryManager` object, from which all memory in the program is allocated. When this object is destroyed, it releases all allocated memory back to the operating system. The second object is the `ErrorLogger` object, which is used by the entire program to log errors. The logger needs memory to store the error information, but releases this memory when the object itself is destroyed. Both objects are lazy-initialization singletons, so they are constructed on demand when they are used for the first time.

At first glance, there is no problem—surely the memory manager will be constructed first, if for no other reason than because the error logger needs it? Therefore, the error logger will be destroyed first and will return all memory to the memory manager. But the actual interaction is more complex. Imagine that not every operation on the error logger needs memory—some messages are just printed without logging. Then, we could have the following sequence of operations:

```
ErrorLogger::instance().MessageNoLog("Starting execution");     // 1
ErrorLogger::instance().Error("Problem found");                 // 2
```

On line one, the `ErrorLogger` singleton is initialized, but it does not need any memory yet, so the memory manager is not initialized. On line two, the `ErrorLogger` is already constructed, so the call just uses that singleton instance. The implementation of `ErrorLogger::Error()` needs memory, and so it calls `MemoryManager`. Since this is the first call to this singleton object, the singleton instance of the `MemoryManager` object is constructed now, and the memory is allocated. `ErrorLogger` stores a pointer to that memory. Now, let's fast-forward to the end of the program—the `MemoryManager` was constructed last, so it will be destroyed first and will release all allocated memory. But we still have an instance of `ErrorLogger`, and it still has that pointer to the memory that it got from the manager! The logger was constructed just before the manager, so now, it is its turn to be destroyed. As a part of its destructor, the logger calls the `MemoryManager` API to return the memory. But the `MemoryManager` object is already destroyed, so we just called a member function on a destroyed object. Furthermore, the memory has already been released to the operating system, so now, `ErrorLogger` has a dangling pointer. That's two actions with undefined behavior, combined.

It is a subtle error that manifests itself in strange ways—if your program crashes at the very end, after it printed its last message, then chances are you have a bug similar to the one we described previously. There is, unfortunately, no general solution to this problem. First of all, there is no way to alter the sequence of static destructors, so the only way to avoid problems caused by this fixed order is to not use static instances at all. We can replace static objects with static pointers, as follows:

```
static Singleton&amp; instance() {
    static Singleton* inst = new Singleton;
    return *inst;
}
```

The difference with the previous implementation is subtle, but significant—the static pointer is still initialized only once, and this happens the first time the function is called. The constructor of the `Singleton` object is called at that time. However, destruction of the pointer does nothing. In particular, it does not call `delete` on the object; we would have to do that ourselves. This gives us a chance to control the destruction order. Unfortunately, in practice, it is very hard to make good use of that chance. Sometimes, reference-counting can be used, but it requires that we somehow count all uses of the singleton object. In the preceding example with the error logger and the memory manager, we would have to maintain a reference count as long as the logger has at least one pointer to the memory it got from the manager. Such implementations are always specific to the particular problem—there is no general way to do this correctly. Even then, these implementations are often complex and hard to test or prove their correctness.

One alternative, which should be considered if the deletion order is becoming a problem, is not to delete at all. In this implementation, the singleton objects are leaked, as the program never destroys them. For some types of resources, this is unacceptable, but it is usually a feasible solution, especially if the only resource managed by these objects is memory: the program is moments away from the end, the memory is about to be collected by the operating system anyway, and releasing the memory at that point is not going to make the program any faster or use any less memory (if the program performs so much work in static destructors that not releasing memory as soon as possible leads to performance problems, then there is a bigger problem with the overall design). The leaky lazy-initialized singleton looks very similar to the Meyers' Singleton, only with the one difference that it uses a local static pointer instead of the local static object:

```cpp
class Singleton {
    public:
    static Singleton& instance() {
        // This is the only difference from Meyers' singleton
        static Singleton* inst = new Singleton;
        return *inst;
    }

    int& get() { return value_; }

    private:
    Singleton() : value_(0) {
        std::cout << "Singleton::Singleton()" << std::endl;
    }
    ~Singleton() {
        std::cout << "Singleton::~Singleton()" << std::endl;
    }
    Singleton(const Singleton&) = delete;
    Singleton& operator=(const Singleton&) = delete;
```

```
    private:
    int value_;
};
```

Except for the lack of deletion, this implementation is identical to the Meyers' Singleton. It has lazy initialization and guarantees that the order of initialization is correct, it is thread-safe, and it has essentially identical performance. Just like the Meyers' Singleton, it incurs the overhead of testing whether the static variable was initialized, and can be made more efficient by storing a local reference to cache the result of the instance() call.

An alternative implementation that should be preferred, when possible, is to explicitly trigger the release of all resources by the static objects at the end of the program. For example, our ErrorLogger object may have a clear() method—when called, it will complete the error logging tasks and release all memory back to the manager; the destructor is then left with nothing to do but destroy the static instance itself. This design relies on the goodwill of the programmer, and so is not enforced by the compiler. Nonetheless, it is a better alternative in many cases.

Summary

In this chapter, we have learned pretty much all there is to know about the singleton, which is a classic object-oriented programming pattern. We have discussed when to consider using the singleton pattern, and when it should be avoided as a sign of a sloppy design. We have considered several possible implementations of the singleton: some are lazily initialized on demand, and others are eagerly initialized up front; some use multiple handle objects that are all equivalent, and others explicitly present the programmer with the single object. We have considered and compared the thread-safety and performance issues with the different implementations and reviewed the potential issues with the order of construction and destruction.

With so many different implementations, the reader can be forgiven for wanting a more definitive recommendation—which singleton should I use? On balance, we are going to recommend the Meyers' Singleton as the first choice. If minimization of the compilation dependencies is an additional goal, or you simply seek to enforce the reference-caching optimization, we recommend the *pimpl* variant of the Meyers' Singleton. Finally, if the deletion order is a problem (and it will be, if there are multiple static objects that store resources that they obtained from other such objects), then the explicit cleanup of the singleton objects is highly preferred. If not possible, the best solution is the leaky Meyers' Singleton (which can be combined with the *pimpl* idiom as well).

The next chapter is a big one—not just in volume, but in importance. The chapter is dedicated to another well-known pattern, the Strategy, but, when used in the domain of C++ generic programming, it becomes one of the most powerful C++ design patterns, that is, Policy-Based design.

Questions

1. What is the singleton pattern?
2. When can the singleton pattern be used, and when should it be avoided?
3. What is lazy initialization, and what problems does it solve?
4. How can we make singleton initialization thread safe?
5. What is the deletion order problem, and what are the solutions?

16
Policy-Based Design

Policy-based design is one of the most well-known C++ patterns. Since the introduction of the standard template library in 1998, few new ideas have been more influential on the way we design C++ programs than the invention of policy-based design.

A policy-based design is all about flexibility, extensibility, and customization. It is a way to design software that can evolve, and can be adapted to the changing needs, some of which could not even be anticipated at the time when the initial design was conceived. A well-designed policy-based system can remain unchanged at the structural level for many years, and serve the changing needs and new requirements without compromise. Unfortunately, it is also a way to build software that could do all of those things if only there was someone who could figure out how it works. The aim of this chapter is to teach the reader to understand and design the systems of the former kind while avoiding the excesses that lead to the disasters of the latter one.

The following topics will be covered in this chapter:

- Strategy pattern and policy-based design
- Compile time policies in C++
- Implementations of policy-based classes
- Guidelines for the use of policies

Technical requirements

The example code for this chapter can be found at the following GitHub link: https://github.com/PacktPublishing/Hands-On-Design-Patterns-with-CPP/tree/master/Chapter16.

Strategy pattern and policy-based design

The classic Strategy pattern is a behavioral design pattern that enables the runtime selection of a specific algorithm for a particular behavior, usually from a predefined family of algorithms. This pattern is also known as the *policy pattern*; the name predates its application to the generic programming in C++. The aim of the Strategy pattern is to allow for more flexibility of the design: in the classic object-oriented Strategy pattern, the decision about which specific algorithm to use is deferred until runtime.

As is the case with many classic patterns, the generic programming in C++ applies the same approach to algorithm selection at compile time—it allows for compile-time customization of specific aspects of the system behavior by selecting from a family of related, compatible algorithms. We will now learn the basics of implementing classes with policies in C++, then proceed to study more complex and varied approaches to policy-based design.

Foundations of policy-based design

The Strategy pattern should be considered whenever we design a system that does certain operations, but the exact implementation of these operations is uncertain, varied, or can change after the system is implemented—in other words, when we know the answer to *what the system must do*, but not *how*. Similarly, the compile-time strategy, or a policy, is a way to implement a class that has a specific function (*what*), but there is more than one way to implement that function (*how*).

Throughout this chapter, we will, to illustrate different ways to use policies, design a smart pointer class. A smart pointer has many other required and optional features besides policies, and we will not cover all of them—for a complete implementation of a smart pointer, the reader is referred to such examples as the C++ standard smart pointers (`unique_ptr` and `shared_ptr`), Boost smart pointers, or the Loki smart pointer (http://loki-lib.sourceforge.net/). The material presented in this chapter will help the reader to understand the choices made by the implementers of these libraries, as well as how to design their own policy-based classes.

A very minimal initial implementation of a smart pointer may look like this:

```
template <typename T>
class SmartPtr {
    public:
    explicit SmartPtr(T* p = nullptr)
        : p_(p) {}
    ~SmartPtr() {
        delete p_;
```

```
    }
    T* operator->() { return p_; }
    const T* operator->() const { return p_; }
    T& operator*() { return *p_; }
    const T& operator*() const { return *p_; }
    private:
    T* p_;
    SmartPtr(const SmartPtr&) = delete;
    SmartPtr& operator=(const SmartPtr&) = delete;
};
```

This pointer has a constructor from the raw pointer of the same type and the usual (for a pointer) operators, that is, * and ->. The most interesting part here is the destructor—when the pointer is destroyed, it automatically deletes the object as well (it is not necessary to check the pointer for the null value before deleting it; the operator delete is required to accept a null pointer and do nothing). It follows, therefore, that the expected use of this smart pointer is as follows:

```
    Class C { ..... };
    {
        SmartPtr<C> p(new C);
        ..... use p .....
    } // Object *p is deleted automatically
```

This is a basic example of the RAII class—the RAII object—the smart pointer, in our case—owns the resource (the constructed object) and releases (deletes) it when the owning object itself is deleted. The common applications, which were considered in detail in Chapter 5, *A Comprehensive Look at RAII*, focus on ensuring that the object that was constructed in the scope is deleted when the program exits this scope, no matter how the latter is accomplished (for example, if an exception is thrown somewhere in the middle of the code, the RAII destructor guarantees that the object is destroyed).

Two more member functions of the smart pointer are noted, not for their implementation, but for their absence—the pointer is made non-copyable as both its copy constructor and the assignment operator are disabled. This detail, which is sometimes overlooked, is of crucial importance for any RAII class—since the destructor of the pointer deletes the owned object, there should never be two pointers that point to, and will attempt to delete, the same object.

The pointer we have here is functional, but the implementation is constraining. In particular, it can own and delete only an object that was constructed with the standard `operator new`, and only a single object. While it could capture a pointer that was obtained from a custom `operator new`, or a pointer to an array of elements, it does not properly delete such objects.

We could implement a different smart pointer for objects that are created on a user-defined heap, and another one for objects that are created in client-managed memory, and so on, one for every type of object construction with its corresponding way of deletion. Most of the code for these pointers would be duplicated—they are all pointers, and the entire pointer-like API will have to be copied into every class. We can observe that all of these different classes are, fundamentally, of the same kind—the answer to the question *what is this type?* is always the same—*it's a smart pointer*. The only difference is in how the deletion is implemented. This common intent with a difference in one particular aspect of the behavior suggests the use of the Strategy pattern. We can implement a more general smart pointer where the details of how to handle the deletion of the object are delegates to one of any number of deletion policies:

```cpp
template <typename T, typename DeletionPolicy>
class SmartPtr {
    public:
    explicit SmartPtr(
        T* p = nullptr,
        const DeletionPolicy& deletion_policy = DeletionPolicy()
        ) : p_(p),
            deletion_policy_(deletion_policy)
    {}
    ~SmartPtr() {
        deletion_policy_(p_);
    }
    T* operator->() { return p_; }
    const T* operator->() const { return p_; }
    T& operator*() { return *p_; }
    const T& operator*() const { return *p_; }
    private:
    T* p_;
    DeletionPolicy deletion_policy_;
    SmartPtr(const SmartPtr&) = delete;
    SmartPtr& operator=(const SmartPtr&) = delete;
};
```

The deletion policy is an additional template parameter, and an object of the type of the deletion policy is passed to the constructor of the smart pointer (by default, such an object is default-constructed). The deletion policy object is stored in the smart pointer and is used in its destructor to delete the object that's being pointed to by the pointer.

The only requirement on the deletion policy type is that it should be callable—the policy is invoked, just like a function with one argument, and the pointer to the object that must be deleted. For example, the behavior of our original pointer that called `operator delete` on the object can be replicated with the following deletion policy:

```
template <typename T>
struct DeleteByOperator {
    void operator()(T* p) const {
        delete p;
    }
};
```

To use this policy, we must specify its type when constructing the smart pointer, and, optionally, pass an object of this type to the constructor, although in this case, the default constructed object will work fine:

```
class C { ..... };
SmartPtr<C, DeleteByOperator<C>> p(new C);
```

If the deletion policy does not match the object type, a syntax error will be reported for the invalid call to `operator()`.

Other deletion policies are needed for objects that were allocated in different ways. For example, if an object is created on a user-given heap object whose interface includes the member functions `allocate()` and `deallocate()` to, respectively, allocate and free memory, we can use the following heap deletion policy:

```
template <typename T>
struct DeleteHeap {
    explicit DeleteHeap(Heap& heap)
        : heap_(heap) {}
    void operator()(T* p) const {
        p->~T();
        heap_.deallocate(p);
    }
    private:
    Heap& heap_;
};
```

On the other hand, if an object is constructed in some memory that is managed separately by the caller, then only the destructor of the object needs to be called:

```
template <typename T>
struct DeleteDestructorOnly {
    void operator()(T* p) const {
        p->~T();
    }
};
```

We mentioned earlier that, because the policy is used as a callable entity, `deletion_policy_(p_)`, it can be of any type that can be called like a function. That includes the actual function:

```
typedef void (*delete_int_t)(int*);
void delete_int(int* p) { delete p; }
SmartPtr<int, delete_int_t> p(new int(42), delete_int);
```

A template instantiation is also a function and can be used in the same way:

```
template <typename T> void delete_T(T* p) { delete p; }
SmartPtr<int, delete_int_t> p(new int(42), delete_T<int>);
```

Of all the possible deletion policies, one is often the most commonly used. In most programs, it will likely be deletion by the default `operator delete` function. If this is so, it makes sense to avoid specifying this one policy every time it's used and make it the default:

```
template <typename T, typename DeletionPolicy = DeleteByOperator<T>>
class SmartPtr {
    .....
};
```

Now, our policy-based smart pointer can be used in exactly the same way as the original version, with only one deletion option:

```
SmartPtr<C> p(new C);
```

Here, the second template parameter is left to its default value, `DeleteByOperator<C>`, and a default constructed object of this type is passed to the constructor as the default second argument.

At this point, we must caution the reader against a subtle mistake that could be made when implementing such policy-based classes. Note that the policy object is captured in the constructor of the smart pointer by a `const` reference:

```
explicit SmartPtr(
    T* p = nullptr,
    const DeletionPolicy& deletion_policy = DeletionPolicy());
```

The `const` reference here is important since a non-const reference cannot be bound to a temporary object (we will consider the r-value references later in this section). However, the policy is stored in the object itself by value, and, thus, a copy of the policy object must be made:

```
template <typename T, typename DeletionPolicy = DeleteByOperator<T>>
class SmartPtr {
    .....
    private:
    DeletionPolicy deletion_policy_;
};
```

It may be tempting to avoid the copy and capture the policy by reference in the smart pointer as well:

```
template <typename T, typename DeletionPolicy = DeleteByOperator<T>>
class SmartPtr {
    .....
    private:
    const DeletionPolicy& deletion_policy_;
};
```

In some cases, this will even work, for example:

```
Heap h;
DeleteHeap<C> del_h(h);
SmartPtr<C, DeleteHeap<C>> p(new (&heap) C, del_h);
```

However, it won't work for the default way to create smart pointers or any other smart pointer that is initialized with a temporary policy object:

```
SmartPtr<C> p(new C, DeleteByOperator<C>());
```

This code will compile. Unfortunately, it is incorrect—the temporary `DeleteByOperator<C>` object is constructed just before the `SmartPtr` constructor is called, but is destroyed at the end of the statement. The reference inside the `SmartPtr` object is left dangling. At first glance, this should not surprise anyone—of course, the temporary object does not outlive the statement in which it was created—it is deleted at the closing semicolon at the latest. A reader who is more versed in subtle language details may ask—doesn't the standard specifically extend the lifetime of a temporary bound to a constant reference? Indeed it does; for example:

```
{
    const C& c = C();
    ..... c is not dangling! .....
} // the temporary is deleted here
```

In this code fragment, the temporary object `C()` is not deleted at the end of the sentence, but only at the end of the lifetime of the reference to which it is bound. So, why didn't the same trick work for our deletion policy object? The answer is, it sort of did—the temporary object that was created when the argument to the constructor was evaluated and bound to the `const` reference argument was not destroyed for the lifetime of that reference, which is the duration of the constructor call. Actually, it would not have been destroyed anyway—all temporary objects that are created during the evaluation of the function arguments are deleted at the end of the sentence containing the function call, that is, at the closing semicolon. The function, in our case, is the constructor of the object, and so the lifetime of the temporaries spans the entire call to the constructor. It does not, however, extend to the lifetime of the object—the `const` reference member of the object is not bound to the temporary object, but to the constructor parameter, which itself is a `const` reference. The lifetime extension works only once—the reference bound to a temporary object extends its lifetime. Another reference that's bound to the first one does nothing else and may be left dangling if the object is destroyed. Therefore, if the policy object needs to be stored as a data member of the smart pointer, it has to be copied.

Usually, policy objects are small, and copying them is trivial. However, sometimes, a policy object may have a non-trivial internal state that is expensive to copy. You could also imagine a policy object that is non-copyable. In these cases, it may make sense to move the argument object into the data member object. This is easy to do if we declare an overload that is similar to a move constructor:

```
template <typename T, typename DeletionPolicy = DeleteByOperator<T>>
class SmartPtr {
    public:
    explicit SmartPtr(T* p,
                      const DeletionPolicy& deletion_policy
        ) : p_(p),
```

```
                deletion_policy_(std::move(deletion_policy))
    {}
    explicit SmartPtr(T* p = nullptr,
                    DeletionPolicy&& deletion_policy = DeletionPolicy()
        ) : p_(p),
            deletion_policy_(std::move(deletion_policy))
    {}
    .....
    private:
    DeletionPolicy deletion_policy_;
};
```

As we said, the policy objects are usually small, so copying them is rarely an issue.

We now have a smart pointer class that has been implemented once, but whose deletion implementation can be customized at compile time by specifying the deletion policy. We could even add a new deletion policy that did not exist at the time the class was designed, and it will work as long as it conforms to the same calling interface. Next, we will consider different ways to implement policy objects.

Implementation of policies

In the previous section, we learned how to implement the simplest policy object. The policy can be of any type as long as it conforms to the interface convention, and is stored in the class as a data member. The policy object is most commonly generated by a template; however, it could be a regular, non-template, object that's specific to a particular pointer type, or even a function. The use of the policy was limited to a specific behavioral aspect, such as deletion of the object owned by the smart pointer.

There are several ways in which such policies can be implemented and used. First of all, let's review the declaration of a smart pointer with a deletion policy:

```
template <typename T, typename DeletionPolicy = DeleteByOperator<T>>
class SmartPtr { ..... };
```

Next, let's look at how we can construct a smart pointer object:

```
class C { ..... };
SmartPtr<C, DeleteByOperator<C>> p(new C, DeleteByOperator<C>());
```

One disadvantage of this design jumps out at once—the type C is mentioned four times in the definition of the object p—it must be consistent in all four places, or the code will not compile. C++17 allows us to simplify the definition somewhat:

```
SmartPtr p(new C, DeleteByOperator<C>());
```

Here, the constructor is used to deduce the parameters of the class template from the constructor arguments, in the manner similar to that of function templates. There are still two mentions of the type C that must be consistent.

One alternative implementation that works for stateless policies as well as for policy objects whose internal state does not depend on the types of the primary template (in our case, the type T of the SmartPtr template) is to make the policy itself a non-template object, but give it a template member function. For example, the DeleteByOperator policy is stateless (the object has no data members) and can be implemented without a class template:

```
struct DeleteByOperator {
    template <typename T>
    void operator()(T* p) const {
        delete p;
    }
};
```

This is a non-template object, so it does not need a type parameter. The member function template is instantiated on the type of object that needs to be deleted—the type is deduced by the compiler. Since the type of the policy object is always the same, we do not have to worry about specifying consistent types when creating the smart pointer object:

```
SmartPtr<C, DeleteByOperator> p(new C, DeleteByOperator()); // Before C++17
SmartPtr p(new C, DeleteByOperator());                      // C++17
```

This object can be used by our smart pointer as it is, with no changes to the SmartPtr template, although we may want to change the default template argument:

```
template <typename T, typename DeletionPolicy = DeleteByOperator>
class SmartPtr { ..... };
```

A more complex policy, such as the heap deletion policy, can still be implemented using this approach:

```
struct DeleteHeap {
    explicit DeleteHeap(SmallHeap& heap)
        : heap_(heap) {}
    template <typename T>
    void operator()(T* p) const {
        p->~T();
```

```
        heap_.deallocate(p);
    }
    private:
    Heap& heap_;
};
```

This policy has an internal state—the reference to the heap—but nothing in this policy object depends on the type T of the object we need to delete, except for the operator() member function. Therefore, the policy does not need to be parameterized by the object type.

Since the main template, SmartPtr, did not have to be changed when we converted our policies from class templates to non-template classes with template member functions, there is no reason why we cannot use both types of policies with the same class. Indeed, any of the template class policies from the previous subsection would still work, so we can have some deletion policies implemented as classes and others as class templates. The latter is useful when the policy has data members whose type depends on the object type of the smart pointer.

If the policies are implemented as class templates, we have to specify the correct type to instantiate the policy for use with each specific policy-based class. In many cases, this is a very repetitive process—the same type is used to parameterize the main template and its policies. We can get the compiler to do this job for us if we use the entire template and not its particular instantiation as a policy:

```
template <typename T, template <typename> class DeletionPolicy =
DeleteByOperator>
class SmartPtr {
    public:
    explicit SmartPtr(T* p = nullptr,
                        const DeletionPolicy<T>& deletion_policy =
DeletionPolicy<T>()
            ) : p_(p),
                deletion_policy_(deletion_policy)
    {}
    ~SmartPtr() {
        deletion_policy_(p_);
    }
    . . . . .
};
```

Note the syntax for the second template parameter—`template <typename> class DeletionPolicy`. This is known as a *template template* parameter—the parameter of a template is itself a template. The `class` keyword is necessary in C++14 and earlier; in C++17, it can be replaced with `typename`. To use this parameter, we need to instantiate it with some type; in our case, it is the main template type parameter `T`. This ensures the consistency of the object type in the primary smart pointer template and its policies, although the constructor argument still must be constructed with the correct type:

```
SmartPtr<C, DeleteByOperator> p(new C, DeleteByOperator<C>());
```

Again, in C++17, the class template parameters can be deduced by the constructor; this works for template template parameters as well:

```
SmartPtr p(new C, DeleteByOperator<C>());
```

The template template parameters seem like an attractive alternative to the regular type parameters when the types are instantiated from a template anyway. Why don't we always use them? It turns out that a template template parameter has one significant limitation—the number of the template parameters has to match the specification precisely, including the default arguments. In other words, let's say I have the following template:

```
template <typename T, typename Heap = MyHeap> class DeleteHeap { ..... };
```

This template cannot be used as a parameter of the preceding smart pointer—it has two template parameters, while we only specified only one in the declaration of `SmartPtr` (a parameter with a default value is still a parameter). In contrast, we can use the instantiation of this template for a smart pointer that has a simple type, not a template, for the `DeletionPolicy`—we just need a class, and `DeleteHeap<int, MyHeap>` will do as good as any.

So far, we have always captured the policy object as a data member of the policy-based class. This approach to integrating classes into a larger class is known as composition. There are other ways in which the primary template can get access to the customized behavior algorithms provided by the policies, which we will consider next.

Use of policy objects

All of our examples until now have stored the policy object as a data member of the class. This is generally the preferred way of storing the policies, but it has one significant downside—a data member always has a non-zero size. Consider our smart pointer with one of the deletion policies:

```
template <typename T>
struct DeleteByOperator {
    void operator()(T* p) const {
        delete p;
    }
};

template <typename T, typename DeletionPolicy = DeleteByOperator<T>>
class SmartPtr {
    .....
    private:
    T* p_;
    DeletionPolicy deletion_policy_;
};
```

Note that the policy object has no data members. However, the size of the object is not zero, but one byte (we can verify that by printing the value of `sizeof(DeleteByOperator<int>)`). This is necessary because every object in a C++ program must have a unique address:

```
DeleteByOperator<int> d1;          // &d1 = ......
DeleteByOperator<long> d2;         // &d2 must be != &d1
```

When two objects are laid out consecutively in memory, the difference between their addresses is the size of the first object (plus padding, if necessary). To prevent both the d1 and d2 objects from residing at the same address, the standard mandates that their size is at least one byte (this requirement will be somewhat relaxed in C++20, which will provide a way to use empty objects as data members without assigning a unique address to each object).

When used as a data member of another class, an object will occupy at least as much space as its size requires, which in our case, is one byte. Assuming that the pointer takes 8 bytes, the entire object is, therefore, 9 bytes long. But the size of an object also has to be padded to the nearest value that meets the alignment requirements—if the address of the pointer has to be aligned on 8 bytes, the object can be either 8 bytes or 16 bytes, but not in-between. So, adding an empty policy object to the class ends up changing its size from 8 bytes to 16 bytes. This is purely a waste of memory and is often undesirable, especially for objects that are created in large numbers, such as pointers. It is not possible to coax the compiler into creating a data member of zero size; the standard forbids it. But there is another way in which policies can be used without the overhead.

The alternative to composition is inheritance—we can use the policy as a base class for the primary class:

```cpp
template <typename T, typename DeletionPolicy = DeleteByOperator<T>>
class SmartPtr : private DeletionPolicy {
    public:
    explicit SmartPtr(T* p = nullptr,
                    DeletionPolicy&& deletion_policy = DeletionPolicy()
        ) : DeletionPolicy(std::move(deletion_policy)),
            p_(p)
    {}
    ~SmartPtr() {
        DeletionPolicy::operator()(p_);
    }
    . . . . .
    private:
    T* p_;
};
```

This approach relies on a particular optimization—if a base class is empty (has no non-static data members), it can be completely optimized out of the layout of the derived class. This is known as the empty base class optimization. It is allowed by the standard, but usually isn't required (C++11 requires this optimization for certain classes, but not for the classes we are using in this chapter). Even though it is not required, it is almost universally done by modern compilers. With empty base class optimization, the size of the derived SmartPtr class is only as large as necessary to hold its data members—in our case, 8 bytes.

When using inheritance for policies, the choice must be made between public or private inheritance. Usually, the policies are used to provide an implementation for a particular aspect of behavior. Such inheritance for implementation is expressed through private inheritance. In some cases, a policy may be used to change the public interface of the class; in this case, public inheritance should be used. For the deletion policy, we are not changing the interface of the class—the smart pointer always deletes the object at the end of its life; the only question is how. Therefore, the deletion policy should use private inheritance.

While the deletion policy using `operator delete` is stateless, some policies have data members that must be preserved from the object given to the constructor. Therefore, in general, the base class policy should be initialized from the constructor argument by copying or moving it into the base class, similarly to the way we initialized the data members. The base classes are always initialized on the member initialization list before the data members of the derived class. Finally, the `base_type::function_name()` syntax can be used to call a member function of a base class; in our case, `DeletionPolicy::operator()(p_)`.

Inheritance or composition are the two choices for integrating the policy class into the primary class. In general, the composition should be preferred, unless there is a reason to use inheritance. We have already seen one such reason—the empty base class optimization. Inheritance is also the necessary choice if we want to affect the public interface of the class.

Our smart pointer is, so far, missing several important features that are commonly found in most smart pointer implementations. One such feature is the ability to release the pointer, that is, to prevent the automatic destruction of the object from taking place. This can be useful if, in some cases, the object is destroyed by some other means, or, alternatively, if the lifetime of the object needs to be extended and its ownership is passed to another resource-owning object. This feature can be easily added to our smart pointer:

```
template <typename T, typename DeletionPolicy, typename ReleasePolicy>
class SmartPtr : private DeletionPolicy {
    public:
    ~SmartPtr() {
        DeletionPolicy::operator()(p_);
    }
    void release() { p_ = nullptr; }
    .....
    private:
    T* p_;
};
```

Now, we can call `p.release()` on our smart pointer, and the destructor will do nothing. Suppose now that not all of our smart pointers need this functionality, and we decided to make it optional. We can add a `ReleasePolicy` template parameter to control whether the `release()` member function is present, but what should it do? We could, of course, move the implementation of `SmartPtr::release()` into the policy:

```
template <typename T>
class WithRelease {
    public:
    void release(T*& p) { p = nullptr; }
};
```

Now, the `SmartPtr` implementation only has to call `ReleasePolicy::release(p_)` to delegate the appropriate handling of `release()` to the policy. But what is the appropriate handling if we do not want to support the release functionality? Our no-release policy can simply do nothing, but this is misleading—the user has the expectation that, if `release()` was called, the object would not be destroyed. We could assert at runtime and terminate the program. This converts a logic error on the part of the programmer—trying to release a no-release smart pointer—into a runtime error. The best way would be for the `SmartPtr` class to not have the `release()` member function at all, if it is not wanted. This way, the incorrect code would be impossible to compile. The only way to do this is to make the policy inject a new public member function into the public interface of the primary template. This can be accomplished using public inheritance:

```
template <typename T, typename DeletionPolicy, typename ReleasePolicy>
class SmartPtr : private DeletionPolicy, public ReleasePolicy { ..... };
```

Now, if the release policy has a public member function called `release()`, then so does the `SmartPtr` class.

This solves the interface problem. Now, there is the small matter of implementation. The `release()` member function has now moved into the policy class, but it must operate on the data member `p_` of the parent class. One way to do this would be to pass a reference to this pointer from the derived class to the base policy class during construction. This is an ugly implementation—it wastes 8 bytes of memory to store a reference to a data member that is *almost right there*, which is stored in the derived class right next to the base class itself. A much better way is to cast from the base class to the correct derived class. Of course, for this to work, the base class needs to know what the correct derived class is. The solution to this problem is the **Curiously Recurring Template Pattern (CRTP)** that we studied in this book: the policy should be a template (so we will need a template template parameter) that is instantiated on the derived class type.

This way, the `SmartPtr` class is both the derived class of the release policy and the template parameter of it:

```
template <typename T,
          typename DeletionPolicy = DeleteByOperator<T>,
          template <typename> class ReleasePolicy = WithRelease>
class SmartPtr :
    private DeletionPolicy,
    public ReleasePolicy<SmartPtr<T, DeletionPolicy, ReleasePolicy>>
{ ..... };
```

Note that the `ReleasePolicy` template is specialized with the concrete instantiation of the `SmartPtr` template, including all its policies, and including the `ReleasePolicy` itself.

Now, the release policy knows the type of the derived class and can cast itself to that type. This case is always safe because the correct derived class is guaranteed by construction:

```
template <typename P> class WithRelease {
    public:
    void release() { static_cast<P*>(this)->p_ = NULL; }
};
```

The template parameter P will be substituted with the type of the smart pointer. Once the smart pointer publicly inherits from the release policy, the public member function, `release()`, of the policy is inherited and becomes a part of the smart pointer public interface.

The last detail concerning the implementation of the release policy has to do with the access. As we've written so far, the data member p_ is private in the `SmartPtr` class and cannot be accessed by its base classes directly. The solution to this is to declare the corresponding base class to be a friend of the derived class:

```
template <typename T,
          typename DeletionPolicy = DeleteByOperator<T>,
          template <typename> class ReleasePolicy = WithRelease>
class SmartPtr :
    private DeletionPolicy,
    public ReleasePolicy<SmartPtr<T, DeletionPolicy, ReleasePolicy>>
{
    .....
    private:
    friend class ReleasePolicy<SmartPtr>;
    T* p_;
};
```

Note that inside the body of the `SmartPtr` class, we do not need to repeat all the template parameters. The shorthand `SmartPtr` refers to the currently instantiated template. This does not extend to the part of the class declaration before the opening brace of the class, so we had to repeat the template parameters when specifying the policy as a base class.

The no-release policy is just as easy to write:

```
template <typename P> class NoRelease {
};
```

There is no `release()` function here, so an attempt to call `release()` on a smart pointer with this policy will not compile. This solves our stated requirement to have a the `release()` public member function only when it makes sense to call one. The policy-based design is a complex pattern, and it is rare to be limited to just one way to do something. There is, perforce, another way to accomplish the same objective, and we will see it later in this chapter.

There is yet another way in which policy objects can sometimes be used. This applies only to policies that have no internal state in any version of the policy, by design. For example, our deletion policies are sometimes stateless, but the one with the reference to the caller's heap is not, so this is a policy that is not always stateless. The release policy can always be considered stateless; there is no reason for us to add a data member to it, but it is constrained to be used through public inheritance because its primary effect is to inject a new public member function. Let's consider another aspect of behavior that we may want to customize—debugging or logging. For debugging purposes, it may be convenient to print when an object is owned by a smart pointer and when it is deleted. We could add a debugging policy to the smart pointer to support this. The debug policy has to do only one thing, and that is to print something when a smart pointer is constructed or destroyed. It does not need access to the smart pointer if we pass the value of the pointer to the printing function. Therefore, we can make the print functions static in the debug policy and not store it in the smart pointer class at all:

```
template <typename T,
          typename DeletionPolicy,
          typename DebugPolicy = NoDebug>
class SmartPtr : private DeletionPolicy {
    public:
    explicit SmartPtr(T* p = nullptr,
                    DeletionPolicy&& deletion_policy = DeletionPolicy()
        ) : DeletionPolicy(std::move(deletion_policy)),
            p_(p)
    {
        DebugPolicy::constructed(p_);
    }
```

```
    ~SmartPtr() {
        DebugPolicy::deleted(p_);
        DeletionPolicy::operator()(p_);
    }
    .....
    private:
    T* p_;
};
```

The debugging policy implementation is straightforward:

```
struct Debug {
    template <typename T> static void constructed(const T* p) {
        std::cout << "Constructed SmartPtr for object "
                << static_cast<const void*>(p) << std::endl;
    }
    template <typename T> static void deleted(const T* p) {
        std::cout << "Destroyed SmartPtr for object "
                << static_cast<const void*>(t) << std::endl;
    }
};
```

We have chosen to implement the policy as a non-template class with template static member functions. Alternatively, we could have implemented it as a template, parametrized with the object type T. The no-debug version of the policy, which is the default, is even simpler. It must have the same functions defined, but they don't do anything:

```
struct NoDebug {
    template <typename T> static void constructed(const T* p) {}
    template <typename T> static void deleted(const T* p) {}
};
```

We can expect the compiler to inline the empty template functions at the call site and optimize the entire call away since no code needs to be generated.

Note that by choosing this implementation of policies, we made a somewhat restrictive design decision—all versions of the debug policy must be stateless. We may, in time, come to regret this decision if we need to, for example, store a custom output stream inside a debug policy, instead of the default std::cout. But even in that case, only the implementation of the smart pointer class will have to change—the client code will continue to work with no changes.

We have considered three different ways to incorporate the policy objects into the policy-based class—by composition, by inheritance (public or private), and compile-time incorporation only, where the policy object does not need to be stored inside the main object at runtime. We will now move on to more advanced techniques for policy-based design.

Advanced policy-based design

The techniques we have introduced in the previous section form the foundation of policy-based design—policies can be classes, template instantiations, or templates (used by template template parameters). The policy classes can be composed, inherited, or used statically at compile time. If a policy needs to know the type of the primary policy-based class, the CRTP can be used. The rest is largely variations on the same theme, as well as tricky ways to combine several techniques to accomplish something new. We will now consider some of these more advanced techniques.

Policies for constructors

Policies can be used to customize almost any aspect of the implementation, as well as to alter the class interface. However, there are unique challenges that arise when we attempt to customize class constructors using policies.

As an example, let's consider another limitation of our current smart pointer. As it stands so far, the object owned by the smart pointer is always deleted when the smart pointer is deleted. If the smart pointer supports release, then we can call the `release()` member function and be wholly responsible for the deletion of the object. But how are we going to ensure this deletion? The most likely way is, we will let another smart pointer own it:

```
SmartPtr<C> p1(new C);
SmartPtr<C> p2(&*p1);    // Now two pointers own one object
p1.release();
```

This approach is verbose and error-prone—we temporarily let two pointers own the same object. If something were to happen at this moment that causes both pointers to be deleted, we would destroy the same object twice. We also have to remember to always release one of these pointers, but only one. We should take the higher level view of the problem—we are trying to pass the ownership of the object from one smart pointer to another.

The better way to do this is by moving the first pointer into the second:

```
SmartPtr<C> p1(new C);
SmartPtr<C> p2(std::move(p1));
```

Now, the first pointer is left in the moved-from state, which we can define (the only requirement is that the destructor call must be valid). We choose to define it to be a pointer that does not own any object, that is, a pointer in the released state. The second pointer receives the ownership of the object and will delete it in due time.

To support this functionality, we must implement the move constructor. However, there may be a reason to sometimes prevent the transfer of ownership. Therefore, we may want to have both movable and non-movable pointers. This calls for yet another policy to control whether moving is supported:

```
template <typename T,
          typename DeletionPolicy = DeleteByOperator<T>,
          typename MovePolicy = MoveForbidden
         >
class SmartPtr .....;
```

For simplicity, we have reverted back to just one other policy—the deletion policy. The other policies we have considered can be added alongside the new MovePolicy. The deletion policy can be implemented in any of the ways we have learned already. Since it is likely to benefit from the empty base optimization, we will stay with the inheritance-based implementation for it. The move policy can be implemented in several different ways, but the inheritance is probably the easiest. We will also assume that the release() facility is always available and move the member function back into the smart pointer class:

```
template <typename T,
          typename DeletionPolicy = DeleteByOperator<T>,
          typename MovePolicy = MoveForbidden
         >
class SmartPtr : private DeletionPolicy,
                 private MovePolicy
{
    public:
    explicit SmartPtr(T* p = nullptr,
                      DeletionPolicy&& deletion_policy = DeletionPolicy()
        ) : DeletionPolicy(std::move(deletion_policy)),
            MovePolicy(),
            p_(p)
    {}
    SmartPtr(SmartPtr&& other)
        : DeletionPolicy(std::move(other)),
          MovePolicy(std::move(other)),
```

```
            p_(other.p_)
    {
        other.release();
    }
    ~SmartPtr() {
        DeletionPolicy::operator()(p_);
    }
    void release() { p_ = NULL; }
    T* operator->() { return p_; }
    const T* operator->() const { return p_; }
    T& operator*() { return *p_; }
    const T& operator*() const { return *p_; }
    private:
    T* p_;
    SmartPtr(const SmartPtr&) = delete;
    SmartPtr& operator=(const SmartPtr&) = delete;
};
```

With both policies integrated using private inheritance, we now have a derived object with several base classes. Such multiple inheritance is fairly common in policy-based design in C++, and should not alarm you. This technique is sometimes known as *mix-in* since the implementation of the derived class is *mixed* from the pieces provided by the base classes. In C++, the term *mix-in* is also used to refer to a totally different inheritance scheme that is related to the CRTP, so the use of this term often creates confusion (in most object-oriented languages, *mix-in* unambiguously refers to the application of multiple inheritance that we can see here).

The new feature in our smart pointer class is the move constructor. The move constructor is unconditionally present in the `SmartPtr` class. However, its implementation requires that all base classes be movable. This gives us a way to disable move support with a non-movable move policy:

```
struct MoveForbidden {
    MoveForbidden() = default;
    MoveForbidden(MoveForbidden&&) = delete;
    MoveForbidden(const MoveForbidden&) = delete;
    MoveForbidden& operator=(MoveForbidden&&) = delete;
    MoveForbidden& operator=(const MoveForbidden&) = delete;
};
```

The movable policy is much simpler:

```
struct MoveAllowed {
};
```

We can now construct a movable pointer and a non-movable pointer:

```
class C { ..... };
SmartPtr<C, DeleteByOperator<C>, MoveAllowed> p = .....;
auto p1(std::move(p));          // OK
SmartPtr<C, DeleteByOperator<C>, MoveForbidden> q = .....;
auto q1(std::move(q));          // Does not compile
```

An attempt to move a non-movable pointer does not compile because one of the base classes, `MoveForbidden`, is non-movable (does not have a move constructor). Note that the moved-from pointer p in the preceding example can be safely deleted, but cannot be used in any other way. In particular, it cannot be dereferenced.

While we are dealing with movable pointers, it would make sense to provide a move assignment operator as well:

```
template <typename T,
          typename DeletionPolicy = DeleteByOperator<T>,
          typename MovePolicy = MoveForbidden
          >
class SmartPtr : private DeletionPolicy,
                 private MovePolicy
{
    public:
    SmartPtr(SmartPtr&& other)
        : DeletionPolicy(std::move(other)),
          MovePolicy(std::move(other)),
          p_(other.p_)
    {
        other.release();
    }
    SmartPtr& operator=(SmartPtr&& other) {
        if (this == &other) return *this;
        DeletionPolicy::operator=(std::move(other));
        MovePolicy::operator=(std::move(other));
        p_ = other.p_;
        other.release();
        return *this;
    }
    .....
};
```

Note the check for the self-assignment—while there is some debate on the subject of the self-move and an update to the standard may be forthcoming, there is a general agreement that the self-move should always leave an object in a well-defined state (the moved-from state is an example of such a state). A no-op self-move is not required, but is valid as well. Also note the way in which the base classes are move-assigned—the easiest way is to invoke the move assignment operator of each base class directly. There is no need to cast the derived class `other` to each of the base types—this is an implicitly performed cast. We must not forget to `release()` the moved-from pointer, otherwise the object owned by these pointers will be deleted twice.

For simplicity, we have ignored all of the policies we introduced earlier. This is fine – not all designs need everything to be controlled by a policy, and, in any case, it is quite straightforward to combine multiple policies. However, it is a good opportunity to point out that different policies are sometimes related—for example, if we use both a release policy and a move policy, the use of a movable move policy implies that the object must support release. Using template metaprogramming, we can force such dependence between the policies.

Note that a policy that needs to disable or enable constructors does not automatically have to be used as a base class—move assignment or construction also moves all data members, and, therefore, a non-movable data member will disable the move operations just as well. The more important reason to use inheritance here is the empty base class optimization.

We have considered making our pointers movable. But what about copying? So far, we have disallowed copying outright—both the copy constructor and the copy assignment operator are deleted in our smart pointer from the very beginning. This makes sense so far—we do not want to have two smart pointers own the same object and delete it twice. But there is another type of ownership where the copy operation makes perfect sense—the shared ownership, such as what's implemented by a reference-counting shared pointer. With this type of pointer, copying the pointer is allowed, and both pointers now equally own the pointed-to object. A reference count is maintained to count how many pointers to the same object exist in the program. When the very last pointer owning a particular object is deleted, so is the object itself, since there are no more references to it.

There are several ways to implement a reference-counted shared pointer, but let's start with the design of the class and its policies. We still need a deletion policy, and it makes sense to have a single policy control the move and the copy operations. For simplicity, we will again limit ourselves to just the policies we are currently exploring:

```
template <typename T,
          typename DeletionPolicy = DeleteByOperator<T>,
          typename CopyMovePolicy = NoMoveNoCopy
```

```
            >
class SmartPtr : private DeletionPolicy,
                 public CopyMovePolicy
{
    public:
    explicit SmartPtr(T* p = nullptr,
                      DeletionPolicy&& deletion_policy = DeletionPolicy()
        ) : DeletionPolicy(std::move(deletion_policy)),
            p_(p)
    {}
    SmartPtr(SmartPtr&& other)
        : DeletionPolicy(std::move(other)),
          CopyMovePolicy(std::move(other)),
          p_(other.p_)
    {
        other.release();
    }
    SmartPtr(const SmartPtr& other)
        : DeletionPolicy(other),
          CopyMovePolicy(other),
          p_(other.p_)
    {
    }
    ~SmartPtr() {
        if (CopyMovePolicy::must_delete()) DeletionPolicy::operator()(p_);
    }
    void release() { p_ = NULL; }
    T* operator->() { return p_; }
    const T* operator->() const { return p_; }
    T& operator*() { return *p_; }
    const T& operator*() const { return *p_; }
    private:
    T* p_;
};
```

The copy operations are no longer unconditionally deleted. Both the copy and the move constructor are provided (the two assignment operators are omitted for brevity, but should be implemented in the same way it was done earlier).

The deletion of the object in the destructor of the smart pointer is no longer unconditional—in the case of the reference-counted pointer, the copying policy maintains the reference count and knows when there is only one copy of the smart pointer for a particular object.

The smart pointer class itself provides the requirements on the policy classes. The no-move no-copy policy must disallow all copy and move operations:

```
class NoMoveNoCopy {
    protected:
    NoMoveNoCopy() = default;
    NoMoveNoCopy(NoMoveNoCopy&&) = delete;
    NoMoveNoCopy(const NoMoveNoCopy&) = delete;
    NoMoveNoCopy& operator=(NoMoveNoCopy&&) = delete;
    NoMoveNoCopy& operator=(const NoMoveNoCopy&) = delete;
    constexpr bool must_delete() const { return true; }
};
```

In addition to that, the non-copyable smart pointer always deletes the object it owns in its destructor, so the `must_delete()` member function should always return `true`. Note that this function must be implemented by all copying policies, even if it is trivial, otherwise the smart pointer class will not compile. However, we can fully expect the compiler to optimize the call away and unconditionally call the destructor when this policy is used.

The move-only policy is similar to the movable policy we had earlier, but now we must explicitly enable the move operations and disable the copy operations:

```
class MoveNoCopy {
    protected:
    MoveNoCopy() = default;
    MoveNoCopy(MoveNoCopy&&) = default;
    MoveNoCopy(const MoveNoCopy&) = delete;
    MoveNoCopy& operator=(MoveNoCopy&&) = default;
    MoveNoCopy& operator=(const MoveNoCopy&) = delete;
    constexpr bool must_delete() const { return true; }
};
```

Again, the deletion is unconditional (the pointer inside the smart pointer object can be null if the object was moved, but this does not prevent us from calling `operator delete` on it). This policy allows the move constructor and the move assignment operator to compile; the `SmartPtr` class provides the correct implementation for these operations, and no additional support from the policy is required.

The reference-counting copying policy is much more complex. Here, we have to decide on the shared pointer implementation. The simplest implementation allocates the reference counter in a separate memory allocation, which is managed by the copying policy. Let's start with a reference-counted copying policy that does not allow move operations:

```
class NoMoveCopyRefCounted {
    protected:
    NoMoveCopyRefCounted() : count_(new size_t(1)) {}
```

```
NoMoveCopyRefCounted(const NoMoveCopyRefCounted& other)
    : count_(other.count_)
{
    ++(*count_);
}
NoMoveCopyRefCounted(NoMoveCopyRefCounted&&) = delete;
~NoMoveCopyRefCounted() {
    --(*count_);
    if (*count_ == 0) {
        delete count_;
    }
}
bool must_delete() const { return *count_ == 1; }
private:
size_t* count_;
};
```

When a smart pointer with this copying policy is constructed, a new reference counter is allocated and initialized to one (we have one smart pointer pointing to the particular object—the one we are now constructing). When a smart pointer is copied, so are all its base classes, including the copy policy. The copy constructor of this policy simply increments the reference count. When a smart pointer is deleted, the reference count is decremented. The very last smart pointer to be deleted also deletes the count itself. The copying policy also controls when the pointed-to object is deleted—it happens when the reference count reaches one, which means that we are about to delete the very last pointer for this object. It is, of course, very important to make sure that the counter is not deleted before the `must_delete()` function is called. This is guaranteed to be true since the destructors of the base classes run after the destructor of the derived class—the derived class of the last smart pointer will see the counter value of one and will delete the object; then, the destructor of the copying policy will decrement the counter once more, see it drop to zero, and delete the counter itself.

With this policy, we can implement shared ownership of an object:

```
SmartPtr<C, DeleteByOperator<C>, NoMoveCopyRefCounted> p1{new C};
auto p2(p1);
```

Now, we have two pointers to the same object, with the reference count of two. The object is deleted when the last of the two pointers is, assuming that no more copies are created beforehand. The smart pointer is copyable, but not movable:

```
SmartPtr<C, DeleteByOperator<C>, NoMoveCopyRefCounted> p1{new C};
auto p2(std::move(p1));    // Does not compile
```

In general, once reference-counted copying is supported, there is probably no reason to disallow move operations, unless they are simply not needed (in which case, the no-move implementation can be slightly more efficient). To support the move, we must give some thought to the moved-from state of the reference-counting policy—clearly, it must not decrement the reference counter when it is deleted, since a moved-from pointer no longer owns the object. The simplest way is to reset the pointer to the reference counter so that it is no longer accessible from the copying policy, but then the copying policy must support the special case of a null counter pointer:

```cpp
class MoveCopyRefCounted {
    protected:
    MoveCopyRefCounted() : count_(new size_t(1)) {}
    MoveCopyRefCounted(const MoveCopyRefCounted& other)
        : count_(other.count_)
    {
        if (count_) ++(*count_);
    }
    ~MoveCopyRefCounted() {
        if (!count_) return;
        --(*count_);
        if (*count_ == 0) {
            delete count_;
        }
    }
    MoveCopyRefCounted(MoveCopyRefCounted&& other)
        : count_(other.count_)
    {
        other.count_ = nullptr;
    }
    bool must_delete() const { return count_ && *count_ == 1; }
    private:
    size_t* count_;
};
```

Finally, a reference-counting copying policy must support the assignment operations as well. These are implemented similarly to the copy or move constructors.

As you have seen, some of the policy implementations can get pretty complex, and their interactions even more so. Fortunately, the policy-based design is particularly well-suited for writing testable objects. This application of policy-based design is so important that it deserves a special mention.

Policies for test

We will now show the reader how to use policy-based design to write better tests. In particular, policies can be used to make the code more testable by means of unit tests. This can be done by substituting a special test-only version of a policy instead of the regular one. Let's demonstrate this on the example of the reference-counting policy from the previous subsection.

The main challenge of that policy is, of course, maintaining the correct reference count. We can easily develop some tests that should exercise all of the corner cases of reference counting:

```
// Test 1: only one pointer
{
    SmartPtr<C, .....> p(new C);
} // C should be deleted here

// Test 2: one copy
{
    SmartPtr<C, .....> p(new C);
    {
        auto p1(p);     // Reference count should be 2
    } // C should not be deleted here
} // C should be deleted here
```

The hard part is actually testing that all of this code works the way it is supposed to. We know what the reference count should be, but we have no way of checking what it really is. We know when the object is supposed to be deleted, but it is hard to verify that it actually was. We will probably get a crash if we delete the object twice, but even that is not certain. It is even harder to catch the case when the object is not deleted at all.

Fortunately, we can use policies to give our tests a window into the internal working of the object. For example, we can create a testable wrapper for the reference-counting policy:

```
class NoMoveCopyRefCounted {
    .....
    protected:
    size_t* count_;
};
class NoMoveCopyRefCountedTest : public NoMoveCopyRefCounted {
    public:
    using NoMoveCopyRefCounted::NoMoveCopyRefCounted;
    size_t count() const { return *count_; }
};
```

Note that we had to change the `count_` data member from private to protected in the main copy policy. We could also declare the test policy a friend, but then we would have to do this for every new test policy. Now, we can actually implement our tests:

```
// Test 1: only one pointer
{
    SmartPtr<C, ..... NoMoveCopyRefCountedTest> p(new C);
    assert(p.count() == 1);
} // C should be deleted here

// Test 2: one copy
{
    SmartPtr<C, ..... NoMoveCopyRefCountedTest> p(new C);
    {
        auto p1(p);     // Reference count should be 2
        assert(p.count() == 2);
        assert(p1.count() == 2);
        assert(&*p == &*p1);
    } // C should not be deleted here
    assert(p.count == 1);
} // C should be deleted here
```

Similarly, we can create an instrumented deletion policy that checks whether the object will be deleted, or record in some external logging object that it was actually deleted and test that the deletion was properly logged.

By now, the reader has likely noticed that the declarations of the policy-based objects can be quite long:

```
SmartPtr<C, DeleteByOperator<T>, MoveNoCopy, WithRelease, Debug> p( .....
);
```

This is one of the most frequently observed problems with the policy-based design, and we should consider some ways to mitigate this problem.

Policy adapters and aliases

Perhaps the most obvious drawback of the policy-based design is the way we have to declare the concrete objects—specifically, the long list of policies that must be repeated every time. Judicious use of default parameters helps to simplify the most commonly used cases. For example, let's look at the following long declaration:

```
SmartPtr<C, DeleteByOperator<T>, MoveNoCopy, WithRelease, NoDebug>
    p( ..... );
```

This can be reduced to the following:

```
SmartPtr<C> p( ..... );
```

This can be done if the defaults represent the most common case of a movable non-debug pointer that uses `operator delete`. However, what is the point of adding the policies if we are not going to use them? A well-thought-out order of policy parameters helps to make the more common policy combinations shorter. For example, if the most common variation is the deletion policy, then a new pointer with a different deletion policy and default remaining policies can be declared without repeating the policies we do not need to change:

```
SmartPtr<C, DeleteHeap<T>> p( ..... );
```

This still leaves the problem of the less commonly used policies. Also, policies are often added later as additional features must be added to the design. These policies are almost always added to the end of the parameter list. To do otherwise would require rewriting every bit of code where a policy-based class is declared to reorder its parameters. However, the late-coming policies are not necessarily less often used, and this evolution of the design may lead to a case where many policy arguments have to be explicitly written, even at their default values, so that one of the trailing arguments can be changed.

While there is no general solution to this problem within the confines of the traditional policy-based design, in practice, there are often few commonly used groups of policies, and then there are some frequent variations. For example, most of our smart pointers may be using `operator delete` and support move and release, but we frequently need to alternate between the debug and non-debug versions. This can be accomplished by creating adapters that convert a class with many policies to a new interface that exposes only the policies we want to change often and pins the rest of the policies to their commonly used values. Any large design will likely need more than one such adapter, as the commonly used sets of policies can vary.

One way to create such an adapter is through inheritance:

```
template <typename T,
          typename DebugPolicy = NoDebug
       >
class SmartPtrAdapter :
public SmartPtr<T, DeleteByOperator<T>, MoveNoCopy, WithRelease,
DebugPolicy>
{.....};
```

This creates a derived class template that pins some of the parameters of the base class template, while leaving the rest parameterized. The entire public interface of the base class is inherited, but some care needs to be taken about the constructors of the base class. By default, they are not inherited, and so the new derived class will have the default compiler-generated constructors. This is probably not something we want. In C++11, this problem is easy to remedy; the `using` declaration brings all base class constructors into the derived class:

```
template <typename T,
          typename DebugPolicy = NoDebug
        >
class SmartPtrAdapter :
public SmartPtr<T, DeleteByOperator<T>, MoveNoCopy,
                  WithRelease, DebugPolicy>
{
    using SmartPtr<T, DeleteByOperator<T>, MoveNoCopy,
                  WithRelease, DebugPolicy>::SmartPtr;
};
```

In C++03, unfortunately, there is no easier way than to repeat all of the constructors we want to forward.

We can now use the new adapter when we need a smart pointer with the preset policies, but quickly change the debug policy:

```
SmartPtrAdapter<C, Debug> p1{new C}; // Debug pointer
SmartPtrAdapter<C> p2{new C};        // Non-debug pointer
```

In C++11, there is an even simpler way to solve the same problem, and that's by using template aliases (sometimes called *template typedefs*):

```
template <typename T,
          typename DebugPolicy = NoDebug
        >
using SmartPtrAdapter =
    SmartPtr<T, DeleteByOperator<T>, MoveNoCopy, WithRelease, DebugPolicy>;
```

The effect of this statement is similar to a regular `typedef`—no new types or templates are created, but there is now an alias to call the existing template by a new name, with some of the template parameters set to the specified values.

As we said from the beginning, the most common application of policies is to select a specific implementation for some aspect of the behavior of the class. Sometimes, such variations in the implementation are reflected in the public interface of the class as well—some operations may make sense only for some implementations, and not for others, and the best way to make sure that an operation that is not compatible with the implementation is not requested is to simply not provide it.

Now, let's revisit the issue of selectively enabling parts of the public interface using policies.

Using policies to control the public interface

We have previously used policies to control the public interface in one of two ways—first, we were able to inject a public member function by inheriting from a policy. This approach is reasonably flexible and powerful, but has two drawbacks—first, once we inherit publicly from a policy, we have no control over what interface gets injected—every public member function of the policy becomes a part of the derived class interface. Second, to implement anything useful this way, we have to let the policy class cast itself to the derived class, and then it has to have access to all of the data members and possibly other policies of the class. The second approach we tried relied on a particular property of the constructors—to copy or move a class, we have to copy or move all of its base classes or data members; if one of them is non-copyable or non-movable, the entire constructor will fail to compile. Unfortunately, it usually fails with a rather non-obvious syntax error—nothing as straightforward as *no copy constructor found in this object*. We can extend this technique to other member functions, for example, to assignment operators, but it gets uglier.

We will now learn a more direct way to manipulate the public interface of a policy-based class. First of all, let's differentiate between conditionally disabling existing member functions and adding new ones. The former is reasonable and generally safe: if a particular implementation cannot support certain operations offered by the interface, they should not be offered in the first place. The latter is dangerous as it allows for the essentially arbitrary and uncontrolled extension of the public interface of the class. Therefore, we will focus on providing the interface for all possible intended uses of a policy-based class, and then disabling parts of that interface when they do not make sense for some choice of policies.

There is already a facility in the C++ language to selectively enable and disable member functions. This facility is most commonly implemented though `std::enable_if`, but the foundation behind it is the SFINAE idiom that we studied in `Chapter 7`, *SFINAE and Overload Resolution Management*.

To illustrate the use of SFINAE to let the policies selectively enable a member function, we're going to optionally disable the `operator->()` in our smart pointer class. This is mostly an illustration—while it is true that the `operator->()` does not always make sense—it can only be used for classes with data members—it is usually not a concern since it will simply not compile if used incorrectly. Nonetheless, it provides a useful example to demonstrate several important techniques.

First of all, let's review the use of `std::enable_if` to enable or disable a particular member function—in general, the expression `std::enable_if<value, type>` will compile and yield the specified `type` if the `value` is `true` (it must be a compile-time, or `constexpr`, Boolean value). If the `value` is false, the type substitution fails (no type result is produced). The proper use for this template metafunction is in an SFINAE context, where the failure of type substitution does not result in a compilation error, but simply disables the function that causes the failure (to be more precise, it removes it from the overload resolution set).

Since all we need to enable or disable member functions using SFINAE is a compile-time constant, we can define our policies with nothing else but a `constexpr` value:

```
struct WithArrow {
    static constexpr bool have_arrow = true;
};

struct WithoutArrow {
    static constexpr bool have_arrow = false;
};
```

Now, we should be able to use the policy to control whether the `operator->()` is included in the public interface of the class:

```
template <typename T,
          typename DeletionPolicy = DeleteByOperator<T>,
          typename ArrowPolicy = WithArrow
         >
class SmartPtr : private DeletionPolicy
{
    public:
    std::enable_if_t<ArrowPolicy::have_arrow, T*> operator->() {
        return p_;
    }
    .....
    private:
    T* p_;
};
```

Here, we use `std::enable_if` to generate the return type of the member function `operator->()`—if we want the function to exist, the return type should be `T*` as intended, otherwise, the return type deduction will fail. Unfortunately, this is not going to be quite as easy as that—the preceding code works fine with the `ArrowPolicy` set to `WithArrow`, but it fails to compile with the `WithoutArrow` policy, even if we do not use the `operator->()`. It appears that, sometimes, substitution failure is an error, SFINAE notwithstanding. The reason for this failure is that SFINAE only works in the template context, so the member function itself has to be a template. The fact that the entire thing is inside a class template is not enough. It is easy enough to convert our `operator->()` to a template member function, but how would we figure out the template parameter type? The `operator->()` takes no arguments, so template type deduction from arguments is not an option. Fortunately, there is another way—template parameters can have default values:

```
template <typename T,
          typename DeletionPolicy = DeleteByOperator<T>,
          typename ArrowPolicy = WithArrow
        >
class SmartPtr : private DeletionPolicy
{
    public:
    .....
    template <typename U = T>
        std::enable_if_t<ArrowPolicy::have_arrow, U*>
        operator->() { return p_; }
    template <typename U = T>
        std::enable_if_t<ArrowPolicy::have_arrow, const U*>
        operator->() const { return p_; }
    private:
    T* p_;
};
```

The preceding example uses C++14 features. In C++11, we have to be slightly more verbose because there is no `std::enable_if_t`:

```
template <typename U = T>
    typename std::enable_if<ArrowPolicy::have_arrow, U*>::type
    operator->() { return p_; }
```

Here, we define the template member function `operator->()` with a template parameter: `U`. There is no way for this parameter to be deduced to be anything other than the default value, which is `T`. Now, SFINAE applies as intended—if `ArrowPolicy::have_arrow` is false, the return type of the `operator->()` cannot be determined, and the entire function is simply eliminated from the public interface of the class.

One case where the `operator->()` can be removed for sure is when the type `T` is not a class—the syntax `p->x` is valid only when the type, `T`, has a member, `x`, and it has to be a class for that. We can, therefore, set the `WithArrow` policy by default for all class types and the `WithoutArrow` policy for all other types (again, using C++14 syntax):

```
template <typename T,
          typename DeletionPolicy = DeleteByOperator<T>,
          typename ArrowPolicy =
              std::conditional_t<std::is_class<T>::value,
                                 WithArrow, WithoutArrow>
          >
class SmartPtr : private DeletionPolicy
{
```

Now that we have a way to disable a member function selectively, we can revisit the conditionally enabled constructors. We can enable and disable constructors as well, the only complication being that the constructors have no return type and we have to hide the SFINAE test somewhere else. In addition, we again have to make the constructor a template, and a very common way of hiding the SFINAE test, such as `std::enable_if`, is to add an extra parameter to the template that is not used and has a default type. It is in deriving that default type that the substitution may conditionally fail:

```
struct MoveForbidden {
    static constexpr bool can_move = false;
};

struct MoveAllowed {
    static constexpr bool can_move = true;
};

template <typename T,
          typename DeletionPolicy = DeleteByOperator<T>,
          typename MovePolicy = MoveForbidden
          >
class SmartPtr : private DeletionPolicy
{
    public:
    template <typename U,
              typename V = std::enable_if_t<MovePolicy::can_move &&
                                            std::is_same<U,
    SmartPtr>::value, U>>
    SmartPtr(U&& other)
        : DeletionPolicy(std::move(other)),
          p_(other.p_)
    {
        other.release();
```

```
    }
    .....
};
```

Our move constructor is now a template that accepts an arbitrary type U (just for a moment) instead of being restricted to the same smart pointer type SmartPtr. It is conditionally enabled if the move policy allows it and (the moment is over) if the type U is really the same type as the SmartPtr itself. In this manner, we have avoided extending the interface with a move constructor from an arbitrary type and still made it a template necessary to permit SFINAE. C++17 allows for a more compact form of the is_same expression—instead of std::is_same<U, SmartPtr>::value, we can write std::is_same_v<U, SmartPtr>.

Now that we have a fully general way to enable or disable specific member functions that work for constructors as well, the reader may be wondering, what was the point of introducing the earlier way? Mostly for simplicity—the enable_if expression has to be used in the right context, and the compiler errors that are generated if anything is even slightly wrong are not pretty. On the other hand, the notion that a non-copyable base class makes the entire derived class non-copyable is very basic and works every time. This technique can even be used in C++03, where SFINAE is much more limited and even harder to get to work correctly. Another reason to at least know the way to inject public member functions through policies is that sometimes the enable_if alternative requires that the entire set of possible functions be declared in the primary class template, and then some can be selectively disabled. Sometimes, that set of functions is self-contradicting and cannot be present all at once. An example is a set of conversion operators. Right now, our smart pointer cannot be converted back into a raw pointer. We could enable such conversions and require them to be explicit, or allow implicit conversions:

```
void f(C*);
SmartPtr<C> p(.....);
f((C*)(p));     // Explicit conversion
f(p);           // Implicit conversion
```

The conversion operators are defined as follows:

```
template <typename T, .....>
class SmartPtr ..... {
    public:
    explicit operator T*() { return p_; }    // Explicit conversion
    operator T*() { return p; }              // Implicit conversion
    .....
    private:
    T* p_;
};
```

We could enable one of these operators using `std::enable_if` and SFINAE, based on a conversion policy. The problem is, we cannot declare both implicit and explicit conversion to the same type, even if one is later disabled. These operators cannot be in the same overload set to begin with. If we want to have an option to select one of them in our smart pointer class, we have to have them generated by the base class policy. Since the policy needs to be aware of the smart pointer type, we have to use the CRTP again. Here is a set of policies to control the conversion from smart pointers to raw pointers:

```
template <typename P, typename T>
struct NoRaw {
};

template <typename P, typename T>
struct ExplicitRaw {
    explicit operator T*() { return static_cast<P*>(this)->p_; }
    explicit operator const T*() const {
        return static_cast<const P*>(this)->p_;
    }
};

template <typename P, typename T>
struct ImplicitRaw {
    operator T*() { return static_cast<P*>(this)->p_; }
    operator const T*() const { return static_cast<const P*>(this)->p_; }
};
```

These policies add the desired public member function operators to the derived class. Since they are templates that need to be instantiated with the derived class type, the conversion policy is a template template parameter, and its use follows the CRTP:

```
template <typename T,
          .....
          template <typename, typename>
              class ConversionPolicy = ExplicitRaw
         >
class SmartPtr : .....,
    public ConversionPolicy<SmartPtr<T, ....., ConversionPolicy>, T>
{
    public:
    .....
    private:
    template<typename, typename> friend class ConversionPolicy;
    T* p_;
};
```

The selected conversion policy adds its public interface, if any, to that of the derived class. One policy adds a set of explicit conversion operators, while the other one provides implicit conversions. Just like in the earlier CRTP example, the base class needs access to the private data members of the derived class. We can either grant friendship to the entire template (and every instantiation of it) or, more verbosely, to the specific instantiation used as the base class for each smart pointer:

```
friend class ConversionPolicy<SmartPtr<T, ....., ConversionPolicy>, T>;
```

We have learned several different ways to implement new policies. Sometimes, the challenge comes in reusing the ones we already have. The next section shows one way to do it.

Rebinding policies

As we have already seen, the policy lists can get quite long. Often, we want to change just one policy and create a class *just like that other one, but with a small change*. There are at least two ways to do this.

The first way is very general but somewhat verbose. The first step is to expose the template parameters as typedefs, or aliases, inside the primary template. This is a good practice, anyway—without such aliases, it is very difficult to find out, at compile time, what a template parameter was in case we ever need to use it outside of the template. For example, we have a smart pointer, and we want to know what the deletion policy was. The easiest way, by far, is with some help from the smart pointer class itself:

```
template <typename T,
          typename DeletionPolicy = DeleteByOperator<T>,
          typename CopyMovePolicy = NoMoveNoCopy,
          template <typename, typename>
            class ConversionPolicy = ExplicitRaw
         >
class SmartPtr : private DeletionPolicy,
                 public CopyMovePolicy,
                 public ConversionPolicy<SmartPtr<T, DeletionPolicy,
                                                  CopyMovePolicy,
                                                  ConversionPolicy>,
                          T>
{
    public:
    using value_t = T;
    using deletion_policy_t = DeletionPolicy;
    using copy_move_policy_t = CopyMovePolicy;
```

```
        template <typename P, typename T1> using conversion_policy_t =
    ConversionPolicy<P, T1>;
        . . . . .
    };
```

Note that we're using two different types of aliases here—for the regular template parameters such as `DeletionPolicy`, we can use a `typedef`, or the equivalent `using` alias. For a template template parameter, we have to use the template alias, sometimes called template `typedef`—to reproduce the same policy with another smart pointer, we need to know the template itself, not the template instantiation, such as `ConversionPolicy<SmartPtr, T>`. For uniformity, we use the alias syntax everywhere. Now, if we need to create another smart pointer with some of the same policies, we can simply query the policies of the original object:

```
    SmartPtr<int, DeleteByOperator<int>, MoveNoCopy, ImplicitRaw>
    p_original(new int(42));
    using ptr_t = decltype(p_original);    // The exact type of p_original
    SmartPtr<ptr_t::value_t, ptr_t::deletion_policy_t,
            ptr_t::copy_move_policy_t, ptr_t::conversion_policy_t> p_copy;
    SmartPtr<double, ptr_t::deletion_policy_t,
            ptr_t::copy_move_policy_t, ptr_t::conversion_policy_t> q;
```

Now, `p_copy` and `p_original` have exactly the same type. There is, of course, an easier way to accomplish that. But the point is, we could alter any one of the types in the list and keep the rest, and get a pointer *just like* `p_original`, *except for one change*. For example, the pointer `q` has the same policies, but points to a `double`.

The latter turns out to be a pretty common case, and there is a way to facilitate the *rebinding* or a template to a different type while keeping the rest of the arguments intact. To do this, the primary template and all its policies need to support such rebinding:

```
    template <typename T>
    struct DeleteByOperator {
        void operator()(T* p) const {
            delete p;
        }
        template <typename U> using rebind_type = DeleteByOperator<U>;
    };

    template <typename T,
            typename DeletionPolicy = DeleteByOperator<T>,
            typename CopyMovePolicy = NoMoveNoCopy,
            template <typename, typename>
                class ConversionPolicy = ExplicitRaw
            >
    class SmartPtr : private DeletionPolicy,
```

```
                    public CopyMovePolicy,
                    public ConversionPolicy<SmartPtr<T, DeletionPolicy,
                                                      CopyMovePolicy,
                                                      ConversionPolicy>,
                                           T>
{
    public:
    .....
    template <typename U> using rebind_type =
        SmartPtr<U, typename DeletionPolicy::template rebind_type<U>,
                 CopyMovePolicy, ConversionPolicy>;
};
```

The `rebind_type` alias defines a new template that has only one parameter—the type we can change. The rest of the parameters come from the primary template itself. Some of these parameters are types that also depend on the primary type `T`, and themselves need rebinding (in our example, the deletion policy). By choosing not to rebind the copy/move policy, we impose a requirement that none of these policies depend on the primary type, otherwise this policy, too, needs to be rebound. Finally, the template conversion policy does not need rebinding—we have access to the entire template here, so it will be instantiated with the new primary type. We can now use the rebinding mechanism to create a *similar* pointer type:

```
SmartPtr<int, DeleteByOperator<int>, MoveNoCopy, ImplicitRaw> p(new
int(42));
using dptr_t = decltype(p)::rebind_type<double>;
dptr_t q(new double(4.2));
```

If we have direct access to the smart pointer type, we can use it for rebinding (for example, in a template context). Otherwise, we can get the type from a variable of this type using `decltype()`. The pointer `q` has the same policies as `p`, but points to a `double`, and the type-dependent policies such as the deletion policy have been updated accordingly.

We have covered the main ways in which the policies can be implemented and used to customize policy-based classes. It is now time to review what we have learned and state some general guidelines for the use of policy-based designs.

Recommendations and guidelines

Policy-based design allows for exceptional flexibility in the creation of finely customizable classes. Sometimes, this flexibility and power become the enemy of a good design. In this section, we will review the strengths and weaknesses of the policy-based design and come up with some general recommendations.

Strengths of the policy-based design

The main advantages of the policy-based design are the flexibility and extensibility of the design. At a high level, these are the same benefits the Strategy pattern offers, only realized at compile-time. The policy-based design allows the programmer to select, at compile time, one of several algorithms for each specific task or operation performed by the system. Since the only constraints on the algorithms are the requirements on the interface that binds them into the rest of the system, it is equally possible to extend the system by writing new policies for the customizable operations.

At a high level, policy-based design allows the software system to be built from components. At a high level, this is hardly a novel idea, certainly not limited to policy-based design. The focus of policy-based design is the use of components to define behavior and implementation of individual classes. There is some similarity between policies and callbacks—both allow a user-specified action to be taken when a particular event takes place. However, the policies are much more general than callbacks—while a callback is a function, policies are entire classes, with multiple functions and, possibly, a non-trivial internal state.

These general concepts translate into a unique set of advantages for the design, mostly centered around the ideas of flexibility and extensibility. With the overall structure of the system and its high-level components are determined by the high-level design, the policies allow for a variety of low-level customizations within the constraints that were imposed by the original design. Policies can extend the class interface (add public member functions), implement or extend the state of the class (add data members), and specify implementations (add private member functions). The original design, in setting the overall structure of the classes and their interactions, in effect authorizes each policy to have one or more of these roles.

The result is an extensible system that can be modified to address evolving requirements, even ones that have not been anticipated or known at the time when the system was designed. The overall architecture remains stable, while the selection of possible policies and the constraints on their interfaces offers a systematic, disciplined way to modify and extend the software.

Disadvantages of policy-based design

The first problem with policy-based design that comes to mind is the one we have already encountered—declarations of policy-based classes with a specific set of policies are extremely verbose, especially if one of the policies at the end of the list has to be changed. Consider the declaration of a smart pointer with all of the policies we have implemented in this chapter, put together:

```
SmartPtr<int, DeleteByOperator<int>, NoMoveNoCopy, ExplicitRaw,
WithoutArrow, NoDebug> p;
```

That's just for a smart pointer—a class with a fairly simple interface and limited functionality. Even though it is unlikely that someone will need one pointer with all of these customization possibilities, the policy-based classes tend to have a lot of policies. This problem may be the most evident, but it is actually not the worst. The template aliases help to give concise names to the few policy combinations that are actually used by a particular application. In the template context, the types of smart pointers used as function arguments are deduced and do not need to be explicitly specified. In regular code, auto can be used to save a lot of typing and also make the code more robust—when the complex type declarations that must be consistent are replaced with an automatic way to generate these consistent types, the errors caused by typing something slightly different in two different places disappear (in general, if there is a recipe to make the compiler generate correct-by-construction code, use it).

The much more significant, if slightly less visible, problem is that all of these policy-based types with different policies are actually different types. Two smart pointers that point to the same object type but have different deletion policies are different types. Two smart pointers that are otherwise the same but have different copying policies are different types. Why is that a problem? Consider a function that is called to work on an object that is passed into the function using a smart pointer. This function does not copy the smart pointer, so it should not matter what the copying policy is—it is never used. And yet, what should the argument type be? There is no one type that can accommodate all smart pointers, even the ones with very similar functionality.

There are several possible solutions here. The most straightforward one is to make all functions that use policy-based types into templates. This does simplify the coding, and it reduces code duplication (at least the source code duplication), but it has its own downsides—the machine code becomes larger since there are multiple copies of every function, and all template code must be in the header files.

The other option is to erase the policy types. We saw the type erasure technique in `Chapter 6`, *Understanding Type Erasure*. Type erasure solves the problem of having many similar types—we could make all smart pointers, regardless of their policies, to be the same type (only to the extent that the policies determine the implementation and not the public interface, of course). However, this comes at a very high cost. One of the main drawbacks of the templates in general, and the policy-based design, in particular, is that templates provide a zero-overhead abstraction—we can express our programs in terms of convenient high-level abstractions and concepts, but the compiler strips it all away, inlines all of the templates, and generates the minimum necessary code. Type erasure not only negates this advantage, but has the opposite effect—it adds a very high overhead of memory allocations and indirect function calls.

The last option is to avoid using policy-based types, at least for some operations. Sometimes, this choice carries a little extra cost—for example, a function that needs to operate on an object but not delete or own it should take the object by reference instead of a smart pointer (see `Chapter 3`, *Memory Ownership*). In addition to clearly expressing the fact that the function is not going to own the object, this neatly solves the problem of what type the argument should be—the reference is the same type, no matter which smart pointer it came from. This is, however, a limited approach—more often than not, we do need to operate on the entire policy-based objects, which are usually much more complex than a simple pointer (for example, custom containers are often implemented using policies).

The final disadvantage is the general complexity of the policy-based types, although such claims should be made with care—the important question is, complexity compared to what? Policy-based designs are usually invoked to solve complex design problems where a family of similar types serves the same overall purpose (*what*), but does so in slightly different ways (*how*). This leads us to the recommendations on the use of policies.

Guidelines for policy-based designs

The guidelines for policy-based designs boil down to managing the complexity and making sure the ends justify the means—the flexibility of the design and the elegance of the resulting solutions should justify the complexity of the implementation and its use.

Since most of the complexity comes from the increasing number of policies, this is the focus of most of the guidelines. Some policies end up putting together very different types that happen to have a similar implementation. The goal of such a policy-based type is to reduce the code duplication. While a worthwhile objective, this is generally not a good enough reason to expose a multitude of disparate policy options to the end user of the type. If two different types or type families happen to have similar implementations, that implementation can be factored out. The private, hidden, implementation-only part of the design can itself use policies if it makes the implementation easier. But these hidden policies should not be selected by the client—the client should specify the types that make sense in the application and the policies that customize the visible behavior. From these types and policies, the implementation can derive additional types as needed. This is no different than calling a common function to, say, find the minimum element in a sequence from several different unrelated algorithms that all happen to need that operation. The common code is not duplicated, but neither is it exposed to the user.

So, when should a policy-based type be broken up into two or more pieces? A good way to look at it is to ask whether the primary type, with a particular set of policies, has a good specific name that describes it. For example, a non-copyable owning pointer, movable or not, is a *unique pointer*—there is only one such pointer for each object at any given time. This is true for any deletion or conversion policy. On the other hand, a reference-counted pointer is a *shared pointer*, again, with any choice of other policies. This suggests that our one smart pointer to end all smart pointers would be, perhaps, better split into two—a non-copyable unique pointer and a copyable shared pointer. We still get some code reuse because the deletion policy, for example, is common to both pointer types, and does not have to be implemented twice. This is, indeed, the choice the C++ standard makes. The std::unique_ptr has only one policy, the deletion policy. The std::shared_ptr also has the same policy and can use the same policy objects, but it is type-erased, so all shared pointers to a particular object are of one type.

But what about other policies? Here, we come to the second guideline—the policies that restrict the use of the class should be justified by the cost of possible errors that are caused by the incorrect use they are trying to prevent. For example, do we really need a non-movable policy? On the one hand, it could prevent a programming error if the ownership of the object absolutely must not be transferred. On the other hand, in many cases, the programmer will simply change the code to use a movable pointer.

Similarly, while it is probably desirable to prevent implicit casting to the raw pointer as a matter of basic coding discipline, there is always a way to convert the smart pointer to the raw one explicitly—if nothing else, `&*p` should always work. Again, the benefits of the carefully restricted interface probably do not justify adding this policy. On the other hand, it makes a great compact learning example for a set of techniques that can be used to create more complex and more useful policies, and so the time we spent learning how this policy works is entirely justified.

Another way to look at the question of what the right set of policies is and what policies should be broken up into separate groups is to go back to the fundamental strength of the policy-based design—the composability of the behavior expressed by different policies. If we have a class with four different policies, each of which can have four different implementations, that is 256 different versions of the class. It is, of course, unlikely that we will need all 256. But the point is, at the time when we implement the class, we do not know which of these versions we will actually need later. We could make a guess and implement only a few most likely ones. If we are wrong, this will result in much code duplication and copy-pasting. With policy-based design, we have the potential to implement any combination of the behavior, without actually having to write them all explicitly up front.

Now that we understand this strength of policy-based designs, we can use it to evaluate a particular set of policies—do they need to be composable? Would we ever need to combine them in different ways? If some policies always come in certain combinations or groups, this calls for automatically deducing these policies from one primary user-specified policy. On the other hand, a set of largely independent policies that can be combined arbitrarily is probably a good set of policies.

Another way to address some of the weaknesses of policy-based design is to try and accomplish the same goal by different means. There is no substitute for the entirety of the

capabilities offered by the policies—the Strategy pattern is there for a reason. However, there are alternative patterns that offer somewhat superficial similarities, and may be used to solve some of the same problems as the policy-based design addresses. We will see one such alternative in `Chapter 17`, *Adapters and Decorators*, when we talk about decorators. Another solution that may look very *policy-like* in a limited domain will be shown in the next section.

Almost policy-based approach

We are now going to look at an alternative to the policy-based design we have been studying so far. It is not as general, but when it works, it can provide all the advantages of the policies, in particular, the composability, without some of the problems. To introduce this new approach, we will consider the problem of designing a custom value type.

A value type, to put it simply, is a type that behaves mostly like an `int`. Often, these types are numbers. While we have a set of built-in types for that, we may want to operate on rational numbers, complex numbers, tensors, matrices, or numbers that have units associated with them (meters, grams, and so on). These value types support a set of operations such as arithmetic operations, comparisons, assignment, and copying. Depending on what the value represents, we may need only a limited subset of these operations—for example, we may need to support addition and multiplication for matrices, but no division, and comparing matrices for anything other than equality probably doesn't make sense in most cases. Similarly, we probably don't want to allow the addition of meters to grams.

More generally, there is often a desire to have a numeric type with a limited interface—we would like it if the operations that we do not wish to allow for the quantity represented by such numbers did not compile. This way, a program with an invalid operation simply cannot be written.

This problem can be tackled with a policy-based approach:

```
template <typename T,
          typename AdditionPolicy, typename ComparisonPolicy,
          typename OrderPolicy, typename AssignmentPolicy, ..... >
class Value { ..... };
```

This implementation runs into the entire set of drawbacks of policy-based design—the policy list is long, all policies must be spelled out, and there aren't any good defaults; the policies are positional, so the type declaration requires careful counting of commas, and, as the new policies are added, any semblance of a meaningful order of policies disappears. Note that we did not mention the problem of different sets of policies creating different types—in this case, this is not a drawback, but the design intent. If we want a type with support for addition and a similar type but without addition, these have to be different types.

Ideally, we would like to just list the properties we want our value to have—I want a value type based on integers that support addition and multiplication and assignment, but nothing else. As it turns out, there is a way to accomplish this.

First, let's think of what such a policy might look like. For example, the policy that enables addition should inject `operator+()` into the public interface of the class (and maybe also `operator+=()`). The policy that makes the value assignable should inject `operator=()`. We have seen enough of such policies to know how they are implemented—they have to be base classes, publicly inherited, and they need to know what the derived class is and cast it to its type, so they have to use CRTP:

```
template <typename T,      // T is the foundation type (like int)
          typename V>      // V is the derived class
struct Incrementable
{
    V operator++() {
        V& v = static_cast<V&>(*this);
        ++v.value_; // This is the actual value
                    // inside the derived class
        return v;
    }
};
```

Now, we need to give some thought to the use of these policies in the primary template. First of all, we want to support the unknown number of policies, in any order. This brings `variadic` templates to mind. However, to use CRTP, the template parameters have to be templates themselves. Then, we want to inherit from an instantiation of each of these templates, however many there are. What we need is a `variadic` template with a template template parameter pack:

```
template <typename T, template <typename, typename> class ... Policies>
class Value : public Policies<T, Value<T, Policies ... >> ...
{    .....    }; // Not three dots!
```

We have to be careful with ellipses (. . .) from now on—in the previous sections, we used . . . . . to indicate *some more code here that we have seen already and don't want to repeat*. But from now on, three dots (. . .) is literally three dots—it's part of the C++ syntax for variadic templates (this is why the rest of this chapter used five dots to indicate *more code* and not three). The preceding declaration introduces a class template called `Value`, with at least one parameter that is a type, plus zero or more template policies, which themselves have two type parameters (again, in C++17, we can also write `typename ... Policies` instead of `class ... Policies`). The `Value` class instantiates these templates with the type `T` and itself, and inherits publicly from all of them.

The `Value` class template should contain the interface that we want to be common for all our value types. The rest will have to come from policies. Let's make the values copyable, assignable, and printable by default:

```
template <typename T, template <typename, typename> class ... Policies>
class Value : public Policies<T, Value<T, Policies ... >> ...
{
    public:
    typedef T value_type;
    explicit Value() : val_(T()) {}
    explicit Value(T v) : val_(v) {}
    Value(const Value& rhs) : val_(rhs.val_) {}
    Value& operator=(Value rhs) { val_ = rhs.val_; return *this; }
    Value& operator=(T rhs) { val_ = rhs; return *this; }
    friend std::ostream& operator<<(std::ostream& out, Value x) {
        out << x.val_; return out;
    }
    friend std::istream& operator>>(std::istream& in, Value& x) {
        in >> x.val_; return in;
    }

    private:
    T val_;
};
```

The stream inserter operators `<<` and `>>` have to be non-member functions, as usual. We use the *friend factory*, which was described in the `Chapter 12`, *Friend Factory* to generate these functions.

Before we can indulge ourselves in implementing all of the policies, there is one more hurdle to overcome. The `val_` value is private in the `Value` class, and we like it this way. However, the policies need to access it and modify it. In the past, we solved this problem by making each policy that needed such access into a friend. This time, we don't even know the names of the policies we may have. After working through the preceding declaration of the parameter pack expansion as a set of base classes, the reader may reasonably expect us to pull a rabbit out of the hat and somehow declare friendship to the entire parameter pack. Unfortunately, we know of no such way. The best solution we can suggest is to provide a set of accessor functions that should be called only by the policies, but there is no good way to enforce that (a name, such as `policy_accessor_do_not_call()`, might go some way to suggest that the user code should stay away from it, but the ingenuity of the programmer knows no bounds, and such hints are not universally respected):

```
template <typename T, template <typename, typename> class ... Policies>
class Value : public Policies<T, Value<T, Policies ... >> ...
{
```

```
    public:
    .....
    T get() const { return val_; }
    T& get() { return val_; }
    private:
    T val_;
};
```

To create a value type with a restricted set of operations, we have to instantiate this template with a list of policies we want, and nothing else:

```
using V = Value<int, Addable, Incrementable>;
V v1(0), v2(1);
v1++;               // Incrementable - OK
V v3(v1 + v2);      // Addable - OK
v3 *= 2;            // No multiplication policies - won't compile
```

The number and the type of policies we can implement is limited mostly by the need at hand (or imagination), but here are some examples that demonstrate adding different kinds of operations to the class.

First of all, we can implement the aforementioned Incrementable policy that provides the two ++ operators, postfix and prefix:

```
template <typename T, typename V>
struct Incrementable
{
    V operator++() {
        V& v = static_cast<V&>(*this);
        ++(v.get());
        return v;
    }
    V operator++(int) {
        V& v = static_cast<V&>(*this);
        return V(v.get()++);
    }
};
```

We can make a separate Decrementable policy for the -- operators, or have one policy for both if it makes sense for our type. Also, if want to increment by some value other than one, then we need the += operators as well:

```
template <typename T, typename V>
struct Incrementable
{
    V& operator+=(V val) {
        V& v = static_cast<V&>(*this);
```

```
        v.get() += val.get();
        return v;
    }
    V& operator+=(T val) {
        V& v = static_cast<V&>(*this);
        v.get() += val;
        return v;
    }
};
```

The preceding policy provides two versions of the `operator+=()`—one accepts the increment of the same `Value` type, and the other of the foundation type `T`. This is not a requirement, and we could implement an increment by values of some other types as needed. We can even have several versions of the increment policy, as long as only one is used (the compiler would let us know if we were introducing incompatible overloads of the same operator).

We can add the operators `*=` and `/=` in a similar manner. Adding binary operators such as comparison operators or addition and multiplication is a little different—these operators have to be non-member functions to allow for type conversions on the first argument. Again, the friend factory pattern comes in handy. Let's start with the comparison operators:

```
template <typename T, typename V>
struct ComparableSelf
{
    friend bool operator==(V lhs, V rhs) { return lhs.get() == rhs.get(); }
    friend bool operator!=(V lhs, V rhs) { return lhs.get() != rhs.get(); }
};
```

When instantiated, this template generates two non-member non-template functions, that is, the comparison operators for variables of the type of the specific `Value` class, the one that is instantiated. We may also want to allow comparisons with the foundation type (such as `int`):

```
template <typename T, typename V>
struct ComparableValue
{
    friend bool operator==(V lhs, T rhs) { return lhs.get() == rhs; }
    friend bool operator==(T lhs, V rhs) { return lhs == rhs.get(); }
    friend bool operator!=(V lhs, T rhs) { return lhs.get() != rhs; }
    friend bool operator!=(T lhs, V rhs) { return lhs != rhs.get(); }
};
```

More often than not, we will likely want both types of comparison at the same time. We could simply put them both into the same policy and not worry about separating them, or we could create a combined policy from the two we already have:

```
template <typename T, typename V>
struct Comparable : public ComparableSelf<T, V>,
                    public ComparableValue<T, V>
{
};
```

The addition and multiplication operators are created by similar policies. They are also friendly non-template non-member functions. The only difference is the return value type—they return the object itself, for example:

```
template <typename T, typename V>
struct Addable
{
    friend V operator+(V lhs, V rhs) { return V(lhs.get() + rhs.get()); }
    friend V operator+(V lhs, T rhs) { return V(lhs.get() + rhs); }
    friend V operator+(T lhs, V rhs) { return V(lhs + rhs.get()); }
};
```

Explicit or implicit conversion operators can be added as well; the policy is very similar to the one we already used for pointers:

```
template <typename T, typename V>
struct ExplicitConvertible
{
    explicit operator T() {
        return static_cast<V*>(this)->get();
    }
    explicit operator const T() const {
        return static_cast<const V*>(this)->get();
    }
};
```

This approach, at first glance, seems to solve most of the drawbacks of the policy-based types (except for one of them being separate types, of course). The order of the policies does not matter—we can specify only the ones we want and not worry about the other ones—what's not to like? There are, however, two fundamental limitations. First of all, the policy-based class cannot refer to any policy by name. There is no longer a slot for `DeletionPolicy` or `AdditionPolicy`. There are no convention-enforced policy interfaces, such as the deletion policy having to be callable. The entire process of binding the policies into the single type is implicit; it's just a superposition of interfaces.

Therefore, we are limited in what we can do using these policies—we can inject public member functions and non-member functions—even add private data members—but we cannot provide an implementation for an aspect of behavior that's determined and limited by the primary policy-based class. As such, this is not an implementation of the Strategy pattern—we are composing the interface (and, necessarily, the implementation) at will, not customizing a specific algorithm.

The second, closely related, limitation is that there are no default policies. The missing policies are just that, missing. There is nothing in their place. The default behavior is always the absence of any behavior. In the traditional policy-based design, each policy slot has to be filled. If there is a reasonable default, it can be specified. Then, that is the policy, unless the user overrides it (for example, the default deletion policy uses `operator delete`). If there is no default, the compiler won't let us omit the policy—we have to give an argument to the template.

The consequences of these limitations reach farther than the reader may think at first glance. For example, it may be tempting to use the `enable_if` technique instead of injecting public member functions through the base class. Then, we could have a default behavior that is enabled if none of the other options are. But it won't work here. We can certainly create a policy that is targeted for use with `enable_if`:

```
template <typename T, typename V> struct Addable
{
    constexpr bool adding_enabled = true;
};
```

But there is no way to use it—we can't use `AdditionPolicy::adding_enabled` because there is no `AdditionPolicy`—all policy slots are unnamed. The other option would be to use `Value::adding_enabled`—the addition policy is a base class of `Value`, and, therefore, all of its data members are visible in the `Value` class. The only problem is that it does not work—at the point where this expression is evaluated by the compiler (in the definition of the `Value` type as the template parameter for the CRTP policies), `Value` is an incomplete type and we cannot access its data members yet. We could evaluate `policy_name::adding_enabled` if we knew what the policy name was. But that knowledge is exactly what we gave up in trade for not having to specify the entire list of policies.

While not, strictly speaking, an application of the Strategy pattern, the alternative to the policy-based design that we have just learned about can be attractive when the policies are primarily used to control a set of supported operations. While discussing the guidelines for policy-based design, we have mentioned that it is rarely worth it to use a policy slot just to provide the additional safety of the restricted interface. For such situations, this alternative approach should be kept in mind.

Summary

In this chapter, we have studied, extensively, the applications of the Strategy pattern (also known as the policy pattern) to C++ generic programming. The combination of the two gives rise to one of the most powerful tools in the arsenal of a C++ programmer—the policy-based design of classes. This approach provides great flexibility by allowing us to compose the behavior of the class from many building blocks, or policies, each of which is responsible for a particular aspect of the behavior.

We have learned different ways to implement policies—these can be templates, classes with template member functions, classes with static functions, and even classes with constant values. Just as varied are the ways that we can use policies through composition, inheritance, or direct access to static members. Policy parameters can be types or templates, each with their own advantages and limitations.

A tool as powerful as policy-based design is also easily misused or applied in poor judgment. Often, such situations arise from the gradual evolution of the software toward more and more complexity. To mitigate such mischance, we have provided a set of guidelines and recommendations that focus on the key advantages that the policy-based design offers to the programmer and suggested the techniques and constraints that maximize such advantages.

We have also considered a more limited design pattern that can sometimes be used to mimic the policy-based approach, without some of its drawbacks. Yet more such limited alternatives will be described in Chapter 17, *Adapters and Decorators*. This chapter is dedicated to the Decorator pattern and the more general Adapter pattern. Both are sort of C++ magic tricks—they make an object appear as something it's not.

Questions

1. What is the Strategy pattern?
2. How is the Strategy pattern implemented at compile time using C++ generic programming?
3. What types can be used as policies?
4. How can policies be integrated into the primary template?
5. What are the main drawbacks of policy-based design?

17
Adapters and Decorators

This chapter takes on two classic patterns in **object-oriented programming** (OOP)—the Adapter pattern and the decorator pattern. These patterns are just two of the original twenty-three design patterns that were introduced in the *Design Patterns – Elements of Reusable Object-Oriented Software* book by Erich Gamma, Richard Helm, Ralph Johnson, and John Vlissides. As an object-oriented language, C++ can take advantage of these patterns as well as any other language. But, as is often the case, generic programming brings some advantages, variations, and, with it, new challenges to the classic patterns.

The following topics are covered in this chapter:

- What are the adapter and decorator patterns?
- What is the difference between the two?
- What design problems can be solved by these patterns?
- How are these patterns used in C++?
- How does generic programming help to design adapters and decorators?
- What other, different, patterns offer alternative solutions to similar problems?

Technical requirements

The example code for this chapter can be found on GitHub at the following link: https://github.com/PacktPublishing/Hands-On-Design-Patterns-with-CPP/tree/master/Chapter17.

The decorator pattern

We will begin this study with the definitions of the two classic patterns. As we will see, on paper, the patterns, as well as the differences between them, are quite clear. Then, C++ comes in and blurs the lines by allowing design solutions that fall somewhere in-between the two. Still, the clarity of these simple cases is helpful, even if it gets muddled as we pile on the complexity. Let's start with what is clear, then.

The decorator pattern is also a structural pattern; it allows a behavior to be added to an object. The classic decorator pattern extends the behavior of an existing operation that's performed by a class. It *decorates* the class with the new behavior and creates an object of the new, decorated type. The decorator implements the interface of the original class and forwards the requests from its own interface to that class, but it also performs additional actions before and after these forwarded requests—these are the *decorations*. Such decorators are sometimes called **class wrappers**.

Basic decorator pattern

We will begin with a C++ example of the decorator pattern that follows the classic definition as closely as possible. For this example, we will imagine designing a fantasy game that's set in medieval times (true to life, only with dragons and elves and so on). Of course, what are medieval times without fighting? And so, in our game, the player has a choice of units appropriate for his/her side, and they can do battle when called on. Here is the basic `Unit` class—at least the combat-related part:

```
class Unit {
    public:
    Unit(double strength, double armor) : strength_(strength),
                                          armor_(armor) {}
    virtual bool hit(Unit& target) { return attack() > target.defense(); }
    virtual double attack() = 0;
    virtual double defense() = 0;
    protected:
    double strength_;
    double armor_;
};
```

The unit has the `strength`, which determines its attack, and the `armor`, which provides defense. The actual values of the attack and the defense are computed by the derived classes—the concrete units—but the combat mechanism itself is right here—if the attack is stronger than the defense, the unit successfully hits the target (this is a very simplistic approach to gaming, of course, but we want to make the examples as concise as possible).

Now, what are the actual units in the game? The pillar of the human armies is the valorous `Knight`. This unit has strong armor and a sharp sword, giving it bonuses to both attack and defend:

```
class Knight : public Unit {
    public:
    using Unit::Unit;
    double attack() { return strength_ + sword_bonus_; }
    double defense() { return armor_ + plate_bonus_; }
    protected:
    static constexpr double sword_bonus_ = 2;
    static constexpr double plate_bonus_ = 3;
};
```

Fighting against the knights are the brutish ogres. The ogres swing simple wooden clubs and wear ragged leather, neither of which are great implements of war, giving them some combat penalties:

```
class Ogre : public Unit {
    public:
    using Unit::Unit;
    double attack() { return strength_ + club_penalty_; }
    double defense() { return armor_ + leather_penalty_; }
    protected:
    static constexpr double club_penalty_ = -1;
    static constexpr double leather_penalty_ = -1;
};
```

On the other hand, ogres are remarkably strong, to begin with:

```
Knight k(10, 5);
Ogre o(12, 2);
k.hit(o);        // Yes!
```

Here the knight, aided by his attack bonus and the enemy's weak armor, will successfully hit the ogre. But the game is far from over. As the units fight, the surviving ones gain experience and eventually become veterans. A veteran unit is still the same kind of unit, but it gains attack and defense bonuses, reflecting its combat experience. Here, we do not want to change any of the class interfaces, but we want to modify the behavior of the attack() and defense() functions. This is the job of the decorator pattern, and what follows is the classic implementation of the VeteranUnit decorator:

```
class VeteranUnit : public Unit {
    public:
    VeteranUnit(Unit& unit, double strength_bonus, double armor_bonus) :
        Unit(strength_bonus, armor_bonus), unit_(unit) {}
    double attack() { return unit_.attack() + strength_; }
    double defense() { return unit_.defense() + armor_; }
    private:
    Unit& unit_;
};
```

Note that this class inherits directly from the Unit class, so in the class hierarchy, it is *to the side* of concrete unit classes such as Knight or Ogre. We still have the original unit that is decorated and becomes the veteran—the VeteranUnit decorator contains a reference to it. The way it is used, then, is to decorate a unit and use the decorated unit from then on, but it does not delete the original unit:

```
Knight k(10, 5);
Ogre o(12, 2);
VeteranUnit vk(k, 7, 2);
VeteranUnit vo(o, 1, 9);
vk.hit(vo);              // Another hit!
```

Here, both our old enemies reached their first veterancy levels, and the victory again goes to the knight. But experience is the best teacher, and our ogre gains another level, and, with it, enchanted runic armor with a massive defense bonus:

```
VeteranUnit vvo(vo, 1, 9);
vk.hit(vvo);            // Miss!
```

Note that we can decorate a decorated object in this design! This is intentional, and the bonuses stack up as the unit gains levels. This time, the experienced fighter's defense proves to be too much for the knight.

As we already mentioned, this is the classic decorator pattern, straight out of the textbook. It works in C++, but with some limitations. The first one is rather evident—even though we want to use the decorated unit once we have it, the original unit must be kept around, and the lifetimes of these objects must be carefully managed. There are practical solutions to such practical problems, but the focus of this book is on combining design patterns with generic programming, and the new design possibilities that pairing creates. Therefore, our creative path takes us elsewhere.

The second problem is more endemic to C++. It is best illustrated by an example. The game's designers have added a special ability to the `Knight` unit—it can charge forward at its enemy, gaining a short-term attack bonus. This bonus is valid only for the next attack, but in the thick of the battle, it may be just enough:

```cpp
class Knight : public Unit {
    public:
    Knight(double strength, double armor) :
        Unit(strength, armor), charge_bonus_(0) {}
    double attack() {
        double res = strength_ + sword_bonus_ + charge_bonus_;
        charge_bonus_ = 0;
        return res;
    }
    double defense() { return armor_ + plate_bonus_; }
    void charge() { charge_bonus_ = 1; }
    protected:
    double charge_bonus_;
    static constexpr double sword_bonus_ = 2;
    static constexpr double plate_bonus_ = 3;
};
```

The charge bonus is activated by calling the `charge()` member function and lasts for one attack, and then it is reset. When the player activates the charge, the game executes the code, which looks something like this:

```cpp
Knight k(10, 5);
Ogre o(12, 2);
k.charge();
k.hit(o);
```

Of course, we would expect the veteran knight to be able to charge forward as well, but here we run into a problem—our code does not compile:

```cpp
VeteranUnit vk(k, 7, 2);
vk.charge(); // Does not compile!
```

The root of the problem is that `charge()` is a part of the interface of the `Knight` class, while the `VeteranUnit` decorator is derived from the `Unit` class. We could move the `charge()` function into the base class, `Unit`, but this is a bad design—`Ogre` is also derived from `Unit`, and ogres cannot charge, so they should not have such an interface (it violates the *is-a* principle of public inheritance).

This is a problem that's inherent in the way we implemented the decorator object—both `Knight` and `VeteranUnit` are derived from the same base class, `Unit`, but they don't know anything about each other. There are some ugly workarounds, but it is a fundamental C++ limitation; it does not handle *cross-casting* well (casting to a type in another branch of the same hierarchy). But what the language takes with one hand, it gives with the other—we have much better tools to deal with this problem, and we are going to learn about these tools next.

Decorators the C++ way

We have encountered two problems while implementing a classic decorator in C++—first of all, the decorated object did not take ownership of the original object, so both must be kept around (this may not be so much a problem as a feature, if the decoration needs to be removed later, which is one of the reasons the decorator pattern is implemented this way). The other problem is that a decorated `Knight` is not really a `Knight` at all, but a `Unit`. We can solve the second problem if the decorator is itself derived from the class that is being decorated. This would imply that the `VeteranUnit` class does not have a fixed base class—the base class should be whatever class is being decorated. This description matches the **Curiously Recurring Template Pattern** (CRTP) to a tee (this C++ idiom was described earlier in this book). To apply CRTP, we need to make the decorator into a template and inherit from the template parameter:

```
template <typename U> class VeteranUnit : public U {
    public:
    VeteranUnit(U&& unit, double strength_bonus, double armor_bonus) :
        U(unit), strength_bonus_(strength_bonus), armor_bonus_(armor_bonus)
    {}
    double attack() { return U::attack() + strength_bonus_; }
    double defense() { return U::defense() + armor_bonus_; }
    private:
    double strength_bonus_;
    double armor_bonus_;
};
```

Now, to promote a unit to the veteran status, we must convert it to the decorated version of the concrete `unit` class:

```
Knight k(10, 5);
Ogre o(12, 2);
k.hit(o);           // Hit!
VeteranUnit<Knight> vk(std::move(k), 7, 2);
VeteranUnit<Ogre> vo(std::move(o), 1, 9);
vk.hit(vo);         // Hit!
VeteranUnit<VeteranUnit<Ogre>> vvo(std::move(vo), 1, 9);
vk.hit(vvo);        // Miss...
vk.charge();        // Compiles now, vk is a Knight too
vk.hit(vvo);        // Hit with the charge bonus!
```

This is the same scenario that we saw at the end of the previous section, but it now uses the template decorator. Notice the differences. First of all, a `VeteranUnit` is a class that's derived from a concrete unit such as `Knight` or `Ogre`. As such, it has access to the interface of the base class: for example, a veteran knight, `VeteranUnit<Knight>`, is a `Knight` too, and has the member function `charge()` inherited from `Knight`. Second, the decorated unit explicitly takes the ownership of the original unit—to create a veteran unit, we have to move the original unit into it (the base class of the veteran unit is move-constructed from the original unit). The original object is left in the unspecified moved-from state, and the only safe action that can be done on this object is a call to the destructor. Note that, at least for the simple implementation of unit classes, the `move` operation is just a copy, so the original object is usable, but you should not rely on it—making assumptions about the moved-from state is a bug waiting to happen.

It is worth pointing out that our declaration of the `VeteranUnit` constructor enforces and requires this ownership transfer. If we try to construct a veteran unit without moving from the original unit, it will not compile:

```
VeteranUnit<Knight> vk(k, 7, 2);     // Does not compile
```

By providing only one constructor that accepts an r-value reference, that is, `Unit&&`, we require that the caller agrees to the transfer of ownership.

So far, for demonstration purposes, we have created all unit objects on the stack as local variables. In any non-trivial program, this is not going to work—we need these objects to stay around, long after the function that created them is done. We can integrate decorator objects and the memory ownership mechanism and ensure that the moved-from original units are deleted after a decorated version is created.

Let's say that ownership is managed throughout the program by unique pointers (each object has a clear owner at any given time). Here is how this can be accomplished. First of all, it is convenient to declare aliases for the pointers we need to use:

```
using Unit_ptr = std::unique_ptr<Unit>;
using Knight_ptr = std::unique_ptr<Knight>;
```

While any unit can be owned by the `Unit_ptr` pointer, we cannot call unit-specific member functions such as `charge()` through it, so we may need pointers to the concrete classes as well. As we will see next, we need to move the object between these pointers. Moving from a pointer to the derived class to the pointer to the base class is easy:

```
Knight_ptr k(new Knight(10, 5));
Unit_ptr u(std::move(k));          // Now k is null
```

Going in the other direction is a little harder; `std::move` will not work implicitly, just like we cannot convert from `Unit*` to `Knight*` without an explicit cast. We need a *moving cast*:

```
template <typename To, typename From>
std::unique_ptr<To> move_cast(std::unique_ptr<From>& p) {
    return std::unique_ptr<To>(static_cast<To*>(p.release()));
}
```

Here, we use `static_cast` to cast to the derived class, which works if the assumed relation (that the base object really is the expected derived object) is correct, otherwise the results are undefined. We can test this assumption at runtime, if we want to, using `dynamic_cast` instead. Here is a version that does the test, but only if asserts are enabled (we could throw an exception instead of the assert):

```
template <typename To, typename From>
std::unique_ptr<To> move_cast(std::unique_ptr<From>& p) {
#ifndef NDEBUG
    auto p1 = std::unique_ptr<To>(dynamic_cast<To*>(p.release()));
    assert(p1);
    return p1;
#else
    return std::unique_ptr<To>(static_cast<To*>(p.release()));
#endif
}
```

If all objects will be owned by instances of a unique pointer, then the `VeteranUnit` decorator has to accept a pointer in its constructor and move the object out of this pointer:

```
template <typename U> class VeteranUnit : public U {
    public:
    template <typename P>
    VeteranUnit(P&& p, double strength_bonus, double armor_bonus) :
        U(std::move(*move_cast<U>(p))),
        strength_bonus_(strength_bonus), armor_bonus_(armor_bonus) {}
    double attack() { return U::attack() + strength_bonus_; }
    double defense() { return U::defense() + armor_bonus_; }
    private:
    double strength_bonus_;
    double armor_bonus_;
};
```

The tricky part here is in the initialization of the base class U of `VeteranUnit<U>`—we have to move the unit from a unique pointer to the base class into a move-constructor of the derived class (there is no way to simply move the object from one unique pointer to another; we need to wrap it into the derived class). We have to do this without leaking any memory, too. The original, unique pointer, is released, so its destructor will do nothing, but our `move_cast` returns a new unique pointer that now owns the same object. This unique pointer is a temporary variable and will be deleted at the end of the initialization of the new object, but not before we use its object to construct a new derived object that is a `VeteranUnit` (the move-initialization of the unit object itself does not save any time versus copy in our case, but it is a good practice in the event a more heavyweight unit object provides an optimized move constructor).

Here is how this new decorator is used in a program that manages resources (units, in our case) by unique pointers:

```
Knight_ptr k(new Knight(10, 5));        // Knight_ptr so we can call charge()
Unit_ptr o(new Ogre(12, 2));            // Could be Orge_ptr if we needed one
Knight_ptr vk(new VeteranUnit<Knight>(k, 7, 2));
Unit_ptr vo(new VeteranUnit<Ogre>(o, 1, 9));
Unit_ptr vvo(new VeteranUnit<VeteranUnit<Ogre>>(vo, 1, 9));
vk->hit(*vvo);                          // Miss
vk->charge();                           // Works because vk is Knight_ptr
vk->hit(*vvo);                          // Hit
```

Note that we did not redefine the hit() function—it still accepts a unit object by reference. This is correct because this function does not take ownership of the object—it merely operates on it. There is no need to pass an owning pointer into it—that would suggest a transfer of ownership.

Note that, strictly speaking, there is very little difference between this example and the last one—the moved-from unit should not be accessed either way. Practically speaking, there is a significant difference—the moved-from pointer no longer owns the object. Its value is null, so any attempt to operate on the original unit after it was promoted will become evident in very short order (the program will dereference a null pointer and crash).

As we have seen, we can decorate an already decorated class, as the effects of the decorators stack up. Similarly, we can apply two different decorators to the same class. Each decorator adds a particular new behavior to the class. In our game engine, we can print the results of each attack, whether or not there was a hit. But if the result does not match the expectations, we don't know why. For debugging, it might be useful to print the attack and defense values. We would not want to do this all the time for all units, but for the part of the code we are interested in, we could use a debugging decorator that adds a new behavior to the units to print the intermediate results of the calculations.

The DebugDecorator uses the same design idea as the previous decorator—it's a class template that generates a class that's derived from the object to be decorated. Its attack() and defense() virtual functions forward the calls to the base class and print the results:

```
template <typename U> class DebugDecorator : public U {
    public:
    using U::U;
    template <typename P> DebugDecorator(P&& p) :
        U(std::move(*move_cast<U>(p))) {}
    double attack() {
        double res = U::attack();
        cout << "Attack: " << res << endl;
        return res;
    }
    double defense() {
        double res = U::defense();
        cout << "Defense: " << res << endl;
        return res;
    }
};
```

When implementing decorators, you should be careful to not inadvertently change the behavior of the base class in unexpected ways. For example, consider this possible implementation of `DebugDecorator`:

```
template <typename U> class DebugDecorator : public U {
    double attack() {
        cout << "Attack: " << U::attack() << endl;
        return U::attack();
    }
};
```

There is a subtle bug here—the decorated object, in addition to the expected new behavior—the printout—hides a change in the original behavior—it calls `attack()` twice on the base class. Not only might the printed value be incorrect if two calls to `attack()` return different values, but also any one-time attack bonuses such as the knight's charge will be canceled.

`DebugDecorator` adds very similar behavior to each member function it decorates. C++ has a rich set of tools that are aimed specifically at improving code reuse and reducing duplication. Let's see if we can do better and come up with a more reusable, universal decorator.

Polymorphic decorators and their limitations

Some decorators are very specific to the classes they modify, and their behavior is narrowly targeted. Others are very general, at least in principle. For example, a debugging decorator that logs function calls and prints return values could be used with any function if we could only implement it correctly.

Such an implementation is pretty straightforward in C++14 or above using `variadic` templates, parameter packs, and perfect forwarding:

```
template <typename Callable> class DebugDecorator {
    public:
    DebugDecorator(const Callable& c, const char* s) : c_(c), s_(s) {}
    template <typename ... Args> auto operator()(Args&& ... args) const {
        cout << "Invoking " << s_ << endl;
        auto res = c_(std::forward<Args>(args) ...);
        cout << "Result: " << res << endl;
        return res;
    }

    private:
    const Callable& c_;
```

```
        const std::string s_;
};
```

This decorator can be wrapped around any callable object or function (anything that can be called with the `()` syntax) with any number of arguments. It prints the custom string and the result of the call. However, writing out the callable type is often tricky—it is much better to get the compiler to do it for us using template argument deduction:

```
template <typename Callable>
auto decorate_debug(const Callable& c, const char* s) {
    return DebugDecorator<Callable>(c, s);
}
```

This template function deduces the type of the `Callable` and decorates it with the debugging wrapper. We can now apply it to any function or object. Here is a decorated function:

```
int g(int i, int j) { return i - j; }    // Some function
auto g1 = decorate_debug(g, "g()");       // Decorated function
g1(5, 2);       // Prints "Invoking g()" and "Result: 3"
```

We can also decorate a callable object:

```
struct S {
    double operator()() const {
        return double(rand() + 1)/double(rand() + 1);
    }
};
S s;                                      // Callable
auto s1 = decorate_debug(s, "rand/rand"); // Decorated callable
s1(); s1();                               // Prints the result, twice
```

Note that our decorator does not take ownership of the callable object (we could write it in such a way that it does so if we wanted to).

We can even decorate a lambda expression, which is really just an implicitly typed callable object. The one in this example defines a callable object with two integer arguments:

```
auto f2 = decorate_debug([](int i, int j) { return i + j; }, "i+j");
f2(5, 3);                    // Prints "Invoking i+j" and "Result: 8"
```

Our decorator has some limitations. First, it falls short when we try to decorate a function that does not return anything, such as the following lambda expression, which increments its argument but returns nothing:

```
auto incr = decorate_debug([](int& x) { ++x; }, "++x");
int i;
incr(i);    // Does not compile
```

The problem lies with the `void res` expression that is coming from the `auto res =` . . . line inside the `DebugDecorator`. This makes sense since we cannot declare variables of the `void` type. The second limitation is that the `auto` return type of our decorator is deduced only *mostly* accurately—for example, if a function returns `double&`, the decorated function will return just `double`. Lastly, wrapping member function calls is possible, but requires a somewhat different syntax.

Now, the template mechanism in C++ is powerful, and there are ways to make our generic decorator even more generic. These ways also make it more complex. Code like this belongs in a library, such as the standard library, but in most practical applications a debugging decorator is not worth such effort.

The other limitation is that the more generic a decorator becomes, the less it can do. As it is, there are very few actions we could take that make sense for calling any function or member function. We could add some debug printouts, and print the result as long as it has the stream output operator defined. We could lock a mutex to protect a non-thread-safe function call in a multi-threaded program. Maybe there are a few more general actions. But, in general, do not get seduced by the pursuit of the most generic code for its own sake.

Whether we have somewhat generic or very specific decorators, we often have the need to add multiple behaviors to an object. We have seen one such example already. Now, let's review the problem of applying multiple decorators more systematically.

Composable decorators

The decorator property that we would like to have here has a name—composability. Behaviors are composable if they can be applied to the same object separately: in our case, if we have two decorators, A and B. Therefore, A(B(object)) should have both behaviors applied. The alternative to composability is the explicit creation of the combined behaviors: to have both behaviors without composability, we would need to write a new decorator, AB. Since writing new code for any combination of several decorators would be impossible even for a relatively small number of decorators, composability is a very important property.

Fortunately, composability is not hard to achieve with our approach to decorators. The CRTP decorators we used in our game design earlier are naturally composable:

```
template <typename U> class VeteranUnit : public U { ... };
template <typename U> class DebugDecorator : public U { ... };
Unit_ptr o(new DebugDecorator<Ogre>(12, 2));
Unit_ptr vo(new DebugDecorator<VeteranUnit<Ogre>>(o, 1, 9));
```

Each decorator inherits from the object it decorates and, thus, preserves its interface, except for the added behavior. Note that the order of the decorators matters since the new behavior is added before or after the decorated call. The `DebugDecorator` applies to the object it decorates and provides debugging for it, so a `VeteranUnit<DebugDecorator<Ogre>>` object would debug the base portion of the object (`Ogre`), which can be useful as well.

Our (somewhat) universal decorators can be composed as well. We already have a debugging decorator that can work with many different callable objects, and we mentioned a possible need to protect these calls with a mutex. We can now implement such a locking decorator in a similar manner (and with similar limitations) to the polymorphic debugging decorator:

```
template <typename Callable> class LockDecorator {
    public:
    LockDecorator(const Callable& c, std::mutex& m) : c_(c), m_(m) {}
    template <typename ... Args> auto operator()(Args&& ... args) const {
        std::lock_guard<std::mutex> l(m_);
        return c_(std::forward<Args>(args) ...);
    }
    private:
    const Callable& c_;
    std::mutex& m_;
};

template <typename Callable>
auto decorate_lock(const Callable& c, std::mutex& m) {
    return LockDecorator<Callable>(c, m);
}
```

Again, we will use the `decorate_lock()` helper function to delegate to the compiler the tedious work of figuring out the right type of the callable object. We can now use a mutex to protect a function call that is not thread-safe:

```
std::mutex m;
auto safe_f = decorate_lock([](int x) { return unsafe_f(x); }, m);
```

If we want to protect a function by a mutex and have a debug printout when it's called, we do not need to write a new *locking debugging decorator*, but instead can apply both decorators in sequence:

```
auto safe_f = decorate_debug(
                decorate_lock(
                    [](int x) { return unsafe_f(x); },
                    m
                ),
                "f(x)");
```

This example demonstrates the benefits of composability—we do not have to write a special decorator for every combination of behaviors (think how many decorators you would have to write for any combination of five different primary decorators if they were not composable!).

This composability is achieved easily in our decorators because they preserve the interface of the original object, at least the part we are interested in—the behavior changes, but the interface does not. When a decorator is used as an original object for another decorator, the preserved interface is once again preserved, and so on.

This preservation of the interface is a fundamental feature of the Decorator pattern. It is also one of its most serious limitations. Our locking decorator is not nearly as useful as it may seem at first glance (so do not go around your code bolting a lock onto every call when you need to make the code thread-safe). As we will see next, not every interface can be made thread-safe, no matter how good the implementation is. That's when we have to change the interface in addition to modifying the behavior.

The Adapter pattern

We ended the last section with the notion that the decorator pattern has particular advantages that come from preserving the decorated interface, and that these advantages can sometimes turn into limitations. The Adapter pattern is a more general pattern that can be used in such cases.

The Adapter pattern is defined very generally—it is a structural pattern that allows an interface of a class to be used as another, different interface. It allows an existing class to be used in code that expects a different interface, without modifying the original class. Such adapters are sometimes called **class wrappers**, since they *wrap* around a class and present a different interface. You may recall that decorators are also sometimes called **class wrappers**, much for the same reason.

However, Adapter is a very general, broad pattern. It can be used to implement several other, more narrowly defined patterns—in particular, the decorator. The decorator pattern is easier to follow, so we dealt with that first. Now, we will move on to the general case.

Basic Adapter pattern

Let's follow on from the final example from the last section—the locking decorator. It calls any function under a lock, so no other function protected by the same mutex can be called on any other thread at the same time. In some cases, this could be enough to make the entire code thread-safe. Often, it is not.

To demonstrate this, we are going to implement a thread-safe queue object. A queue is a moderately complex data structure, even without thread safety, but, fortunately, we do not need to start from scratch—we have `std::queue` in the C++ standard library. We can push objects onto the queue and take them from the queue in first-in-first-out order, but only on one thread—it is not safe to push two objects onto the same queue from two different threads at the same time, for example. But we have a solution for that—we can implement a locking queue as a decorator for the basic one. Since we are not concerned about the empty base optimization here (`std::queue` is not an empty class) and we have to forward every member function call, we do not need the inheritance and can use composition instead. Our decorator will contain the queue and the lock. Wrapping the `push()` method is easy. There are two versions of `push()` in `std::queue`—one moves the object and one copies it. We should protect both with the lock:

```
template <typename T> class locking_queue {
    using mutex = std::mutex;
    using lock_guard = std::lock_guard<mutex>;
    using value_type = typename std::queue<T>::value_type;
    void push(const value_type& value) {
        lock_guard l(m_);
        q_.push(value);
    }
    void push(value_type&& value) {
        lock_guard l(m_);
        q_.push(value);
    }
    private:
    std::queue<T> q_;
    mutex m_;
};
```

Now, let's turn our attention to getting elements off the queue. The standard queue has three relevant member functions—first, there is `front()`, which lets us access the front element of the queue, but does not remove it from the queue. Then, there is `pop()`, which removes the front element but returns nothing (it gives no access to the front element—it just removes it). Both of these functions should not be called if the queue is empty—there is no error checking, but the result is undefined.

Finally, there is the third function, `empty()`; it returns false if the queue is not empty, and then we can call `front()` and `pop()`. If we decorate them with locking, we will be able to write code like the following:

```
locking_queue<int> q;
q.push(5);
... some time later in the program ...
if (!q.empty()) {
    int i = q.front();
    q.pop();
}
```

Each function is thread-safe by itself. The entire combination of them is not. It is important to understand why. First, we call `q.empty()`. Let's assume that it returns `false`, so we know there is at least one element on the queue. We go on to access it on the next line by calling `q.front()`, which returns 5. But this is just one of many threads in the program. Another thread is going through the same code at the same time (enabling this behavior is the point of the exercise). That thread, too, calls `q.empty()` and also gets `false`—as we just said, there is an element in the queue, and we have done nothing to remove it yet. The second thread also calls `q.front()` and gets 5 as well. That is already a problem—two threads each tried to take an element from the queue, but got the same one instead. But it gets worse—our first thread now calls `q.pop()` and removes 5 from the queue. The queue is now empty, but the second thread does not know about this—it called `q.empty()` earlier. Therefore, the second thread now calls `q.pop()` as well, this time on an empty queue. The best-case scenario here is that the program will crash right away.

We have just seen a specific case of a general problem—a sequence of actions, each of which is thread-safe, but is not thread-safe as a whole. In fact, this *locking queue* is entirely useless, and there is no way to write thread-safe code with it. What we need is a single thread-safe function that performs the entire transaction under one lock, as a single uninterruptible action (such transactions are called **atomic**). The transaction, in our case, is the removal of the front element if it's present, and some kind of error diagnostic if it's not. The `std::queue` interface does not provide such a transactional API.

So, now, we need a new pattern—one that transforms the existing interface of a class to our needs for a different interface. This cannot be done with the decorator pattern, but this is exactly the problem that the Adapter pattern solves. Now that we have agreed that we need a different interface, we just have to decide what it should be. Our single new `pop()` member function should do all of this—if the queue is not empty, it should remove the first element from the queue and return it, by copy or move, to the caller. If the queue is empty, it should not alter the state of the queue at all, but should somehow notify the caller that the queue was empty. One way to do this is to return two values—the element itself (if there is one) and a Boolean value that tells us whether the queue was empty or not. Here is the `pop()` part of the locking queue, which is now an adapter, not a decorator:

```
template <typename T> class locking_queue {
    ... the push() is unchanged ...
    bool pop(value_type& value) {
        lock_guard l(m_);
        if (q_.empty()) return false;
        value = std::move(q_.front());
        q_.pop();
        return true;
    }
    private:
    std::queue<T> q_;
    mutex m_;
};
```

Note that we do not need to change `push()`—the single function call already does everything we need, so that part of the interface is just forwarded one-to-one by our adapter. This version of `pop()` returns `true` if it removed an element from the queue, and `false` otherwise. If `true` is returned, the element is saved into the provided argument, but if `false` is returned, the argument is unchanged. If the element type `T` is move-assignable, a move will be used instead of copy.

This is, of course, not the only possible interface for such an atomic `pop()`. Another way would be to return both the element and the Boolean value as a pair. One significant difference is that there is now no way to leave the element unchanged—it's the return value and it always has to be something. The natural way is to default-construct the element if there isn't one on the queue:

```
template <typename T> class locking_queue {
    ... the push() is unchanged ...
    std::pair<value_type, bool> pop() {
        lock_guard l(m_);
        if (q_.empty()) return { value_type(), false };
        value_type value = std::move(q_.front());
```

```
        q_.pop();
        return { value, true };
    }
    private:
    std::queue<T> q_;
    mutex m_;
};
```

There is now a restriction on the element type `T`—it has to be default-constructible. Depending on the application code that needs this queue, one of the interfaces may be preferable, and so there are other ways to design it as well. In all cases, we end up with two member functions, `push()` and `pop()`, that are protected by the same mutex. Now, any number of threads can execute any combination of these operations at the same time, and the behavior is well-defined. This means that the `locking_queue` object is thread-safe.

Converting an object from its current interface to the interface needed by a particular application, without rewriting the object itself, is the purpose and use of the Adapter pattern. All kinds of interface may have to be converted, and so there are many different types of adapter. We will learn about some of them in the next section.

Function adapters

We have just seen a class adapter that changes the interface of a class. Another kind of interface is a function (a member or a non-member function). A function has certain arguments, but we may want to call it with a different set of arguments. This would need an adapter. One common application of such adapters is known as currying one (or more) of the function's arguments. All it means is that we have a function of several arguments, and we fix the value of one of these arguments, so we don't have to specify it on every call. One example would be if we have `f(int i, int j)`, but we want `g(i)`, which is the same as `f(i, 5)`, only without typing the `5` every time.

Here is a more interesting example that we are actually going to work our way through and implement an adapter. The `std::sort` function takes an iterator range (the sequence to sort), but it can also be called with three arguments—the third one is the comparison object (by default, `std::less` is used, which, in turn, calls `operator<()` on the objects being sorted).

We want something else now—we want to compare floating-point numbers *fuzzily*, with tolerance—if the two numbers x and y are close enough to each other, then we don't consider one to be less than the other. Only when x is much less than y do we want to enforce the sorted order where x comes before y.

Here is our comparison functor (a callable object):

```
struct much_less {
    template <typename T>
    bool operator()(T x, T y) {
        return x < y &&
            std::abs(x - y) > tolerance*std::max(std::abs(x), std::abs(y));
    }
    static constexpr double tolerance = 0.2;
};
```

This comparison object can be used with a standard sort:

```
std::vector<double> v;
std::sort(v.begin(), v.end(), much_less());
```

However, if we need this kind of sort often, we may want to curry the last argument and make ourselves an adapter that has just two arguments, the iterators, and the sorting function implied. Here is such an adapter—it is very simple:

```
template<typename RandomIt>
void sort_much_less(RandomIt first, RandomIt last) {
 std::sort(first, last, much_less());
 }
```

Now, we can call a sort function with two arguments:

```
std::vector<double> v;
sort_much_less(v.begin(), v.end());
```

Now, if we often call sort in this manner to sort the entire container, we may want to change the interface once again and make another adapter:

```
template<typename Container> void sort_much_less(Container& c) {
    std::sort(c.begin(), c.end(), much_less());
}
```

Now, the code in our program looks even simpler:

```
std::vector<double> v;
sort_much_less(v);
```

It is important to point out that C++14 provides an alternative for writing such simple adapters that should, in general, be preferred; we can use a lambda expression, as follows:

```
auto sort_much_less = [](auto first, auto last) {
    return std::sort(first, last, much_less());
};
```

The container adapter is just as easy to write:

```
auto sort_much_less = [](auto& container) {
    return std::sort(container.begin(), container.end(), much_less());
};
```

Note that you cannot have both of these in the same program under the same name—lambda expressions cannot be *overloaded* in this manner; they are actually not functions at all, but rather objects.

Coming back to the matter of calling a function with some arguments fixed, or bound, to constant values, we should say add this is such a common need that the C++ standard library provides a standard customizable adapter for this purpose, std::bind. Here is an example that shows us how it is used:

```
using namespace std::placeholders; // For _1, _2 etc
int f3(int i, int j, int k) { return i + j + k; }
auto f2 = std::bind(f3, _1, _2, 42);
auto f1 = std::bind(f3, 5, _1, 7);
f2(2, 6);                        // Returns 50
f1(3);                           // Returns 15
```

This standard adapter has its own *mini-language*—the first argument to std::bind is the function to be bound, while the rest are its arguments, in order. The arguments that should be bound are replaced by the specified values. The arguments that should remain free are replaced by the placeholders _1, _2, and so on (not necessarily in that order; that is, we can also change the order of the arguments). The returned value is of an unspecified type and has to be captured using auto.

As useful as std::bind is, it does not free us from the need to learn how to write our own function adapters—its greatest limitation is that std::bind cannot bind template functions. We cannot write the following:

```
auto sort_much_less = std::bind(std::sort, _1, _2, much_less()); // No!
```

This does not compile. Inside a template, we can bind the specific instantiation of it, but, at least in our sorting example, this really does not buy us anything:

```
template<typename RandomIt> void sort_much_less(RandomIt first,
                                                RandomIt last) {
    auto f = std::bind(std::sort<RandomIt, much_less>, _1, _2,
                   much_less());
    f(first, last, much_less());
}
```

So far, we have considered only adapters that convert runtime interfaces, which are the interfaces we call when the program is executed. However, C++ has compile-time interfaces as well—one of the prime examples that we considered in the last chapter was policy-based design. These interfaces are not always exactly what we need them to be, so we have to learn to write compile-time adapters next.

Compile-time adapters

In `Chapter 16`, *Policy-Based Design*, we learned about policies, which are building blocks for classes—they let the programmer customize the implementation for a particular behavior. As an example, we can implement this policy-based smart pointer that automatically deletes the object it owns. The policy is the particular implementation of the deletion:

```
template <typename T,
          template <typename> class DeletionPolicy = DeleteByOperator>
class SmartPtr {
    public:
    explicit SmartPtr(
        T* p = nullptr,
        const DeletionPolicy<T>& deletion_policy = DeletionPolicy<T>()
        ) : p_(p),
            deletion_policy_(deletion_policy)
    {}
    ~SmartPtr() {
        deletion_policy_(p_);
    }
    ... pointer interface ...
    private:
    T* p_;
    DeletionPolicy<T> deletion_policy_;
};
```

Note that the deletion policy is itself a template—this is a *template* parameter. The default deletion policy is to use `operator delete`:

```
template <typename T>
struct DeleteByOperator {
    void operator()(T* p) const {
        delete p;
    }
};
```

However, for objects allocated on a user-given heap, we need a different deletion policy that returns the memory to that heap:

```
template <typename T>
struct DeleteHeap {
    explicit DeleteHeap(MyHeap& heap)
        : heap_(heap) {}
    void operator()(T* p) const {
        p->~T();
        heap_.deallocate(p);
    }
    private:
    MyHeap& heap_;
};
SmartPtr<int, DeleteHeap<int>> p; // This pointer uses DeleteHeap policy
```

This policy is not very flexible, however—it can handle heaps of only one type—MyHeap. We can make the policy more general if we make the heap type the second template parameter. As long as the heap has the `deallocate()` member function to return memory to it, we can use any heap class with this policy:

```
template <typename T, typename Heap>
struct DeleteHeap {
    explicit DeleteHeap(Heap& heap)
        : heap_(heap) {}
    void operator()(T* p) const {
        p->~T();
        heap_.deallocate(p);
    }
    private:
    Heap& heap_;
};
```

Of course, if we have a heap class that uses another name for this member function, we can use a class adapter to make that class work with our policy, too. But we have a larger problem—our policy does not work with our smart pointer. The following code does not compile:

```
SmartPtr<int, DeletelHeap> p;    // Does not compile
```

The reason is again the interface mismatch, only now it is a different kind of interface—the `template <typename T,`
`template <typename> class DeletionPolicy> class SmartPtr {};` template expects the second argument to be a template with one type parameter. Instead, we have the `DeleteHeap` template with two type parameters. This is just like trying to call a function that has one parameter but uses two arguments—it won't work. We need an adapter to convert our two-parameter template into a one-parameter one, and we have to fix the second argument to a particular heap type (but we do not need to rewrite the policy if we have multiple heap types, we just need to write several adapters). We can create this adapter, `DeleteMyHeap,` using a template alias:

```
template <typename T> using DeleteMyHeap = DeleteHeap<T, MyHeap>;
```

We could also use inheritance and forward the constructors of the base class to the derived adapter class:

```
template <typename T>
struct DeleteMyHeap : public DeleteHeap<T, MyHeap> {
    using DeleteHeap<T, MyHeap>::DeleteHeap;
};
```

This second version is, obviously, much longer. However, we have to learn both ways of writing template adapters because the template alias has one major limitation. To illustrate it, let's consider another example where an adapter is needed. We will begin by implementing a stream insertion operator for any STL-compliant sequence container whose elements have such an operator defined. It is a simple function template:

```
template <template <typename> class Container, typename T>
std::ostream& operator<<(std::ostream& out, const Container<T>& c) {
    bool first = true;
    for (auto x : c) {
        if (!first) out << ", ";
        first = false;
        out << x;
    }
    return out;
}
```

This `template` function has two type parameters, the container type and the element type. The container is itself a template with one type parameter. The compiler deduces both the container type and the element type from the second function argument (the first argument in any `operator<<()` is always the stream). We can test our insertion operator on a simple container:

```
template <typename T> class Buffer {
    public:
    explicit Buffer(size_t N) : N_(N), buffer_(new T[N_]) {}
    ~Buffer() { delete [] buffer_; }
    T* begin() const { return buffer_; }
    T* end() const { return buffer_ + N_; }
    ...
    private:
    const size_t N_;
    T* const buffer_;
};
Buffer<int> buffer(10);
... fill the buffer ...
cout << buffer;    // Prints all elements of the buffer
```

But this is just a toy container, and is not very useful. What we really want is to print elements of a real container, such as `std::vector`:

```
std::vector<int> v;
... add some values to v ...
cout << v;
```

Unfortunately, this code does not compile. The reason is that `std::vector` is not really a template with one type parameter, even though we used it as such. It has two parameters—the second is the allocator type. There is a default for this allocator, which is why we can write `std::vector<int>` and it compiles. But, even with this default argument, this is still a template with two parameters, while our stream insertion operator is declared to accept container templates with only one parameter. Again, we can solve the problem by writing an adapter (most STL containers are used with the default allocator anyway). The easiest way to write this adapter is with an alias:

```
template <typename T> using vector1 = std::vector<T>;
vector1<int> v;
...
cout << v;    // Does not compile either
```

Unfortunately, this does not compile either, and now we can show the template alias limitation that we alluded to earlier—template aliases are not used in template argument type deduction. When the compiler attempts to figure out the template argument types for the call of `operator<<()` with the arguments `cout` and `v`, the template alias `vector1` is *invisible*. In this case, we have to use a derived class adapter:

```
template <typename T> struct vector1 : public std::vector<T> {
    using std::vector<T>::vector;
};
vector1<int> v;
...
cout << v;
```

We have now seen how we can implement decorators to augment class and function interfaces with the desired behavior, and how to create adapters when the existing interface is not suitable for a particular application. Decorator, and, even more so, Adapter, are very general and versatile patterns that can be used to solve many problems. It should come as no surprise that, often, a problem can be solved in more than one way, so there is a choice of patterns to use. In the next section, we will see one such case.

Adapter versus policy

The adapter and the policy (or strategy) patterns are some of the more general patterns, and C++ adds generic programming capabilities to these patterns. This tends to extend their usability and sometimes blurs the lines between the patterns. The patterns themselves are defined very distinctly—policies provide custom implementations while adapters change the interface and add functionality to the existing interface (the latter is a decorator aspect, but, as we have seen, most decorators are implemented as adapters). We also saw in the last chapter than C++ broadens the capabilities of policy-based design; in particular, policies in C++ can add or remove parts of the interface as well as control the implementation. So, while patterns are different, there is significant overlap in the types of problem they can be used for. In the last chapter, we saw an example of a policy-based restricted value type: a type that is, at least conceptually, a number *like an int*, but has an interface we can define piece by piece—comparable, ordered, addable, but no multiplication or division, for example. Now that we have learned about adapters, it is tempting to apply them to the same problem—we will start with a basic value type that supports almost nothing in its interface, and then we can add the desired capabilities, one by one.

Here is our initial `Value` class template:

```
template <typename T> class Value {
    public:
    typedef T basic_type;
    typedef Value value_type;
    explicit Value() : val_(T()) {}
    explicit Value(T v) : val_(v) {}
    Value(const Value& rhs) : val_(rhs.val_) {}
    Value& operator=(Value rhs) { val_ = rhs.val_; return *this; }
    Value& operator=(basic_type rhs) { val_ = rhs; return *this; }
    friend std::ostream& operator<<(std::ostream& out, Value x) {
        out << x.val_; return out;
    }
    friend std::istream& operator>>(std::istream& in, Value& x) {
        in >> x.val_; return in;
    }

    protected:
    T val_;
};
```

It is copyable, assignable, and printable (we could have moved some of those capabilities into adapters as well). There is nothing else we can do with this class—no comparisons for equality or inequality, no arithmetic operations. However, we can create an adapter that adds the comparison interface:

```
template <typename V> class Comparable : public V {
    public:
    using V::V;
    typedef typename V::value_type value_type;
    typedef typename value_type::basic_type basic_type;
    Comparable(value_type v) : V(v) {}
    friend bool operator==(Comparable lhs, Comparable rhs) {
        return lhs.val_ == rhs.val_;
    }
    friend bool operator!=(Comparable lhs, Comparable rhs) {
        return lhs.val_ != rhs.val_;
    }
    friend bool operator==(Comparable lhs, basic_type rhs) {
        return lhs.val_ == rhs;
    }
    friend bool operator==(basic_type lhs, Comparable rhs) {
        return lhs == rhs.val_;
    }
    friend bool operator!=(Comparable lhs, basic_type rhs) {
        return lhs.val_ != rhs;
    }
```

```
        friend bool operator!=(basic_type lhs, Comparable rhs) {
            return lhs != rhs.val_;
        }
    };
```

This is a class adapter—it is derived from the class it is augmenting with new capabilities, so it inherits all of its interface and adds some more—the complete set of comparison operators. We are familiar with the way these adapters are used:

```
using V = Comparable<Value<int>>;
V i(3), j(5);
i == j;    // False
i == 3;    // True
5 == j;    // Also true
```

That is one capability. What about some more? No problem—the `Ordered` adapter can be written very similarly, only it provides the operators `<`, `<=`, `>`, and `>=`:

```
template <typename V> class Ordered : public V {
    public:
    using V::V;
    typedef typename V::value_type value_type;
    typedef typename value_type::basic_type basic_type;
    Ordered(value_type v) : V(v) {}
    friend bool operator<(Ordered lhs, Ordered rhs) {
        return lhs.val_ < rhs.val_;
    }
    friend bool operator<(basic_type lhs, Ordered rhs) {
        return lhs < rhs.val_;
    }
    friend bool operator<(Ordered lhs, basic_type rhs) {
        return lhs.val_ < rhs;
    }
    ... same for the other operators ...
};
```

We can combine the two adapters—as we say, they are composable, and they work in any order:

```
using V = Ordered<Comparable<Value<int>>>;  // Or Comparable<Ordered<...>
V i(3), j(5);
i == j;    // False
i <= 3;    // True
```

It is no more difficult to implement adapters for addition or multiplication:

```
template <typename V> class Addable : public V {
    public:
    using V::V;
    typedef typename V::value_type value_type;
    typedef typename value_type::basic_type basic_type;
    Addable(value_type v) : V(v) {}
    friend Addable operator+(Addable lhs, Addable rhs) {
        return Addable(lhs.val_ + rhs.val_);
    }
    friend Addable operator+(Addable lhs, basic_type rhs) {
        return Addable(lhs.val_ + rhs);
    }
    friend Addable operator+(basic_type lhs, Addable rhs) {
        return Addable(lhs + rhs.val_);
    }
    ... same for - ...
};

template <typename V> class Multipliable : public V {
    public:
    using V::V;
    typedef typename V::value_type value_type;
    typedef typename value_type::basic_type basic_type;
    Multipliable(value_type v) : V(v) {}
    friend Multipliable operator*(Multipliable lhs, Multipliable rhs) {
        return Multipliable(lhs.val_ * rhs.val_);
    }
    ... same for other variants of * and / ...
};
```

Now, we have finally reached the limit of what can be done, at least easily, with the Adapter pattern:

```
using V = Multipliable<Addable<Value<int>>>;
V i(5), j(3), k(7);
i + j;                  // OK
i * j;                  // OK
(i + j) * (k + 3);      // Not OK
```

The problem here is that the i + j expression uses the operator + that comes from the Addable adapter, and this operator returns an object of type Addable<Value<int>>. The multiplication operator expects the Multipliable<Addable<Value<int>>> type, and will not accept the *partial* type (there is no implicit conversion from a base class to the derived one). We could solve this problem by reversing the order of Multipliable and Addable, but then the expression (i * j) + (i / k) would break, for a similar reason.

This is the limitation of composable adapters—they work great until the interface they add has to return an adapted type. We had no problems with comparison operators returning bool, but once we have to return the adapted type itself, the composability breaks down. There are some workarounds to that problem, but they are very complex and have side-effects. Once we reach this point, the policy-based solution from Chapter 16, *Policy-Based Design*, looks so much simpler:

```
template <typename T, template <typename, typename> class ... Policies>
class Value : public Policies<T, Value<T, Policies ... >> ...
{ ..... };
using V = Value<int, Addable, Multipliable, Ordered>; // Works in any order
```

Now, as we discussed at the end of Chapter 16, *Policy-Based Design*, that solution has its own drawbacks. Such is the nature of the problems we have to solve as software engineers—once a problem becomes complex enough, it can be solved, frequently using more than one design, and each approach has its own advantages and limitations. There is no way we can compare every two patterns that can be used to create two very different designs that address the same need, at least not in a book of any finite size. By presenting and analyzing these examples, we hope to equip the reader with the understanding and the insight that will be helpful in evaluating similarly complex and varied design options for real-life problems.

Summary

We have studied two of the most commonly used patterns—not just in C++, but in software design in general. The Adapter pattern offers an approach to solving a wide class of design challenges. These challenges have only the most general property in common—given a class, a function, or a software component that provides certain functionality, we must solve a particular problem, and build a solution for a different, related problem. The decorator pattern is, in many ways, a subset of the Adapter pattern, which is restricted to augmenting the existing interface of the class of a function with new behavior.

We have seen that the interface conversion and modification done by the adapters and decorators can be applied to interfaces at every stage of the program's life—while the most common use is to modify runtime interfaces so that a class can be used in a different context, there are also compile-time adapters for generic code that allow us to use a class as a building block or a component of a larger, more complex, class.

The Adapter pattern can be applied to many very different design challenges. The varied nature of these challenges and the generality of the pattern itself often mean that an alternative solution is possible. Such alternatives often use a completely different approach—an entirely different design pattern—but end up providing similar behavior. The difference lies in trade-offs, additional conditions, and limitations imposed by the chosen approach to the design, and the possibilities of extending the solution in different ways. To this end, this and the previous chapters offer a comparison of two very different design approaches to the same problem, complete with an evaluation of the strengths and drawbacks of both options.

The next and final chapter introduces a pattern that is large, complex and has several interacting components—an appropriate pattern to be left for our grand finale—the Visitor pattern.

Questions

1. What is the Adapter pattern?
2. What is the decorator pattern and how does it differ from the Adapter pattern?
3. The classic OOP implementation of the decorator pattern is usually not recommended in C++. Why not?
4. When should the C++ class decorator use inheritance or composition?
5. When should the C++ class adapter use inheritance or composition?
6. C++ provides a general function adapter for currying function arguments, `std::bind`. What are its limitations?
7. C++11 provides template aliases that can be used as adapters. What are their limitations?
8. Both the adapter and policy patterns can be used to add or modify the public interface of a class. Give are some reasons for preferring one over the other.

18
The Visitor Pattern and Multiple Dispatch

The Visitor pattern is another classic object-oriented design pattern, one of the 23 patterns introduced in the book *Design Patterns – Elements of Reusable Object-Oriented Software*, by Erich Gamma, Richard Helm, Ralph Johnson, and John Vlissides. It was one of the more popular patterns during the golden age of object-oriented programming since it can be used to make large class hierarchies more maintainable. In recent years, the use of Visitor in C++ declined, as large complex hierarchies became less common, and the Visitor pattern is a fairly complex pattern to implement. Generic programming—in particular, the new language features added in C++11 and C++14—makes it easier to implement and maintain the Visitor classes, while the new applications of the old pattern have served to rekindle some of the fading interest in it.

The following topics will be covered in this chapter:

- The Visitor pattern
- Implementations of Visitor in C++
- The use of generic programming to simplify the Visitor classes
- The use of Visitor for composite objects
- Compile-time Visitor and reflection

Technical requirements

The example code for this chapter can be found at the following GitHub link: `https://github.com/PacktPublishing/Hands-On-Design-Patterns-with-CPP/tree/master/Chapter18`.

The Visitor pattern

The Visitor pattern stands out from the other classic object-oriented patterns due to its complexity. On the one hand, the basic structure of the Visitor pattern is quite complex and involves many coordinated classes that must work together to form the pattern. On the other hand, even the description of the Visitor pattern is complex—there are several very different ways to describe the same pattern. Many patterns can be applied to multiple kinds of problems, but the Visitor pattern goes beyond that—there are several ways to describe what it does that use completely different languages, talk about seemingly unrelated problems, and overall have nothing in common. However, they all describe the same pattern. Let's start by examining the many faces of the Visitor pattern, and then move on to the implementation.

What is the Visitor pattern?

The Visitor pattern is a pattern that separates the algorithm from the object structure, which is the data for this algorithm. Using the Visitor pattern, we can add a new operation to the class hierarchy without modifying the classes themselves. The use of the Visitor pattern follows the **open/closed principle** of the software design—a class (or another unit of code, such as a module) should be closed for modifications; once the class presents an interface to its clients, the clients come to depend on this interface and the functionality it provides. This interface should remain stable; it should not be necessary to modify the classes in order to maintain the software and continue its development. At the same time, a class should be open for extensions—new functionality can be added to satisfy new requirements. As with all very general principles, a counter-example can be found where the rigorous application of the rule is worse than breaking it. Again, as with all general principles, its value lies not in being an absolute rule for every case, but rather a *default* rule, a guideline that should be followed in the absence of a good reason not to; the reality is that the majority of everyday work is *not special* and the result is better if this principle is followed.

When viewed this way, the Visitor pattern allows us to add functionality to a class or the entire class hierarchy without having to modify the class. This feature can be particularly useful when dealing with public APIs—the users of the API can extend it with additional operations without having to modify the source code.

A very different, more technical way to describe the Visitor pattern is to say that it implements **double dispatch**. This requires some explanation. Let's start with the regular virtual function calls:

```
class Base {
    virtual void f() = 0;
};
class Derived1 : public Base {
    void f() override;
};
class Derived2 : public Base {
    void f() override;
};
```

If we invoke the b->f() virtual function through a pointer to the b base class, the call is dispatched to Derived1::f() or Derived2::f(), depending on the real type of the object. This is the **single dispatch**—the function that is actually called is determined by a single factor, the type of the object.

Now let's assume that the f() function also takes an argument, and it is also a pointer to a base class:

```
class Base {
    virtual void f(Base* p) = 0;
};
class Derived1 : public Base {
    void f(Base* p) override;
};
class Derived2 : public Base {
    void f(Base* p) override;
};
```

The actual type of the *p object is also one of the derived classes. Now, the b->f(p) call can have four different versions; both the *b and *p object can be of either of the two derived types. It is reasonable to want the implementation to do something different in each of these cases. This would be double dispatch—the code that runs, in the end, is determined by two separate factors. Virtual functions do not provide a way to implement double dispatch directly, but the Visitor pattern does exactly that.

When presented this way, it is not obvious that the **double-dispatch** Visitor pattern has anything to do with the **operation-adding** Visitor pattern. However, they are exactly the same pattern, and the two requirements are really one and the same. Here is a way to look at it that might help—if we want to add an operation to all classes in a hierarchy, that is equivalent to adding a virtual function, so we have one factor controlling the final disposition of each call, the object type. But, if we can effectively add virtual functions, we can add more than one—one for each operation we need to support. The type of the operation is the second factor controlling the dispatch, similar to the argument to the function in our previous example. Thus, the operation-adding visitor is able to provide double dispatch. Alternatively, if we had a way to implement double dispatch, we could do what the Visitor pattern does—effectively add a virtual function for each operation we want to support.

Now that we know what the Visitor pattern does, it is reasonable to ask, *why* would we want to do it? *What* is the use of double dispatch?, and why would we want *another way* to add a virtual function substitute to a class when we can just add a *genuine* virtual function? Setting aside the case of the public API with unavailable source code, why would we want to add an operation *externally* instead of implementing it in every class? Consider the example of the serialization/deserialization problem. Serialization is an operation that converts an object into a format that can be stored or transmitted (for example, written into a file). Deserialization is the inverse operation—it constructs a new object from its serialized and stored image. To support serialization and deserialization in the straightforward, object-oriented way, each class in the hierarchy would need two methods, one for each operation. But what if there is more than one way to store an object? For example, we may need to write an object into a memory buffer, to be transmitted across the network and deserialized on another machine. Alternatively, we may need to save the object to disk, or else we may need to convert all objects in a container to a markup format such as JSON. The straightforward approach would have us add a serialization and a deserialization method to every object for every serialization mechanism. If a new and different serialization approach is needed, we have to go over the entire class hierarchy and add support for it.

An alternative is to implement the entire serialization/deserialization operation in a separate function that can handle all classes. The resulting code is a loop that iterates over all objects, with the large decision tree inside of it. The code must interrogate every object and determine its type, for example, using dynamic casts. When a new class is added to the hierarchy, all serialization and deserialization implementations must be updated to handle the new objects.

Both implementations are difficult to maintain for large hierarchies. The Visitor pattern offers a solution—it allows us to implement a new operation—in our case, the serialization—outside of the classes and without modifying them, but also without the downside of a huge decision tree in a loop. (note that the Visitor pattern is not the only solution to the serialization problem; C++ offers other possible approaches as well, but we focus on the Visitor pattern in this chapter).

As we stated at the beginning, Visitor pattern is a complex pattern with a complex

description. We can best handle this difficult pattern by studying concrete examples, starting from the very simple ones in the next section.

Basic Visitor in C++

The only way to really understand how the Visitor pattern operates is to work through an example. Let's start with a very simple one. First, we need a class hierarchy:

```
class Pet {
    public:
    virtual ~Pet() {}
    Pet(const std::string& color) : color_(color) {}
    const std::string& color() const { return color_; }
    private:
    std::string color_;
};

class Cat : public Pet {
    public:
    Cat(const std::string& color) : Pet(color) {}
};

class Dog : public Pet {
    public:
    Dog(const std::string& color) : Pet(color) {}
};
```

In this hierarchy, we have the `Pet` base class and several derived classes for different pet animals. Now we want to add some operations to our classes, such as *feed the pet* or *play with the pet*. The implementation depends on the type of the pet, so these would have to be virtual functions if added directly to each class. This is not a problem for such simple class hierarchy, but we are anticipating the future need for maintaining a much larger system in which modifying every class in the hierarchy is going to be expensive and time consuming. We need a better way, and we begin by creating a new class, `PetVisitor`, which will be applied to every `Pet` object (visit it) and perform the operations we need. First, we need to declare the class:

```
class Cat;
class Dog;
class PetVisitor {
    public:
    virtual void visit(Cat* c) = 0;
    virtual void visit(Dog* d) = 0;
};
```

We had to forward-declare the `Pet` hierarchy classes because `PetVisitor` has to be declared before the concrete `Pet` classes. Now we need to make the `Pet` hierarchy visitable, which means we do need to modify it, but only once, regardless of how many operations we want to add later. We need to add a virtual function to accept the Visitor pattern to every class that can be visited:

```
class Pet {
    public:
    virtual void accept(PetVisitor& v) = 0;
    .....
};

class Cat : public Pet {
    public:
    void accept(PetVisitor& v) override { v.visit(this); }
    .....
};

class Dog : public Pet {
    public:
    void accept(PetVisitor& v) override { v.visit(this); }
    .....
};
```

Now our `Pet` hierarchy is visitable, and we have an abstract `PetVisitor` class. Everything is ready to implement new operations for our classes. (note that nothing we have done so far depends on what operations we are going to add; we have created the visiting infrastructure that has to be implemented once). The operations are added by implementing concrete Visitor classes derived from `PetVisitor`:

```
class FeedingVisitor : public PetVisitor {
    public:
    void visit(Cat* c) override {
        std::cout << "Feed tuna to the " << c->color() << " cat"
                << std::endl;
    }
    void visit(Dog* d) override {
        std::cout << "Feed steak to the " << d->color() << " dog"
                << std::endl;
    }
};

class PlayingVisitor : public PetVisitor {
    public:
    void visit(Cat* c) override {
        std::cout << "Play with feather with the " << c->color() << " cat"
                << std::endl;
    }
    void visit(Dog* d) override {
        std::cout << "Play fetch with the " << d->color() << " dog"
                << std::endl;
    }
};
```

Assuming the visitation infrastructure is already built into our class hierarchy, we can implement a new operation by implementing a derived Visitor class, and all its virtual functions overrides for `visit()`. To invoke one of the new operations on an object from our class hierarchy, we need to create a visitor and visit the object:

```
Cat c("orange");
FeedingVisitor fv;
c.accept(fv);    // Feed tuna to the orange cat
```

The latest example of the call is too simple in one important way—at the point of calling the visitor, we know the exact type of the object we are visiting. To make the example more realistic, we have to visit an object polymorphically:

```
std::unique_ptr<Pet> p(new Cat("orange"));
.....
FeedingVisitor fv;
p->accept(fv);
```

Here we do not know at compile time the actual type of the object pointed to by p; at the point where the visitor is accepted, p could have come from different sources. While less common, the visitor can also be used polymorphically:

```
std::unique_ptr<Pet> p(new Cat("orange"));
.....
std::unique_ptr<PetVisitor> v(new FeedingVisitor);
.....
p->accept(*v);
```

When written this way, the code highlights the double-dispatch aspect of the Visitor pattern—the call to accept() ends up dispatched to a particular visit() function based on two factors—the type of the visitable *p object and the type of the *v visitor. If we wish to stress this aspect of the Visitor pattern, we can invoke the visitors using a helper function:

```
void dispatch(Pet* p, PetVisitor* v) { p->accept(*v); }
Pet* p = .....;
PetVisitor* v = .....;
dispatch(p, v);      // Double dispatch
```

We now have the most bare-bones example of the classic object-oriented visitor in C++. Despite its simplicity, it has all the necessary components; an implementation for a large real-life class hierarchy and multiple visitor operations has a lot more code, but no new kinds of code, just more of the things we have already done. This example shows both aspects of the Visitor pattern; on the one hand, if we focus on the functionality of the software, with the visitation infrastructure now in place, we can add new operations without any changes to the classes themselves. On the other hand, if we look just at the way the operation is invoked, the accept() call, we have implemented double dispatch.

We can immediately see the appeal of the Visitor pattern, we can add any number of new operations without having to modify every class in the hierarchy. If a new class is added to the Pet hierarchy, it is impossible to forget to handle it—if we do nothing at all to the visitor, the accept() call on the new class will not compile since there is no corresponding visit() function to call. Once we add the new visit() overload to the PetVisitor base class, we have to add it to all derived classes as well; otherwise, the compiler will let us know that we have a pure virtual function without an override. The latter is also one of the main disadvantages of the Visitor pattern—if a new class is added to the hierarchy, all visitors must be updated, whether the new classes actually need to support these operations or not. For this reason, it is sometimes recommended to use the visitor only on *relatively stable* hierarchies that do not have new classes added often. There is also an alternative visitor implementation that somewhat mitigates this problem; we will see it later in this chapter.

The example in this section is very simple—our new operations take no arguments and return no results. We will now consider whether these limitations are significant, and how they can be removed.

Visitor generalizations and limitations

Our very first visitor, in the previous section, allowed us to effectively add a virtual function to every class in the hierarchy. That virtual function had no parameters and no return value. The former is easy to extend; there is no reason at all why our `visit()` functions cannot have parameters. Let's expand our class hierarchy by allowing our pets to have kittens and puppies. This extension cannot be done using only the Visitor pattern—we don't just need to add new operations, but also new data members to our classes. The Visitor pattern can be used for the former, but the latter requires code changes. A policy-based design could have let us factor this change out into a new implementation of an existing policy if we had the foresight to provide the appropriate policy. We do have a separate chapter on Chapter 16, *Policy-Based Design* in this book, so here we will avoid mixing several patterns together and just add the new data members:

```
class Pet {
    public:
    . . . .
    void add_child(Pet* p) { children_.push_back(p); }
    virtual void accept(PetVisitor& v, Pet* p = nullptr) = 0;
    private:
    std::vector<Pet*> children_;
};
```

Each parent `Pet` object tracks its child objects (note that the container is a vector of pointers, not a vector of unique pointers, so the object does not own its children, but merely has access to them). We have also added the new `add_child()` member function to add objects to the vector. We could have done this with a visitor, but this function is non-virtual, so we have to add it only once to the base class, not to every derived class—the visitor is unnecessary here. The `accept()` function has been modified to have an additional parameter that would have to be added to all derived classes as well, where it is simply forwarded to the `visit()` function:

```
class Cat : public Pet {
    public:
    Cat(const std::string& color) : Pet(color) {}
    void accept(PetVisitor& v, Pet* p = nullptr) override {
        v.visit(this, p);
    }
};
```

```
class Dog : public Pet {
    public:
    Dog(const std::string& color) : Pet(color) {}
    void accept(PetVisitor& v, Pet* p = nullptr) override {
        v.visit(this, p);
    }
};
```

The `visit()` function also has to be modified to accept the additional argument, even for the visitors that do not need it. Changing the parameters of the `accept()` function is, therefore, an expensive global operation that should not be done often, if at all. Note that all overrides for the same virtual function in the hierarchy already have to have the same parameters. The Visitor pattern extends this restriction to all operations added using the same base Visitor object. A common workaround for this problem is to pass parameters using aggregates (classes or structures that combine multiple parameters together). The `visit()` function is declared to accept a pointer to the base aggregate class, while each visitor receives a pointer to a derived class that may have additional fields, and uses them as needed.

Now our additional argument is forwarded through the chain of virtual function calls to the visitor, where we can make use of it. Let's create a visitor that records the pet births and adds new pet objects as children to their parent objects:

```
class BirthVisitor : public PetVisitor {
    public:
    void visit(Cat* c, Pet* p) override {
        assert(dynamic_cast<Cat*>(p));
        c->add_child(p);
    }
    void visit(Dog* d, Pet* p) override {
        assert(dynamic_cast<Dog*>(p));
        d->add_child(p);
    }
};
```

Note that if we want to make sure that there are no biological impossibilities in our family tree, the verification has to be done at run time—at compile time, we do not know the actual types of the polymorphic objects. The new visitor is just as easy to use as the ones from the last section:

```
Pet* parent;      // A cat
BirthVisitor bv;
Pet* child(new Cat("calico"));
parent->accept(bv, child);
```

Once we have established the parenthood relationships, we may want to examine our pet families. That is another operation we want to add, which calls for another Visitor:

```cpp
class FamilyTreeVisitor : public PetVisitor {
    public:
    void visit(Cat* c, Pet*) override {
        std::cout << "Kittens: ";
        for (auto k : c->children_) {
            std::cout << k->color() << " ";
        }
        std::cout << std::endl;
    }
    void visit(Dog* d, Pet*) override {
        std::cout << "Puppies: ";
        for (auto p : d->children_) {
            std::cout << p->color() << " ";
        }
        std::cout << std::endl;
    }
};
```

We have hit a slight problem, though, because as written, the code will not compile. The reason is that the `FamilyTreeVisitor` class is trying to access the `Pet::children_` data member, which is private. This is another weakness of the Visitor pattern—from our point of view, the visitors add new operations to the classes, just like virtual functions, but from the compiler's point of view they are completely separate classes, not at all like member functions of the `Pet` classes and have no special access. Application of the Visitor pattern usually requires that the encapsulation is relaxed in one of two ways—we can either allow public access to the data (directly or through accessor member functions) or declare the Visitor classes to be friends (which does require changes to the source code). In our example, we will follow the second route:

```cpp
class Pet {
    .....
    friend class FamilyTreeVisitor;
};
```

Now the family tree visitor works as expected:

```cpp
Pet* parent;            // A cat
.....
FamilyTreeVisitor tv;
parent->accept(tv);     // Prints kitten colors
```

Unlike `BirthVisitor`, `FamilyTreeVisitor` does not need the additional argument.

Now we have visitors that implement operations with parameters. What about the return values? Technically, there is no requirement for the `visit()` and `accept()` functions to return `void`. They can return anything else. However, the limitation that they have to all return the same type usually makes this capability useless. Virtual functions can have covariant return types, where the base class virtual function returns an object of some class and the derived class overrides return objects derived from that class, but even that is usually too limiting. There is another, much simpler solution—the `visit()` functions of every Visitor object have full access to the data members of that object. There is no reason why we cannot store the return value in the Visitor class itself and access it later. This fits well with the most common use where each visitor adds a different operation and is likely to have a unique return type, but the operation itself usually has the same return type for all classes in the hierarchy. For example, we can make our `FamilyTreeVisitor` count the total number of children and return the value through the Visitor object:

```
class FamilyTreeVisitor : public PetVisitor {
    public:
    FamilyTreeVisitor() : child_count_(0) {}
    void reset() { child_count_ = 0; }
    size_t child_count() const { return child_count_; }
    private:
    size_t child_count_;
};
FamilyTreeVisitor tv;
parent->accept(tv);
std::cout << tv.child_count() << " kittens total" << std::endl;
```

This approach imposes some limitations in multithreaded programs—the visitor is now not thread-safe since multiple threads cannot use the same Visitor object to visit different pet objects. The most common solution is to use one Visitor object per thread, usually a local variable created on the stack of the function that calls the visitor. If this is not possible, more complex options are available to give the visitor a per-thread (thread-local) state, but the analysis of such options lies outside of the scope of this book. On the other hand, sometimes we want to accumulate results over multiple visitations, in which case the previous technique of storing the result in the Visitor object works perfectly. Also note that the same solution can be used to pass arguments into the Visitor operations, instead of adding them to the `visit()` functions; we can store the arguments inside the Visitor object itself, and then we don't need anything special to access them from the visitor. This technique works particularly well when the arguments don't change on every invocation of the visitor, but may vary from one Visitor object to another.

Let's return for a moment and examine the `FamilyTreeVisitor` implementation again. Note that it iterates over the child objects of the parent object and calls the same operation on each one, in turn. It does not, however, process the children of the child object—our family tree is only one-generation deep. The problem of visiting objects that contain other objects is very general and occurs rather often. Our motivational example from the very beginning of this chapter, the problem of serialization, demonstrates this need perfectly—every complex object is serialized by serializing its components, one by one, and they, in turn, are serialized the same way, until we get all the way down to the built-in types like `int` and `double`, which we know how to read and write. The next section deals with visiting of the complex objects in a more comprehensive way than what we have done so far.

Visiting complex objects

In the last section, we saw how the Visitor pattern allows us to add new operations to the existing hierarchy. In one of the examples, we visited a complex object that contained pointers to other objects. The visitor iterated over these pointers, in a limited way. We are now going to consider the general problem of visiting objects that are composed of other objects, or objects that contain other objects and build up to the demonstration of a working serialization/deserialization solution at the end.

Visiting composite objects

The general idea of visiting complex objects is quite straightforward—when visiting the object itself, we generally do not know all the details of how to handle each component or contained object. But there is something else that does—the visitor for that object type is written specifically to handle that class and nothing else. This observation suggests that the correct way to handle the component objects is to simply visit each one, and thus delegate the problem to someone else (a generally powerful technique, in programming and otherwise).

Let's first demonstrate this idea on the example of a simple container class, such as the `Shelter` class, which can contain any number of pet objects representing the pets waiting for adoption:

```
class Shelter {
    public:
    void add(Pet* p) {
        pets_.emplace_back(p);
    }
```

```
        void accept(PetVisitor& v) {
            for (auto& p : pets_) {
                p->accept(v);
            }
        }
    private:
        std::vector<std::unique_ptr<Pet>> pets_;
};
```

This class is essentially an adapter to make a vector of pet objects visitable (we have discussed the Adapter pattern in detail in the eponymous chapter). Note that the objects of this class do own the pet objects they contain—when the Shelter object is destroyed, so are all the Pet objects in the vector. Any container of unique pointers is a container that owns its contained objects; this is how polymorphic objects should be stored in a container, such as std::vector (For non-polymorphic objects we can store objects themselves, but that won't work in our case, objects derived from Pet are of different types.)

The code relevant to our current problem is, of course, Shelter::accept(), which determines how a Shelter object is visited. As you can see, we do not invoke the Visitor on the Shelter object itself. Instead, we delegate the visitation to each of the containing objects. Since our Visitors are already written to handle Pet objects, nothing more needs to be done. When a Shelter is visited by, say, FeedingVisitor, every pet in the shelter gets fed, and we didn't have to write any special code to make it happen.

Visitation of composite objects is done in a similar manner—if an object is composed of several smaller objects, we have to visit each of these objects. Let's consider an object representing a family with two family pets, a dog and a cat (the humans who serve the pets are not included in the following code, but we assume they are there too):

```
class Family {
    public:
    Family(const char* cat_color, const char* dog_color) :
        cat_(cat_color), dog_(dog_color)
    {}
    void accept(PetVisitor& v) {
        cat_.accept(v);
        dog_.accept(v);
    }
    private:    // Other family members not shown for brevity
    Cat cat_;
    Dog dog_;
};
```

Again, visiting the family with a visitor from the `PetVisitor` hierarchy is delegated so that each `Pet` object is visited, and the visitors already have everything they need to handle these objects (of course, a `Family` object could accept visitors of other types as well, we would have to write separate `accept()` methods for them).

Now, at last, we have all the pieces we need to tackle the problem of serialization and deserialization of arbitrary objects. The next subsection shows how this can be done using the Visitor pattern.

Serialization and deserialization with Visitor

The problem itself was described in details in the previous section—for serialization, each object needs to be converted to a sequence of bits, and these bits need to be stored or copied or sent. The first part of the action depends on the object (each object is converted differently) but the second part depends on the specific application of the serialization (saving to disk is different from sending across the network). The implementation depends on two factors, hence the need for double dispatch, which is exactly what the Visitor pattern provides. Furthermore, if we have a way to serialize some object and then deserialize it (reconstruct the object from the sequence of bits), we should use the same method when this object is included in another object.

To demonstrate serialization/deserialization of a class hierarchy using the Visitor pattern, we need a more complex hierarchy than the toy examples we have used so far. Let's consider this hierarchy of two-dimensional geometric objects:

```
class Geometry {
    public:
    virtual ~Geometry() {}
};

class Point : public Geometry {
    public:
    Point() = default;
    Point(double x, double y) : x_(x), y_(y) {}
    private:
    double x_;
    double y_;
};

class Circle : public Geometry {
    public:
    Circle() = default;
    Circle(Point c, double r) : c_(c), r_(r) {}
```

```
        private:
        Point c_;
        double r_;
    };

    class Line : public Geometry {
        public:
        Line() = default;
        Line(Point p1, Point p2) : p1_(p1), p2_(p2) {}
        private:
        Point p1_;
        Point p2_;
    };
```

All objects are derived from the abstract `Geometry` base class, but the more complex object contains one or more of the simpler objects; for example, `Line` is defined by two `Point` objects. Note that, at the end of the day, all our objects are made of `double` numbers, and, therefore, will serialize into a sequence of numbers. The key is knowing which `double` represents which field of which object; we need this to restore the original objects correctly.

To serialize these objects using the Visitor pattern, we follow the same process we used in the last section. First, we need to declare the base Visitor class:

```
    class Visitor {
        public:
        virtual void visit(double& x) = 0;
        virtual void visit(Point& p) = 0;
        virtual void visit(Circle& c) = 0;
        virtual void visit(Line& l) = 0;
    };
```

There is one additional detail here—we can also visit double values, each visitor would need to handle them appropriately (write them or read them, and so on). Visiting any geometry object will result, eventually, in visiting the numbers it is composed of.

Our base `Geometry` class and all classes derived from it need to accept this visitor:

```
    class Geometry {
        public:
        virtual ~Geometry() {}
        virtual void accept(Visitor& v) = 0;
    };
```

There is, of course, no way to add an `accept()` member function to double, but we won't have to. The `accept()` member functions for the derived classes, each of which is composed of one or more numbers and other classes, visit every data member in order:

```
void Point::accept(Visitor& v) {
    v.visit(x_);      // double
    v.visit(y_);      // double
}
void Circle::accept(Visitor& v) {
    v.visit(c_);      // Point
    v.visit(r_);      // double
}
void Point::accept(Visitor& v) {
    v.visit(p1_);     // Point
    v.visit(p2_);     // Point
}
```

The concrete Visitor classes, all derived from the base `Visitor` class, are responsible for the specific mechanisms of serialization and deserialization. The order in which the objects are broken down into their parts, all the way down to the numbers, is controlled by each object, but the visitors determine what is done with these numbers. For example, we can serialize all objects into a string using the formatted I/O (similar to what we get if we print the numbers into `cout`):

```
class StringSerializeVisitor : public Visitor {
    public:
    void visit(double& x) override { S << x << " "; }
    void visit(Point& p) override { p.accept(*this); }
    void visit(Circle& c) override { c.accept(*this); }
    void visit(Line& l) override { l.accept(*this); }
    std::string str() const { return S.str(); }

    private:
    std::stringstream S;
};
```

The string is accumulated in `stringstream` until all necessary objects are serialized:

```
Line l(.....);
Circle c(.....);
StringSerializeVisitor serializer;
serializer.visit(l);
serializer.visit(c);
std::string s(serializer.str());
```

Now that we have the objects printed into the s string, we can restore them from this string, perhaps on a different machine (if we arranged for the string to be sent there). First, we need the deserializing Visitor:

```
class StringDeserializeVisitor : public Visitor {
public:
    StringDeserializeVisitor(const std::string& s) { S.str(s); }
    void visit(double& x) override { S >> x; }
    void visit(Point& p) override { p.accept(*this); }
    void visit(Circle& c) override { c.accept(*this); }
    void visit(Line& l) override { l.accept(*this); }

private:
    std::stringstream S;
};
```

This Visitor reads the numbers from the string and saves them in the variables given to it by the object that is visited. The key to successful deserialization is to read the numbers in the same order as they were saved—for example, if we started by writing coordinates X and Y of a point, we should construct a point from the first two numbers we read and use them as coordinates X and Y. If the first point we wrote was the endpoint of a line, we should use the point we constructed as the endpoint of the new line. The beauty of the Visitor pattern is that the functions that do the actual reading and writing don't need to do anything special to preserve this order—the order is determined by each object and is guaranteed to be the same for all visitors (the object makes no distinction between the specific visitors, and doesn't even know what kind of visitor is it). All we need to do is to visit the objects in the same order they were serialized in:

```
Line l1;
Circle c1;
StringDeserializeVisitor deserializer(s);    // String from serializer
deserializer.visit(l1);                       // Restored Line l
deserializer.visit(c1);                       // Restored Circle c
```

So far, we have known which objects are serialized and in what order. Therefore, we can deserialize the same objects in the same order. A more general case is when we don't know what objects to expect during deserialization—the objects are stored in a visitable container, similar to the Shelter in the earlier example, which has to ensure that the objects are serialized and deserialized in the same order. For example, consider this class, which stores a geometry represented as an intersection of two other geometries:

```
class Intersection : public Geometry {
public:
    Intersection() = default;
    Intersection(Geometry* g1, Geometry* g2) : g1_(g1), g2_(g2) {}
```

```
    void accept(Visitor& v) override {
        g1_->accept(v);
        g2_->accept(v);
    }
    private:
    std::unique_ptr<Geometry> g1_;
    std::unique_ptr<Geometry> g2_;
};
```

Serialization of this object is straightforward—we serialize both geometries, in order, by delegating the details to these objects—we cannot call `v.visit()` directly because we do not know the types of the `*g1_` and `*g2_` geometries, but we can let these objects dispatch the call as appropriate. But deserialization, as written, will fail—the geometry pointers are `null`, there are no objects allocated yet, and we do not know what type of objects should be allocated. Somehow, we need to encode the types of objects in the serialized stream first, then construct them based on these encoded types. There is another pattern that offers the standard solution for this problem, and that is the Factory pattern (it is quite common to have to use more than one design pattern when building a complex system).

There are several ways in which this can be done, but they all boil down to converting types to numbers and serializing those numbers. In our case, we have to know the complete list of geometry types when we declare the base `Visitor` class, so we can also define an enumeration for all these types at the same time:

```
class Geometry {
    public:
    enum type_tag { POINT = 100, CIRCLE, LINE, INTERSECTION };
    virtual type_tag tag() const = 0;
};

class Visitor {
    public:
    static Geometry* make_geometry(Geometry::type_tag tag);
    virtual void visit(Geometry::type_tag& tag) = 0;
    .....
};
```

It is not essential that enum type_tag be defined inside the Geometry class, or that the make_geometry factory constructor be a static member function of the Visitor class. They can be declared outside of any class as well, but the virtual tag() method that will return the correct tag for every derived geometry type needs to be declared exactly as shown. The tag() overrides must be defined in every derived Geometry class, for example, the Point class:

```
class Point : public Geometry {
    public:
    .....
    type_tag tag() const override { return POINT; }
};
```

Other derived classes have to be similarly modified.

Then we need to define the factory constructor:

```
Geometry* Visitor::make_geometry(Geometry::type_tag tag) {
    switch (tag) {
        case Geometry::POINT: return new Point;
        case Geometry::CIRCLE: return new Circle;
        case Geometry::LINE: return new Line;
        case Geometry::INTERSECTION: return new Intersection;
    }
}
```

This factory function constructs the right derived object depending on the specified type tag. All that is left is for the Intersection object to serialize and deserialize the tags of the two geometries that form the intersection:

```
class Intersection : public Geometry {
    public:
    void accept(Visitor& v) override {
        Geometry::type_tag tag;
        if (g1_) tag = g1_->tag();
        v.visit(tag);
        if (!g1_) g1_.reset(Visitor::make_geometry(tag));
        g1_->accept(v);
        if (g2_) tag = g2_->tag();
        v.visit(tag);
        if (!g2_) g2_.reset(Visitor::make_geometry(tag));
        g2_->accept(v);
    }
    .....
};
```

First, the tags are sent to the visitor. The serializing visitor should write the tags along with the rest of the data:

```
class StringSerializeVisitor : public Visitor {
    public:
    void visit(Geometry::type_tag& tag) override {
        S << size_t(tag) << " ";
    }
    .....
};
```

The deserializing visitor has to read the tag (actually, it reads a `size_t` number and converts it to the tag):

```
class StringDeserializeVisitor : public Visitor {
    public:
    void visit(Geometry::type_tag& tag) override {
        size_t t;
        S >> t;
        tag = Geometry::type_tag(t);
    }
    .....
};
```

Once the tag is restored by the deserializing visitor, the `Intersection` object can invoke the factory constructor to construct the right geometry object. Now we can deserialize this object from the stream, and our `Intersection` is restored as an exact copy of the one we serialized. Note that there are other ways to package visiting the tags and the calls to the factory constructor; the optimal solution depends on the roles of different objects in the system—for example, the deserializing visitor may construct the objects based on tag instead of the composite object that owns these geometries. The sequence of events that need to take place, however, remains the same.

So far, we have been learning about the classic object-oriented Visitor pattern. Before we see what the C++-specific twists on the classic pattern are, we should learn about another type of visitor that addresses some of the inconveniences in the Visitor pattern.

Acyclic Visitor

The Visitor pattern, as we have seen it so far, does what we wanted it to do. It separates the implementation of the algorithm from the object that is the data for the algorithm, and it allows us to select the correct implementation based on two run-time factors—the specific object type and the concrete operation we want to perform, both of which are selected from their corresponding class hierarchies. There is, however, a fly in the ointment—we wanted to reduce complexity and simplified the code maintenance, and we did, but now we have to maintain two parallel class hierarchies, the visitable objects, and the visitors, and the dependencies between the two are non-trivial. The worst part of these dependencies is that they form a cycle—the Visitor object depends on the types of the visitable objects (there is an overload of the `visit()` methods for every visitable type), and the base visitable type depends on the base visitor type. The first half of this dependency is the worst. Every time a new object is added to the hierarchy, every visitor must be updated. The second half does not take much action from the programmer as new visitors can be added at any time and without any other changes—this is the whole point of the Visitor pattern. But there is still the compile-time dependency of the base visitable class, and, perforce, all derived classes, on the base Visitor class. Were the Visitor class to change, every file that uses one of the visitable classes would need to be recompiled. The visitors are, for the most part, stable in their interface and implementation, except for one case—adding a new visitable class. Thus, the cycle in action looks like this—a new class is added to the hierarchy of the visitable objects. The Visitor classes need to be updated with the new type. Since the base Visitor class was changed, the base visitable class and every line of code that depends on it must be recompiled, including the code that does not use the new visitable class, only the old ones. Even using forward declarations whenever possible does not help—if a new visitable class is added, all the old ones must be recompiled.

The additional problem of the traditional Visitor pattern is that every possible combination of the object type and the visitor type must be handled. Often there are cases when some combinations do not make sense, and certain objects will never be visited by some types of visitors. But we cannot take advantage of this as every combination must have a defined action (the action could be very simple, but still, every Visitor class must have the full set of `visit()` member functions defined).

The Acyclic Visitor pattern is a variant of the Visitor pattern that is specifically designed to break the dependency cycle and allow partial visitation. The base visitable class for the Acyclic Visitor pattern is the same as for the regular Visitor pattern:

```
class Pet {
    public:
    virtual ~Pet() {}
    virtual void accept(PetVisitor& v) = 0;
```

```
      . . . . .
};
```

However, that is where the similarity ends. The base Visitor class does not have the
`visit()` overloads for every visitable. In fact, it has no `visit()` member function at all:

```
class PetVisitor {
    public:
    virtual ~PetVisitor() {}
};
```

So, who does the visiting then? For every derived class in the original hierarchy, we also
declare the corresponding Visitor class, and that is where the `visit()` function is:

```
class Cat;
class CatVisitor {
    public:
    virtual void visit(Cat* c) = 0;
};

class Cat : public Pet {
    public:
    Cat(const std::string& color) : Pet(color) {}
    void accept(PetVisitor& v) override {
        if (CatVisitor* cv = dynamic_cast<CatVisitor*>(&v))
            cv->visit(this);
        else { // Handle error
            assert(false);
        }
    }
};
```

Note that each visitor can visit only the class it was designed for—the `CatVisitor` visits
only `Cat` objects, the `DogVisitor` visits only `Dog` objects, and so on. The magic is in the
new `accept()` function—when a class is asked to accept a visitor, it first uses the
`dynamic_cast` to check whether this is the right type of visitor. If it is, all is well, and the
visitor is accepted. If it isn't, we have a problem and must handle the error (the exact
mechanism of error handling depends on the application; for example, an exception can be
thrown). The concrete Visitor classes, therefore, must be derived from both the common
`PetVisitor` base class and the class-specific base class such as `CatVisitor`:

```
class FeedingVisitor : public PetVisitor, public CatVisitor, public
DogVisitor {
    public:
    void visit(Cat* c) override {
        std::cout << "Feed tuna to the " << c->color() << " cat"
                << std::endl;
```

```
    }
    void visit(Dog* d) override {
        std::cout << "Feed steak to the " << d->color() << " dog"
                  << std::endl;
    }
};
```

Each concrete visitor class is derived from the common visitor base and from every per-type visitor base (`CatVisitor`, `DogVisitor`, and so on) for every type that must be handled by this visitor. On the other hand, if this visitor is not designed to visit some of the classes in the hierarchy, we can simply omit the corresponding visitor base, and then we won't need to implement the virtual function override either:

```
class BathingVisitor : public PetVisitor,
                       public DogVisitor { // But no CatVisitor
public:
    void visit(Dog* d) override {
        std::cout << "Wash the " << d->color() << " dog" << std::endl;
    }
    // No visit(Cat*) here!
};
```

The invocation of the Acyclic Visitor pattern is done in exactly the same way as with the regular Visitor pattern:

```
std::unique_ptr<Pet> c(new Cat("orange"));
std::unique_ptr<Pet> d(new Dog("brown"));

FeedingVisitor fv;
c->accept(fv);
d->accept(fv);

BathingVisitor bv;
//c->accept(bv); // Error
d->accept(bv);
```

If we try to visit an object that is not supported by the particular Visitor, the error is detected. Therefore, we have solved the problem of partial visitation. What about the dependency cycle? That is taken care of as well—the common `PetVisitor` base class does not need to list the complete hierarchy of visitable objects, and the concrete visitable classes depend only on their per-class visitors, but not on any visitors for other types. Therefore, when another visitable object is added to the hierarchy, the existing ones do not need to be recompiled.

The Acyclic Visitor pattern looks so good that one has to wonder, *why not use it all the time instead of the regular Visitor pattern?* There are a few reasons. First of all, the Acyclic Visitor pattern uses `dynamic_cast` to cast from one base class to another (sometimes called cross-cast). This operation is typically more expensive than the virtual function call, so the Acyclic Visitor pattern is slower than the alternative. Also, the Acyclic Visitor pattern requires a Visitor class for every visitable class, so twice as many classes, and it uses multiple inheritance with a lot of base classes. That second issue is not much of a problem for most modern compilers, but many programmers find it difficult to deal with multiple inheritance. Whether the first issue—the runtime cost of the dynamic cast—is a problem depends on the application, but it is something you need to be aware of. On the other hand, the Acyclic Visitor pattern really shines when the visitable object hierarchy changes frequently or when the cost of recompiling the entire code base is significant.

You may have noticed one more issue with the Acyclic Visitor pattern —it has a lot of boilerplate code. Several lines of code have to be copied for every visitable class. In fact, the regular Visitor pattern suffers from the same problem in that implementing either kind of visitor involves a lot of repetitive typing. But C++ has a special set of tools to replace code repetition by code reuse: that is exactly what generic programming is for. We shall see next how the Visitor pattern is adapted to modern C++.

Visitors in modern C++

As we have just seen, the Visitor pattern promotes separation of concerns; for example, the order of serialization and the mechanism of serialization are made independent, and a separate class is responsible for each. The pattern also simplifies code maintenance by collecting all code that performs a given task into one place. What the Visitor pattern does not promote is code reuse with no duplication. But that's the object-oriented Visitor pattern , before C++. Let's see what we can do with the generic capabilities of C++, starting from the regular Visitor pattern .

Generic Visitor

We are going to try to reduce the boilerplate code in the implementation of the Visitor pattern. Let's start with the `accept()` member function, which must be copied into every visitable class; it always looks the same:

```
class Cat : public Pet {
    void accept(PetVisitor& v) override { v.visit(this); }
};
```

This function cannot be moved to the base class because we need to call the visitor with the actual type, not the base type—visit() accepts Cat*, Dog*, and so on; not Pet*. We can get a template to generate this function for us if we introduce an intermediate templated base class:

```
class Pet {      // Same as before
    public:
    virtual ~Pet() {}
    Pet(const std::string& color) : color_(color) {}
    const std::string& color() const { return color_; }
    virtual void accept(PetVisitor& v) = 0;
    private:
    std::string color_;
};

template <typename Derived>
class Visitable : public Pet {
    public:
    using Pet::Pet;
    void accept(PetVisitor& v) override {
        v.visit(static_cast<Derived*>(this));
    }
};
```

The template is parameterized by the derived class. In this regard, it is similar to the **Curiously Recurring Template Pattern (CRTP)**, but here we do not inherit from the template parameter—we use it to cast the this pointer to the correct derived class pointer. Now we just need to derive each pet class from the right instantiation of the template, and we get the accept() function automatically:

```
class Cat : public Visitable<Cat> {
    using Visitable<Cat>::Visitable;
};

class Dog : public Visitable<Dog> {
    using Visitable<Dog>::Visitable;
};
```

That takes care of the half of the boilerplate code—that inside the derived visitable objects. Now there is only the other half left: that inside the Visitor classes, were we have to type the same declaration over and over again for every visitable class. We can't do much about the specific visitors; after all, that's where the real work is done, and, presumably, we need to do different things for different visitable classes (otherwise why use double dispatch at all?)

However, we can simplify the declaration of the base Visitor class if we introduce this generic Visitor template:

```
template <typename ... Types>
class Visitor;

template <typename T>
class Visitor<T> {
    public:
    virtual void visit(T* t) = 0;
};

template <typename T, typename ... Types>
class Visitor<T, Types ...> : public Visitor<Types ...> {
    public:
    using Visitor<Types ...>::visit;
    virtual void visit(T* t) = 0;
};
```

Note that we have to implement this template only once: not once for each class hierarchy, but once forever (or at least until we need to change the signature of the visit() function, for example, to add arguments). This is a good generic library class. Once we have it, declaring a visitor base for a particular class hierarchy becomes so trivial that it feels anticlimactic:

```
using PetVisitor = Visitor<class Cat, class Dog>;
```

Notice the somewhat unusual syntax with the class keyword—it combines the template argument list with a forward declaration and in equivalent to the following:

```
class Cat;
class Dog;
using PetVisitor = Visitor<Cat, Dog>;
```

How does the Generic Visitor base work? It uses the variadic template to capture an arbitrary number of type arguments, but the primary template is only declared, not defined. The rest are specializations. First, we have the special case of one type argument. We declare the pure visit() virtual member function for that type. Then we have a specialization for more than one type argument, where the first argument is explicit, and the rest are in the parameter pack. We generate the visit() function for the explicitly specified type and inherit the rest of them from an instantiation of the same variadic template but with one less argument. The instantiation is recursive until we are down to only one type argument, and then the first specialization is used.

Now that we have the boilerplate visitor code generated by templates, we can also make it simpler to define concrete visitors.

Lambda Visitor

Most of the work in defining a concrete visitor is writing the code for the actual work that has to happen for every visitable object. There is not a lot of boilerplate code in a specific visitor class. But sometimes we may not want to declare the class itself. Think about lambda expressions—anything that can be done with a lambda expression can also be done with an explicitly declared callable class because lambdas are (anonymous) callable classes. Nonetheless, we find lambda expressions very useful for writing one-off callable objects. Similarly, we may want to write a visitor without explicitly naming it—a lambda Visitor. We would want it to look something like this:

```
auto v(lambda_visitor<PetVisitor>(
    [](Cat* c) {
        std::cout << "Let the " << c->color() << " cat out"
                  << std::endl;
    },
    [](Dog* d) {
        std::cout << "Take the " << d->color() << " dog for a walk"
                  << std::endl;
    }
));
pet->accept(v);
```

There are two problems to be solved—how to create a class that handles a list of types and corresponding objects (in our case, the visitable types and the corresponding lambdas), and how to generate a set of overloaded functions using lambda expressions.

The former problem will require us to recursively instantiate a template on the parameter pack, peeling off one argument at a time. The solution to the latter problem is similar to the overload set of the lambda expression, which was described in the chapter on class templates. We could use the overload set from that chapter, but we can use the recursive template instantiation that we need anyway, to build the overloaded set of functions directly.

There is going to be one new challenge in this implementation—we have to process not one but two lists of types. The first list has all visitable types in it; in our case, `Cat`, `Dog`. The second list has the types of the lambda expressions, one for each visitable type. We have not seen a variadic template with two parameter packs yet, and for a good reason—it is not possible to simply declare `template<typename ... A, typename ... B>` as the compiler would not know where the first list ends and the second begins. The trick is to hide one, or both lists of types inside other templates. In our case, we already have the `Visitor` template that is instantiated on the list of visitable types:

```
using PetVisitor = Visitor<class Cat, class Dog>;
```

We can extract this list from the `Visitor` template and match each type with its lambda expression. The partial specialization syntax used to process two parameter packs in sync is tricky, so we will work through it in steps. First of all, we need to declare the general template for our `LambdaVisitor` class:

```
template <typename Base, typename ... >
class LambdaVisitor;
```

Note that there is only one general parameter pack here, plus the base class for the visitor (in our case, it will be `PetVisitor`). This template must be declared, but it is never going to be used—we will provide a specialization for every case that needs to be handled. The first specialization is used when there is only one visitable type and one corresponding lambda expression:

```
template <typename Base, typename T1, typename F1>
class LambdaVisitor<Base, Visitor<T1>, F1> : private F1, public Base {
    public:
    LambdaVisitor(F1&& f1) : F1(std::move(f1)) {}
    LambdaVisitor(const F1& f1) : F1(f1) {}
    void visit(T1* t) override { return F1::operator()(t); }
};
```

This specialization, in addition to handling the case where we have only one visitable type, is used as the last instantiation in every chain of recursive template instantiations. Since it is always the first base class in the recursive hierarchy of `LambdaVisitor` instantiations, it is the only one that directly inherits from the base Visitor class such as `PetVisitor`. Note that, even with a single `T1` visitable type, we use the `Visitor` template as a wrapper for it. This is done in preparation for the general case where we will have a list of types whose length is unknown. The two constructors store the `f1` lambda expression inside the `LambdaVisitor` class, using move instead of copy if possible. Finally, the `visit(T1*)` virtual function override simply forwards the call to the lambda expression. It may appear simpler, at first glance, to inherit publicly from `F1` and just agree to use the functional calling syntax (in other words, to rename all calls to `visit()` to calls to `operator()` everywhere). This is not going to work; we need the indirection because the `operator()` instance of the lambda expression itself cannot be a virtual function override. By the way, the `override` keyword here is invaluable in detecting bugs in the code where the template is not inherited from the right base class or the virtual function declarations do not match exactly.

The general case of any number of visitable types and lambda expressions is handled by this partial specialization, which explicitly deals with the first types in both lists, then recursively instantiates itself to process the rest of the lists:

```
template <typename Base,
          typename T1, typename ... T,
          typename F1, typename ... F>
class LambdaVisitor<Base, Visitor<T1, T ...>, F1, F ...> :
    private F1, public LambdaVisitor<Base, Visitor<T ...>, F ...>
{
    public:
    LambdaVisitor(F1&& f1, F&& ... f) :
        F1(std::move(f1)),
        LambdaVisitor<Base, Visitor<T ...>, F ...>(std::forward<F>(f) ...)
    {}
    LambdaVisitor(const F1& f1, F&& ... f) :
        F1(f1),
        LambdaVisitor<Base, Visitor<T ...>, F ...>(std::forward<F>(f) ...)
    {}
    void visit(T1* t) override { return F1::operator()(t); }
};
```

Again, we have two constructors that store the first lambda expression in the class and forward the rest to the next instantiation. One virtual function override is generated on each step of the recursion, always for the first type in the remaining list of the visitable classes. That type is then removed from the list, and the processing continues in the same manner until we reach the last instantiation, the one for a single visitable type.

Since it is not possible to explicitly name the types of lambda expressions, we also cannot explicitly declare the type of the lambda visitor. Instead, the lambda expression types must be deduced by the template argument deduction, so we need a `lambda_visitor()` template function that accepts multiple lambda expression arguments and constructs the `LambdaVisitor` object from all of them:

```
template <typename Base, typename ... F>
auto lambda_visitor(F&& ... f) {
    return LambdaVisitor<Base, Base, F ...>(std::forward<F>(f) ...);
}
```

Now we have a class that stores any number of lambda expressions and binds each one to the corresponding `visit()` override, we can write lambda visitors just as easily as we write lambda expressions:

```
void walk(Pet& p) {
    auto v(lambda_visitor<PetVisitor>(
            [](Cat* c) {
```

```
            std::cout << "Let the " << c->color() << " cat out"
                      << std::endl; },
        [](Dog* d) {
            std::cout << "Take the " << d->color() << " dog for a walk"
                      << std::endl; }
    ));
    p.accept(v);
}
```

Note that, because of the way we declare the `visit()` function in the same class that inherits from the corresponding lambda expression, the order of the lambda expression in the argument list of the `lambda_visitor()` function must match the order of classes in the list of types in `PetVisitor` definition. This restriction can be removed, if desired, at the cost of some additional complexity of the implementation.

We have now seen how the common fragments of the visitor code can be turned into reusable templates, and how this, in turn, lets us create a lambda visitor. But we have not forgotten the other visitor implementation we learned in this chapter, the Acyclic Visitor pattern. Let's see how it, too, can benefit from the modern C++ language features.

Generic Acyclic Visitor

The Acyclic Visitor pattern does not need a base class with the list of all visitable types. However, it has its own share of the boilerplate code. First of all, each visitable type needs the `accept()` member function, and it has more code than the similar function in the original Visitor pattern:

```
class Cat : public Pet {
    public:
    void accept(PetVisitor& v) override {
        if (CatVisitor* cv = dynamic_cast<CatVisitor*>(&v))
            cv->visit(this);
        else { // Handle error
            assert(false);
        }
    }
};
```

Assuming that the error handling is uniform, this function is repeated over and over for different types of visitors, each corresponding to its visitable type (such as `CatVisitor` here). Then there is the per-type Visitor class itself, for example:

```
class CatVisitor {
    public:
    virtual void visit(Cat* c) = 0;
};
```

Again, this code is pasted all over the program, with slight modifications. Let's convert this error-prone code duplication into easy to maintain reusable code.

Again, we will need to create some infrastructure first. The Acyclic Visitor pattern bases its hierarchy on a common base class for all visitors, such as the following:

```
class PetVisitor {
    public:
    virtual ~PetVisitor() {}
};
```

Note that there is nothing specific to the `Pet` hierarchy here. With a better name, this class can serve as a base class for any visitor hierarchy:

```
class VisitorBase {
    public:
    virtual ~VisitorBase() {}
};
```

We also need a template to generate all these Visitor base classes specific to visitable types, to replace the near-identical `CatVisitor`, `DogVisitor`, and so on. Since all that is needed from these classes is the declaration of the pure virtual `visit()` method, we can parameterize the template by the visitable type:

```
template <typename Visitable>
class Visitor {
    public:
    virtual void visit(Visitable* p) = 0;
};
```

The base visitable class for any class hierarchy now accepts the visitors using the common `VisitorBase` base class:

```
class Pet {
    .....
    virtual void accept(VisitorBase& v) = 0;
};
```

Instead of deriving each visitable class directly from `Pet` and pasting a copy of the `accept()` method, we introduce an intermediate template base class that can generate this method with the correct types:

```
template <typename Visitable>
class PetVisitable : public Pet {
    public:
    using Pet::Pet;
    void accept(VisitorBase& v) override {
        if (Visitor<Visitable>* pv = dynamic_cast<Visitor<Visitable>*>(&v))
            pv->visit(static_cast<Visitable*>(this));
        else { // Handle error
            assert(false);
        }
    }
};
```

This is the only copy of the `accept()` function we need to write, and it contains the preferred error handling implementation for our application to deal with the cases when the visitor is not accepted by the base class (recall that Acyclic Visitor allows partial visitation, where some combinations of the visitor and the visitable are not supported).

The concrete visitable classes inherit from the common `Pet` base class indirectly, through the intermediate `PetVisitable` base class, which also provides them with the visitable interface. The argument to the `PetVisitable` template is the derived class itself (again, we see the CRTP in action):

```
class Cat : public PetVisitable<Cat> {
    using PetVisitable<Cat>::PetVisitable;
};

class Dog : public PetVisitable<Dog> {
    using PetVisitable<Dog>::PetVisitable;
};
```

It is, of course, not mandatory to use the same base class constructors for all derived classes, as custom constructors can be defined in every class as needed.

The only thing left is to implement the Visitor class. Recall that the specific visitor in the Acyclic Visitor pattern inherits from the common visitor base and each of the visitor classes representing the supported visitable types. That is not going to change, but we now have a way to generate these visitor classes on demand:

```
class FeedingVisitor :
    public VisitorBase, public Visitor<Cat>, public Visitor<Dog>
{
    public:
    void visit(Cat* c) override {
        std::cout << "Feed tuna to the " << c->color() << " cat"
                << std::endl;
    }
    void visit(Dog* d) override {
        std::cout << "Feed steak to the " << d->color() << " dog"
                << std::endl;
    }
};
```

Let's look back at the work we have done—the parallel hierarchy of visitor classes no longer needs to be typed explicitly, instead, they are generated as needed. The repetitive `accept()` functions are reduced to the single `PetVisitable` class template. Still, we have to write this template for every new visitable class hierarchy. We can generalize this too, and create a single reusable template for all hierarchies, parameterized by the base visitable class:

```
template <typename Base, typename Visitable>
class VisitableBase : public Base {
    public:
    using Base::Base;
    void accept(VisitorBase& vb) override {
        if (Visitor<Visitable>* v = dynamic_cast<Visitor<Visitable>*>(&vb))
            v->visit(static_cast<Visitable*>(this));
        else { // Handle error
            assert(false);
        }
    }
};
```

Now, for every visitable class hierarchy, we just need to create a template alias:

```
template <typename Visitable>
using PetVisitable = VisitableBase<Pet, Visitable>;
```

We can make one more simplification and allow the programmer to specify the list of visitable classes as a list of types, instead of inheriting from `Visitor<Cat>`, `Visitor<Dog>`, and so on, as we have done previously. This requires a variadic template to store the list of types. The implementation is similar to the `LambdaVisitor` instance we saw earlier:

```
template <typename ... V> struct Visitors;

template <typename V1>
struct Visitors<V1> : public Visitor<V1>
{};

template <typename V1, typename ... V>
struct Visitors<V1, V ...> : public Visitor<V1>, public Visitors<V ...>
{};
```

We can use this wrapper template to shorten the declarations of the specific visitors:

```
class FeedingVisitor :
    public VisitorBase, public Visitors<Cat, Dog>
{
    .....
};
```

If desired, we can even hide `VisitorBase` in the definition of the `Visitors` template for the single type argument.

We have now seen both the classic object-oriented Visitor pattern and its reusable implementations, made possible by the generic programming tools of C++. In the earlier chapters, we have seen how some patterns can be applied entirely at compile time. Let's now consider whether the same can be done with the Visitor pattern.

Compile-time Visitor

In this section, we will analyze the possibility of using the Visitor pattern at compile time, in a similar fashion to, say, the application of the Strategy pattern that leads to policy-based design.

First of all, the multiple dispatch aspect of the Visitor pattern becomes trivial when used in the template context:

```
template <typename T1, typename T2> auto f(T1 t1, T2 t2);
```

A template function can easily run a different algorithm for any combination of the `T1` and `T2` types. Unlike the run-time polymorphism implemented with the virtual functions, dispatching the call differently based on two or more types comes at no extra cost (other than writing the code for all the combinations we need to handle, of course). Based on this observation, we can easily mimic the classic Visitor pattern at compile time:

```
class Pet {
    std::string color_;
    public:
    Pet(const std::string& color) : color_(color) {}
    const std::string& color() const { return color_; }
    template <typename Visitable, typename Visitor>
        static void accept(Visitable& p, Visitor& v) { v.visit(p); }
};
```

The `accept()` function is now a template, and a static member function—the actual type of the first argument, the visitable object derived from the `Pet` class, will be deduced at compile time. The concrete visitable classes are derived from the base class the usual way:

```
class Cat : public Pet {
    public:
    using Pet::Pet;
};

class Dog : public Pet {
    public:
    using Pet::Pet;
};
```

The visitors do not need to be derived from a common base since we now resolve the types at compile time:

```
class FeedingVisitor {
    public:
    void visit(Cat& c) {
        std::cout << "Feed tuna to the " << c.color() << " cat"
                << std::endl;
    }
    void visit(Dog& d) {
        std::cout << "Feed steak to the " << d.color() << " dog"
                << std::endl;
    }
};
```

The visitable classes can accept any visitor that has the correct interface, that is, `visit()` overloads for all classes in the hierarchy:

```
Cat c("orange");
Dog d("brown");

FeedingVisitor fv;
Pet::accept(c, fv);
Pet::accept(d, fv);
```

Of course, any function that accepts the visitor arguments and needs to support multiple visitors would have to be made a template as well (it is no longer sufficient to have a common base class, that only helps to determine the actual object type at run time).

The compile-time visitor solves the same problem as the classic visitor, it allows us to effectively add new member functions to a class without editing the class definition. It does, however, look much less exciting than the run-time version.

More interesting possibilities arise when we combine the Visitor pattern with the Composition pattern. We had done this once already when we discussed the visitation of complex objects, especially in the context of the serialization problem. The reason this is particularly interesting is that it relates to the connection with one of the few *big-ticket* features missing in C++; namely, the reflection. Reflection in programming is the ability of a program to examine and introspect its own source and then generate new behavior based on this introspection. Some programming languages, such as Delphi or Python, have native reflection capability, but C++ does not. The reflection is useful for solving many problems: for example, the serialization problem could be easily solved if we could make the compiler iterate over all data members of the object and serialize each one, recursively, until we reach the built-in types. We can implement something similar using a compile-time Visitor pattern.

Again, we will consider the hierarchy of geometric objects. Since everything is now happening at compile time, we are not interested in the polymorphic nature of the classes (they could still use virtual functions if needed for runtime operations; we just won't be writing them or looking at them in this section). For example, here is the `Point` class:

```
class Point {
    public:
    Point() = default;
    Point(double x, double y) : x_(x), y_(y) {}
    template <typename This, typename Visitor>
    static void accept(This& t, Visitor& v) {
        v.visit(t.x_);
        v.visit(t.y_);
    }
```

```
        private:
        double x_;
        double y_;
    };
```

The visitation is provided via the `accept()` function, as before, but it is class-specific now. The only reason we have the first template parameter, `This`, is to support both const and non-const operations easily: `This` can be `Point` or `const Point`. Any visitor to this class is sent to visit the two values that define the point, `x_` and `y_`. The visitor must have the appropriate interface, specifically, the `visit()` member function that accepts `double` arguments. Like most C++ template libraries, including the **Standard Template Library (STL)**, this code is held together by conventions—there are no virtual functions to override or base classes to derive from, only the requirements on the interface of each class involved in the system. The more complex classes are composed of the simpler ones; for example, here is the `Line` class:

```
class Line {
    public:
    Line() = default;
    Line(Point p1, Point p2) : p1_(p1), p2_(p2) {}
    template <typename This, typename Visitor>
    static void accept(This& t, Visitor& v) {
        v.visit(t.p1_);
        v.visit(t.p2_);
    }
    private:
    Point p1_;
    Point p2_;
};
```

The `Line` class is composed of two points. At compile time, the visitor is directed to visit each point. That is the end of the involvement of the `Line` class; the `Point` class gets to determine how it is visited (as we have just seen, it also delegates the work to another visitor). Since we are not using runtime polymorphism anymore, the container classes that can hold geometries of different types now have to be templates:

```
template <typename G1, typename G2>
class Intersection {
    public:
    Intersection() = default;
    Intersection(G1 g1, G2 g2) : g1_(g1), g2_(g2) {}
    template <typename This, typename Visitor>
    static void accept(This& t, Visitor& v) {
        v.visit(t.g1_);
        v.visit(t.g2_);
    }
```

```
    private:
    G1 g1_;
    G2 g2_;
};
```

We now have visitable types. We can use different kinds of visitors with this interface, not just serialization visitors. However, we are focused on serialization now. Previously, we have seen a visitor that converts the objects into ASCII strings. Now let's serialize our objects as binary data, continuous streams of bits. The serialization visitor has access to a buffer of a certain size and writes the objects into that buffer, one `double` at a time:

```
class BinarySerializeVisitor {
    public:
    BinarySerializeVisitor(char* buffer, size_t size) :
        buf_(buffer), size_(size)
    {}
    void visit(double x) {
        if (size_ < sizeof(x))
            throw std::runtime_error("Buffer overflow");
        memcpy(buf_, &x, sizeof(x));
        buf_ += sizeof(x);
        size_ -= sizeof(x);
    }
    template <typename T> void visit(const T& t) { T::accept(t, *this); }
    private:
    char* buf_;
    size_t size_;
};
```

The deserialization visitor reads memory from the buffer and copies it into the data members of the objects it restores:

```
class BinaryDeserializeVisitor {
    public:
    BinaryDeserializeVisitor(const char* buffer, size_t size) :
        buf_(buffer), size_(size)
    {}
    void visit(double& x) {
        if (size_ < sizeof(x))
            throw std::runtime_error("Buffer overflow");
        memcpy(&x, buf_, sizeof(x));
        buf_ += sizeof(x);
        size_ -= sizeof(x);
    }
    template <typename T> void visit(T& t) { T::accept(t, *this); }
    private:
    const char* buf_;
```

```
        size_t size_;
};
```

Both visitors process built-in types directly by copying them to and from the buffer, while letting the more complex types decide how the objects should be processed. In both cases, the visitors throw an exception if the size of the buffer is exceeded. Now we can use our visitors to, for example, send objects through a socket to another machine:

```
// On the sender machine:
Line l = .....;
Circle c = .....;
Intersection<Circle, Circle> x = .....;
char buffer[1024];
BinarySerializeVisitor serializer(buffer, sizeof(buffer));
serializer.visit(l);
serializer.visit(c);
serializer.visit(x);

..... send the buffer to the receiver .....

// On the receiver machine:
Line l;
Circle c;
Intersection<Circle, Circle> x;
BinaryDeserializeVisitor deserializer(buffer, sizeof(buffer));
deserializer.visit(l);
deserializer.visit(c);
deserializer.visit(x);
```

While we cannot implement universal reflection without language support, we can have the classes reflect on their content in limited ways, such as this composite visitation pattern. There are also few variations on the theme that we can consider.

First of all, it is conventional to make the objects that have only one *important* member function callable; in other words, instead of calling the member function, we invoke the object itself using the function call syntax. This convention dictates that the visit() member function should be called operator() instead:

```
class BinarySerializeVisitor {
    public:
    void operator()(double x);
    template <typename T> void operator()(const T& t);
    .....
};
```

The visitable classes now call the visitors like functions:

```
class Point {
    public:
    static void accept(This& t, Visitor& v) {
        v(t.x_);
        v(t.y_);
    }
    .....
};
```

It may also be convenient to implement wrapper functions to invoke visitors on more than one object:

```
SomeVisitor v;
Object1 x; Object2 y; .....
visitation(v, x, y, z);
```

This is easy to implement using a variadic template:

```
template <typename V, typename T>
void visitation(V& v, T& t) {
    v(t);
}
template <typename V, typename T, typename ... U>
void visitation(V& v, T& t, U& ... u) {
    v(t);
    visitation(v, u ...);
}
```

The compile-time visitors are, in general, easier to implement because we don't have to do anything clever to get the multiple dispatch, as the templates provide it out of the box. We just need to come up with the interesting applications of the pattern, such as the serialization/deserialization problem we just explored.

Summary

We have learned about the Visitor pattern and the different ways it can be implemented in C++. The classic object-oriented Visitor pattern allows us to effectively add a new virtual function to the entire class hierarchy without changing the source code of the classes. The hierarchy must be made visitable, but after that, any number of operations can be added, and their implementation is kept separate from the objects themselves. In the classic Visitor pattern implementation, the source code containing the visited hierarchy does not need to be changed, but it does need to be recompiled when a new class is added to the hierarchy. The Acyclic Visitor pattern solves this problem, but at the cost of the additional dynamic cast. On the other hand, the Acyclic Visitor pattern also supports partial visitation—ignoring some visitor/visitable combinations—while the classic Visitor pattern requires that all combinations must at least be declared.

For all visitor variants, the tradeoff for the extensibility is the need to weaken the encapsulation and, frequently, grant external visitor classes access to what should be private data members.

The Visitor pattern is often combined with other design patterns, in particular, the Composition pattern, to create complex visitable objects. The composite object delegates the visitation to its contained objects. This combined pattern is particularly useful when an object must be decomposed into its smallest building blocks; for example, for serialization.

The classic Visitor pattern implements the double dispatch at run-time—during execution, the program selects which code to run based on two factors, the types of the visitor and the visitable objects. The pattern can be similarly used at compile time, where it provides a limited reflection capability.

This chapter on the Visitor pattern concludes this book dedicated to the C++ idioms and design patterns. But, like new stars, the birth of new patterns never stops—new frontiers and new ideas bring with them new challenges to be solved, the solutions are invented, and they evolve and develop, until the programming community collectively arrives at something we can point to and say, with confidence, *this is usually a good way to handle that problem*. We elaborate on the strengths of this new approach, consider its drawbacks, and give it a name, so we can concisely refer to the entire set of knowledge about the problem, the solutions, and the caveats. With that, a new pattern enters our design toolset and our programming vocabulary.

Questions

1. What is the Visitor pattern?
2. What problem does the Visitor pattern solve?
3. What is double dispatch?
4. What are the advantages of the Acyclic Visitor pattern?
5. How does the Visitor pattern help implement serialization?

Assessments

Chapter 1

- What is the importance of objects in C++?

    Objects and classes are the building blocks of a C++ program. By combining data and algorithms (*code*) into a single unit, the C++ program represents the components of the system that it models, as well as their interactions.

- What relation is expressed by public inheritance?

    Public inheritance represents an *is-a* relationship between objects—an object of the derived class can be used as if it was an object of the base class. This relation implies that the interface of the base class, with its invariants and restrictions, is also a valid interface for the derived class.

- What relation is expressed by private inheritance?

    Unlike public inheritance, private inheritance says nothing about the interfaces. It expresses a *has-a* or *is implemented in terms of* relationship. The derived class reuses the implementation provided by the base class. For the most part, the same can be accomplished by composition. Composition should be preferred when possible; however, empty base optimization and (less often) virtual method overrides are valid reasons to use private inheritance.

- What is a polymorphic object?

    A polymorphic object in C++ is an object whose behavior depends on its type, and the type is not known at compile time (at least at the point where the behavior in question is requested). An object that is referred to as a base class object can demonstrate the behavior of the derived class if that is its true type. In C++, polymorphic behavior is implemented using virtual functions.

Chapter 2

- What is the difference between a type and a template?

    A template is not a type; it is a *Factory* for many different types with similar structures. A template is written in terms of generic types; substituting concrete types for these generic types results in a type generated from the template.

- What kinds of templates does C++ have?

    There are class, function, and variable templates. Each kind of template generates the corresponding entities—functions in the case of function templates, classes (types) from class templates, and variables from variable templates.

- What kinds of template parameters do C++ templates have?

    Templates can have type and non-type parameters. Type parameters are types. Non-type parameters can be integral or enumerated values or templates (in the case of variadic templates, the placeholders are also non-type parameters).

- What is the difference between a template specialization and a template instantiation?

    A template instantiation is the code generated by a template. Usually, the instantiations are implicit; the use of a template forces its instantiation. An explicit instantiation, without use, is also possible; it generates a type or a function that can be used later. An explicit specialization of a template is a specialization where all generic types are specified; it is not an instantiation, and no code is generated until the template is used. It is only an alternative recipe for generating code for these specific types.

- How can you access the parameter pack of the variadic template?

    Usually, the parameter pack is iterated over using recursion. The compiler will typically inline the code generated by this recursion, so the recursion exists only during compilation (as well as in the head of the programmer reading the code). In C++17 (and, rarely, in C++14), it is possible to operate on the entire pack without recursion.

- What are lambda expressions used for?

  Lambda expressions are essentially a compact way to declare local classes that can be called like functions. They are used to effectively store a fragment of code in a variable (or, rather, associate the code with a variable) so that this code can be called later.

Chapter 3

- Why is it important to clearly express memory ownership in a program?

  Clear memory ownership, and by extension, resource ownership, is one of the key attributes of a good design. With clear ownership, resources are certain to be created and made available in time for when they are needed, maintained while they are in use, and released/cleaned up when no longer needed.

- What are the common problems arising from unclear memory ownership?

  The most common problems are resource leaks, including memory leaks; dangling handles (resource handles, such as pointers, references, or iterators, pointing to resources that do not exist); multiple attempts to release the same resource; and multiple attempts to construct the same resource.

- What types of memory ownership can be expressed in C++?

  Non-ownership, exclusive ownership, shared ownership, as well as conversion between different types of ownership and transfer of ownership.

- How do you write non-memory-owning functions and classes?

  Ownership-agnostic functions and classes should refer to objects by raw pointers and references.

- Why should exclusive memory ownership be preferred to shared ownership?

  Exclusive memory ownership is easier to understand and follow the control flow of the program. It is also more efficient.

- How can we express exclusive memory ownership in C++?

  Preferably, by allocating the object on the stack or as a data member of the owning class (including container classes). If reference semantics or certain move semantics are needed, a unique pointer should be used.

- How can we express shared memory ownership in C++?

  Shared ownership should be expressed through a shared pointer such as `std::shared_ptr`.

- What are the potential downsides of shared memory ownership?

  Shared ownership in a large system is difficult to manage and may delay deallocation of resources unnecessarily. It also has a non-trivial performance overhead, compared to exclusive ownership. Maintaining shared ownership in a thread-safe concurrent program requires very careful implementation.

Chapter 4

- What does swap do?

  The swap function exchanges the state of the two objects. After the swap call, the objects should remain unchanged, except for the names they are accessed by.

- How is swap used in exception-safe programs?

  Swap is usually employed in programs that provide commit-or-rollback semantics; a temporary copy of the result is created first, then swapped into its final destination only if no errors were detected.

- Why should the swap function be non-throwing?

  The use of swap to provide commit-or-rollback semantics assumes that the swap operation itself cannot throw an exception or otherwise fail and leave the swapped objects in an undefined state.

- Should a member or a non-member implementation of swap be preferred?

  A non-member swap function should always be provided, to ensure that the calls to non-member swap are executed correctly. A member swap function can also be provided, for two reasons—first, it is the only way to swap an object with a temporary, and second, the swap implementation usually needs access to the private data members of the class. If both are provided, the non-member function should call the member swap function on one of the two parameters.

- How do standard library objects implement swap?

  All STL containers and some other standard library classes provide a member function `swap()`. In addition, the non-member `std::swap()` function template has standard overloads for all STL types.

- Why should the non-member swap function be called without the `std::` qualifier?

  The `std::` qualifier disables the argument-dependent lookup and forces the default `std::swap` template instantiation to be called, even if a custom swap function was implemented with the class. To avoid this problem, it is recommended to also provide an explicit instantiation of the `std::swap` template.

Chapter 5

- What are the *resources* that a program can manage?

  Memory is the most common resource, but any object can be a resource. Any virtual or physical quantity that the program operates on is a resource.

- What are the main considerations when managing resources in a C++ program?

  Resources should not be lost (leaked). If a resource is accessed through a handle, such as a pointer or an ID, that handle should not be dangling (referring to a resource that does not exist). Resources should be released when they are no longer needed, in the manner that corresponds to the way they were acquired.

- What is RAII?

    Resource Acquisition Is Initialization is an idiom; it is the dominant C++ approach to resource management, where each resource is owned by an object, acquired in the constructor, and released in the destructor of that object.

- How does RAII address the problem of leaking resources?

    An RAII object should always be created on the stack or as a data member of another object. When the flow of the program leaves the scope containing the RAII object or the larger object containing the RAII object is deleted, the destructor of the RAII object is executed. This happens regardless of how the control flow leaves the scope.

- How does RAII address the problem of dangling resource handles?

    If each resource is owned by an RAII object and the RAII object does not give out raw handles (or the user is careful to not clone the raw handle), the handle can only be obtained from the RAII object and the resource is not released as long as that object remains.

- What are RAII objects provided by the C++ standard library?

    The most frequently used is `std::unique_ptr` for memory management; `std::lock_guard` is used to manage mutexes.

- What precautions must be taken when writing RAII objects?

    As a rule, RAII objects must be non-copyable. Moving an RAII object transfers the ownership of the resource; the classic RAII pattern does not support this, so most RAII objects should be non-movable (differentiate between `std::unique_ptr` and `const std::unique_ptr`).

- What happens if releasing a resource fails?

    RAII has difficulty handing release failures, because exceptions cannot propagate from the destructors, and hence there is no good way to report the failure to the caller. For that reason, failing to release a resource often results in undefined behavior (this approach is sometimes taken by the C++ standard as well).

Chapter 6

- What is type erasure really?

  Type erasure is a programming technique where the program, as written, does not show an explicit dependence on some of the types it uses.

- How is type erasure implemented in C++?

  Part of the implementation always involves a polymorphic object and a virtual function call or a dynamic cast. Usually, this is combined with generic programming to construct such polymorphic objects.

- What is the difference between hiding a type behind `auto` and erasing it?

  A program may be written in a way that avoids explicit mention of most types. The types are deduced by template functions and declared as `auto` or as template-deduced `typedef` types. However, the actual types of the objects that are hidden by `auto` still depend on all types the object operates on (such as the `deleter` type for a pointer). The erased type is not captured by the object type at all. In other words, if you could get the compiler to tell you what this particular `auto` stands for, all types would be explicitly there. But if the type was erased, even the most detailed declaration of the containing object will not reveal it (such as `std::shared_ptr<int>`—this is the entire type, the deleter type is not there).

- How is the concrete type reified when the program needs to use it?

  One of two ways—the programmer can assert a specific type based on some prior knowledge (such as a specific context or a runtime value of some variable), or the type can be used polymorphically, through a common interface.

- What is the performance overhead of type erasure?

  There is always an extra indirection and the pointer associated with it. Almost all implementations use runtime polymorphism (virtual functions or dynamic casts), which increases both the time (indirect function calls) and memory (virtual pointers). The greatest overhead usually comes from additional memory allocations, necessary for constructing polymorphic objects whose size is not known at compile time. If such allocations can be minimized and the additional memory made local to the object, the total overhead at runtime may be quite small (the overhead in memory remains and is often increased by such optimizations).

Chapter 7

- What is the overload set?

  For each function call, it is the set of all functions with the specified name that are accessible from the call location (the accessibility may be affected by the namespaces, nested scopes, and so on).

- What is overload resolution?

  It is the process of selecting which function in the overload set is going to be called, given the arguments and their types.

- What are type deduction and type substitution?

  For template functions and member functions (and class constructors in C++17), type deduction determines the types of the template parameters from the types of the function arguments. For each parameter, it may be possible to deduce the type from several arguments. In this case, the results of this deduction must be the same, otherwise the type deduction fails.

  Once the template parameter types are deduced, the concrete types are substituted for the template parameters in all arguments, the return type, and the default arguments. This is type substitution.

- What is SFINAE?

  Type substitution, described previously, can result in invalid types, such as a member function pointer for a type that has no member functions. Such substitution failures do not generate compilation errors; instead, the failing overload is removed from the overload set.

- In what contexts can the potentially invalid code be present and not trigger a compilation error unless that code is actually needed?

  This is only in the function declaration (return type, parameter types, and default values). Substitution failures in the body of the function chosen by the overload resolution are hard errors.

- How can we determine which overload was chosen without actually calling it?

  If each overload returns a different type, these types can be examined at compile time. The types must have some way to distinguish them, for example, a different size or different values of embedded constants.

- How is SFINAE used to control conditional compilation?

  It is used with great care and caution. By deliberately causing substitution failures, we can direct the overload resolution toward a particular overload. Generally, the desired overload is preferred unless it fails; otherwise, the variadic overload remains and is chosen, indicating that the expression we wanted to test was invalid. By differentiating between the overloads using their return types, we can generate a compile-time (`constexpr`) constant that can be used in conditional compilation.

Chapter 8

- How expensive is a virtual function call and why?

  While not very expensive in absolute numbers (a few nanoseconds at most), a virtual function call is several times more expensive than a non-virtual one and could easily be an order of magnitude or more slower than an inline function call. The overhead comes from the indirection: a virtual function is always invoked by a function pointer, and the actual function is unknown at compile time and cannot be inlined.

- Why does a similar function call, resolved at compile time, have no such performance overhead?

    If the compiler knows the exact function that is going to be called, it can optimize away the indirection and may be able to inline the function.

- How can we make compile-time polymorphic function calls?

    Just like the runtime polymorphic calls are made through the pointer to the base class, the static polymorphic calls must also be made through a pointer or reference to the base class. In the case of CRTP and static polymorphism, the base type is actually a whole collection of types generated by the base class template, one for each derived class. To make a polymorphic call, we have to use a function template that can be instantiated on any of these base types.

- How can we use CRTP to expand the interface of the base class?

    When the derived class is called directly, the use of CRTP is quite different from the compile-time equivalent of the virtual functions. It becomes an implementation technique, where a common functionality is provided to multiple derived classes and each one expands and customizes the interface of the base class template.

Chapter 9

- Why do functions with many arguments of the same or related types lead to fragile code?

    It is easy to miscount arguments, change the wrong argument, or use an argument of the wrong type that happens to convert to the parameter type. Also, adding a new parameter requires changing all function signatures that must pass these parameters along.

- How do aggregate argument objects improve code maintainability and robustness?

    The argument values within the aggregate have explicit names. Adding a new value does not require changing the function signatures. Classes made for different groups of arguments have different types and cannot be accidentally mixed.

- What is the named argument idiom and how does it differ from aggregate arguments?

  The named argument idiom permits use of temporary aggregate objects. Instead of changing each data member by name, we write a method to set the value of each argument. All such methods return a reference to the object itself and can be chained together in one statement.

- What is the difference between method chaining and cascading?

  Method cascading applies multiple methods to the same object. In a method chain, in general, each method returns a new object and the next method applies to it. Often, method chaining is used to cascade methods; in this case, all chained methods return the reference to the original object.

Chapter 10

- How can we measure the performance of a small fragment of code?

  Micro-benchmarks can measure the performance of small fragments of code in isolation. To measure the performance of the same fragment in the context of a program, we have to use a profiler.

- Why are small and frequent memory allocations particularly bad for performance?

  Processing small amounts of data usually involves a correspondingly small amount of computing and is therefore very fast. Memory allocation adds a constant overhead, not proportional to the data size. The relative impact is larger when the processing time is short. In addition, memory allocation may use a global lock or otherwise serialize multiple threads.

- What is local buffer optimization and how does it work?

  Local buffer optimization replaces external memory allocation with a buffer that is a part of the object itself. This avoids the cost, and the overhead, of an additional memory allocation.

- Why is the allocation of an additional buffer inside an object effectively *free*?

  The object has to be constructed and the memory for it must be allocated, regardless of whether any secondary allocations happen. This allocation has some cost—more if the object is allocated on the heap and less if it's a stack variable—but that cost must be paid before the object can be used. Local buffer optimization increases the size of the object and therefore of the original allocation, but that usually does not significantly affect the cost of that allocation.

- What is short string optimization?

  Short string optimization involves storing string characters in a local buffer contained inside the string object, up to a certain length of the string.

- What is small vector optimization?

  Small vector optimization involves storing a few elements of the vector's content in a local buffer contained in the vector object.

- Why is local buffer optimization particularly effective for callable objects?

  Callable objects are usually small, and hence require only a small local buffer. In addition, calling a remote callable object involves an extra indirection, often accompanied by a cache miss.

- What are the trade-offs to consider when using local buffer optimization?

  Local buffer optimization increases the size of all objects of a class with a local buffer, whether this buffer is used or not. If most allocations end up larger than the size of the local buffer, that memory is wasted. Increasing the local buffer size allows storing more data locally, but also increases the total memory use.

- When should an object not be placed in a local buffer?

  Local buffers, and any data placed in them, always have to be copied or moved when the containing object is copied or moved. In contrast, remote data that is pointed to by a pointer never needs to be moved and may not need to be copied if the object that owns the data supports sharing (for example, using reference counting). Moving or copying the data will invalidate any pointers or iterators pointing to it and may throw exceptions. This limits what guarantees the class can provide for its behavior when copied or moved. If stricter guarantees are required, local buffer optimization may be impossible or limited for this class.

Chapter 11

- What is an error-safe, or exception-safe, program?

  An error-safe program maintains a well-defined state (a set of invariants) even if it encounters an error. Exception safety is a particular kind of error safety; it assumes that errors are signaled by throwing expressions. The program must not enter an undefined state when an (allowed) expression is thrown. An exception-safe program may require that certain operations do not throw exceptions.

- How can we make a routine that performs several related actions in an error-safe manner?

  If a consistent state must be maintained across several actions, each of which may fail, then the prior actions must be undone if a subsequent action fails. This often requires that the actions do not commit fully until the end of the transaction is reached successfully. The final commit operation must not fail (for example, throw an exception), otherwise error safety cannot be guaranteed. The rollback operation also must not fail.

- How does RAII assist in writing error-safe programs?

   RAII classes ensure that a certain action is always taken when the program leaves a scope, such as a function. With RAII, the closing action cannot be skipped or bypassed, even if the function exits the scope prematurely with an early return or by throwing an exception.

- How does the ScopeGuard pattern generalize the RAII idiom?

   The classic RAII needs a special class for every action. ScopeGuard automatically generates an RAII class from an arbitrary code fragment (at least, if lambda expressions are supported).

- How can a program automatically detect when a function exits successfully and when it fails?

   If the status is returned through error codes, it cannot. If all errors in the program are signaled by exceptions and any return from a function is a success, we can detect at runtime whether an exception was thrown. The complication is that the guarded operation may itself take place during stack unwinding caused by another exception. That exception is propagating when the guard class has to decide whether the operation succeeded or failed, but its presence does not indicate the failure of the guarded operation (it may indicate that something else failed elsewhere). Robust exception detection must keep track of how many exceptions are propagating at the beginning and at the end of the guarded scope, which is possible only in C++17 (or using compiler extensions).

- What are the advantages and drawbacks of a type-erased ScopeGuard?

   The ScopeGuard classes are usually template instantiations. This means that the concrete type of the ScopeGuard is unknown to the programmer, or at least difficult to specify explicitly. The ScopeGuard relies on lifetime extension and template argument deduction to manage this complexity. A type-erased ScopeGuard is a concrete type; it does not depend on the code it holds. The downside is that type erasure requires runtime polymorphism and, most of the time, a memory allocation.

Chapter 12

- What is the effect of declaring a function *friend*?

    A non-member friend function has the same access to the members of the class as a member function.

- What is the difference between granting friendship to a function and a function template?

    Granting friendship to a template makes every instantiation of this template a friend; this includes instantiations of the same template but with different, unrelated, types.

- Why are binary operators usually implemented as non-member functions?

    Binary operators implemented as member functions are always called on the left-hand-side operand of the operator, with no conversions allowed for that object. Conversions are allowed for the right-hand-side operand, according to the type of the argument of the member operator. This creates an asymmetry between expressions such as x+2 and 2+x, where the latter cannot be handled by a member function since the type of 2 (int) does not have any.

- Why is the inserter operator always implemented as a non-member function?

    The first operand of the inserter is always the stream, not the object that is printed. Therefore, a member function would have to be on that stream, which is a part of the standard library; it cannot be extended by the user to include user-defined types.

- What is the main difference between argument conversions for template and non-template functions?

    While the details are complex, the main difference is that user-defined conversions (implicit constructors and conversion operators) are considered when calling non-template functions but, for template functions, the argument types must match the parameter types (almost) exactly, and no user-defined conversions are permitted.

- How can we make the act of instantiating the template also generate a unique non-template, non-member function?

  Defining an in situ `friend` function (with the definition immediately following the declaration) in a class template causes every instantiation of that template to generate one non-template, non-member function with the given name and parameter types in the containing scope.

Chapter 13

- Why does C++ not allow a virtual constructor?

  There are several reasons, but the simplest is that the memory must be allocated in the amount `sizeof(T)`, where `T` is the actual object type, and the `sizeof()` operator is `constexpr` (a compile-time constant).

- What is the Factory pattern?

  The Factory pattern is a creational pattern that solves the problem of creating objects without having to explicitly specify the type of the object.

- How can we use the Factory pattern to achieve the effect of a virtual constructor?

  While in C++ the actual type has to be specified at construction point, the Factory pattern allows us to separate the point of construction from the place where the program has to decide what object to construct and to identify the type using some alternative identifier, a number, a value, or another type.

- How can we achieve the effect of a virtual copy constructor?

  The virtual copy constructor is a particular kind of factory where the object to construct is identified by the type of another object we already have. A typical implementation involves a virtual `clone()` method that is overridden in every derived class.

- How can we use the Template and Factory patterns together?

  The Template pattern describes the design where the overall control flow is dictated by the base class, with derived classes providing customizations at certain predefined points. In our case, the overall control flow is that of a factory construction, and the customization point is the act of construction of an object (memory allocation and constructor invocation).

Chapter 14

- What is a behavioral design pattern?

  A behavioral pattern describes a way to solve a common problem by using a specific method to communicate between different objects.

- What is the template method pattern?

  The template method pattern is a standard way to implement an algorithm that has a rigid *skeleton* or the overall flow of control, but allows for one or more customization points for specific kinds of problems.

- Why is the template method considered a behavioral pattern?

  The template method lets the subclasses (derived types) implement specific behaviors of the otherwise generic algorithm. The key to this pattern is the way the base and the derived types interact.

- What is the inversion of control and how does it apply to the template method?

  The more common hierarchical approach to design sees the low-level code provide *building blocks* from which the high-level code builds the specific algorithm by combining them in a particular flow of control. In the template pattern, the high-level code does not determine the overall algorithm and is not in control of the overall flow. The lower-level code controls the algorithm and determines when the high-level code is called to adjust specific aspects of the execution.

- What is the non-virtual interface?

  It is a pattern where the public interface of a class hierarchy is implemented by non-virtual public methods of the base class and the derived classes contain only virtual private methods (as well as any necessary data and non-virtual methods needed to implement them).

- Why is it recommended to make all virtual functions in C++ private?

  A public virtual function performs two separate tasks: it provides the interface (since it is public) and also modifies the implementation. A better separation of concerns is to use virtual functions only to customize the implementation and to specify the common interface using the non-virtual functions of the base class.

- When should virtual functions be protected?

  Once the NVI is employed, virtual functions can usually be made private. One exception is when the derived class needs to invoke a virtual function of the base class to delegate part of the implementation. In this case, the function should be made protected.

- Why can the template method not be used for destructors?

  Destructors are called in *nested* order, starting from the most derived class. When the destructor for the derived class is done, it calls the destructor of the base class. By that time, the *extra* information that the derived class contained is already destroyed, and only the base portion is left. If the base class destructor were to call a virtual function, it would have to be dispatched to the base class (since the derived class is gone by then). There is no way for the base class destructor to call the virtual functions of the derived class.

- What is the fragile base class problem and how can we avoid it when employing the template method?

  The fragile base class problem manifests itself when a change to the base class unintentionally breaks the derived class. While not specific to the template method, it affects, potentially, all object-oriented designs, including ones based on the template pattern. In the simplest example, changing the non-virtual public function in the base class in a way that changes the names of the virtual functions called to customize the behavior of the algorithm will break all existing derived classes because their current customizations, implemented by the virtual functions with the old names, would suddenly stop working. To avoid this problem, the existing customization points should not be changed.

Chapter 15

- What is the Singleton pattern?

  The Singleton pattern enforces the uniqueness of an object; only one instantiation of a particular object can exist in the entire program.

- When can the Singleton pattern be used and when should it be avoided?

  In a poorly designed program, a Singleton can be used as a substitute for a global variable. To justify its use, there have to be additional reasons for the uniqueness of the object. These reasons can reflect the nature of the reality that is modeled by the program (one car per driver and one Sun in the solar system) or an artificially imposed design restriction (one central source of memory for the whole program). In either case, the programmer should consider how likely it is that the requirements will change and multiple instances will be needed, and weigh it against the work necessary to maintain more complex code with multiple instances before they are needed.

- What is lazy initialization and what problems does it solve?

  A lazily initialized object is constructed when it is used for the first time. Lazy initialization can be deferred for a long time, and possibly never happen at all, if a particular run of the program does not need this object. The opposite is eager initialization, which happens in a predefined order whether the object is needed or not.

- How can we make singleton initialization thread-safe?

  In C++11 and later, that is very simple: initialization of the local static variables is guaranteed to be thread-safe.

- What is the deletion order problem and what are the solutions?

  Even after the order of initialization problem is solved, there could be a problem with the order of deletion—a static object could be deleted while another static object still has a reference or a pointer to the first object. There is no general solution to this problem. Explicit cleanup is preferred; otherwise, leaking resources from the static objects is often the "least worst" alternative.

Chapter 16

- What is the Strategy pattern?

  The Strategy pattern is a behavioral pattern that allows the user to customize a certain aspect of the behavior of the class by selecting an algorithm that implements this behavior from a set of provided alternatives, or by providing a new implementation.

- How is the Strategy pattern implemented at compile time using C++ generic programming?

  While the traditional OOP Strategy applies at runtime, C++ combines generic programming with the Strategy pattern in a technique known as policy-based design. In this approach, the primary class template delegates certain aspects of its behavior to the user-specified policy types.

- What types can be used as policies?

  In general, there are almost no restrictions on the policy type, although the particular way in which the type is declared and used imposes certain restrictions by convention. For example, if a policy is invoked as a function, then any callable type can be used. On the other hand, if a specific member function of the policy is called, the policy must necessarily be a class and provide the required member function. Template policies can be used as well but must match the specified number of template parameters exactly.

- How can policies be integrated into the primary template?

  The two primary ways are composition and inheritance. Composition should generally be preferred; however, many policies in practice are empty classes with no data members and can benefit from empty base class optimization. Private inheritance should be preferred unless the policy must also modify the public interface of the primary class. Policies that need to operate on the primary policy-based class itself often have to employ CRTP. In other cases, when the policy object itself does not depend on the types used in the construction of the primary template, the policy behavior can be exposed through a static member function.

- What are the main drawbacks of policy-based design?

  The primary drawback is complexity, in various manifestations. Policy-based types with different policies are, generally, different types (the only alternative, type erasure, usually carries a prohibitive runtime overhead). This may force large parts of the code to be templated as well. Long lists of policies are difficult to maintain and use correctly. For this reason, care should be taken to avoid creating unnecessary or hard to justify policies. Sometimes a type with two sufficiently unrelated sets of policies is better to be split into two separate types.

Chapter 17

- What is the Adapter pattern?

    Adapter is a very general pattern that modifies an interface of a class or a function (or a template, in C++) so it can be used in a context that requires a different interface but similar underlying behavior.

- What is the Decorator pattern and how does it differ from the Adapter pattern?

    The Decorator pattern is a more narrow pattern; it modifies the existing interface by adding or removing behavior, but does not convert an interface into a completely different one.

- The classic OOP implementation of the Decorator pattern is usually not recommended in C++. Why not?

    In the classic OOP implementation, both the decorated class and the Decorator class inherit from a common base class. This has two limitations; the most important one is that the decorated object preserves the polymorphic behavior of the decorated class but cannot preserve the interface that is added in a concrete (derived) decorated class and was not present in the base class. The second limitation is that the Decorator is specific to a particular hierarchy. We can remove both limitations using the generic programming tools of C++.

- When should the C++ class Decorator use inheritance or composition?

    In general, a Decorator preserves as much of the interface of the decorated class as possible. Any functions the behavior of which is not modified are left unchanged. For that reason, public inheritance is commonly used. If a Decorator has to forward most calls to the decorated class explicitly, then the inheritance aspect is less important and composition or private inheritance can be used.

- When should the C++ class adapter use inheritance or composition?

    Unlike Decorators, adapters usually present a very different interface from that of the original class. Composition is often preferred in this case. The exception is compile-time adapters that modify the template parameters but otherwise are essentially the same class template (similar to template aliases). These adapters must use public inheritance.

- C++ provides a general function adapter for currying function arguments, `std::bind`. What are its limitations?

  The main limitation is that it cannot be applied to template functions. It also cannot be used to replace function arguments with expressions containing those arguments.

- C++11 provides template aliases that can be used as adapters. What are their limitations?

  Template aliases are never considered by the argument type deduction when function templates are instantiated. Both adapter and policy patterns can be used to add or modify the public interface of a class.

- What are some of the reasons to prefer one over the other?

  Adapters are easy to stack (compose) to build a complex interface one function at a time. The features that are not enabled do not need any special treatment at all; if the corresponding adapter is not used, then that feature is not enabled. The traditional policy pattern requires predetermined slots for every pattern. With the exception of the default arguments after the last explicitly specified one, all policies, even the default ones, must be explicitly specified. On the other hand, the adapters in the middle of the stack do not have access to the final type of the object, which restricts the interface. The policy-based class is always the final type, and using CRTP, this type can be propagated into the policies that need it.

Chapter 18

- What is the Visitor pattern?

  The Visitor pattern provides a way to separate the implementation of algorithms from the objects they operate on; in other words, it is a way to add operations to classes without modifying them by writing new member functions.

- What problem does the Visitor pattern solve?

  The Visitor pattern allows us to extend the functionality of class hierarchies. It can be used when the source code of the class is not available for modification or when such modifications would be difficult to maintain.

- What is double dispatch?

  Double dispatch is the process of dispatching a function call (selecting the algorithm to run) based on two factors. Double dispatch can be implemented at runtime using the Visitor pattern (virtual functions provide the single dispatch) or at compile time using templates or compile-time visitors.

- What are the advantages of the Acyclic Visitor?

  The classic visitor has a circular dependency between the visitor class hierarchy and the visitable class hierarchy. While the visitable classes do not need to be edited when a new visitor is added, they do need to be recompiled when the visitor hierarchy changes. The latter must happen every time a new visitable class is added, hence a dependency circle. The Acyclic Visitor breaks this circle by using cross-casting and multiple inheritance.

- How does the Visitor pattern help implement serialization?

  A natural way to accept a visitor into an object composed of smaller objects is to visit each of these objects one by one. This pattern, implemented recursively, ends up visiting every built-in data member contained in an object and does so in a fixed, predetermined order. Hence, the pattern maps naturally onto the requirement for serialization and deserialization, where we must deconstruct an object into a collection of built-in types, then restore it.

Other Books You May Enjoy

If you enjoyed this book, you may be interested in these other books by Packt:

Hands-On System Programming with C++
Dr. Rian Quinn

ISBN: 9781789137880

- Understand the benefits of using C++ for system programming
- Program Linux/Unix systems using C++
- Discover the advantages of Resource Acquisition Is Initialization (RAII)
- Program both console and file input and output
- Uncover the POSIX socket APIs and understand how to program them
- Explore advanced system programming topics, such as C++ allocators
- Use POSIX and C++ threads to program concurrent systems
- Grasp how C++ can be used to create performant system applications

The Modern C++ Challenge

Marius Bancila

ISBN: 9781788993869

- Serialize and deserialize JSON and XML data
- Perform encryption and signing to facilitate secure communication between parties
- Embed and use SQLite databases in your applications
- Use threads and asynchronous functions to implement generic purpose parallel algorithms
- Compress and decompress files to/from a ZIP archive
- Implement data structures such as circular buffer and priority queue
- Implement general purpose algorithms as well as algorithms that solve specific problems
- Create client-server applications that communicate over TCP/IP
- Consume HTTP REST services
- Use design patterns to solve real-world problems

Leave a review - let other readers know what you think

Please share your thoughts on this book with others by leaving a review on the site that you bought it from. If you purchased the book from Amazon, please leave us an honest review on this book's Amazon page. This is vital so that other potential readers can see and use your unbiased opinion to make purchasing decisions, we can understand what our customers think about our products, and our authors can see your feedback on the title that they have worked with Packt to create. It will only take a few minutes of your time, but is valuable to other potential customers, our authors, and Packt. Thank you!

Index

Made in the USA
Las Vegas, NV
22 July 2022

52034465R00282